Competition Policy for
Small Market Economies

Competition Policy for Small Market Economies

MICHAL S. GAL

HARVARD UNIVERSITY PRESS

Cambridge, Massachusetts, and London, England   2003

Library of Congress Cataloging-in-Publication Data

Gal, Michal S.
  Competition policy for small market economies / Michal S. Gal.
    p.   cm.
  Includes bibliographical references and index.
  ISBN 0-674-01049-3 (cloth : alk. paper)
  1. Competition. 2. States, Small—Economic conditions. I. Title.

  HF1414.G35 2003
  338.6'048—dc21   2002027506

Contents

Preface

This book is concerned with the question of whether the size of an economy matters for competition policy. The answer, I submit, is a definite yes: size *does* matter, and to a considerable extent.

The idea for this book and the need for it struck me while I was practicing law in Israel. Although Israel is a small economy, characterized by highly concentrated markets protected by entry barriers, almost all of the court decisions at that time looked to EC and U.S. court decisions and scholarly writings for guidance and applied their principles almost blindly. The difference in market conditions between these two large economies and that of Israel was rarely taken into account. This seemed contrary to basic economic principles: competition policy strives to maintain market conditions that are conducive for competition. Whether firms compete is very much a factor of the structure of the markets in which they operate. Structure, in turn, is highly influenced by the natural conditions of the market, mainly the degree of concentration and the height of entry barriers. As both are usually higher in small economies than in large ones, this should be taken into account in the formulation and application of competition law. I decided to return to academia and research this question. This book is the fruit of that research.

The economic paradigms on which the competition policies of large economies are based do not necessarily apply to small economies. The main fact that creates the need to tailor competition policy to economic size is that competition laws often consist of "one-size-fits-all" formulations. These formulations are designed to achieve the goals of the law in each category of cases to which they apply, while recognizing that some false positives and some false negatives may occur at the margin. The marginal cases of large economies constitute, however, the mainstream cases for small economies. The effect of small size is similar to that of a magnifying glass: special market phenomena become more significant as extremes become the rule. This requires small economies to change the focus of their competition laws to regulate their markets efficiently.

Although several major economic studies have focused on the special characteristics of small economies, there has been no comprehensive attempt to evaluate the implications of those characteristics on competition policy in small economies. In this book I seek to analyze systematically the competition policy implications of small size. The need to recognize the effects of size on optimal competition policy has been strengthened by the positive steps taken by both the World Trade Organization and an organization comprised of most competition authorities toward the harmonization of competition laws. To be welfare-enhancing, such laws should take into account differences between jurisdictions, including differences that result from their markets' natural economic conditions, which may affect the formulation, interpretation, and application of their competition laws.

I am relieved to have more than the time allotted to Academy Award winners to express their thanks, as over the period it has taken me to write this book many people have provided insightful guidance on many difficult questions.

My research on the subject began at the Graduate School of the University of Toronto Faculty of Law, where I benefited greatly from the teaching and the inspiring guidance of Frank Mathewson, Ralph Winter, and Hudson Janisch, who have also provided some perceptive and useful criticisms of the manuscript from which this book was distilled. Above all, I wish to express my heartfelt appreciation to my teacher, supervisor, mentor, colleague, and friend Michael J. Trebilcock for his invaluable guidance and comments and his constant encouragement and support throughout my work. Michael's criticism and wisdom, his personal involvement in all stages of my work, and the belief he showed in my capabilities throughout this research were second to none. I will forever be indebted to him. The John M. Olin Law and Economics Program at the University of Toronto provided invaluable financial support.

The major part of this book was written during the time I spent as a visiting scholar at the Columbia University Law School and later as a research fellow at NYU's Center for Law and Business. Both have been extremely instructive to my research by making me feel very welcome and by providing me with the physical and financial resources necessary to engage in extensive research. I have also benefited greatly from personal interaction with many faculty members and visiting scholars. While it is impossible to name them all, I would like to mention in particular Ron Gilson, Victor Goldberg, Harvey Goldschmid, Jeff Gordon, Merit Janow, Avery Katz, John Manning, and Carol Sanger at Columbia. Victor Goldberg also provided extremely useful and perceptive comments on previous drafts of an extended manuscript.

Within NYU's School of Law my debts are likewise considerable. Eleanor Fox and Bill Allen have been wonderful mentors and friends. Eleanor's perceptive and thoughtful suggestions, as well as her kindness and support, have been highly instrumental to my work. I have also greatly benefited from Bill's innovative spirit, sharp mind, and warm heart. Barry Adler, Yochai Benkler, Rob Daines, Marcel Kahan, and Louis Kornhauser have provided invaluable support by their encouragement and open doors.

I have also benefited from helpful discussions and valuable suggestions on parts of this book from Amitai Aviram, Adi Ayal, Michael Birenhack, Leonard Cheng, Russell Damtoft, Elizabeth Davidson, Ed Iacobucci, Niva Elkin-Koren, Allan Fels, John Fingleton, Idit Froim, Barry Hawk, Ehud Kamar, Bill Kovacic, David Lewis, Menachem Perlman, Peter Roth, Steven Salop, Oz Shy, Raymond Pierce, Dror Strum, David Tadmor, and Roger Ware. Many of them are also close friends. Many thanks are due to participants in the stimulating faculty seminars at Columbia University, the University of Michigan, University of Pennsylvania, and University of Toronto, and George Mason University on a paper that embodied a much-condensed version of this book.

Susan Atkins at NYU has provided invaluable administrative assistance. Keren Wainberg and Boris Sherman rendered excellent research assistance in the last stages of preparing this book for print.

Both worked long hours in search of ever-evasive references and sources. To the anonymous readers who reviewed the manuscript for Harvard University Press, I express my thanks for their valuable suggestions and for the supportive spirit in which they were made. Michael Aronson, Benno Weisberg, Amanda Heller, and Kate Brick of Harvard University Press contributed valuable editorial suggestions. I am also indebted to my friends and colleagues at Haifa University whose friendship and understanding allowed me to devote time to preparing the book for print.

I would also like to thank the *Southern California Law Review* for its permission to reprint some parts of this book, which first appeared as "Size Does Matter: The Effects of Market Size on Optimal Competition Policy," 74 *Southern California Law Review* 1437 (2001).

Last, but in no way least, I am grateful to my family. To my personal source of strength, my husband, Avigdor, for whom research is a life mission, and who has constantly reminded me of life's real priorities. To my children, Jonathan and Natalie. To my parents, Etty and Avraham Shitzer, whose belief in my abilities is nothing less than astounding. To my brother and sister, Eran and Mayrav. This book is dedicated to all of them.

Competition Policy for
Small Market Economies

Introduction

For the most part, the literature on competition policy focuses on large economies, such as the United States and the European Community. This is not surprising, as their competition policies have been a major tool for achieving economic and other social goals for several decades, and given the size of the markets regulated by these policies. Yet the economic paradigms on which such competition policies are based do not necessarily apply to the many small market economies that exist around the world and that have adopted or are contemplating the adoption of a competition policy. As I argue in this book, the size of a market necessarily affects the competition policy it should adopt.[1]

Definition of a Small Market Economy

Let me first define what constitutes a small economy. For the purposes of this book, a small economy is an independent sovereign economy that can support only a small number of competitors in most of its industries. This definition already captures one of the economic consequences of small size: the highly concentrated nature of most of the industries, which is a determining feature for applying competition policy.

Market size is influenced by three main factors: population size, population dispersion, and openness to trade.[2] Small population size limits demand and reduces the number of firms that can efficiently serve the market. Population dispersion over a large geographic area may create several small local markets within a geographically large jurisdiction. The size of an economy is also influenced by a combination of additional economic, geographic, technological, legal, and political factors that create market boundaries and restrain the entry of potential competitors into the market. Primarily, the relevance of the jurisdiction in economic analysis is dependent on the international environment in which it is positioned, including its trade agreements or arrangements with other economies. Liechtenstein, Andorra, and Monaco, for example, are so economically integrated with their larger neighboring states that they can be economically regarded as part of their markets. In these jurisdictions a considerable degree of openness to trade negates a conclusion of smallness based on population size alone. These examples signify why the definition focuses on economies rather than on jurisdictions.

The definition of a small economy is arbitrary in the sense that there is no magic number that distinguishes a small economy from a large one. Jurisdictions can be placed on a continuum according to their size. Some are very small, such as Jersey (with a population of approximately 90,000) and Malta (400,000). These are also, geographically, island economies. For political reasons Israel can also be considered an island economy with a larger population of about 6 million. Australia is much larger (19.5 million), but can still qualify as a small economy because most of its industries are characterized by concentrated market structures. The dispersion of its population over a comparatively large geographic area (albeit mostly around several urban centers) serves to create market regionalization. This fact, coupled with its distance from its major trading partners, creates problems typical of small economies. Of course, the smaller the economy, the more concentrated its industries are likely to be and vice versa. Yet all small economies are characterized by monopolistic or oligopolistic structures in most of their industries. For the sake of simplicity, I shall not differentiate between degrees of smallness, unless necessary.

It should also be emphasized that for an economy to be considered small, not all its industries need be highly concentrated. Some industries, such as retail services, are highly competitive even in small economies. Conversely, firms located in small economies might compete in and even dominate world markets. In such cases, the size of the domestic population or its dispersion does not constrain the scale and scope of production of such firms. Nonetheless, when such firms are the exception rather than the rule, the jurisdiction should still be defined as a small economy. The fact that some domestic firms are internationally competitive does not alter the fact that most domestic markets are highly concentrated. Moreover, the domestic markets in which such firms operate may also be concentrated.

The Relevance of Jurisdictional Borders

As international trade among countries is steadily rising, one can reasonably question the relevance of jurisdictional borders to competition policy. More large firms are becoming multinational, and multinational firms based in different countries crisscross national boundaries in establishing networks of subsidiaries. Major international trade agreements have been signed and implemented. All these trends throw firms based in different national markets, including those based in small economies, into increased competition with one another.

Yet the borders of a jurisdiction often create a point of discontinuity. They represent a change in the degree of mobility of almost all factors of production. These boundaries may result from natural trade barriers. For example, language differences may create trade barriers when language is an important element of the product (e.g., computer keyboards and software). Trade barriers may also result from geographic boundaries (e.g., maritime borders, high mountain chains, secluded areas) that create high transportation costs. Transportation and adaptation costs are especially influential when low-priced, high-shipment-cost, or perishable products are involved. Australia's distance from major exporters, for example, is great enough to make natural protection quite substantial.[3] Trade is also limited when producers must be in close proximity to the ultimate consumers. This condition is most typical in service industries such as retail trade, personal service establishments, and the curative and other professions. Political conditions may also influence trade levels—accentuating geographic isolation both by closing certain passages to trade and by preventing trade between adjacent jurisdictions.[4] For example, eastern European countries were traditionally closed to competition from many other countries owing to political and ideological differences. Differing tastes or cultural preferences may also affect trade levels.

These natural trade barriers are often compounded by policy choices such as tariffs, quotas, limits to the convertibility of currencies and transfer of credits, and even the standardization of consumer choice created by the central authority. Trade levels are also affected by domestic laws and regulations such as those regulating dumping liability, preferential treatment in government tenders for local products, and intellectual property rights protection. Entry barriers that face domestic and foreign producers alike, such as brand name recognition and sunk costs, also affect trade.

These barriers are not uniform in degree, either between jurisdictions or at different periods in time. The relevance of the jurisdiction in economic analysis is thus dependent, inter alia, on its agreements or arrangements with other jurisdictions with which it has economic contacts, actual or potential. A liberal trade policy may make the jurisdiction de facto less relevant as a unit in economic analysis. Yet openness to trade is quite often a limited tool that does not remove many trade boundaries. Accordingly, many economies are still small in size.

The Need for a Specially Tailored Competition Policy

Small economies need a competition policy that is specifically tailored to their markets. As Chapter 1 demonstrates, small economies face different welfare maximization issues than do large ones. A critical feature of small economies is the concentrated nature of many of their markets, resulting from the presence of scale economies and high entry barriers. Smallness has adverse implications for domestic market structure and performance. The size of some industries is sub-optimal to the extent that limited demand constrains the development of a critical mass of domestic productive activities necessary to achieve the lowest costs of production. But even when productive efficiency can be achieved, small economies cannot support more than a few competitors in most of their industries. Competition is often characterized by monopoly or oligopoly protected by high entry barriers. These market conditions have an adverse impact on prices and output levels of many goods and services, that may carry over to vertically interconnected industries. This in turn implies that finding the balance between productive efficiency and competitive conditions in small economies is challenging. In the presence of scale economies, a balance should be struck between firms large and integrated enough to enjoy these economies and firms numerous enough and with sufficient opportunity for effective rivalry.

These salient characteristics require small economies to devise appropriate endogenous policies that offset at least some of the adverse effects of their small size. Competition policy can either increase or reduce the disadvantages of small size. To reduce them, competition policy has to be designed to deal effectively with the unique obstacles to competition that are inherent in an economy, including those that stem from small size. Even small economies that enjoy some unusual comparative advantage must have the capacity to benefit from these hazards of fortune and to make them a basis for sustained economic development. Moreover, in small economies the importance of an appropriately structured and efficiently enforced competition policy may be greater than in large economies. Given that the market's invisible hand[5] has a much weaker self-correcting tendency, the costs of improper design and application of competition laws might be higher in both the short and the long run.

To be sure, many of the principles and doctrines that apply to large economies apply equally to small ones. The goal of competition policy, which is aimed at creating and maintaining the conditions for workable competition to maximize social welfare, and its main tool and ideological choice—a market economy—are similar in both large and small economies. Yet the comparative prevalence of concentrated market structures in a small economy creates trade-offs that require a different set of rules to regulate the conduct of market participants. The need for different rules arises from the existence of one-size-fits-all formulations that are based on general presumptions about market conduct, which are informed, in turn, by the natural conditions of the market. Small size affects competition laws from their goals to their rules of thumb. For example, a rule that categorically prohibits the creation of joint ventures that might increase the market power of the parties would not enable firms located in small economies to utilize one of the most important methods open to them for increasing their productive and dynamic efficiency and thereby overcome the inherent limitations arising from smallness.

The need to apply to small economies a different set of rules from those that maximize the overall welfare of large ones can also be explained by using the theory of the second best.[6] The theory postulates that if there exists an optimum under certain conditions, once even one of the conditions is not fulfilled, the old optimum is no longer necessarily the most efficient solution. The new optimum would not necessarily even be in the same direction and magnitude as the old one. This can be demonstrated by an example. The U.S. competition authorities use concentration indices as a prima facie indicator of the competitive effects of a merger. These indicators are important since they create a presumption of illegality. The Herfindahl-Hirschman Index (HHI) is one such tool, which indicates the level of concentration in a market based on both the number of firms operating in it and their relative market shares. The U.S. competition authorities have chosen an HHI level that is met, for example, by any merger in a market with five equal firms. This HHI indicates mergers that are likely to be anti-competitive, unless the defendant can prove otherwise. This index is based on generalized predictions of gains from size as well as behavioral assumptions about the market. Small economies would not achieve efficient results by applying the same concentration levels, as most of their industries would be caught under them, and a presumption of illegality, which is usually hard to combat, would arise in most mergers. Yet the second-best optimum will not necessarily be achieved by reducing the HHI levels in proportion to the reduction in the size of the economy. The reason is quite simple: at smaller firm sizes it can no longer be assumed that scale and scope economies have been exhausted, and concentration might be necessary to achieve productive and dynamic efficiency. Moreover, concentration affects the conduct and performance of firms in direct as well as indirect ways such that no simple formula exists to predict the effects of more limited demand on them.

One may question the justification for a competition policy in small economies, especially very small ones. The costs of adopting and implementing a competition policy may be regarded as a tax that must be justified by offsetting benefits before it is implemented. The smaller the economy, the higher the costs per capita of implementing a competition policy because certain expenses should be incurred regardless of population size. A second reason for the relatively high costs of competition policy in small economies is that concentrated markets pose relatively more competition policy issues than less concentrated markets.

At the same time, however, the benefits that competition policy may offer to small economies are much greater, relatively, than those to be gained in larger, less concentrated markets. The natural conditions of many markets in small economies that tend to limit competition increase the need to regulate the conduct of market players to ensure that competition occurs in those industries in which competition is feasible, that limits are set on the conduct of firms operating in markets that are not self-regulating, and that importers do not behave anti-competitively. Even in monopolistic or oligopolistic markets, competition policy can significantly improve market performance by reducing the opportunities and the incentives of firms to abuse their market power, either commercially or politically. Competition laws are also an indispensable ingredient of economic liberalization. They are part of the basic organizing principles of a society relying primarily on contract rights and private ownership to allocate resources, distribute wealth, and motivate innovation. Beyond purely economic reasons, a culture of competition is positively linked to other social goals, including employment and democracy. Abuse of dominance or cartelization of newspapers or TV stations, for example, may have significant negative effects on the freedom of speech, which is one of the basic tenets of democracy. Microeconomic policy, including competition policy, may also become more important when a small economy limits its discretion with regard to macroeconomic tools, such as its currency. The adoption of the basic principles of competition policy is often also a precondition for trading with large economies, such as the EC. Should small economies decide to forgo the adoption of competition policy principles, they may lose the many benefits that trade may offer, including the increase in demand enjoyed by exporting firms and the strengthening of incentives of domestic firms facing foreign competition to increase productive and dynamic efficiency. Often the adoption of competition principles is thus a strong force for efficiency in small economies. Such principles also create a basis for a stronger and better law as the competition agency becomes integrated into the international competition community, develops more specific competition rules, and creates public awareness of the benefits of stronger competition.[7]

The competition policy of small economies may thus have relatively higher costs but also higher payoffs than that of large ones. To reduce enforcement costs, the competition authorities of small economies should choose their cases cautiously so as to ensure that the benefits—

both to the specific industry at hand and from setting guiding principles for other market participants—justify the costs. The establishment of a competition regime at a regional rather than a national level also offers a means by which small jurisdictions may reduce the costs of applying a competition policy.[8] A supranational competition authority that implements and enforces the competition rules in all jurisdictions involved may counteract the adverse scale effects of small size by reducing implementation costs for all the jurisdictions. The successful implementation of such regimes requires, however, that all jurisdictions concede their authority on competition matters to the supranational authority. To reduce costs significantly, all jurisdictions should also have relatively similar characteristics and policy goals.

Regional agreements are especially useful for micro-states, which may lack the necessary technical and financial means to implement a full-blown competition policy on their own. Yet even when regional agreement are not feasible, micro-states should, nonetheless, seek to promote a culture of competition through the adoption of some of the fundamental tenets of competition policy, such as measures against hard-core cartels and blatant abuses of dominance. Such measures would enable them to combat some of the major problems associated with market power instead of leaving them to the limited regulatory powers of the market. They would also allow for the shaking up of established and close-knit business elites, given the severe problems of impartiality and stagnation of existing structures that often characterize small economies.

The Current State of Competition Policy in Small Economies

Most small economies give no systematic weight to considerations of size in their competition policy. Many do not go beyond rhetorical acknowledgment of their special economic traits in designing and applying their antitrust laws. Rather, they adopt or rely on the statutes and established case law of large economies, mostly of the EC. This approach has many recognizable advantages, such as a ready basis for the law, a large body of comprehensive case law and commentary, and network externalities. The main pitfall of such an approach is that insufficient weight is given to the unique characteristics of small economies.

Surprisingly, although several major economic studies have focused on the special economic characteristics of small economies,[9] there has been no comprehensive attempt to evaluate the implications of those characteristics on their competition laws. This book provides systematic guidance on the effects of small size for competition policy in small economies. It places under the magnifying glass the implications of size on competition policy. While the main focus is on the issues that call for special attention or different regulatory tools, it also identifies areas of law in which the applicability of the competition policy of large jurisdictions poses no special problems based on differences in market size.

The need for this research has intensified in recent years. Political trends toward separating formerly large jurisdictions into smaller ones and the move toward more market-oriented economies have made competition policy an important and indispensable tool in the formation of these economies. The shift from direct management of the economy in favor of an increased reliance on the market has led to the adoption of competition laws as an integral part of economic reform measures in many jurisdictions. In the early 1980s there were approximately twenty jurisdictions with competition laws. Twenty years later there were approximately ninety-eight jurisdictions with competition laws, and this number continues to rise. Many of the jurisdictions that have recently adopted a competition policy are small.[10] In addition, only in recent years have many jurisdictions, especially small ones, acknowledged the need for competition laws that would regulate their markets by maximizing the use of the market's invisible hand. In other jurisdictions competition laws that were only partially enforced in the past are currently being implemented with more vigor. These trends increase the need for a study of the implications of small size on one of the main economic tools used in market economies: competition policy.

Although size is only one of a set of parameters that affect optimal competition policy, the importance of an analytical framework that analyzes the implications of size as a stand-alone factor stems from four different sources. First, in many small economies the goals of economic efficiency take center stage. Size is undoubtedly an important parameter in this framework. Analysis of the case law of small economies clearly indicates that disregarding the effects of small size on optimal competition policy may prevent small economies from achieving their stated policy goals.

Second, considerations of economic size are much too often overlooked by policy makers, agencies, and courts. This stems, usually, from the lack of awareness of the economic consequences of small size (beyond rhetoric alone) and the lack of an analytical source that would provide guidance on the subject.

Third, and most important, even if policy makers in small economies eventually decide that it will be in their best interest to adopt the laws of large economies, this decision must be based on a clear understanding of the implications of such a decision for their economies. Understanding the specific economic implications of small size is a crucial element in making an informed decision about which competition principles to adopt.

Finally, the importance of the study of optimal competition policy in small economies also derives from the recent trend toward the harmonization and convergence of competition policies on a global scale. Two events have pushed convergence to the forefront. The first is the recognition of the World Trade Organization (WTO) Ministerial Conference of the need for a "multilateral framework to enhance the contribution of competition policy to international trade and development."[11] The second is the establishment of an International Competition Network by the competition authorities of most jurisdictions for the enhancement of international cooperation and the reduction of trade barriers.[12]

One of the major risks of the harmonization process is that in the rush to harmonize, the effects of harmonized laws on small economies will be overlooked. Small economies undoubtedly stand to benefit from convergence of competition policies. Harmonization of competition policies will, inter alia, reduce the transaction costs of importers that may otherwise find it unprofitable to invest in learning and complying with the competition policies of small economies. It will also reduce the costs of domestic exporters of exporting to large economies. At the same time, the special characteristics of small economies should not be overlooked in formulating the harmonized laws, as otherwise they may lose some of the benefits of harmonization. To give but one example, rules that combat the anti-competitive conduct of international firms by the extraterritorial application of domestic competition rules may create problems of enforcement in small economies that often lack the ability to create a credible threat to large international firms. Any arrangement relating to competition policy at the international level should take due account of such considerations. Moreover, even if a harmonized law is eventually adopted, market size may continue to affect the interpretation and enforcement policy of small economies. International firms doing business in small economies would need to be sensitive to these differences.

Additional Factors That Affect Optimal Competition Policy

Undoubtedly, economic size is not the only parameter that influences the design of competition policy. Competition policies do not apply in a vacuum. Rather, they are a product of a combination of economic, ideological, philosophical, historical and political factors. Accordingly, the environment in which competition policies are applied might differ significantly from one jurisdiction to another. For example, the east European countries that adopted competition policy as part of a move from a fundamentally communitarian and socialistic set of national values may wish to apply their competition laws differently than a country that has adopted it as part of a highly individualistic, freedom-of-contract set of values. The ideological values on which competition policy is based might also affect its goals. One of the main goals of South African competition policy, for example, is distributive: to ensure the dispersion of economic power among previously deprived citizens. This goal may well overshadow efficiency objectives.[13] Transitional economies also raise a unique set of issues, including the phased application of competition policy principles and the need to educate the public in their benefits.

While such factors must be taken into account in shaping optimal competition policy, they are outside the scope of this book, as transitional, ideological, and political economy issues are not necessarily unique to small economies. Yet whatever the ideological basis on which competition policy is based, policy makers and interpreters of competition policy in small economies must have a clear understanding of the implications of the special economic characteristics of their markets for framing optimal competition policy. Otherwise, the social costs of their policies would be obscured. This book provides guidelines for such an analysis.

Similarly, competition operates within a framework defined by the general laws and by social conventions. Many domestic policies, such as intellectual property, subsidy and tax, licensing, and health and environmental policies, set some of the ground rules for market activities and, accordingly, affect the scope for competition.[14] For example, intellectual property policy may create legal monopolies justified by the need to enhance dynamic efficiency in the long run. Competition policy should take into account the effects of such policies in designing an overall framework in which firms operate. Since, however, such policies are usually taken as a given in competition law settings, and they usually do not differ significantly in small and large economies, this book is confined to the question of the proper role of competition laws within such frameworks.

I begin by focusing on the economic characteristics of small-scale market economies. Economic analysis serves to answer two questions that are germane to the debate: Which market conditions and trade practices are characteristic of small economies? And how large are the gains and costs of these market phenomena? The answers to these questions provide the basis for the policy issues addressed in subsequent chapters, which focus on how the competition laws of small economies should be designed and implemented.

The Economic Characteristics of Small Market Economies

The theory of competition is a fundamental feature of our free market society. From the time of Adam Smith until today, competition has been viewed as an important tool for achieving social welfare as well as other social goals. As Kenneth Train observes: "Competition, in theory if not always in practice, is nothing short of a miracle. Each firm tries to make as much profit as possible without regard (at least directly) for social welfare. Each consumer maximizes his own utility, ignoring others. Yet the result is that social welfare, in the Pareto sense, becomes as great as possible. This consistency of private goals with social goals—the existence of the 'invisible hand' that molds privately motivated actions into socially desirable outcomes—serves as the rationale for a 'free market.'"[1]

The economic theory underlying competition laws is based on the belief that the market's invisible hand is, potentially at least, a far more powerful guardian of the social welfare than any other form of regulation. Competition draws competitors into the market to remove excess profit. It stimulates incumbents to greater productive and dynamic efficiency. It weeds out the inefficient by the objective test of market survival, and it assures the optimal allocation of resources into production activities. Competition is also trusted because there is little basis for faith that regulators possess the knowledge and the motivation required to fine-tune business behavior on behalf of consumers.

Whether firms compete is very much a matter of the natural conditions of the markets in which they operate, and natural conditions are highly influenced by the size of the market. The natural conditions of many markets in small economies differ greatly from the assumptions of the textbook economic models of perfect or contestable competition. There is generally some departure from these models that cannot be glossed over or rectified. Richard Caves and others have argued that the fundamental structural traits of smallness of an economy demand that particular functions in standard economic models be specified differently from those cited in studies of large economies.[2]

Accordingly, this chapter presents the key economic characteristics of small market economies. It analyzes the basic causes and consequences of concentrated industries, as are commonly found in small economies. As I will show, small market size affects the three main indicators of social welfare: allocative, productive, and dynamic efficiency. Allocative efficiency refers to the economy-wide allocation of resources. Ideally, the allocation of resources should reflect real, relative resource costs of producing the goods or services in each sector of the economy and the relative utility or satisfaction to each consuming unit of the various goods and services that are available. Productive efficiency addresses the question of whether any given level of output is being produced at lowest cost. Dynamic efficiency focuses on whether there are appropriate incentives to increase productivity and to engage in innovative activity that may yield less expensive or better goods.

Research has shown that there are three main economic characteristics of small economies: high industrial concentration levels, high entry barriers, and below-MES (minimum efficient scale) levels of production. These characteristics result from the basic handicap of small economies: the large size of minimum efficient scales of production relative to demand. These characteristics and their implications for the conduct and performance of firms operating in small economies are the focus of this chapter.

Naturally, no two small economies are alike. They differ in their characteristics and policies. Some of these differences are the result of the natural conditions of the market, such as geographic isolation and the availability of raw materials. Others are attributable to governmental economic policies such as tax and trade regulations. Accordingly, smallness is always a matter of degree. Nonetheless, some regularities of economic phenomena can be found in all small economies. Predictions are therefore robust in the sense that they hold across all small economies.

Although all the economic studies I surveyed have been conducted on small jurisdictions rather than small economies, their outcomes can generally be easily translated to fit the latter. The reason is that they were either conducted on jurisdictions with absolutely small population and high natural and artificial barriers to foreign trade (e.g., Israel) or jurisdictions with dispersed population and high entry barriers to foreign trade (e.g., Australia). Similarly, all studies cited on the Canadian economy relate to the period before its trade barriers were significantly lowered. Despite Canada's large landmass, much of the Canadian population is concentrated in several urban regions, and this serves to create market regionalization.

The special economic characteristics of small economies were first explored in depth in studies prepared for a symposium on this issue organized by the International Economic Association[3] and studies commissioned by a Canadian Royal Committee in the late 1970s to research the economic justifications and implications of the high levels of corporate concentration in the nation's markets.[4] These studies, by some of the top economic industrial organization experts in North America, including Richard Caves, Michael Porter, and Michael Spence,[5] are among the seminal works on the economic characteristics of small economies. These sources remain the principal substantive basis for later studies, which have generally verified their results.

The Main Economic Characteristics of Small Economies

The Basic Handicap: High Levels of MES
Relative to Demand

The main handicap resulting from small size is the need of firms operating in many markets to produce at levels that cater to a large portion of demand to achieve minimum efficient scales of operation. MES is the scale of operation at which average unit costs of production are first minimized and is largely dependent on production techniques.[6] Naturally, the smaller the market demand, the fewer the MES units that can operate profitably in it. This can be illustrated by a simplified example. Suppose a firm has to produce at least 10,000 units to achieve lowest costs, and domestic demand is 50,000; then the market can economically support five efficiently sized firms. If demand is only 10,000, the market can support only one efficiently sized firm. Limited demand in small economies implies that the number of MES firms that the domestic market can support will be smaller than that supported by large economies.[7]

Scale economies are the main determinant of MES of operation.[8] Scale economies are unit-cost reductions achieved through the production of more of an output, which are internal to the firm. Accordingly, they carry an inherent tendency to decrease average unit costs until the level of output that minimizes average costs (MES) is attained. Economies of scale consist of three main categories: product-specific economies, associated with the volume of any single product made and sold; plant-specific economies, associated with total output (possibly encompassing many products) of an entire plant or plant complex; and firm-scale economies, associated with the scale of the company.

Product-specific economies are created when increased volumes of production of a specific product tend to decrease the average total cost per unit. They often result from production technologies that necessitate large investments merely to be able to produce the product. When output expands, these fixed costs are spread over more units, such that the average cost per unit declines in inverse relation to the number of units produced. Product economies may also result from increased specialization of machinery and labor. With a larger output, downtime for changes between products using the same machinery is reduced. Product economies also have a dynamic dimension: when complex process adjustments must be worked out through trial and error, unit costs fall as workers and operators learn by doing or develop cost-cutting measures and quality control in production. Where product economies exist, plants constructed for higher levels of output of the same product will have lower average costs than smaller plants.

Plant-specific economies of scale arise from indivisibilities in plant management, maintenance, repair, inventories of raw materials, shipping, construction, and the like. For example, economies of massed reserves permit a large plant to retain proportionately fewer repairmen to hedge against randomly occurring breakdowns. Plant-specific economies may extend to output levels exceeding the threshold at which economies for any single product are exhausted. In such circumstances, it will be more efficient for a plant to produce multiple products.

Firm-scale economies reflect the relationship between the absolute size of the firm and the efficiency with which it can operate. The factors that lead to economies at the firm level are generally considered to include management, finance, research and development, advertising, distribution, export activities, and risk taking for large projects, as well as overhead expenses such as insurance and legal services. Scope economies may also exist at the firm level, that is, savings in transaction costs that result from the advantages of intra-firm trade over market relations. Economies of scope may thus justify vertical integration of two or more functions down the production and distribution chain in one firm.[9]

Scale economies are not necessarily inexhaustible. Normally there will be some scale at which all relevant advantages of large size are attained and at which unit costs reach their minimum value. Beyond the minimum point, unit costs may be constant for some output or may rise. Diseconomies of scale, when costs rise as output is increased, may result, for example, when it becomes difficult for the top management to exercise control over the entire organization.

Productive efficiency requires that a firm exhaust all scale economies. The realization of scale economies might create entry barriers, that is, factors that impede or prevent the entry of new firms into an industry or the expansion of existing ones.[10] An entrant with plants of less than MES will face cost disadvantages vis-à-vis firms with MES plants. If MES is large relative to demand and the cost penalties for operating below MES are substantial, a new firm would have to enter the market at such a large scale that the combined output of all the firms operating in the market could be sold only at substantially reduced prices, perhaps even below average total cost, unless another firm were to exit the market or reduce its output. When there are economies of firm size encompassing broader organizational economies, this may act as a barrier to entry at the broader enterprise level.

A precondition for this result is that some of the costs involved in building MES plants are sunk, that is, they are committed to a specific activity and are unrecoverable by their use for another economic activity.[11] Accordingly, they impose a high risk that the excess of prospective revenues over variable costs might be insufficient to cover sunk costs, in part because of the actions of incumbents that have already incurred these high costs. Entry can thus be expected to be profitable only if the size and probability of expected profits in the event of success outweigh the unrecoverable entry costs that will be lost if the firm fails as a result, inter alia, of the retaliatory strategies of incumbents that have already committed sunk costs.[12]

Scale economies may also affect the choice of technology of firms. When more efficient production technologies become profitable only after a very large output relative to demand, it might be more profitable to install a different technology that, though less efficient, has lower production costs for the range of output that satisfies demand. Below-MES equipment not only may be a current handicap for firms but also may persist when demand increases and can support a more efficient technology, as it may be costly for incumbent entrepreneurs to change their technology choice. As we shall see, scale economies might also impede the creation of indigenous research and development, technology acquisition, and technical progress.

The effects of scale economies may extend far beyond a specific industry if the good or the service it provides serves as an intermediate product in the production of other goods. Even if demand for a final product is large enough to provide adequate market outlets for the output of at least one optimum-sized plant, demand may still be below MES for the efficient production of intermediate products necessary for the production of the final product. Accordingly, industrial interdependence greatly increases the scale of the output necessary for the full exploitation of economies of scale.[13] This basic handicap of small economies results in the three characteristics we examine next.

High Industrial Concentration Levels

The relatively large size of MES compared to demand creates high industrial concentration levels in many industries in small economies. Industrial concentration signifies the static concentration of an industry as determined by the number and size of firms operating in it. While in large economies minimum efficient scales tend to be too small relative to most markets to warrant high levels of concentration, in small economies the number of MES firms many markets can support is much smaller, and accordingly industrial concentration is likely to be much higher. In other words, in a small economy the market structure has to be more concentrated to exploit MES.

How high industrial concentration must be to secure production efficiency depends, primarily, on the balance between technology and demand. At the extreme, when MES is larger than market demand, the market can support only one plant, or cannot support any plant at all. Production MES can also support only one plant when MES is equal to or slightly smaller than demand. In most situations a small economy can support a few efficient plants. A study conducted by F. M. Scherer and others on twelve manufacturing industries indicated that in the United States plant-scale economies compel moderately tight oligopoly only in the refrigerator industry (a maximum of seven efficient single-plant sellers). In smaller nations, however, the conflict between competitive structure and production efficiency was much sharper. Out of the twelve industries studied, Sweden had three natural monopolies (brewing, refrigerators, and cigarettes) and four more natural duopolies. In Canada, production conditions at the plant level were favorable to some degree of competitive structures only in the shoe and weaving industries.[14] Accordingly, to the extent that industrial concentration is influenced by the efficiency imperatives associated with plant- and product-scale economies, industrial concentration is higher the smaller the market.

Actual industrial concentration levels in a market are also influenced by firm-scale economies. If such economies extend beyond the plant level, efficiency dictates that an even smaller number of firms operate in the industry, each operating several MES plants. Studies of firm concentration levels in different economies have confirmed that smaller economies have a smaller number of firms per industry than larger economies. To illustrate, a study conducted by Zeev Galmor on 210 Israeli manufacturing industries indicated that monopolies (defined as industries in which the leading firm's share in total sales was at least 50 percent) occupied 33 percent of the industries, and oligopolies (defined as industries in which the share of the three leading firms in total sales was at least 70 percent) occupied 20 percent.[15] The same phenomenon was observed in other small economies, including Canada[16] and Australia.[17] Table 1.1 compares industrial concentration levels of the three leading firms in a survey of twelve industries in 1970, based on studies by Scherer and others and Michael Schefer.[18] The correlation between concentration levels and population size is striking.

Simply put, industrial concentration levels of an industry are

Table 1.1 Industrial concentration levels and population size: survey of twelve manufacturing industries in 1970

Country	Concentration of the three leading firms		Population	
	%	Index	In millions	Index[a]
United States	41.1	100	204	100
West Germany	56.1	136	61	129
Britain	60.4	147	55	133
France	66.3	161	51	135
Canada	70.8	172	21	175
Sweden	83.4	203	8	256
Israel	91.0	221	3	480

a. The index of the inverted logarithm of the population.

heavily influenced by the size of the domestic market. The smaller the economy, the higher the level of concentration, as most of its markets cannot accommodate many viable competitors, ceteris paribus. Conversely, scale economies are less important as a constraint on the structure of large economies. Another important factor that determines actual concentration levels in an industry is the toughness of price competition.[19] Accordingly, there exists a reverse link from conduct to structure.

Yet even in small economies, high concentration levels appear only in some segments of the economy. In some industries scale economies are relatively low and thus are capable of supporting numerous enterprises. Retailing and personal services markets, for example, are usually also characterized by low minimum scales of operation. The structure of these industries is generally not affected by market size.

Moreover, the negative relationship between market size and concentration holds best for homogeneous goods industries in which sunk costs are exogenously determined by the nature of the underlying technology. In such settings, given any particular configuration of MES, an expansion in the size of the market will raise the equilibrium number of firms entering the market, thus leading to a fall in concentration.[20] As John Sutton has shown, this relationship is not so strong lemand in order to achieve minimum costs, when establishing cilities involves high sunk costs.

ll size may also impose a *supply constraint* on factors of pro-on. Small population size may constrain the availability of la-especially skilled labor, at least in the short run. Moreover, many ll economies are also small in geographic size, which often im-s a limited and less diversified supply of natural, irreproducible re-urces, such as minerals. This raises the costs of producing goods ilizing these resources, which in turn reduces demand and the num-er of MES firms the market can support. The concentration of la-bor and other economic resources in a few economic activities in which the small economy enjoys a marked comparative advantage in world markets (e.g., oil in Arab countries, shipping in Norway, finan-cial services in the Cayman Islands), albeit necessary to overcome the handicap of smallness, may further imply that few other resources are left for other domestically located activities. Specialization may thus make further diversification and production within a small economy difficult because it creates significant barriers to entry for alternative activities, particularly with respect to scarce technical skills and hu-man capital, but also land and natural resources.[22]

Small size may create additional barriers to entry if *vertically linked markets* are concentrated and controlled by competitors. The exis-tence of high MES levels in one market might create high entry barri-ers in a vertically linked market if it required a new entrant to enter more than one market in the chain of manufacturing and distribution or if it significantly raised its costs of production relative to the costs of its rivals.[23]

Size may also affect *cultural variety*. Some scholars argue that small economies are on average more likely than large ones to have a rela-tively homogeneous culture. This may prove beneficial to competi-tion, as cultural similarity limits the variety of competitive ventures that can exist in the market and enables firms to serve a larger portion of demand with homogeneous products.[24] It has also been argued that small size, through social homogeneity and identity, facilitates rela-tively greater consensus in decision making such that small economies are more responsive to change and are more flexible in the pursuit of shared objectives, which support the process of economic growth.[25] At the same time, small size may make competition too personal, for

for industries in which endogeno...
advertising and research and deve...
role. In such industries, the larger th...
profits achievable—the greater might...
competitive escalation in outlays of er...
costs raises the equilibrium level of sunk...
firms—and thus reduces the number of fi...
ket—in step with increases in market size.^{2}...
dicts only a lower bound to industry concentr...
group of industries. The lower this minimal equ...
the theory constrains concentration levels.

At the same time, Sutton's findings have impo...
for small economies as they may suggest a bottlenec...
advertising-intensive retail sector, much more signifi...
MES considerations would have implied. A competit...
of advertising outlays will necessarily lead to a situation i...
a small number of firms survive and dominate the retail s...
the market. Increases in advertising outlays thereby accentu...
could otherwise have been a modestly concentrated marke...
market conditions can lead to the exercise of market power by t...
tailing firms, with adverse effects on their suppliers and consume...

High industrial concentration levels at the national level of a sm...
economy may also affect the contestability of local or regional mar...
kets, where they exist (a condition most apparent in service industries
and distribution outlets). If there are scale economies at the national
level, the number of firms competing for each local market might be
lower in small economies than in large ones, and thus provide less
constraint on incumbent firms. Assume, for example, that a small
town has room for only one bank branch. If the branch tries to charge
high prices, it might lose its business to another bank that will come in
and establish its own branch, so long as sunk costs and other entry
barriers are not substantial. The toughness of competition for establishing a local branch might be reduced as the number of potential
competitors for the market is reduced.

High Entry Barriers

Most industries in small economies are also characterized by high entry barriers. As noted earlier, the main entry barrier is created by the
need to produce or provide a service at levels that cater to a large por-

example, when the business elite is small and businessmen are careful not to enter one another's domain.[26]

Small size may also inhibit *institutional and technological change*. In large economies the breadth and diversity of the economy facilitates private efforts to create new and better products: there are more resources to invest in research, an experimental field wide enough to try a greater number of new products, and more trained people who may develop new ideas. When the acceptance of a new product by consumers is uncertain, a producer in a small economy faces higher risks than a producer operating in a large economy given the different magnitudes of potential demand, especially for new products with high elasticity of demand. All else being equal, the dynamic forces of variety and change that foster competition tend to be stronger in large economies than in small ones.[27]

Below-MES Levels of Production and Low Levels of Specialization

The problems of high industrial concentration levels and high entry barriers in small economies are often further accentuated by below-MES levels of production. To the extent that small size constrains the development of even one firm of efficient scale, a firm operating in the domestic market alone cannot reach the levels of production that would enable it to take advantage of scale economies and thus minimize its costs by producing at the most efficient levels. Yet even in industries in which market demand is sufficiently large to support several MES plants, a problem of production at below-MES scale still exists. A recurring observation in studies of small economies is that a considerable fraction of all output is produced in below-MES volumes and plants.[28] For example, if demand is 20,000 and MES is 10,000, two firms with a production of 9,000 might operate in the market. It has also been shown that firms (and plants) in small economies generally have an output of products much more diverse than that of similar-sized firms (and plants) in large economies.[29] These observations were most notable in industries that were sheltered from international trade.

Below-MES operation can have a significant impact on the efficiency and international competitiveness of domestic firms if penalties for such operation are significant. Because each plant is smaller or produces a more diverse line of products than similar-sized plants in large economies, it employs less specialized equipment, has a higher proportion of setup and downtime costs, and experiences fewer of the economies of scale that arise from "learning by doing."[30] This has been recognized as a critical cause of small economies' inefficiencies.[31]

In their seminal study *The Tariff and Competition in Canada,*[32] conducted on a sample of sixteen Canadian manufacturing industries during the 1960s (before trade barriers were significantly reduced), H. C. Eastman and Stephan Stykolt found that in half of the industries, 50 percent of the capacity or more was of inefficient size. In only three industries was 80 percent or more of the capacity of efficient size. They concluded that a significant percentage of Canadian production came from plants of technically inefficient size. Consequently, Canadian industries were overcrowded with below-MES plants that had short production runs, thereby incurring excessive costs of production. The large number of industries that produced inefficient capacity was especially striking because a similar phenomenon appeared to be absent in the United States, where on average 80 percent of firms in all manufacturing industries operated MES plants. As a result, real costs of production were higher in Canada.[33] Comparative studies also support the hypothesis that firms in small economies operate with plants of below-MES size, especially in industries in which economies of scale are very large.[34] This problem is accentuated by the fact that cost penalties for diseconomies of scale are often highly significant.

There are numerous reasons for the persistence of small and diversified plants in small economies. Without a doubt the most important explanatory variable is market size relative to MES. Building a small plant and building a diversified one are alternative ways of adapting to limited demand in a small market. Plants of a given size in a small economy are thus more diversified than plants of similar size elsewhere, because the other alternative open to firms is to make their plants more specialized but smaller still.[35] The second variable is the cost penalties incurred by production at below-MES levels. Operation at such scale is more likely when the long-run unit production cost function is relatively flat than when unit costs fall sharply with increased plant size.

Transportation costs, that is, the costs of delivering output to customers or bringing customers to the place where service is provided, may also explain the existence of below-MES plants, especially when customers are dispersed over a wide geographic area and transportation costs are high relative to the value of the commodity. Thus, when the geographic territory served is large and dispersed, it may be more profitable to operate several below-MES spatially dispersed plants that realize multi-plant economies than a single larger MES-sized centralized unit. Multi-plant economies arise when a multi-plant enterprise can produce more cheaply that an enterprise with only one plant.[36] Transportation costs, population density, and other factors that affect total average costs of production and distribution are, of course, country- or region-specific. Nonetheless, when transportation involves fixed costs, the effect of such costs is much more pronounced in a small market in which demand for each product is lower than in a large market.

The diversity of production within a plant might also be a response to the market demand that firms either supply a full range of products or face substantial demand penalties, commanding a price premium sufficiently high to offset production scale economy sacrifices.[37] In addition, consumers in some small markets, particularly industrial buyers, exhibit a preference for some diversity in supply sources of similar products, even if it means fragmenting what could otherwise be a more efficient, albeit tighter, market structure and causing unit costs to be higher. Consumers may value both the security against total interruption of supplies and the bargaining power conferred on them by being able to play one producer off against another.[38]

Product differentiation, whereby the product of one firm is not identical to that of its rivals, is another significant cause of below-MES scales of production. It may lead to the installation of small-scale capacity if, through product differentiation, firms are able to carve out for themselves a small but profitable niche in the market. The lower the buyers' elasticities of substitution between brands, the less elastic the demand curve facing the individual producer, and the lower the cost penalties for operating at below-MES scales of production.[39] Eastman and Stykolt have found that differentiation tends to reduce efficiency, as it is a barrier not only to the entry of new firms but also to the expansion of existing ones.[40] The product diversification sword can, nonetheless, cut both ways. By making entry into an industry difficult for potential entrants, it may allow established firms to grow with the market until eventually they reach efficient size.

Historical legacies from periods when MES was much smaller may also help explain the persistence of small plants, especially in industries with durable, capital-intensive production equipment. The speed at which such legacies are shed depends on the vigor of competition. Vigorous competition stimulates modernization, whereas cartelization retards it. Additional ad hoc reasons for the survival of sub-MES facilities include governmental policies and taxes graduated in favor of small suppliers. For example, in Australia past state policies of subsidizing local industrial development have promoted the construction of branches of each industry in each state. As a consequence, Australia's manufacturing centers were nonspecialized, and the typical industry was spread rather evenly among them.[41]

Some dynamic factors also influence plant and product capacities. One such factor is the adjustment lags of constructing MES-sized plants. The essence of the problem is that investment occurs in discrete lumps, providing an increment of capacity that will satisfy growing demand for some time to come. The decision maker must trade off achieving scale economies against the cost of carrying excess capacity temporarily or sustaining a temporary capacity deficit. The smaller the market for any given growth rate, the more time it takes to accumulate a demand increment sufficient to absorb the capacity of a large new MES plant.[42] Moreover, market prices set after expansion depend on the setup costs only indirectly, that is, only by way of their influence on the expansion decisions of firms in the first stage. It follows that mistakes involving adding excessive capacity may lead to losses, as prices set at the second stage may not suffice to cover the setup costs incurred in entering the industry.[43] Firms in industries with high MES are more vulnerable to such mistakes.

Another important dynamic factor is the high level of interdependence between firms in small, concentrated markets. Here I suggest only the bare bones of the argument, which is elaborated later on. Simply put, the smaller the number of firms operating in a market and the higher the barriers to entry, the greater the influence of each firm on the market equilibrium. Firms recognize this interdependence and seek cooperative policies that are more profitable to each of them than when each firm aggressively looks for a larger market share. Accordingly, profit maximization in an oligopolistic market often requires unaggressive competitive behavior with respect to strategic decisions such as price and capacity. To be sure, interdependent behavior does not necessarily justify below-MES production. Firms do not seek to raise their own costs. The relatively large size of production MES, however, may blunt incentives to adopt efficiency-enhancing measures and may lead to output levels that are below MES.

Whatever the effect of these factors in a given industry, one conclusion is clear: scales of production, as well as industrial concentration levels, are not completely constrained to their present level by production economies. Yet, as studies have shown, transportation costs, market density, product differentiation, and other variables account for much less variance in MES-deflated plant sizes than do market size and seller concentration variables.[44]

High Levels of Aggregate Concentration

The interdependence between market players might extend in a small economy beyond the scope of a specific industry. Aggregate concentration, that is, the percentage of economic activity accounted for by the largest firms in the economy, is substantially higher in small economies than in large ones. Although firms in small economies can be small in comparison to the average firms of large economies, they are large relative to the overall size of the small economy or relative to the sizes of individual industries within it.[45] This concentration factor is sometimes enhanced by a network of business connections between dominant firms.

The size of the economy also significantly affects the internal structure of these large enterprises. In large economies, a large enterprise may be a domestic firm that limits itself wholly to a single large industry. If an economy is small, a domestic firm can become large only by diversification (unless, of course, export is possible). The reciprocal attachments between separate business units of a large enterprise enable the realization of firm-scale economies.

A primary concern raised by high levels of aggregate concentration and large firm size is that decisions made by large corporations may have consequences that extend well beyond specific industries to produce political and social as well as "purely" economic results. Economic concerns about large absolute firm size derive from the potential for competitive disadvantages bestowed on the smaller firms by limited capital, distribution, and advertising channels and production factors. For example, when distribution channels are limited owing to economies of scale, control of a distribution channel by a conglomerate may well grant its components a comparative advantage over their rivals. A potentially important social implication of major concentrations of corporate power is the influence exerted by corporations on public authorities and public opinion. The fear is that large, economically powerful enterprises will influence the government by sheer economic force. This might extend to a loss of democracy.[46]

The Effects of Small Size on the Nature of Competition and the Performance of Firms

The unique characteristics of small economies may affect the quality of competition and the performance of firms in many of their industries. They create three structures which raise competition policy considerations that are more prominent in small economies: natural monopoly, single-firm dominance, and oligopoly. Here I briefly review the conduct and performance of firms under these market structures, which will be further elaborated in the following chapters. The chains of causality do not flow only in one direction, however. Market structure is affected by the toughness of competition in the market, which is dependent not only on market concentration and entry barriers but also on competition policy.

Natural Monopoly Conduct and Performance

The unifying characteristic of natural monopoly markets is the ability of a single firm to provide a good or a service at a lower cost than would a set of firms in the market. Natural monopolies may result from unique natural conditions. They may also result from large internal economies of scale relative to demand. The level of output necessary to meet demand can thus be achieved more cheaply by a single firm than by any combination of several firms. In other words, the cost function of the firm is sub-additive. Under such conditions, production by a single firm is technologically more efficient, as it prevents the wasteful duplication of fixed costs. Accordingly, in natural monopoly markets no competition is feasible in the market, although competition *for* the market may take place. In most cases, however, market forces alone cannot constrain natural monopolies. Small market size, by increasing the size of MES relative to demand, increases the prevalence of natural monopolies.[47]

Natural monopolies, however, do not have to share the benefits of their efficiency with consumers. Rather, they have economic incentives to charge monopoly rates and to restrict output. Monopoly pricing is their most recognized evil. Under perfect competition, output of a commodity expands until price falls to the point just equal to each firm's marginal cost of production. When the monopoly is not constrained by competition for its market, its output will be smaller and its price higher, given that it faces a downward-sloping demand curve and the more it sells, the lower the price it receives (assuming no price discrimination is possible). At the limit, the monopolist will equate marginal cost and marginal revenue to maximize its profits. This in turn reduces economic efficiency by distorting resource allocation away from the maximum satisfaction of consumer wants. The amount by which the decrease in consumer surplus exceeds the increase in profit is known as the "deadweight loss," since it is a loss to consumers without an offsetting gain to producers. Monopoly pricing also creates a wealth transfer from consumers to the monopolist, in that consumers surrender to the monopolist some of the surplus they would have enjoyed in a competitive market.

In addition to cost distortions on the demand side, monopolies may cause cost distortions on the supply side. It has been suggested that firms under competitive pressure will be more driven to succeed at keeping costs low, while monopolists will tend to pay less attention to cost-cutting strategies and engage in slack, thus having a greater tendency to let costs rise, leading to what is often called "X-inefficiency."[48] This, in turn, creates production inefficiency.

Monopoly might also create rent-seeking costs, that is, the wasteful expenditures of money and effort incurred to secure or maintain a monopoly position.[49] In natural monopoly markets these costs are incurred to win competition for the market and, once monopoly has been achieved, to secure this position from more efficient competitors. While rent-seeking behavior certainly wastes some of the monopoly profits, no general assumption can be made about what fraction of the monopoly profits should be counted as a welfare loss. Richard Posner has argued that at the limit, the social loss from rent-seeking behavior is equal to the total expected monopoly profits.[50] Yet it may well be that firms will have to spend much less than the expected monopoly rent to obtain a monopoly position in a market. Even under the model's assumptions, the maximum individual expenditure will always be that of the second-best firm, since beyond that point the eventual monopolist will win. Also, it may become apparent early in the race that one firm possesses greater advantages than others. At that point, other firms will presumably exit the market, thereby reducing the size of the loss. Moreover, not all expenses are necessarily socially wasteful. The prospect of receiving monopoly profits may motivate firms to develop new products, improve existing products, or invent lower-cost technologies.[51]

Natural monopolies may also possess strong incentives to impede innovation and thus reduce the rate of economic progress. As the natural monopoly has already captured the entire market, it has disincentives to innovate or to use new technologies that will decrease economies of scale.[52] Yet if a new technology reduces production costs without reducing economies of scale, then the natural monopolist may have stronger incentives to develop and apply this technology than a firm in a competitive market, given that the spillover effects of such innovation are fewer than in a competitive market, in which there is a greater likelihood that another firm will capture some of the innovation's benefits. Monopoly is also unlikely to reduce innovation when it faces competition for its markets, since a monopolist fearing entry into its markets may increase innovative efforts to defeat such competition.

Apart from these purely economic effects of natural monopoly, non-economic arguments for and against natural monopoly have also been advocated. Some commentators argue that smallness and disparity of firms should be protected, based on goals such as the distribution of opportunities, the dispersal of economic power, and extended product selection. If the natural monopoly firm is large relative to other firms operating in the market, it may also suffer from the costs of bigness surveyed earlier. Yet some non-economic benefits accrue from the fact that there is only one set of production or distribution facilities in a given industry instead of parallel sets. This is especially true when the duplication of facilities is disturbing in an environmental, visual, or physical sense.

Turning again to conduct, we see that natural monopolies have incentives to create artificial barriers to entry into their markets to reduce the risks of being replaced by a more efficient firm. They also have incentives to impede entry into their domain once they lose their "naturalness." If the natural monopolist is vertically integrated to some competitors in the competitive segments of its industry or in another industry, it may also have incentives to extend its monopoly power to, and to exploit it in, those segments. The economic incentives for such actions involve driving out a competitor, with a view to recouping all lost revenues of the natural monopoly segment by charging high costs after the rival's exit from the market (predatory actions in their broad sense). Such conduct is profitable if the monopolist is prevented in some way from extracting monopoly profits through its natural monopoly facilities.

Dominant Firm Conduct and Performance

The small size of the market may also increase the prominence of single-firm dominance.[53] Dominance may result from the production of a superior product in a market with differentiated products. It may also result from a technological comparative advantage in the production, marketing, or distribution process that the dominant firm enjoys over its rivals. When scale economies are prevalent, the firm that attains such economies may enjoy lower costs over its rivals. Fringe firms may then produce highly differentiated products that allow them to overcome their cost disadvantages, or survive under the monopoly price umbrella with higher costs. Dominance can also result from additional entry barriers. For example, when production inputs or distribution channels are limited, firms that control the necessary intermediate goods or services may achieve dominance more easily. The small size of a market increases the prevalence of the two latter conditions that lead to market dominance. It also reduces the self-correcting power of market forces to erode dominance.

Dominant firms may create all the costs of natural monopoly: monopoly pricing, rent-seeking costs, X-inefficiency, limited product selection, impediments to innovation, and the economic and social costs of bigness. Dominance also creates strong incentives and opportunities for the anti-competitive use of market power by the erection of artificial barriers to entry that prevent more efficient firms from entering the market or prevent the expansion of existing firms in the market. Such strategic exclusionary conduct leads rival firms (even more efficient ones) to shrink their output, and enables the monopolist to raise its own price. The efficiency loss involves both the deadweight loss and the loss in production and dynamic efficiency. It also creates distribution of surplus from consumers to producers.

Oligopoly Conduct and Performance

Most industries in small economies are highly concentrated under an oligopolistic structure: a few firms, protected by high entry barriers, produce a large proportion of the industry's output. The main concern raised by this market structure is that firms may have incentives and opportunities to engage in collusive or cooperative conduct. As markets become more concentrated, the behavior of firms changes as they become more aware of the competitive reaction of their rivals to their output and price decisions, and it becomes easier for firms to coordinate these decisions among themselves. Profit maximization under oligopolistic structures often implies an engagement in unaggressive competitive behavior with respect to strategic decisions such as price and the introduction of new capacity which approximates monopoly decisions. Oligopolistic firms might find it profitable to collude, explicitly or implicitly. Alternatively, cooperative policies may merely reflect a mutual recognition that a price cut by one firm will be quickly matched by competitors and will not lead to a significantly greater sales volume in the long run.

The link between conduct and structure in oligopolistic markets is, however, not determinate. There are several possible equilibria, ranging from competitive to monopolistic prices. At one extreme, firms may collude to set near-monopoly prices. At the other extreme, they may engage in cutthroat competition that drives prices and profits in the short run below even those that would prevail in a perfectly competitive industry. Which end of the spectrum an oligopolistic industry will operate on depends on the market conditions that determine the ease of coordination among firms.

Although oligopolists in small economies still face the whole range of possible equilibria, some features of small economies influence the tendencies toward and probabilities of certain outcomes. Most important, small size may increase seller concentration and the height of natural barriers to entry, the two most important conditions for coordination among rivals. Small size may also facilitate coordination or collusion if the economy is characterized by homogeneous culture and customs, as similarity limits the variety of competitive ventures that must be coordinated. In addition, if we accept the view that the dynamic forces of variety and change tend to be weaker in small economies than in large ones, cooperation is strengthened by such trends.

Existing enterprises can flourish with less fear of entry of a new competitor utilizing new and more efficient technologies.

Coordination or collusion among oligopolists can create supracompetitive pricing and limited output as well as some of the additional costs of monopoly, surveyed above. It may also create production inefficiency, and is an important explanatory variable for production at below-MES scale. The choice between higher cost and lower price (which results from increased output) is an impediment to the installation of new capacity. The result of interdependence of firms in many industries in a small market is that both established and new firms may add units of inefficient size to the industry's capacity in order not to increase output—and thus reduce price—significantly. Of course, such behavior does not necessarily justify production below MES production level. Yet the relatively large size of production MES compared to demand may blunt incentives of oligopolists to adopt efficiency-enhancing measures and thus create, in many situations, output levels that are below MES production levels. Firms will operate at below MES so long as the profits involved in such operation are higher than the additional cost involved in operating at sub-MES levels.[54] The smaller the market, the more likely it is that the level of output per firm will be below the MES of production.

Let me illustrate with an example. Assume that three relatively equal firms produce sugar in an industry, and barriers to entry are high, such that oligopolists are not concerned about the entry of new firms or the expansion of fringe ones. All oligopolists currently produce at below-MES levels of production that do not enable them to minimize their costs. As David Gilo observes, an oligopolist's decision whether to install additional capacity in its existing plants that would enable it to produce at MES production levels depends on its estimates of the effect of additional capacity on the price of the product, on the one hand, and on its estimates of the effect of such additional capacity on its production costs, on the other. If the firm believes that the introduction of additional capacity might lead to lower prices, it may choose to continue to operate a plant too small to exhaust economies of scale. Oligopolists may thus collectively accept market shares that do not justify construction of MES plants for any firm in the industry as part of their recognition of their interdependence. Firms might even use technology that minimizes unit costs, given the low collusive level of output. Such behavior may be seen as a commitment device that facilitates cooperation among oligopolists.[55] Small economies may thus simultaneously deter firms from growing to more efficient size, discourage firms from adopting cost-reducing measures, and maintain high prices in the industry. The stability of such oligopoly is likely to be great because of the difficulty of introducing efficient capacity by either existing or new firms.

Oligopolistic interdependence might also lead to operation at below-MES levels in dynamic settings by affecting the oligopolist's decision to add capacity to meet increased demand. Scherer and others support this conclusion with the following example. Suppose that overall market demand growth creates room for one new MES plant every two years, and the market is supplied by four evenly matched firms. Ideally each firm ought to build a new plant every eight years on a two-year rotation. But the coordination required to implement such phasing can be prohibited by the competition authorities, and even when formal cooperation is permitted, oligopolistic rivals might be unwilling to wait long intervals for increments of growth; nor do they trust one another in matters of such strategic importance to forgo a share of current growth in the expectation that they will have their turn later. Rather, they are apt to expand more or less continuously to maintain their accustomed market shares. Each, then, faces a trade-off between carrying excess capacity for a protracted period or sacrificing scale economies and cost-cutting. The excess capacity–scale economy trade-off is more likely to be resolved in favor of sub-MES plants or plant additions the smaller the absolute demand growth increment accruing to a firm in any given time period. These considerations lead to the expectation that average plant size will be larger the larger the market in relation to the MES and the higher the seller concentration. The concentration/plant size relationship may break down, however, if sellers are prone to ignore their interdependence and struggle through price competition to build and absorb the output of large plants.[56]

Horizontal merger is an alternative way for firms in oligopolistic markets to expand and realize scale economies. Firms in oligopolistic markets might prefer mergers to internal growth, as a merger does not affect aggregate output and thus is not deterred by the detrimental effects of increased output on price. At the same time, such mergers might allow the merging firms to attain or strengthen market power or to increase the interdependence in the market. Efficient merger policy is thus extremely important for small economies.

The entry decisions of new firms into an industry and the levels of capacity introduced by such entry are similar, in many respects, to those of existing competitors. They depend on the interplay between the height of entry barriers into the market and in particular the setup costs incurred at entry and the intensity of price competition that firms face at the post-entry stage. The tougher the post-entry price competition, the lower the profits to be had and the lower the incentives to enter. For example, if incumbents operate at MES levels that are high relative to the demand in the industry, and if the cost penalties for operating below MES are substantial, a new firm would have to enter the market at such a large scale that the combined output could be sold only at substantially reduced prices, perhaps even below cost. Such a market will, most likely, not attract entry. In some situations, however, it will be profitable for firms to enter the market and for incumbents to accommodate entry. This is the case, for example, when the entrant possesses a cost advantage over incumbent firms.

In addition to problems of large-scale entry of new firms, fringe entry at below-MES scale, under the high price umbrella created by the oligopolists, may also occur. Small size and large MES may, nonetheless, reduce fringe entry, as the higher the cost penalties that will be incurred by operating below MES, the larger the cost disadvantage these fringe firms will have, and the less likely such entry is.[57] These cost penalties can be compensated, however, by some strategies that tend to create market niches luring small-scale entrants, such as product differentiation. All things being equal, in small economies fringe entry of domestic firms is less profitable than in a large economy if MES is large relative to demand facing the fringe firm. If, however, most or all incumbent firms operate at below MES levels and diseconomies of scale are large, then fringe entry is more likely. This might create a market structure that is overcrowded with many fringe firms operating below production MES.[58]

The Effects of Open Trade Policy on Small Economies

Trade policy is one of the most effective tools available to small economies for dealing with the consequences of their small size. Openness to trade holds promise for solving some of the efficiency problems of small economies but leaves others to be resolved by other methods, mainly competition policy.

The export of products produced in small economies into foreign markets can solve some of the efficiency problems of small economies by changing the pricing, technology, and capacity decisions of domestic firms. Accessibility to export markets has one predominant effect on domestic ones: it enlarges their scope. When a domestic industry can economically sell abroad, the foreign export markets are added to the aggregate demand the industry faces. An expansion of the market could induce the creation of plants and product runs of larger size and the achievement of lower average costs of production by domestic firms. It may also change the technology choices of market players by allowing them to utilize efficient production methods that require a large output in order to be profitable.[59]

Export possibilities may also affect the price of domestic products. If the exporter is constrained from price discrimination, such as by anti-dumping laws, then the domestic price will usually equal the export price. If, however, the exporter is not constrained in such a manner, then the profit-maximizing strategy of a dominant or oligopolistic domestic firm may entail charging higher prices in the domestic market while charging world market prices in the export markets. Such discriminatory pricing can be facilitated if cost barriers to the reimportation of goods are high. Yet the lower production costs of domestic firms may still lower the firms' profit-maximizing price in the domestic market.

The small scale of a domestic market also affects the range of products it exports. Exports of small economies usually concentrate on a limited number of products in which they enjoy a comparative advantage over their trading partners.[60] These are often value-added niche sectors that accord with small economies' comparative advantage such as human capital rather than scale-extensive activities. Not surprisingly, in many export industries transportation costs are nonexistent or relatively minor, such as financial services (Jersey, Malta, Cyprus) and computer software research and development (Israel).[61] This specialization in a relatively narrow range of activities further implies that the production structure is comparatively undiversified, since there is not much room for more industries operating at the large scales necessary for export markets. Interestingly, the relatively strong reliance of a small economy on one or more export activities might give it an advantage over large economies as its vested interests create a commitment device to its customers for the continued operation of the activity.

Trade opportunities are, however, not without their limits. Several factors influence the ability and the incentives of firms in small markets to export their products. Most important, it may not be economical for domestic firms to export their products. Domestic firms will be motivated to export so long as the production price is lower than the foreign market price plus transportation costs to the markets of destination as well as other costs that must be incurred by the firm when exporting its products into another market, such as exchange rates and so on. Transport prices may be high per unit cost unless the firm exports large cargoes. Thus, if the foreign price is not high enough, no trade will take place.

Also, a domestic firm wishing to achieve efficient scale by exporting might be vulnerable to entry barriers in the importing country and thus face a high risk factor in building efficient plants.[62] Large-scale production methods require a market outlet that is large, homogeneous, and stable over time. The uncertainties of political interventions and tariff changes, as well as the risks of the convertibility of currencies, of differing rates of inflation, and of consequent difficulties in maintaining competitive prices, are such as to make investment in exports appreciably more risky than serving the domestic market. Trade agreements provide some insurance against these hazards of export trade. This problem can also be partly solved if the exporter has alternative opportunities to export its products into other jurisdictions. Some firms may also prefer not to export to avoid foreign dumping duties. If firms are deterred from charging prices abroad that fall below domestic prices, then they may forgo exportation, depending on the more profitable strategy. Fear among domestic firms of retaliation from leading rivals abroad may also lead to respect for national borders.[63]

Imports may also significantly affect a small economy's performance.[64] Imports, or even their potential, may induce domestic firms to refrain from supracompetitive pricing and even to operate at efficient scales of production. Foreign firms' production price plus transportation, tariff, and adaptation costs as well as other costs that must be incurred to import into the domestic market (the "foreign delivered price") usually create an upper limit on domestic firms' prices. When the foreign delivered price equals the domestic industry's lowest production costs, inefficient domestic producers would be obliged to lower costs to survive against foreign competition. This may require them to produce at MES. Imports thus provide contestability, which in turn creates more efficient but sometimes more concentrated domestic markets. When domestic production costs exceed the foreign delivered price, imports may wipe out the domestic firms.

When scale economies in the domestic market are substantial so that producers are few and perfect competition cannot prevail, the analysis is more complicated. A potential entrant will take into account the effect of entering the market at the domestic price. It may enter at a smaller scale than it would if the market were competitive, so as not to affect the domestic price significantly. The domestic industry might still be wasting resources by producing at inefficient scale because of the interdependence of firms.

Small size may also affect the character of imports. Suppose that every variety of a good is produced subject to the same production function and at identical costs in each country. Only the more popular varieties of a differentiated good tend to be produced in small economies, with specialized varieties in small demand produced in the large economies and exported to smaller ones. The main reason for this is that producers in the large economy enjoy the advantage of access to more customers who can be served (by assumption) at low transportation costs within national boundaries. Accordingly, foreign firms exporting into small economies have usually reached efficient scales of production. Thus, so long as the foreign landed price is below the domestic price, these products will most likely be imported and sold at a price between the foreign landed price and the former domestic price, depending on the number of foreign firms competing to supply the domestic market.[65] When, however, the domestic industry enjoys cost advantages over its foreign rivals, the product or service can be produced domestically in competition with relatively more costly imports. Substantial exposure to import competition should thus increase the varieties of a given product in a small economy and also the size of domestic firms.

As with exports, imports do not offer a panacea for a small economy's inefficiencies. The extent to which external trade can provide an effective escape from the penalties of smallness is limited by a number of factors. Importing firms face the additional burden of transportation costs and often also adaptation costs and tariffs. These barriers might inhibit trade by making it uneconomical to export into small economies if they raise the foreign delivered price above the domestic price. In particular, the limited size of domestic demand might not enable foreign firms to realize import economies that would allow them to compete effectively with domestic firms. Unless import scale economies encompass several products, the lower the quantity imported, the higher the fixed costs per unit and the higher the foreign landed price. The higher these additional costs, the more protected domestic firms are from foreign competition, and the less they are constrained in their conduct. Moreover, the decisions of foreign firms to enter the domestic market may be influenced by the effect that the foreign producers perceive their entry will have on domestic prices in oligopolistic markets.[66] Finally, from an economy-wide perspective, strong reliance on imports exposes the economy to the risk of exogenous shocks in the global trading system.[67] So long as political independence is desired, there will be justification for keeping within domestic boundaries industries whose products are indispensable and whose whole supply might be cut off. A small economy may also wish to limit imports because of non-economic considerations, such as defense and national security, the closing of domestic plants in unemployment-ridden areas, stability of supply of certain products, and building a technological infrastructure.

As with exports, if foreign importers can segregate the foreign market from the domestic market, they might also profit from a discriminating strategy according to which they will charge higher prices in the domestic market than in their home or international markets. The exercise of market power in the supply of a particular good or service means that the small economy is effectively paying a higher price, which may also have adverse effects on other industries in which the traded good or service is an intermediate input. The supracompetitive price charged by a foreign firm, once it has eliminated all of its domestic competitors, can even be higher than the price charged by domestic producers before international trade occurred.

A study undertaken on the Isle of Man, an independent state lying in the Irish Sea between Britain and Northern Ireland, provides some interesting insights on the limited effects of trade on small open economies. The Isle of Man experiences price levels for consumer goods that are some 10 percent higher than those in nearby regions of the British mainland. Transport costs were found to account for only a relatively small part of the observed price differentials (up to 30 percent). The major causes of price differentials were found to include high stockholding and inventory costs that result from the need to import in economically sized consignments and the desire to obtain bulk purchase discounts from suppliers for quantities that are large relative to local demand; the failure to exploit scale economies in wholesaling and retailing sectors owing to small size; and imperfect competition among firms owing to concentrated market structures protected by entry barriers.[68] This research implies that simply increasing trade will not be sufficient to improve efficiency. What is required is a broader policy that increases productive efficiency and reduces the ability of firms to exploit their market power. Although the Isle of Man is a micro-state, the findings may carry over to relatively larger economies.

An alternative way open to importers to enter a small economy is through the establishment of local subsidiaries. Foreign control can take one of two forms: acquisition of control over existing domestic firms or the creation of new firms in the domestic market. In the first case, large foreign firms can increase the income-earning ability of a small domestic enterprise by incorporating it into a larger complex and giving it access to the advantages of firm-scale economies. Such conduct also preserves the typically close interdependence of firms and has the least effect on prices and industry structure. In the second case, the entry of a foreign firm adds a new market player to the industry. The choice between these two options is based on the same analysis noted with regard to large-scale entry into oligopolistic markets. In addition to the benefits stronger competition creates, the existence of foreign subsidiaries in a small economy may benefit the economy through access to technological innovations. This benefits the domestic market in several ways, including the introduction of domestic workers to new techniques and technologies, elevating the small country's prospects for its own future innovations, and limiting oligopolistic coordination if it introduces heterogeneity in costs or in products.

The foregoing analysis demonstrates that the structure and performance of a small economy are influenced by its international trade. Trade policy is thus an important tool available to small economies for improving market performance.[69] When trade is substantial, it might even negate a presumption of smallness resulting from the size of the domestic population.

There is a clear interaction between trade and competition policy. When trade barriers are reduced, competition policy plays an important role in facilitating trade by reducing private barriers to the entry of foreign importers and to the export of products from within national boundaries.[70] The freer the trade, the stronger the incentives of firms to re-erect barriers and keep their historical advantage. Competition policy can create a level playing field by ensuring foreign firms' access to the domestic market. Such access should ensure that foreign producers have the ability to compete with domestic producers on fair and equal terms. This involves not only the "formal" right to compete in the domestic market but also the creation and enforcement of rules of conduct prohibiting anti-competitive behavior, such as abuse of monopoly power, and discouraging collusive, exclusionary, or predatory practices. For example, when distribution or marketing channels are limited, competition policy has an important role in ensuring that foreign importers have the same access to these channels as do domestic producers. Competition policy has an additional important role in preventing anti-competitive conduct among foreign firms trading in the domestic market as well as anti-competitive agreements between domestic and foreign firms that affect the markets.

When trade barriers are high, competition policy is an important tool for regulating the conduct of firms in small and closed or semi-closed markets. Competition policy also plays a critical role when unrestricted exposure to international trade is not sufficient to solve efficiency problems. As we have seen, the abolition of trade barriers does not always lead to such an expansion of markets for domestic producers that the number of competitors facing them would become large and competition would take place. The existence of significant costs of trading means that firms in small economies often do not compete in a market larger than the domestic market. It may well be that competing imports act like a fringe of small domestic rivals rather than a force linking domestic prices to those of the world market, and the pro-competitive effect of participating in export markets is curbed when domestic sellers can practice price discrimination against domestic buyers. These efficiency concerns remain, owing to factors such as high adaptation and transportation costs, timeliness of supply, and the inherent nature of service markets. Thus, measures to reduce seller concentration, entry barriers, or firms' opportunities to collude still hold promise for securing more efficient market performance.[71] In other words, even in a small market with a liberal trade policy, competition policy has a crucial role for increasing efficiency in the market by reducing or eliminating abuses of dominant position and the incentives of firms to collude, and by ensuring that domestic firms have incentives to achieve productive and dynamic efficiency in light of aggressive international competition.

The symbiosis between competition and trade policies in a small market emphasizes the need for their alignment. An interesting indicator of the interdependence between trade and competition policies is evident in the provisions of the Canadian Competition Act, which enable the competition authorities to recommend the removal of customs duties that prevent or lessen competition. Section 31 of the act, for example, empowers the Governor in Council to remove or reduce customs duties whenever, as a result of an inquiry under the act, a judgment of a court, or a decision of the Competition Tribunal, such trade liberalization is required for remedying anti-competitive situations.[72] Such a trade liberalization remedy should be preferred to a conduct-oriented remedy because the former offers the prospect of new entry while the latter does not. This provision has rarely been used, however.[73] Other sections of the act encourage the tribunal to take a trade-liberalizing initiative in that it is empowered to make conditional orders requiring structural remedies unless within a reasonable time custom duties have been removed, reduced, or remitted or restrictions on imports have been reduced or removed.[74] Trade restrictions that are endogenous policy choices made by the small economy's government may also create a self-inflicted tension with competition policy. It is somewhat problematic for a government to bring action (or enable third parties to bring action) against domestic firms for anti-competitive behavior that is a direct result of the inherent characteristics of a small market and that could be solved through the introduction of trade.

Conclusion

Small market size creates a complex trade-off among the three components of efficiency. If a given number of firms can operate efficiently in the market, *productive efficiency* requires that the market contain only this number of firms, all operating at efficient scales. Productive efficiency in a small economy usually implies that concentration should be higher than in large ones, as fewer MES plants and firms can be supported by the market if export is limited.

At the same time, productive efficiency imperatives often cause industrial concentration in a small economy to be high enough to allow some market power to be realized. Efficiency can be adversely affected by patterns of market behavior to which firms in highly concentrated industries are prone. Under monopolistic or oligopolistic market structures, firms have incentives and opportunities to engage in conduct that leads to higher profits and, in many cases, higher costs. Further, entry barriers play an important role in anti-competitive strategies, especially when irreversibility or information asymmetry exist. This, in turn, creates adverse effects on *allocative efficiency.* Moreover, high concentration bears an uncertain relationship to productive efficiency because noncompetitive behavior in concentrated industries can impair it and lead to below-MES levels of production.

Market size also affects *dynamic efficiency,* which involves research and development expenditures designed to create new products and processes as well as technology transfers. Technological change has long been recognized as an important feature of efficiency: innovations serve to lower production costs, which in turn may serve to enhance allocative efficiency within society by freeing resources for use in other industries, and may enhance the quality of the products and the competitiveness and comparative advantage of the innovative firm.[75]

In today's world of rapid technological change, superior technological innovativeness is also crucial for international competitiveness. Absent strategic control of some natural resource (such as petroleum or tourist sites), high material standards of living can be enjoyed only when advanced technologies are mastered,[76] as a comparative advantage is important for economic growth, a balanced government budget, and a stable balance of payments. Widespread mastery of advanced industrial technology may also have positive spillover effects as it increases the capabilities of domestic firms to achieve ever more powerful evolutions, thereby accelerating technical progress.[77] Firms in small economies, however, generally exhibit extremely low levels of continuous research and development on products and processes.[78] The cost disadvantage that this low level of R&D imposes on domestic firms is often significant.

Many empirical studies have tried to determine the complex relationships among market structure, firm size, and technological change.[79] Innovative activity is responsive to both supply and demand conditions.[80] Small size may affect both. If demand is limited, this may affect the level of the appropriable benefits expected to flow from innovation and reduce incentives to innovate. On the supply side, there is a pervasive duality to the effects of both firm size and market structure on innovative efforts. Some researchers have argued that large firm size is more conducive to innovative activity than small firm size.[81] The essence of this argument is that large size is necessary to realize scale economies involved in research, and to allow firms to appropriate sufficient rewards to justify innovative activity. Yet large size can also be a disadvantage in facilitating innovation. In a large corporation the decision to proceed with R&D has to filter through a long chain of command, which may increase the chance that an idea will be rejected. Most studies conclude that R&D increases more than proportionally with scale up to a certain size and then decreases as a proportion of sales. Scherer concluded that "[a] little bit of bigness . . . is good for invention and innovation."[82]

In a small economy "a little bit of bigness" implies high levels of industrial concentration. There is a consensus that concentration aids innovation up to a threshold level, after which there is no further positive relationship. Firms in concentrated markets with little fear of outside entry do not have strong incentives to innovate.[83] Rather, they may attempt to prolong the life of their fixed assets by slowing the rate of adoption of new technology. Such firms may, nonetheless, have incentives to obtain new products and processes through licensing that are unlikely to disturb the existing equilibrium of the industry, or that may give them a significant comparative advantage over their rivals.[84] Small economies may therefore be caught between the necessity of having large firms in order to have successful R&D programs and the fact that such large firms usually imply the existence of high concentration levels, which have proven to exert a depressing effect on innovation. One way to overcome these problems is, of course, to expand the size of the market by exports.[85]

In summary, the small size of an economy places a handicap on its economic performance. The small number of firms in many domestic markets means that competition is likely to be limited, given the existence of disproportionately more natural monopolies, dominant firms, and oligopolies than in large economies. Their presence can be expected to have an adverse impact on the prices of many goods and services over and above those caused by diseconomies of scale. Thus, small economies suffer both from the inability to realize some scale economies and from the lack of competitive conditions in many of their industries.

Market forces alone cannot achieve efficiency in small markets that operate mainly by private ordering through decentralized market exchanges and that are characterized by high concentration levels and high barriers to entry. In the absence of appropriate regulation, market forces will not, in many cases, sustain a desirable degree and form of competitive discipline among firms in the economy. Even openness to trade is limited in its effect on a small economy, when trade barriers are such that domestic players are not significantly affected in their size and price choices by world markets. When this proves to be the case, competition policy has an important role in placing pro-efficiency pressures on domestic producers. Competition policy in a small economy is thus a critical instrument with respect to determining domestic market structure and conduct and the intensity of competition.

Structural and conduct-oriented measures enforced under the aegis of competition law can improve industrial efficiency, impair it, or simultaneously engender mixed effects. I turn next to competition policies that most effectively deal with the special characteristics of small market economies. The empirical conclusions about the structural and performance characteristics of small markets that were explored in this chapter will be translated into competition policy choices.

CHAPTER TWO

The General Implications of Small Size for Competition Policy

Competition laws are part of a set of legal rules that aim at maximizing social welfare. They do so by determining the rules of the game by which competition takes place and by distinguishing normally advantageous competitive behavior from anti-competitive conduct. The basic tool that is used to achieve this aim is the creation of an economic environment in which firms can compete on merit, and consumers can derive the benefits that the market can deliver.

Competition policy is applied to economic situations. It should thus be carefully designed to take into consideration the special characteristics of the market to which it is applied. Even when conditions for perfect competition do not exist, substantial improvements over the market performance that would have prevailed in the absence of regulation can be achieved by seeking the regulatory framework that is best suited for maximizing the benefits of markets to society.

Accordingly, the empirical conclusions about the structural and conduct characteristics of small market economies, which were explored and analyzed in Chapter 1, should be translated into policy choices. In this chapter I explore the basic policy choices that need to be incorporated into competition policy in small economies.[1] The first section focuses on the goals of competition policy in a small economy. As I will argue, a small economy cannot afford to be vague in setting its goals, but rather should set clear and determinate goals that focus on achieving economic efficiency. The following sections survey in a general manner the dilemmas of competition policy that are unique, or more pronounced, in small economies as well as the basic principles that should be applied to solve these dilemmas. These principles will serve as a framework for the rest of the book. The next three chapters are organized along the market structures that are prevalent in small economies—monopoly, natural monopoly, and oligopoly. Chapter 6 focuses on mergers that create such market structures.

The main assessment criterion used in these discussions is the ability of the regulatory method to enhance and maximize domestic economic welfare. The regulatory regime should create incentives for industries not only to achieve allocational efficiency but also to minimize production costs and engage in innovation so long as the incremental costs of those efforts are exceeded by the value of the cost savings thus achieved.

Certainty is an additional assessment criterion. Reasonably clear rules that are consistently applied are important because they allow firms to assess their legal risk a priori and to adjust their competitive behavior accordingly.[2] Clear rules may also reduce the costs of administering competition policy. Administerability issues will also be taken into account.

The Goals of Competition Policy

In a small economy it is vital that the goals of competition policy be clearly, consciously, and unambiguously defined, and that economic efficiency be given primacy over other goals. Goals signal to market participants, as well as to the relevant authorities, how the law should be interpreted and implemented. While goals should always be clear, the special characteristics of small economies increase the need for clarity. The reason is that in small economies, striking a balance between competing goals raises particularly difficult trade-offs that may create high degrees of uncertainty.

Competition policy is basically designed to protect, promote, and encourage the competitive process. Competition is valued for its effectiveness as a dynamic device for efficiently allocating society's resources and for enforcing market discipline by market pressure from alternative sources of supply and the desire to keep ahead of rivals. Competition may also be valued for other reasons that are more social and political (what I will call social goals): it disperses wealth and opportunity. Were it possible to achieve all the goals of competition policy simultaneously, this analysis would have been an easy one. The problem is that these goals conflict in many situations that are common in small economies. We should therefore adopt a broader social perspective that aims to maximize the aggregate benefits to society which in some cases may come at the expense of specific goals.

Small economies should strive to achieve economic efficiency as their main goal because they cannot afford a competition policy that is prepared to sacrifice economic efficiency for broader policy objectives. Most important, when social goals conflict with economic efficiency, courts either cannot materially promote them or can do so only at unacceptable costs. Undeviating pursuit of wealth dispersion and small size of firms at the expense of efficiency will be costly in small economies because inefficient firms will be preserved in the market, and thus the market will operate inefficiently. If such protection were nonetheless pursued, it would have to involve the whole scope of the market, since sporadic protection of small firms would make little contribution to social goals. Systematic protection, however, would impose unacceptably high economic costs on the economy. Also, competition law efforts to preserve small business units over more efficient larger rivals would often be futile without costly ongoing regulation, because these inefficient firms would either exit the market or grow internally to efficient sizes. But even if efforts to preserve small-sized firms were not futile, they would involve the courts in essentially political decision making for which there are no appropriate legal criteria, and in a costly regulatory, supervisory role for which they are ill equipped. Thus the protection of competitors instead of competition would appear to be costly as well as producing arbitrary results that would make competition law unpredictable and obscure clear thinking about its proper and attainable objectives. Even when there is no evident conflict, injection of social goals, by broadening the proscriptions of business conduct, would multiply legal uncertainties.[3] In addition, such protection of small firms harms consumers who, on average, are likely to be less wealthy than the owners of small businesses, especially when such businesses are protected by competition law.

Moreover, even if the protection of small businesses *were* our chosen goal, competition policy should not be chosen as the method to achieve it. Competition law, as its name indicates, is aimed at facilitating competition among potential rivals. It strives to achieve this goal by reducing artificial barriers to competition and by allowing market participants to interact independently. Tax measures, for example, might be better tools for achieving such goals. Finally, monopoly, or rather the incentive to become one, is an important "engine" that facilitates competition. Limiting business size per se thus conflicts with the basic principles on which competition policy is based.

Although these arguments apply to any economy, regardless of its size, smallness intensifies the primacy of efficiency. In large economies social goals are served, to a considerable extent, by the competition policies that promote economic efficiency and progressiveness. The goals of dispersed power and better business opportunities are achieved, in many cases, by a competition policy that eliminates monopoly not attributable to economies of scale or superior skill and prevents mergers, agreements, or practices that obstruct competition. But even if competition policy makes concessions to social goals, the few instances of market imperfections in a largely competitive environment are not apt to have much adverse incremental impact on the distribution of income and the maintenance of small, dispersed firms. In a small economy, by contrast, economies of scale in production or distribution reduce, by definition, the number of firms necessary to supply any given demand, and may reduce or altogether eliminate competition in the affected market. Accordingly, economic and social objectives may substantially diverge when efficiency dictates displacement of small firms by larger business units.

Moreover, in small economies the argument that the protection of small business is based on individual choice is limited. Once we constrain the size each business can achieve and limit its ability to take advantage of the natural conditions of the market, we inevitably constrain the freedom of choice.

Finally, the importance of economic efficiency as a primary objective becomes highlighted in a small economy in which interdependencies in the interests of various stakeholders are likely to be more significantly affected by a particular market transaction. This reality increases the probability of lobbying, rent-seeking behavior, and political posturing aimed at the "safeguarding" or pursuit of other objectives that a public benefit or interest criterion promotes if not facilitates. If competition policy is influenced by non-economic considerations, the risk of costly industrial policy in the guise of competition policy becomes high.[4] At the same time, however, efficiency considerations might bring about the creation of larger enterprises, which may exert political pressure to use the competition law system strategically as a method for achieving private interest advantages. Efficiency might therefore have to be qualified by public choice considerations in dealing with very large and influential enterprises.

Accordingly, in small economies social goals should be given little or no independent weight in formulating competition policy. This is not to say that when non-economic considerations exist, such as the need to produce a certain product within jurisdictional borders for security reasons, they should be disregarded. Yet these considerations should be limited in their extent and specifically set out in the proper legislation.

The primacy of economic efficiency has been recognized in several small economies. For example, it was expressed in the amendment to the New Zealand Commerce Act that came into force in May 2001. The amendment replaced the statement of purpose that was included in the title of the act to read: "to promote competition in markets *for the long-term benefit of consumers*" (the words that were added by the amendment are emphasized). The change, according to the explanatory note, clarifies that competition is not an end in itself but a means to promote the long-term benefit of consumers and New Zealanders as a whole.[5] A clear goal provision can signal the legislator's intent to regulators as well as to market participants.

Unfortunately, however, this has not been the case in all small economies. Many laws enumerate a long list of potentially conflicting goals, much like the purpose clause of the Canadian Competition Act, which enumerates four different goals. It provides that the act should maintain and encourage competition in Canada "in order to promote efficiency and adaptability of the Canadian economy, in order to expand opportunities for Canadian participation in world markets while at the same time recognizing the role of foreign competition in Canada, in order to ensure that small and medium sized enterprises have an equitable opportunity to participate in the Canadian economy and in order to provide consumers with competitive prices and product choices."[6] Assuming that the purpose clause is not merely a harmless statutory placebo intended to reassure all relevant political constituencies of the good intentions of the act, its goals might be said to conflict. The first, second, and fourth goals may be read as emphasizing efficiency. The third goal may be read as another aspect of efficiency: to promote efficiency, conditions of workable competition should be created, whenever possible, by ensuring that the number of firms operating in the market will be large. But it can also be construed as a public interest argument based on the need to ensure that small firms have an "equitable" share of economic activity. The second interpretation is strengthened by the argument that the legislature does not waste its words and thus would not have included this goal if it did not add to the other goals. Achieving all of the enumerated objectives simultaneously may thus be unrealistic, as several are inherently contradictory.[7]

Stating no goals, or stating the goals too broadly or elusively, may also be problematic. The Israeli Restrictive Trade Practices Act,[8] for example, does not include an explicit goals provision. Several provisions signal that its ultimate goal is to regulate market conduct in accordance with the "public interest." Public interest, however, is a very broad notion, elusive in meaning, which may relate to a diversity of economic as well as non-economic goals that may be inconsistent in some respects. The rhetoric used by the courts as well as the director of the Competition Authority signals that the act's goal is mainly economic: to eliminate obstacles to market competition, which is vital to the proper functioning of the market, and to regulate the operation and creation of economic entities that possess monopoly power.[9] Nevertheless, such broad economic language, which manipulates the rhetoric of competition without penetrating the underlying substance, does not necessarily limit the possible interpretation of the law's provisions.

Yet even if economic efficiency is the ultimate goal, it is difficult, if not impossible, to create a purpose clause that will direct enforcers and market participants to a conclusive interpretation in all cases. The intermediate objectives of economic efficiency and progressiveness are composed of allocative, productive, and dynamic efficiency. In some settings, and especially in concentrated markets, all three cannot simultaneously be realized, and when this is so, competition policy faces complex economic trade-offs. It is with these trade-offs that the rest of this book is concerned.

Recognizing the Relative Importance of Productive Efficiency Considerations

We have seen the conflict that small size creates among productive, dynamic, and allocative efficiency. The dilemma for competition policy is how to reconcile the technical constraints that productive efficiency places on the number of sellers with the assumed undesirability of a certain type of industry behavior created by high degrees of concentration on allocative and dynamic efficiency.

One implication of the fact that in small economies large firm or plant size might be required in order to achieve MES is that high levels of industrial concentration may be a necessary evil in order to achieve productive efficiency. Accordingly, a small economy should not pursue a policy that views high concentration levels as undesirable per se. Rather, competition policy should be sympathetic toward the enhancement of output by individual firms, through either internal growth, mergers, or joint ventures, which allows for the exhaustion of economies that were not exhausted by the previous market structure and could not be exhausted in less anti-competitive ways. For instance, the merger of ownership of plants or firms of sub-optimal size, operating in the same market, may promote the consolidation of plant or firm capacity and the eventual achievement of economies of large scale.

The drawback of such a policy is, of course, higher levels of concentration. One social cost of higher concentration levels might be the increase in the market power of firms and with it their ability to charge prices much above costs, which in turn decreases allocative efficiency. Higher concentration levels are not a free good also because of income distributions caused by increased market power, the impact that widespread cartelization can have on dampening entrepreneurial vigor, and the social and political malaise that follows from excessive concentration of economic power. How much weight one wishes to place on such costs is a question of values. Yet the efficiency benefits from mergers and internal growth in small markets can be sufficiently compelling in at least a subset of cases that policy makers ought not to reject these possibilities out of hand.

Competition policy should thus strive to strike the optimal balance between structural efficiency and competitive vigor so that firms may operate at efficient scales and pass at least some of the benefits of greater efficiency on to consumers. The key question is a matter of degree: How sizable are the benefits compared to the drawbacks of larger size of operation? Some mergers, for example, may lead not to the consolidation of production but rather to higher prices through the exercise of greater market power by the newly created firm. It is an appropriate goal of public policy to prevent such mergers. Other mergers might create economies of scale while increasing the market power of the merging parties. This increase in market power, however, may be a minor consideration if oligopolistic or monopolistic conditions are already present and prices are already at high levels. Thus, when competition fails—because markets are so small in relation to MES that tight oligopoly is inevitable—permitting still higher seller concentration levels to develop and to achieve productive efficiency can sometimes be warranted. Concentration in such situations provides a second-best solution to the plant-specific scale economies problem.

Similar dilemmas arise in the regulation of cooperative agreements among rivals, such as specialization agreements or joint ventures and strategic alliances for shared research and development, production, or marketing functions. Such agreements raise trade restraint concerns, especially those involving the facilitation or enhancement of cooperation among competitors in an already concentrated market. At the same time, cooperative agreements may enable a group of firms to carry on an activity on a more efficient scale; to reduce information or transaction costs; to engage in expensive, innovative projects; or to eliminate free rider problems. Absent such agreements, many firms in small economies will incur high costs and might abandon these projects altogether, thereby reducing dynamic, productive, and even allocative efficiency.

Accordingly, small economies should reject a policy that views agreements that have the potential to increase productive or dynamic efficiency as illegal per se. Rather, they should opt for a rule that balances possible efficiency enhancements against the anti-competitive effects of the cooperative conduct and allow arrangements in which the benefits offset the restrictions on competition. The solutions to such dilemmas are developed throughout the chapters that follow.

The Limited Effectiveness of Structural Remedies

Another implication of the basic dilemma created by small size is that structural remedies to lower seller concentration should be limited when scale economies are significant. Structural remedies, such as the dissolution of monopolistic or oligopolistic structures by reducing concentration, may help reduce the feasibility of market power, collusion, and interdependent behavior. At the same time, they usually involve a trade-off between enhancing competition and exploiting potential cost efficiencies that flow from MES of production, when applied in small economies. Even if firms can be broken up into smaller parts, market demand might constrain the number of efficient units so that oligopolistic conditions would prevail. Moreover, structural remedies based on mere size alone might deter or prevent highly efficient dominant firms from competing aggressively or from taking advantage of their economies of scale or of scope, or their new product development. In addition, structural remedies might not be effective without costly ongoing regulation, as small inefficient firms would not survive in a free market and would eventually grow to larger sizes that allow them to take advantage of scale economies. Accordingly, small economies should generally reject laws that prohibit large size per se or that adopt structural solutions to all market power issues. Nevertheless, where structural remedies may achieve efficient results in small economies, they should be seriously considered. Given the many problems involved in conduct regulation, structural measures may provide an important solution.

The Relative Significance of Conduct Regulation

A policy that is more lenient toward mergers and the internal growth of firms must be accompanied by legal rules minimizing the effect of more concentrated market structures on industry efficiency. Competition policy in a small economy should thus aim to minimize the undesirable economic effects of concentrated market structures and support the dynamic, long-run market forces that lead to more efficient market structures.

One method of achieving this goal is to apply strict rules to collusive anti-competitive behavior. Such a policy may help break down oligopolistic coordination and induce oligopolists to operate at higher levels of output and at lower prices than they would have in the absence of legal consequences. This, in turn, will enhance efficiency.

Similarly, a strict policy should be adopted toward exclusionary practices with no offsetting benefits when practiced by monopolies. Given the prevalence of dominant firms in small economies and the length of time it might take market forces to erode them, a small economy cannot afford to leave the regulation of monopoly power to market forces alone. Competition policy must focus particularly on deterring the creation and maintenance of artificial barriers to entry in order to permit new firms to enter and to expand in monopolistic industries and increase competition. New entrants must have the opportunity to enter a market without handicaps other than those arising from the first-mover advantages enjoyed by existing competitors, such as well-established ties with consumers and skilled employees. Adoption of a strict anti–exclusionary conduct policy is one method for achieving this goal. Another involves ensuring the disclosure of accounting and profit information by the dominant firm so that it becomes more difficult for it to hide areas of rapid growth or high profitability behind a protective shield of consolidated reporting. These methods and additional ones are elaborated below.

The Difficulty of Applying Simplistic Rules in Small Economies

An important effect of the economic conditions of small economies is that they cannot afford to transplant simplistic competition policies applied in large economies. In a large economy, simplistic rules that tend to deny categorically that real benefits can come from concentration-increasing measures have little effect on efficiency. This is because high concentration levels are rare, and most production takes place under conditions sufficiently competitive that the benefits from further concentration must on average be quite small. In a small economy, however, it is much less clear that single-minded reliance on competitive forces is the best policy. Competition is not always more conducive to the efficiency of the market. Rather, there exists a substantial array of cases in which high seller concentration could lead to larger, more efficient production. Thus, competition policy in small economies requires the balancing of competing considerations that need to build on more than the simple and categorical rules that can often be used in large economies.

One prominent example is the role of structural considerations as a basis for a policy toward mergers in some large economies. Simple structural measures are commonly the main indicators of market power associated with mergers. Sometimes the high concentration levels resulting from a merger will be sufficient reason for blocking it. Yet concentration measures alone are not a good guide for competition policy for small economies. Rather, measures of levels of concentration should be balanced with productive efficiency considerations dictated by market size.

Unfortunately, the trade-offs facing competition policy in a small economy may make it more difficult to set general rules that can serve as a basis for a policy. To illustrate, there can be no a priori indication as to whether or not market structures that lead to a significant increase in seller concentration in a market are, on balance, undesirable. Thus, a fuller specification of a more appropriate model is called for.

Areas of Competition Policy Not Affected by Market Size

To be sure, the basic economic theory that serves as the basis for competition policy in large economies can apply equally to small ones. Although a small economy may require a more careful balancing among allocative, productive, and dynamic efficiencies, differences in size have no effect on many areas of competition policy. These include predominately anti-competitive practices with limited or no offsetting efficiency effects. The most striking example is the conduct of a collusive oligopoly that does not bring about any efficiencies by allowing its members to realize scale economies. The size of the economy need not materially affect the policy toward such collusive conduct, given that it is against the public interest in an economy of any size. The same is true for abuse-of-dominance offenses that enable incumbent monopolists to create artificial barriers to entry that are not justified by offsetting efficiencies.

It is nonetheless true that the prevalence of collusive conduct or abuse of dominance is generally much higher in small economies than large ones and that the remedies should usually be conduct-oriented rather than structural. Some offenses, such as exclusive dealing, tying, and refusal to deal, may affect competition more severely in a small economy (quantitatively), although the nature of the effect is similar in both large and small jurisdictions (qualitatively). To illustrate, in small economies, exclusive dealing may more often effectively foreclose some markets for potential competitors. Where, for example, a monopolistic supplier of an intermediate good undertakes not to sell its products to another distributor, a monopoly is effectively created in the market for the final goods, a situation tantamount to vertical integration. As many more markets in the small economy are monopolistic, exclusive-dealing has stronger effects on a small economy than on a larger, less concentrated one. By a series of regional exclusive dealing contracts with major wholesalers or retailers, a manufacturer in a concentrated market can make entry of new firms into the industry more difficult and can even drive existing firms out of it. In large economies, by contrast, the effect of exclusive dealing is usually much more limited, as agreements with several dealers will still leave a sufficient number of uncommitted distributors.[10] Also, in a small economy a relatively small capital requirement or a rise in costs created by exclusionary conduct might constitute a barrier to entry, as there is a greater risk than in a large economy that demand would not be sufficient to yield a normal return.

Here I have outlined the basic principles for competition policy in small economies. In the following chapters I apply them to different market structures in order to formulate a coherent and efficient competition policy.

CHAPTER THREE

The Regulation of Single-Firm Dominance

The costs of single-firm dominance have long been recognized. Such costs may include, but are not limited to, allocative inefficiency resulting from monopoly pricing and output decisions, the potential for productive inefficiency, limited product selection, and the costs of rent-seeking behavior. Large firms may also be able to exert political influence on regulators and legislatures disproportionate to their absolute size. Such costs accrue when dominant firms become immune, to a large degree, to the competitive process and its discipline. As market dominance is quite common in small economies, it is one of the most important issues with which their competition policies must deal. Accordingly, in this chapter I focus on the choice of policy instruments necessary to regulate the economic power of single-firm dominance. Such regulation is as significant a variable as the choice of technology in determining the economic outcomes in small economies.

As I will argue throughout this chapter, small economies require a different focus and emphasis in their competition laws than do large economies to provide efficient and effective solutions to the regulatory challenges posed by dominant firms. In the first section I define dominant position in a market, showing that the *typical* market shares that may serve as a prima facie indicator of market power should be lower in small economies than in large ones. The second section analyzes the regulation of mere dominance and monopoly pricing. Several guidelines for regulating mere monopolies are suggested, when such regulation is applied. The third section focuses on the exclusionary conduct of dominant firms which constitutes an abuse of that dominance. I identify several types of conduct that should be analyzed differently in small economies than in large ones.

Dominant Position Defined

As Confucius once said, if names are not correct, language will not be in accordance with the truth of things. Hence, I first introduce the relevant terminology. Dominant firms are generally defined according to the degree of their market power. Market power is a central feature in competition law analysis. With limited exceptions, if a firm (or a group of firms, acting jointly) does not have significant market power, its conduct is irrelevant for competition law purposes. Accordingly, how one determines whether and to what extent market power exists in particular circumstances is an important issue.

What, then, is the degree of market power the abuse of which should be deemed anti-competitive? As George Hay suggests, the key questions can be formulated accordingly:

1. What is market power?
2. What is the relevant market?
3. How do we determine the degree of market power in the market?
4. What is the threshold degree of market power necessary to infer a dominant position?[1]

While the answers to the first three questions are usually not unique to one jurisdiction or another, differences in economic size should influence the answer to the fourth question. As the answer to it will depend on the factors that determine the answers to the first three questions, we shall first consider them briefly.

Market power is the ability of a firm (or a group of firms, acting jointly) to raise price above the competitive level without losing so many sales so rapidly that the price increase is unprofitable and must be rescinded.[2] The market power of the firm depends on the barriers to entry or expansion of competitors, which enable it to raise prices persistently above its marginal cost without attracting new entry or expansion. Examples of such barriers include superior production techniques, access to limited supplies of raw materials, economies of scale, and legal barriers such as trade restrictions and licensing requirements. With low entry barriers, prices substantially above economic costs attract other firms to pursue a share of those profits by entering or expanding in the market, subsequently pushing prices down toward competitive levels.

The first step in determining whether a firm has market power is to define the relevant market. The delineation of the relevant market is important because it is only in reference to the supply or acquisition of some defined goods or services that a firm's market power can be assessed. The test is basically one of substitutability, in terms of both supply and demand. Thus, the relevant market is the arena within which significant substitution in consumption or production occurs. A narrow or a broad definition of the relevant market affects the analysis of a dominant position. For example, if the market is defined too narrowly, then almost every firm will have high market shares in its area of operation, which might, in turn, serve as prima facie indicators of market power.

Should the relevant market be defined differently in small economies than in large ones? The answer is negative. The crux of the analysis, in small and large economies alike, is the degree of substitutability in the relevant market. Nonetheless, it is important, especially in small economies, to define markets as including current or potential imports, which are real and significant substitutes for domestic products.[3] Otherwise, the market power of domestic firms will be systematically exaggerated.[4]

Once the relevant market is defined, the next step is to calculate the degree of market power of the firm. One method is to use the Lerner index, which indicates the proportional derivation of price at the firm's profit-maximizing output from the firm's marginal cost at that output. The Lerner index can be calculated by using three factors: market demand elasticity, supply elasticity of competing or fringe firms, and the relevant firm's market share.[5] The elasticity of demand signifies the rate of substitution of consumers to other products, at a given price level. The higher the substitutability, the higher the elasticity of demand and the lower the market power of the firm, ceteris paribus. Supply elasticity signifies the ease of entry or expansion of current or potential competitors into the market. It is influenced by the height of entry barriers into the relevant firm's market. Absent entry barriers, a firm cannot control prices in the long run, no matter how large its current market share, because potential competitors will enter and bid down the price. Supply elasticity can be low owing to some technological incapability of firms to expand output rapidly (e.g., economies of scale, the limited availability of raw materials, legal barriers). Firms may also be disinclined to expand for reasons of oligopolistic interdependence. The third factor, market share, defines the share of the allegedly dominant firm in the relevant market. This share is usually calculated on the basis of total production, but it can also be based on other factors, such as production capacity. William Landes and Richard Posner suggested that the market power of a firm be computed as follows: $Li = Si / (Edm + Esj(1 - Si))$ where Li is the Lerner index of firm i, Si is the market share of firm i, Edm is the market elasticity of demand, and Esj is the elasticity of supply of competing or fringe firms.[6]

This formula is not, however, very practical, as it is unlikely that there will be precise estimates of elasticity of supply and demand. Hence, many jurisdictions adopt a more pragmatic approach, suggested by Landes and Posner, that relies on market share as the primary determinant of market power. Inferences of market power are based on a firm's market share, on the assumption that the relevant elasticities are not unusually high or low. When it can be shown that the assumption is false, appropriate adjustments are made. When, for example, demand is highly inelastic because there are not even remotely close substitutes for the product in question, a firm's market share will tend to understate the degree of its market power. In such cases the firm may possess dominant market power notwithstanding the fact that its market share is somewhat less than the usual benchmark. Similarly, when the supply elasticity of the remaining firms is unusually low, a given market share would signify more market power than in the usual case, and vice versa. In the extreme, if barriers to entry are very low, historical market shares have no significance at all.[7]

The market share–based approach to determining market power has many advantages, as dominant position is easily inferred from market share data that are generally readily available, whereas demand and supply elasticities are not easily determinable. Market shares also create administrative convenience and reduce litigation costs, as no lengthy proceedings or economic analyses are necessary to determine market power. In addition, they signal to market participants, though without precision, their "safe harbors." At the same time, the approach has significant flaws. One of the main criticisms points to the fact that this approach might produce highly inaccurate results, especially in differentiated product markets, where market definition—and thus shares in the relevant market—are necessarily based on somewhat arbitrary estimations of market boundaries, and the result is necessarily inaccurate.[8] Corrections based on supply and demand elasticities are not easily applied. Econometric estimates of demand elasticities, when available, are more informative than market shares in determining market power. Such estimates may not, however, always be available. Accordingly, I do not argue for the adoption of the market share–based approach. I do, however, discuss this approach, as it is commonly used in all jurisdictions.

At the same time, however, in some circumstances market shares serve as more than a surrogate for market power. Rather, the ability of a firm to engage in exclusionary practices stems from its portion of the relevant market. Fidelity rebate schemes, whereby the dominant firm reduces its price if the customer buys most or all of its demand from the monopolist, may, for example, succeed in maintaining or enhancing the monopolist's market power precisely because they are based on the existing high market share of the dominant firm. Quantity rebate schemes, which offer a lower price on the total sale provided the customer meets a certain quantity threshold, may also have similar effects.

The Israeli case of *Yediot*[9] serves as an interesting example. The newspaper Yediot Aharonot enjoys a monopoly position in the market for daily newspapers in Hebrew. Its market share at the relevant period was approximately 50 percent, while the market shares of its two major competitors were approximately 25 percent and 10 percent. Yediot engaged in a target discount strategy whereby it more than tripled the commission to its distributors (from 15 percent to 50 percent of the price of the newspaper), provided they continued to buy at least the number of newspapers they had bought in the past, and that no unsold newspapers were returned to it. The court found the policy to be anti-competitive as it created an economic incentive for the distributors to sell as many copies of Yediot as they could, thereby reducing the number of other newspapers sold (e.g., by positioning Yediot more prominently or by supplying other newspapers only on specific demand). One of the main reasons that led to this finding was the fact that this policy gave Yediot an advantage that was based not on the superiority of its product but rather on its current market shares. Its competitors could not offset the effects of Yediot's strategy by engaging in a similar policy because of their low market shares. As the number of copies of Yediot sold was regularly double the number sold by its biggest competitor, the latter would have had to give its distributors larger discounts in order to create a similar incentive for them to sell its newspaper.[10] Furthermore, the distributors might reject a similar strategy by Yediot's rivals' in order to safeguard their long-term relationship with the market leader. Similarly, Microsoft's strategy of limiting the compatibility of its operating system with its rivals' software applications was rational only because it already had high market shares in a market characterized by significant network effects.[11]

Market power in a relevant market is a matter of degree. It is not a single quantum but rather a spectrum, ranging from the very slight to the very substantial. The degree of market power necessary for a firm to be said to have a dominant position in its market, that is, the degree of market power that should be deemed potentially actionable by competition laws in single-firm violations, is of great importance. How much market power is sufficient to warrant possible intervention under the competition laws is a question of legal policy. All jurisdictions have adopted high thresholds of market power, such as "significant," "dominant," or "monopoly" power.

Should small economies adopt lower thresholds of dominant market power than larger economies? When the law uses open terminology that allows the courts to take into account all factors that determine market power (i.e., market share, supply elasticity, and demand elasticity), there should be no difference between small and large economies, given that the factors in the equation for calculating market power will denote the different circumstances in such markets.

When market shares are used as a prima facie indicator of market power, however, in small economies the *typical* market share that will signify market dominance should be lower than in large ones. The reason is that elasticity of supply will usually be lower, given the prevalence of scale economies and entry barriers in small economies. In other words, the smaller the economy, the higher the typical barriers to entry (lower elasticity of supply), and therefore the lesser the constraints that potential entry places on a firm that tries to raise prices above marginal cost, and the lower the market shares necessary to infer dominant market power. For the same reason, in small economies current market shares are a better indicator of the market power of a firm than in large ones.

The logic behind this argument is that when entry barriers are high, the dominant firm is less constrained in its conduct by potential entrants.[12] For example, when large scale economies exist, the dominant firm may be the only one able to enjoy low production costs, while fringe firms compete with higher-production-cost products under its price umbrella or compete with highly differentiated products. Also, firms operating in the market acknowledge their interdependence and are more prone to follow the price leadership of a dominant firm. While market share serves only as a prima facie indicator of market power, in general in a small economy it may be presumed that, owing to its small size, there will not be many competing firms in the remaining parts of the market. Thus, in small economies a given market share will *usually* signify more market power than in a large one, all else being equal.

Of course, this is true only as a general presumption, given the possibility of adjustments when other factors, such as the elasticity of demand or supply, differ significantly from the norm. The Australian case of *Mark Lyons*[13] serves as a good illustration of this point. There, the defendant was the only supplier of Salomon Alpine ski boots. The plaintiff, whose dealership with the defendant had been terminated, was a ski equipment retailer that operated ski shops and also organized warehouse sales of ski equipment. The court found that Salomon possessed a dominant position in the ski equipment market, despite the fact that its market share was roughly a third of the market. The court stated that Salomon's market power resulted from the fact that Salomon was widely regarded as the market leader in terms of innovative ideas and because 90 percent of Australian ski retailers found it necessary to stock Salomon ski boots.

Small economies should also adopt a refined approach to a presumption of market power based on market structure alone. Presumptions of market power should be based not only on the market share of the allegedly dominant firm in absolute terms but also on its market share relative to the market share of its largest competitors. The proposed refinement is necessary especially when the threshold market share necessary for a presumption of monopoly power is equal to or lower than 50 percent. A very fragmented competitive fringe, for example, may also indicate stronger market power of the dominant firm.[14]

Are the approaches to market power adopted by the competition laws of small and large economies compatible with this analysis? As I have noted, the precise point at which market power becomes substantial is hard to define. That is why most competition laws use open terminology, leaving much discretion to the courts or the competition authorities. The EC and New Zealand's competition laws require a "dominant position" in the relevant market;[15] the U.S. Sherman Act requires "monopoly power";[16] the Canadian Competition Act uses terms such as "substantial or complete control [of] a class or species of business"[17] or "major supplier of a product in a market";[18] the Australian Trade Practices Act requires "a substantial degree of power."[19] The Israeli Trade Restrictive Practices Act is unique in that it predefines threshold market shares that indicate a "significant influence on the market."[20]

In most jurisdictions, market share alone is not an indicator of market power. The relative effect of percentage command of the market varies with other factors, including the height of barriers to entry into the market, demand elasticity, market fragmentation, abnormal profits, corporate conduct, and historic trend. This open-ended approach allows authorities and courts to define dominant position in accordance with the specific circumstances in the relevant market. Nonetheless, most courts usually rely on market shares that persist for some time as a primary indicator of market power, and interpret this information in each case by reference to the qualitative indicia of the market's elasticity of demand and supply.[21] Table 3.1 summarizes the market shares typically necessary to establish a dominant position.[22] It clearly indicates that most small economies take their lower typical market shares into account. The New Zealand case law is unique in that it has adopted a rigid and rigorous test for dominance that sets a higher threshold than that adopted in the EC and in Australia, although its markets are typically smaller than those of Australia, and much smaller than those in the EC. Arguably, New Zealand's rigorous and restrictive test is a result of the "dictionary approach" to dominance adopted by its Court of Appeal,[23] which unfortunately

Table 3.1 Market power thresholds in different jurisdictions

Jurisdiction (listed by size)	Dominant position definition	Market share threshold	Role of threshold (mandatory or suggestive)
United States	Monopoly power	Usually 70–75%; rarely below 50%[a]	S
EC	Dominant position	45–55%[b]	S
Canada	Substantial control	87% high enough. Predatory pricing guidelines, 35%[c]	S
Australia	Substantial degree of power	60% large enough. 7–15% too low[d]	S
New Zealand	Dominant position	Higher than in Australia and the EC[e]	S
Israel	Significant influence on the market	50%[f]	M (unless minister declares lower)
Malta	Dominant position	40%[g]	M (unless proven to be lower)
Cyprus	Dominant position	Follow the EC	S

a. When market share is 70–50%, courts usually seek corroborating evidence for the existence of market power. P. Areeda, H. Hovenkamp, and J. L. Solow, *Antitrust Law,* vol. 2A (Boston: Little, Brown, 1995), para. 532b; William M. Landes and Richard A. Posner, "Market Power in Antitrust Cases," 94 *Harv. L. Rev.* 937, 951 (1981).

b. *Hoffman La Roche v. Commission* [1979] 1 ECR 461; *AKZO Chemie BV v. Commission* (C-62/86) [1991] ECR I-3359, para. 60, [1993] 5 CMLR 215; *Hilty AG v. Commission* (T-30/89) [1991] ECR II-1439 [1992] 4 CMLR 16. Although the EC is a large market, the lower thresholds for dominant position may result from the fact that the Treaty of Rome's fundamental emphasis is on facilitating trade between member states.

c. *Canada (Director of Investigation and Research) v. Laidlaw Waste Systems Ltd.* (1992), 40 CPR (3d) 289, 325. It is difficult to base any conclusions regarding the degree of market power necessary to establish a dominant position on existing Canadian case law given that in all cases the monopolists had a very large market share. Director of Investigation and Research, *Predatory Pricing Guidelines* (1992).

d. *Williams v. Papersave Pty Ltd.* (1987) ATPR 40–781 and (1987) ATPR 40–818; *D&R Byrnes (Nominees) Pty Ltd. v. Central Queensland Meat Export Co. Pty Ltd.* (1990) ATPR 41–028. The threshold was lowered from "in a position substantially to control a market" to "a substantial degree of power in a market."

e. *Telecom Corporation of New Zealand Ltd. v. Clear Communications Ltd.* [1992] 3 NZLR 429 (CA).

f. Restrictive Trade Practices Act of 1988, Sec. 26.

g. The Maltese Competition Act of 1994 defines dominant position as control of over 40% of the market. Although the law allows for a market analysis proof that a lower market share is sufficient for a finding of dominance, the 40% market share is a nonrebuttable presumption when one would have liked to prove the opposite.

serves as a good example of the pitfalls of using open terminology for dominance.

Some jurisdictions, including Israel, Malta, and Norway, use preestablished market shares to define monopoly. The Israeli law, for example, creates a nonrebuttable presumption that control of more than 50 percent of the relevant market is a monopoly. Why has the Israeli legislator chosen 50 percent as the appropriate benchmark? The explanatory memorandum to the act states that "experience has shown that a market share of at least 50 percent signals control of the Israeli market."[24] In special cases, however, the Minister of Commerce may reduce this market share threshold for specific industries. For example, the minister lowered the benchmark from 50 percent to 30 percent in the gas market, in which three almost equal-sized firms operated.[25]

The use of predefined market shares as the sole indicator of a dominant position has the same advantages as an approach that uses market share as prima facie evidence of market power. Yet an approach to market dominance that is based solely on market share suffers from several pitfalls. Most important, as noted earlier, because market share is only one of several factors that determine market power, inferences of power from share alone can be misleading. Another problem with a definition of dominance that is based solely on market share arises when a firm prices its products at a high level, just sufficient to reduce its market share below the benchmark, possibly to avoid being labeled a monopolist. Such pricing creates a deadweight loss, in addition to that resulting from the regular pricing tactics of a monopolist. If the other firms in the market were to follow the same pricing policy, the result would be a price level higher than the previous monopoly level, and with worse output effects, especially because inefficient entrants would be attracted to the market by the price umbrella held over their heads by the existing firms. A more efficient approach would use market share benchmarks as merely presumptive evidence of market power and allow the defendant to rebut this presumption by bringing other evidence, such as the height of barriers to entry and demand substitutability.

The Israeli Competition Tribunal has found an interesting way to circumvent some of the pitfalls of a market-share approach to dominance. In a 2000 decision,[26] the tribunal required proof of market power that went beyond market share to prove a causal connection between the harm to competition and the conduct of the alleged monopoly in all cases in which no statutory presumption of abuse exists. This decision negates, to a large extent, the benefits of a market share approach to dominance, as all the other determinants of market power must be proved by the plaintiff, even if through the back door. A prima facie rule that requires the firm to negate a presumption of dominance based on market share is preferable.

To summarize, the legal concept of monopoly is not restricted to the pure case of one firm controlling 100 percent of the market but may include a dominant firm facing a fringe of smaller competitors or even one smaller competitor. The decisive factor is the existence of a power to raise prices above the competitive level for a significant period of time. There is no single correct formulation of market dominance. Nonetheless, the foregoing analysis points to differences between large and small economies. In a small economy, lower market shares can imply stronger market power than in a large economy, all else being equal. Also, in a small economy, current market shares are a better indicator of the market power of a firm than in a large one.

Regulation of Mere Monopoly

Continued dominance of an industry by a single firm that has obtained and maintained its monopoly position by lawful means ("mere monopoly") has long posed difficult questions for competition law. Single-firm dominance, whatever its origin, commonly results in economic as well as non-economic costs. These costs do not necessarily flow from or may not be accompanied by exclusionary or predatory conduct and thus cannot be reached by conventional conduct-based regulation. Rather, the monopolist's decisions that lack an anti-competitive element are in essence identical to those of firms operating in a competitive industry. For example, all firms set price and output at their profit-maximizing level. In a monopoly market these prices are above marginal cost. But such monopoly pricing is simply a rational exploitation of the profit potential of the current market structure, obtained and maintained lawfully.

Accordingly, one of the most important debates regarding monopolized markets involves the regulation of mere monopoly per se, that is, without need of proof of anti-competitive conduct or intent. Instead, the law is triggered by predetermined market structure factors, such as the size of the dominant firm or its performance variables. The premise of "no-fault" regulatory propositions is that there is no wrongdoing worthy of condemnation, but that the government is acting to correct a socially costly market imperfection. Yet it makes no economic sense to regulate mere monopoly unless one can be sure that such regulation would not alter socially desirable behavior of firms or would not be too costly.

We now turn to the considerations and trade-offs involved in mere monopoly regulation. First I describe the various considerations on which the decision whether to regulate mere monopoly rests. The effect of the size of the economy on the applicability and on the relative weight of such considerations is then examined. Finally, I present and analyze the efficacy of the different methods used to regulate mere monopoly.

Conventional Economic Considerations for Dealing with Mere Monopoly

The social costs of monopoly are often independent of the manner in which the monopoly was historically achieved or of its current engagement in predatory or exclusionary conduct. Even an innocently obtained monopoly can and likely will engage in monopoly pricing, and even dominant firms that do not engage in anti-competitive conduct may produce social losses that far exceed any gains. Why not, then, regulate mere monopoly? In this section we examine the basic considerations on which the policy toward mere monopoly usually rests.[27] It is the relative weight given to each of these considerations that ultimately determines the position to be taken toward mere monopoly. As the next section shows, the relative weight of such considerations changes with the size of the economy. This in turn may lead to the adoption of different regulatory solutions in different-sized economies.

Whether regulation is justified depends, primarily, on the *costs to society* from mere monopoly, which were surveyed previously. Regulation of mere monopoly attempts to reduce at least some of these costs. Regulation of monopoly as such, however, involves important trade-offs and practical problems. Accordingly, a key consideration is the perceived *strength of the self-correcting powers* of the market in the absence of restrictive practices. When competitive conditions may develop, monopoly power will tend to attract new firms into the market that seek to enjoy the high profits available. Such new entry, or the fear of it, will constrain the monopolist's ability to raise prices or otherwise use its market power. Competition may thus be regarded as a dynamic process that sometimes contains the seeds of its own short-term destruction but also contains the seeds for the revival of competition in the long run.

Some economists place significant emphasis on the ability of market forces to deal effectively with monopolies. One of the most vehement opponents of a no-fault monopoly approach is Robert Bork. Bork argued that ignoring the route by which size was achieved is a fundamental error, as inferences about the economic effects of market power properly flow from the origins of such power.[28] The maintenance of size against the eroding forces of the market over a long period of time does not indicate market failure, but rather it indicates either an absence of restriction of output, or superior efficiency, or both. Such arguments ignore possible market failures that do not allow market forces to perform their self-correcting task efficiently and expeditiously. There might be several reasons, other than superior performance, for the persistence of market power, mainly high entry barriers. Furthermore, dominance does not necessarily imply prior or existing superiority on any absolute scale. It might well be that existing and potential rivals, on whom the responsibility for the self-policing function rests, are or may have been inept, especially during the critical formative stages of an industry's development.[29]

Yet even if market forces cannot efficiently erode existing market power, mere monopoly regulation involves serious trade-offs. First and foremost, restraining monopolists that achieved their position solely by fair competition *distorts the incentives* of firms to be more efficient or to create superior products in order to become or to remain a monopoly (the "disincentive effect"). Firms approaching the anti-monopoly rule threshold may have incentives to hold back by forgoing opportunities that allow them to achieve further advantage from their abilities. The effect might be impaired innovative performances, low levels of research and development, and productive inefficiency.

The question is how likely and how significant this disincentive effect will be. Phillip Areeda and Herbert Hovenkamp suggest that the answer depends primarily on the nature of the market and the position of the firm in it at the time when highly successful competitive strategies are identified or implemented. Generally, the greater the effect that competitive conduct has on gaining a dominant position, the greater the disincentive to engage in such conduct. There also exists a positive correlation between the potency of the remedies provided by the mere monopoly rule and the disincentive effect. But even if the competitive move were to subject the firm to regulation, deliberate reduction of research and development enhances the risk of an even greater loss in market position.[30]

Several ways have been suggested to mitigate this disincentive effect, such as deferring relief against mere monopoly until it is apparent that market forces cannot eradicate it. This would allow the firm to retain the supracompetitive profits earned before its monopoly position was detected and remedied while at the same time allowing market forces to perform their role whenever possible.[31] Yet such a regulatory lag might not be a complete answer to the disincentive problem. In the first place, it is an inadvertent method of injecting a profit incentive, as there is no expressed recognition that profits are legitimate and acceptable as a method of encouraging a monopolist to improve its performance. More important, one cannot be sure that the opportunity, provided by the regulatory lag, to obtain monopoly profits is sufficient to avoid serious disincentive effects.[32]

Once we view competition as a process in which firms are urged to take part and compete, regulation of mere monopoly may also be seen as an *inequitable denial of earned rewards*. Yet the question still remains: How high are the acceptable profits that the dominant firm can earn both before and after it is subject to regulation?

Another factor, though of less significance, involves the circular effects of a structure-based policy toward dominance on *the enforcement of other competition law violations*. The inability to deal effectively with established monopoly may result in excessive expansion of anti-merger enforcement.[33] Strong anti-merger policy is not without its costs. It might prevent pro-competitive mergers and divert incentives to merge into incentives to invest inefficiently in internal growth.

Regulation also imposes *direct administrative costs* on both the regulator and the regulated firm. A related and highly significant consideration involves the *efficacy of government intervention*. Government intervention is wasteful when it cannot or does not improve economic performance sufficiently to offset the costs of regulation. The efficacy of government intervention depends on the mode of intervention. Intervention proposals focus on two main options: restructuring of the industry by dissolution of the dominant firm or conduct regulation. Both remedies involve additional considerations beyond those already outlined.

Structural remedies combat monopoly by restructuring the dominant firm so that at least two viable competitors will compete in the market. When applied correctly, structural remedies are most effective in regulating monopolies. To combat monopoly effectively, the regulator must divide the firm in such a way that the monopolized product itself is subsequently produced by two or more competitive firms selling in the same geographic market.

Structural remedies are *not* feasible, however, when monopoly is economically justified or because restructuring would be contrary to other policy objectives. To restructure an inevitable monopoly is pointless and inefficient. After deconcentration, either some firm would expand to take advantage of the opportunity for lower costs with larger output until the market was again concentrated, or the market would operate permanently at an unnecessarily high level of costs. Similarly, when dominance is based on valid intellectual property rights, breakup of dominant firms is contrary to the public policy on which such rights are based.

Even if a structural remedy were feasible, it would still involve the *direct costs of breakup* as well as the costs of inefficient or ineffective restructuring. A major drawback of restructuring involves the difficulties in evaluating scale and scope economies, and in balancing their loss against the gains from a more competitive structure. One method that has been proposed to overcome this problem is the inclusion of an efficiency defense in the mere monopoly rule. Efficiency defenses might, however, be hard to apply. Efficiency cannot easily be quantified, and it is extremely difficult to prove the exact extent of the losses that would be incurred through a proposed dissolution. Accordingly, defendants would be unlikely to carry the burden of persuasion of efficiency defenses successfully. Placing the burden of proof on the government reduces the problem of inefficient restructurings. The main drawback of this method, however, is that the relevant information is usually controlled by the monopolist. Restructuring should thus be considered only when it is likely to improve net economic performance or serve other social objectives substantially, after the costs of restructuring are taken into account.

Conduct regulation strives to set the monopolist's decisions (e.g., price, output, quality) at an economically efficient level, or at least closer to the competitive level. Regulation can take one of many forms. It may involve price, output, and quality or other trade terms, or only one of these parameters; it may create a civil or a criminal violation or may subject a monopoly to regulation per se; regulation may apply to all strategies that deviate from a competitive benchmark or may condemn only rare occasions when the difference between the competitive benchmark and the regulated parameter is deemed excessive. Although these differences are appreciable, conduct regulation has many common elements.

While conduct regulation sets the performance variables of dominant firms at more efficient levels, it suffers from some inherent costs. First and foremost, pricing and output regulation *distorts the price signals* in the market, and in so doing impedes the dynamic adjustment process that might restore competition in the long run. Monopoly pricing acts as a signal to other market participants that higher-than-usual profits can be reaped in a certain industry. These participants may then enter the market in order to enjoy such profits, and prices will eventually be bid down to competitive levels. The profit-maximizing price is thus necessary to make competitive market forces function effectively. When high price is used as a signal of high quality, pricing regulation distorts such price signals to consumers. If, however, contestability is limited in the market, such considerations should be given little weight.

Another major consideration focuses on the institutional limitations of an outside agency to regulate efficiently the decisions of a private firm. In a simplified way, regulation can be viewed as a game between the firm and the regulator, in which the firm is intent on profit maximization while the regulator seeks to maximize social welfare. One of the main difficulties that the regulator faces in achieving optimal regulation is that of *asymmetric information.* The fact that regulators are one step removed from the operations of the productive entity necessarily limits their access to the needed information and their ability to evaluate such information. The result may be that substantial monopoly profits are hidden from regulators. Nonetheless, some part of the monopoly profits are reduced.

Regulation might also be limited by the *institutional apparatus* by which the policy is implemented. When regulatory powers are vested in the courts, judicial decrees must be tailored to what they can supervise. As Donald Turner has argued, courts that would attempt to prevent monopoly pricing by setting lower price levels would be forced to act as public utility commissions.[34] An injunction that would simply prohibit the defendant from further charging monopoly prices would be too vague. It would not give an efficient indication for the correct set of prices that would be deemed lawful. An order requiring the monopolist to set price equal to marginal cost would be very hard to enforce, given all the factors that affect the cost function of the firm, and would have to be constantly adjusted to changes in the cost function. Accordingly, such an order cannot be effectively enforced with good prospects for materially solving the resource allocation problems without involving the courts in a regulatory function. In addition, courts would also have to be involved in regulating quality. As we shall see, an administrative regulatory process may solve some of these problems.

The issue of whether to regulate mere monopoly is also influenced by the scope of the additional regulatory powers of competition authorities and the courts. When such bodies are empowered to prohibit practices that may create market power (preventing mergers, regulating attempts to monopolize by anti-competitive methods), regulation of mere monopoly is deemed less important than when regulation is confined to limiting the exercise of already achieved dominance.

Another factor not to be overlooked in evaluating pricing and output regulation involves its impact on the incentives of firms to integrate vertically in order to circumvent pricing regulation. Vertical integration that is not justified by scope economies may create inefficient results and thus increases the need for closer regulation of a vertically integrated monopolist. The decision whether to price-regulate should also rest on the ability of competition courts and authorities to perform the task effectively.

In summary, condemning or regulating mere monopoly involves serious trade-offs between conflicting considerations. The debate centers mainly on the perceived costs of monopoly, the relative effect of the self-correcting tendencies of the market, the magnitude of the disincentive effects, and the costs of government intervention. We now turn to the effect of the size of the economy on such considerations.

The Effect of Small Size on the Comparative Weight of Conflicting Considerations

The size of the economy affects the comparative weight of some of the considerations that determine whether or not to regulate mere monopoly. First and foremost, the market's self-correcting tendencies are more pronounced in large economies than in small ones. In large economies such tendencies are believed to deal effectively with most unnatural monopolies.

The United States serves as a good example of a large economy that relies on the market's self-correcting tendencies to regulate mere monopolies. Judicial interpretation of the antitrust rules has focused on the presence or absence of exclusionary or predatory conduct in obtaining or in maintaining monopoly power (the behavioral approach).[35] The Supreme Court specifically stated that dominance based on "a superior product, business acumen, or historic accident" does not constitute a violation, and the burden of proof that such conditions do not exist rests on the plaintiff; neither do related phenomena, such as large market share, monopoly pricing, and restricted output, which were not achieved by anti-competitive means.[36]

This permissive approach toward mere monopoly rests primarily on the belief in the self-correcting tendencies of the market as well as the rarity of dominance in U.S. markets. Areeda and Hovenkamp express the view adopted in the U.S. *Standard Oil* case,[37] as follows: "If the law can prevent artificial barriers to such new entry, then the self-correcting forces of the marketplace will impede the attainment and maintenance of monopoly power except where the monopolist is beyond cavil because it was, or continues to be, so efficient and progressive as to out-compete all actual or potential rivals. The rarity of the last exception and the *force of the self-correcting tendency* are powerfully suggested by the relative rarity of persistent single-firm domination in our major national markets."[38]

This, however, cannot as easily be said of small economies, in which the self-correcting forces of the market have a much more limited effect. This results from high barriers to entry into many industries. High entry barriers make it easier to achieve market power and might also prevent the erosion of monopoly power for unacceptably long periods of time. Thus, concentration once achieved may not be easily undone in a short period of time. A firm may remain dominant for long periods despite the lack of continuing superior performance.

In addition, the relative effects of single-firm dominance on a small economy might be much more pronounced than on a large one. To be sure, a large economy may suffer a stronger economic impact of dominance, in absolute terms, than a small one, given the extent of its markets. But the prevalence of dominance in a larger number of industries in a small economy might create a much more significant proportional impact of market power.

Finally, the impact of the disincentive effect created by mere monopoly regulation on small economies differs from its effect on large ones. On the one hand, the more concentrated a market, the greater the possibility that discovery and exploitation of a competitive advantage might lead to a monopoly, and the greater the likelihood that the firm will be cautious about seeking or exploiting such advantages if mere monopoly is regulated. Hence the greater possibility that regulation would have a strong deterrent effect on small, concentrated economies. On the other hand, given the prevalence of scale economies in small economies, dominant positions might be unavoidable with or without engaging in competitive moves. In such cases, mere monopoly regulation has a limited effect on the firms' incentives to engage in additional competitive moves. Accordingly, when monopoly is based on scale and scope economies, dominant position will most likely be unavoidable, and the disincentive effect may not be significant. Also, the disincentive effect can be reduced by following the guidelines to conduct regulation suggested in the next section.

Given these considerations, a small economy requires a more serious deliberation of proposals to regulate mere monopoly. Such issues cannot be brushed aside under the assumption that market forces will take their course in due time. A competition law that is based on the assumption that workable competition is technically feasible and will enhance efficiency is a limited tool. In small economies a dominant position can be acquired quite easily, even without anti-competitive conduct. And once such a position is acquired, it is very difficult to erode it. Regulation of mere monopoly may well be justified if applied correctly.

Analysis of Different Approaches to Regulating Mere Monopoly

Generally speaking, there are two main approaches for regulating mere monopoly. The first, structural, method empowers the courts to break up a monopoly or to regulate it when specified market structure or firm performance preconditions are met. The second method finds abuse of dominant position when the monopolist has engaged in some monopoly pricing, output, or other strategies. The conduct is directly prohibited, subject to criminal, quasi-criminal, or civil sanctions in cases of violations. In this section I analyze and compare the two.

Whatever the regulatory method, we shall see that the attainment or maintenance of a monopoly position per se should not be prohibited. Otherwise, the dynamic process of competition will be severely injured, especially in markets in which scale and scope economies make monopoly almost inevitable.

Breakup or Conduct Regulation of Mere Monopoly

The mere monopoly regulation approach does not require proof of intent or anti-competitive conduct. Instead, regulation is based on market structure or firm performance. A common way to regulate mere monopoly is by subjecting the monopoly to conduct regulation. High prices, restricted output, or other specified trading conditions constitute a cause for regulation, with no need to prove intent or anti-competitive conduct. Rather, the law focuses solely on the harm to consumers.

Conduct regulation has been adopted in many small economies, including Malta, New Zealand, and Israel. Although all jurisdictions do not require proof of anti-competitive conduct or intent as a prerequisite to regulation, other aspects of conduct regulation diverge significantly from one jurisdiction to another (e.g., scope of regulated conduct, procedure, experience and expertise of regulators, nature of remedy). The efficacy of conduct regulation depends, inter alia, on these factors. To provide an empirical basis for the analysis that follows, I survey several examples of regulatory regimes along a continuum from the most interventionist approach to the least.

The Israeli law is highly interventionist in that it grants the Director of the Competition Authority wide discretionary powers to regulate the conduct of a mere monopolist. The director may mandate the monopolist to take any steps necessary to eliminate the current or future harm to the public or to competition resulting from the monopolist's conduct or existence.[39] One common remedy is the issuance of decrees or decisions that regulate aspects of the monopolist's business, such as quality of service, hours of operation, and credit terms.[40] Price regulation is only rarely used, given the difficulties involved in setting efficient prices and the fact that a specific law sets maximum prices of certain products and services.[41] The director's decisions are subject to appeal to the Competition Tribunal.[42] It is noteworthy that until the law was changed several years ago, these regulatory powers were vested in the tribunal.

The conduct of a dominant firm is also regulated in the United Kingdom. There, too, the emphasis is on the way in which monopoly power has been used rather than on anti-competitive intent. The objective is to intervene in markets once it has been determined that monopoly power has been exercised in a way contrary to the public interest. The British system is based on a highly discretionary and pragmatic administrative system. The Competition Commission may investigate industries to determine whether a dominant position is being exploited contrary to the public interest.[43] The process is highly expert and discretionary, involving hearings and gatherings of fact. Its findings are then reported to the Secretary of State and, when appropriate, contain recommendations for action. When, for example, it finds prices or profits to be excessive, it may recommend price or profit regulation.[44] The secretary may then instruct the Director General of the Office of Fair Trading—whose role is to supervise and oversee competition and consumer policy in Britain—to seek undertakings from the dominant firm with a view to promoting the public interest. Failing this, an order may be made directing the dominant firm to take, or refrain from taking, certain actions. There is no participation by judicial bodies in this procedure. The procedure is limited, however, by the inability of the commission to initiate an investigation of industries that are not referred to it by the director general,[45] and by the absolute discretion of the secretary as to whether to follow the recommendations.

Malta also regulates monopoly pricing. The Maltese Competition Act empowers the director of the Office for Fair Competition to issue price orders prescribing the maximum price at which essential goods or services may be sold of offered.[46] Within six months of its publication, the commission, which is in essence an administrative tribunal with at least one economist on its panel, must review the price order. In the interregnum period, until the commission has reached its decision, the order is in force. Once the commission finds the price order appropriate and necessary, it remains in force for a year after its decision. The director has used this power to regulate the price of products of several monopolies, such as local beer. This system enjoys the advantage of immediacy of a price order but limits judicial supervision.

Part IV of the New Zealand Commerce Act enables goods or services to be placed under direct price control by the Commerce Commission when the Minister of Commerce determines that there is limited competition in the market and it is necessary or desirable for prices to be controlled in the interests of users, consumers, or suppliers and the governor-general so declares. The price orders may refer specifically or generally to goods or services and may apply to specific areas, specific characteristics of goods or services, and specific persons. These price control measures are purely prospective.[47] Yet regulation is quite limited as it requires a positive act of the Governor-General and the Minister of Commerce before price is controlled.[48]

Conduct regulation combats mere monopoly by setting trade terms closer to competitive levels. It is an important tool for regulating monopoly conduct that does not constitute abuse of monopoly power, especially when monopoly cannot be easily eroded owing to the natural conditions of the market. It should, nonetheless, be fashioned carefully to limit the disincentive effect of firms operating in the market and other obstacles to conduct regulation.

To combat limitations of traditional competition law regulation resulting from the institutional apparatus of courts, conduct regulation should be performed by the competition authorities. As all jurisdictions that apply conduct regulation have recognized, an administrative and highly discretionary procedure conducted by a competition authority may avoid many of the institutional limitations inherent in the traditional judicial regulatory process, such as proof-related and procedural requirements, which may not be relevant to the economic impact of the conduct. Such a procedure is also timelier and may be more expert, provided that the competition authority is given sufficient resources and is staffed by economic experts. The competition authority may also be better than a direct regulator as it avoids the regulatory capture problems because it is not dependent on a specific industry for its existence. At the same time, the decisions of the authority must be subject to a timely and substantive judicial review by an expert court. It is also important that the competition authority be an autonomous agency headed by a non-political director.[49]

The scope of the regulation is another important parameter that affects its efficacy. The wider the scope, the higher the probability of creating a disincentive effect, but at the same time the better the tools to reduce the costs of monopoly. As I have indicated, jurisdictions differ in the scope of their conduct regulation provisions. These range from the potential regulation of any conduct that harms the public interest (United Kingdom) to the regulation of price only (Malta, New Zealand). The scope of the regulation should be set by weighing its disincentive effect against its benefits. The wider-scoped regulation might be preferable to pricing regulation as the monopolist can at least partially combat the effects of pricing regulation by changing other aspects of its products, such as their quality. Thus to be effective, regulation should include all aspects of the regulated product. Also, regulation of conduct other than price can combat specific practices from their incipiency. For example, it may include regulation of trade terms in standard contracts of the dominant firm that might harm its customers applied before the contracts are signed.

Whatever the scope of regulation, clear guidelines should be set as to how the regulator should use its powers so that firms know in advance what to expect. Most important, regulation should be limited to cases in which the inefficiency created by the dominant firm is significant. Another guideline should limit regulation only to cases in which there is no possibility for reviving competition among existing firms or facilitating new entry in due time. While none of the laws specifically differentiate between monopolies that can be eroded by market forces and those that cannot, the wide discretion granted to the regulator should be interpreted as disallowing it to intervene when the market is not disabled in the foreseeable future. Otherwise such regulation is likely to further remove the possibilities for the natural operation of the self-correcting market mechanism.

It should also be ensured that conduct regulation of mere monopoly is not used unless other regulatory means are less effective in restraining the monopolist. The regulator should thus be prevented from using its regulatory powers over mere monopoly instead of challenging alleged anti-competitive conduct under the abuse-of-dominance provisions. An exception occurs when the legislator has specifically included certain types of conduct, which would normally constitute an abuse, under the conduct regulation procedures. The Israeli law, for example, specifically empowers the director to mandate a monopolist to subject its typical contracts to the scrutiny of a special contracts court to ensure that the monopolist is not imposing unfair trade terms on its trading partners. The director may also require the monopolist to meet the specifications of published standards for its products.[50] Such a requirement may deter a dominant firm from raising rivals' costs by changing its standards after a rival has invested significant resources in facilities that adhere to the old standard. A dominant firm might have an incentive to do so if it were to compete in a downstream market in which it had no monopoly power and it was prevented from realizing monopoly profits through its monopoly arm. These regulatory powers enable the early detection and prohibition of abusive trade terms, before they have had any effect on the market.

An additional guideline should require the regulator to distinguish, whenever possible, between monopolies based on superior efficiency and those that are not. To limit the disincentive effect, a monopolist that achieved its position through superiority should be given sufficient time to reap at least some monopoly profits to justify its efforts and reward it for its superiority. Monopolies based on intellectual property rights should generally not be price-regulated.

Even if such regulation is not adopted, small economies should seriously consider creating a mechanism for learning in a timely manner about dominant firms' actions in order to determine their legality. Some jurisdictions use a registration or notification system to aid them in the administrative process of regulating monopolies. Austria, for example, has adopted a system of compulsory notification and registration of market-dominating enterprises.[51] In Israel the director may declare a firm a monopoly if it meets the legal definition of monopoly.[52] The declaration is published in public records and the firm is notified. The main advantage of a registration or declaratory system is that the enterprises and the public are notified about the existence of market-dominating enterprise. In Israel the declaration may also be used as a rebuttable presumption of monopoly in any legal proceeding against the monopolist.[53]

Some jurisdictions further impose on monopolies legal obligations to notify the competition authorities of certain types of agreements they have entered into or certain types of conduct they have engaged in, such as expansion of output or a refusal to supply a competitor.[54] Such notification requirements provide an administrative tool that enhances the ability of the competition authority as well as private litigants to provide a timely check on certain types of conduct of the monopolist in order to prevent clearly abusive practices from their incipiency. The method is effective if it enhances the transparency of the monopolist's conduct and reveals facts of which the enforcement agencies and the public have insufficient knowledge. Moreover, it provides the dominant firm with a constant reminder that its conduct is under surveillance and may also increase the predictability of the legal status of its actions—at least a "quick look" check, as in most jurisdictions inaction by the competition authorities does not constitute an affirmation of the legality of the conduct. It may also provide private parties with the information necessary to make better decisions as to whether or not they can compete with the dominant firm on merit. While such systems have many benefits, caution should be exercised not to make the notification system too burdensome, in order to minimize the deterrence of pro-competitive business activity.

Another method of increasing early detection of abuses and reducing the ability of managers to engage in anti-competitive conduct involves compliance programs, such as have been adopted in Canada and Israel. Under Israeli law, the manager of a firm as well as the manager of the business division that has engaged in anti-competitive conduct are personally liable for the offense, unless they prove that they did not know of the conduct and had taken every reasonable measure to prevent it.[55] To help managers meet the last requirement, the Competition Authority enables large, dominant firms to take part in a voluntary compliance program. Under this program each firm is required to appoint a compliance officer, whose job it is to ensure that all managers are aware of the competition laws and that the firm does not violate the law. The firm may also submit to the Competition Authority queries on the legality of potentially abusive conduct before it is adopted. These programs have succeeded in substantially lessening the occurrence of abusive conduct from its incipiency.

Another method of regulating mere monopoly is by divestiture. In Israel, for example, the Competition Tribunal is authorized to break up a monopoly, upon request of the director of the Competition Authority, if harm to the public from its existence is significant and cannot be dealt with by less drastic measures.[56] Restructuring options include transfer of some of the monopolist's assets to a separate firm, or any other means chosen by the tribunal. Since the power of restructuring was granted to the tribunal in 1988, no breakup had been requested or mandated as of January 2003. This may result from the fact that restructuring is a remedy of last resort, to be used only when conduct regulation fails to regulate the monopolist effectively and the public is significantly harmed. Alternatively, structural remedies may be limited in regulating monopolies in small economies. For restructuring to be efficient, the dominant firm has to be divided into two or more viable firms without jeopardizing scale or scope economies. In a small economy such breakup may not be possible in many markets. In the extreme, where the market can support only one firm, dissolution is not economically feasible. In many other situations breakup of a dominant firm into smaller units may create a concentrated market structure (duopoly or oligopoly) that is also prone to monopolistic exploitation. Yet even when a structural remedy can be efficient, it should be applied only when the costs created by the monopoly power are high, conduct regulation is ineffective, and the dominant firm's market position is unlikely to be eroded in the foreseeable future.

Trade Terms as Abuse of Dominant Position

Some jurisdictions treat certain trade terms, most commonly monopoly pricing and output limitation strategies, as abuse of monopoly power. This approach has been widely adopted by many jurisdictions, including Malta, Cyprus, Sweden, Israel, and most EC members. Like mere monopoly conduct regulation, this approach assumes much in way of the ability of courts to distinguish monopoly trade conditions from competitive ones. Unlike mere monopoly regulation, however, it condemns certain types of conduct as being anti-competitive. The strengths as well as the weaknesses of this approach can be illustrated by the experience of jurisdictions that have adopted this approach. Regulation can be implicit or explicit.

Many small economies explicitly prohibit "inequitable" trading conditions set by a monopolist. Most of these provisions are based on section 82(a) of the EC Treaty of Rome, which prohibits "directly or indirectly imposing unfair . . . prices or other unfair trading conditions." The treaty has been interpreted as prohibiting, inter alia, monopolistic trade conditions, with no need to prove that competition has been harmed. The prohibition is thus a consumer protection measure rather than a device to protect competition, much like mere monopoly conduct regulation.

The objection to "unfair" trading conditions is that the monopolist is using its monopoly position to "reap trading benefits that it would not have reaped if there had been normal and sufficiently effective competition."[57] It follows that the monopolist bears a special duty not to exploit its monopoly power fully and not to create too great a short-run allocative inefficiency in the market. The position adopted by the EC toward monopoly pricing can be explained in part on several grounds. First, the Treaty of Rome does not apply to the acquisition of a dominant position. This in turn requires a stricter policy toward the consequences of market power, including monopoly pricing. Second, the EC is less skeptical than other jurisdictions about the efficiency of regulation. Third, the prohibition builds on the fundamental European dislike of bigness and on the goal of allowing small enterprises the "freedom to compete," as stated in the preamble to the treaty. Although the treaty can also be read as aiming to achieve economic efficiency, a free market economy, and a desire to raise European businesses to standards capable of competing on world levels, the commission and the European Court of Justice (ECJ) sometimes restrain big businesses in order to assist small ones in competing.

The legal standards applicable to unfair trade conditions are not defined by the law and have been left to judicial interpretation. Allegations of excessive pricing were considered by the ECJ in four major cases.[58] Monopoly pricing was first considered by the ECJ in *General Motors*.[59] Belgium had delegated to automobile manufacturers' representatives the duty to inspect and issue certificates of conformity to all vehicles entering the country. General Motors charged a very high fee for this service, thus creating entry barriers for parallel imports from Germany. When its customers complained, GM immediately gave refunds. The commission found that GM had a dominant position in granting certificates of conformity for its automobiles crossing the Belgian border,[60] and that the high fee constituted an abuse of dominant position. GM sued for annulment. On the question of abuse, the ECJ determined that a firm could abuse its dominant position by charging a price "which is excessive in relation to the economic value of the service provided, and which has the effect of curbing parallel imports by neutralizing the possibly more favorable level of prices applying to other sales areas in the Community, or by leading to unfair trade."[61] In that case the excessiveness of the price was deduced from the fact that, on receiving complaints, GM had reduced it to 25 percent of its original value. In *British Leyland*[62] the ECJ reaffirmed the principle that a price is excessive if it bears no reasonable relation to the economic value of the product supplied.

In *United Brands*[63] the ECJ gave some insights into the character of the offense. The court required the commission to consider any objective justification for price differentials, such as production costs, distribution costs, and marketing. If no objective justifications can explain the price difference, then the question becomes "whether a price has been imposed which is either unfair in itself or when compared to competing products."[64] The court's test for excessive pricing was whether the absence of effective competition enabled the dominant firm to reap abnormal trading benefits. In *Tournier*[65] the ECJ held that when a dominant firm's charges are "appreciably higher" than corresponding charges in other member states, that will be prima facie evidence of abusive conduct.

Monopoly pricing is also attacked, though indirectly, by prohibitions placed on limitations of output by dominant firms. Section 82(b) of the Treaty of Rome prohibits limiting production, markets, or technical developments to the prejudice of consumers.

The EC's condemnation of monopoly pricing illuminates the practical problems involved in monitoring the pricing decisions of dominant firms. Two main problems arise: determining the costs and profits of the dominant firm and determining when a price is excessive. On the first issue, difficulties arise in determining cost-price differences. This is especially true when long-term investments are made or when the court must apportion production costs of complex corporate structures with a wide product range or multinational production facilities.

On the second issue, excessiveness of price was never clearly determined. The ECJ defined a price as excessive when it has no reasonable relation to economic value. Even if the price is *excessive* in itself, the court stated, it should be considered whether it is *unfair* either in itself or in comparison to that of competing products. None of the prongs of this decision provide clear guidance. It is unclear where to draw the line between high and excessive price and what margin of profit a dominant firm should be allowed. Comparison to prices charged by other competitors may also not be helpful, since small or inefficient competitors might have different cost structures. Moreover, competitors might take advantage of the monopolist's price umbrella, so that comparison of the dominant firm's price with its competitor's price may be irrelevant.[66]

These formidable problems of identification and surveillance have led the commission to devote only minimal resources to monopoly pricing cases. The commission has acknowledged the difficulty of ascertaining in any given case whether an abusive price has been set, for "there is no objective way of establishing exactly what price covers costs plus a reasonable profit margin."[67] The prohibition is thus generally used, in the EC and elsewhere, only in flagrant cases of excessive prices. At the same time, the number and type of cases litigated does not necessarily indicate the influence the law has on the undertakings operating in the market. It might well be that the prohibition has influenced firms not to charge the highest prices they could obtain from the market.

An interesting attempt to solve the lack of clarity involved in monopoly pricing prohibitions has been tried in Malta, which has adopted an abuse-of-dominance prohibition taken almost verbatim from the Treaty of Rome. Its law also refers to the case law of the European Commission and the ECJ for further defining and supplementing its provisions. The Maltese Competition Act attempts to solve the definitional problem of excessive pricing by including a nonexhaustive list of factors, taken mostly from EC case law, which the Maltese Commission is obliged to consider. These include the relation of price to production costs and to prices being charged by other producers in the local market or by the same undertakings in analogous foreign markets, the risks associated with bringing the product into the market, the expected, probable, or possible charges in the market for the product, and the importance of the product to consumers.[68] The Maltese commission is thus required to make an in-depth market analysis to determine excessive pricing. Yet even this extensive list of factors does not succeed in completely clarifying the concept of an "unfair" price.

The prohibition against certain monopoly pricing strategies can also be created implicitly by case law, under other abuse-of-dominance provisions. Although I deal with such provisions more extensively later on, one observation is warranted here. Abuse-of-dominance provisions focus on the conduct of a monopolist that is exclusionary or predatory in nature, in other words, conduct that is aimed at creating an advantage for the monopolist that is not based on natural market conditions or its superior performance. The ultimate goal of such conduct is to drive competitors out of the market or to raise rivals' costs in order to gain power over price. Thus, monopoly pricing is the ultimate goal of such strategies. It is sometimes confused with mere monopoly pricing.

Most confusion arises in vertical integration cases in which the monopolist is partially integrated into the competitive downstream (or upstream) market or attempts to integrate fully into it. In constructive refusals to deal, monopoly pricing of an intermediate good by a monopolist that also competes with its customers in a competitive market is aimed at forcing its competitors out of the market or at imposing a "price squeeze" that has the effect of raising rivals' costs. But because monopoly pricing is the expected behavior of a monopolist, refusals to deal cannot be distinguished only by the ultimate pricing conduct. The monopolistic purpose of eliminating competition or raising rivals' costs must not be discerned from the mere charging of a high price. Not all courts succeed, however, in distinguishing between the two.

As Kathryn McMahon has shown, the Australian experience illustrates this point.[69] The test adopted by Australian courts to distinguish monopolistic behavior from competitive conduct in abuse-of-dominance cases is whether similar conduct could have been engaged in by a firm operating in a competitive market.[70] It focuses on the linkage between substantial market power and the conduct complained of, and is based on the assumption that any action that is uncharacteristic of a competitive firm is an unlawful exercise of market power. This competitive environment test has been interpreted broadly enough to condemn some monopoly pricing strategies per se. A monopoly position allows a monopolist to restrict output and increase price even if such a position was obtained or is maintained without anti-competitive conduct, whereas in a competitive market it is assumed that a price consistent with profit maximization of the firm is also the competitive market price. Thus on the competitive environment standard, setting price above the competitive market price may be treated as a misuse of market power.[71]

Despite statements to the contrary, in applying the competitive environment standard Australian courts have, in fact, condemned monopoly pricing per se. This can be illustrated by the *ASX Operations* decision.[72] AXSO (the wholly owned subsidiary of ASX) supplied stock exchange information to retail financial information companies such as the respondent, Pont Data, but also to its own retail services. Pont Data alleged that ASX had charged high prices for its services that amounted to a refusal to deal. The court applied the competitive environment test and found that ASX had abused its monopoly power by imposing an excessive fee structure, because in a competitive market the defendant would be highly unlikely to refuse to sell its products through competing distributors. The decision lacked an economic analysis to distinguish between a monopolistic purpose of eliminating competition or raising rivals' costs from the mere collection of monopoly profits that might eventually attract new entry. Rather, the court relied on subjective purposes and statements of intention found in internal company memoranda and affidavits. Further, the evidence demonstrated that there was vigorous and efficient competition and even an increase in competitors in the retail market, and therefore no lessening of competition. Yet the court ultimately found that the imposition of these high prices constituted an anti-competitive purpose notwithstanding the absence of any anti-competitive analysis.

Consequently, the Australian experience provides an example of how a failure to articulate economic analysis, together with reliance on subjective intentions, can lead to an implicit prohibition of mere monopoly pricing. Yet it must be emphasized that both these cases involved vertically integrated firms that competed with their customers. Such situations require non-trivial economic analysis to differentiate between mere monopoly pricing and monopoly pricing as a means toward an anti-competitive end, which may have led the courts to rely on readily observable indicators of the alleged conduct, such as monopolistic prices.

Comparing Mere Monopoly Regulation to Direct Prohibitions

Both mere monopoly regulation and regulation through the abuse-of-dominance provisions take active steps to regulate the conduct of monopolies per se in order to reduce their costs. Both assume much in the ability of the regulator to regulate the monopolist's trade decisions better than the free market. Both take limited account of the fact that in some circumstances high prices may be regarded as pro-competitive in that they will attract new entry. The two can, nonetheless, be distinguished conceptually, procedurally, and on the basis of their disincentive effect. On the one hand, regulation of mere monopoly is based on the premise that there is no wrongdoing by the monopolist.

The law merely provides administrative powers to intervene in predefined cases. A prohibition, on the other hand, is based on the premise that the monopolist has illegally abused its power. This difference may affect the incentives of parties to engage in the regulated conduct, as firms may take positive steps not to be labeled law violators as well as to avoid the quasi-criminal or the civil fines imposed by abuse provisions. Abuse prohibitions may thus create a stronger disincentive effect.

This conceptual difference between the two regulatory methods also affects their scope and their remedies. A law prohibiting certain conduct must be much more definitive and explicit than one regulating mere monopoly. This in turn limits the flexibility of the regulator to deal effectively with a wide array of conduct resulting from a dominant position. It also affects the ability of the regulator to reach an informal settlement with the dominant firm. When a mere regulatory system is adopted, many jurisdictions take formal action only after informal settlement attempts have failed. When the law contains a direct prohibition, however, the regulator enjoys less flexibility, especially when the dominant firm has engaged in a criminal or quasi-criminal offense.

The two approaches also differ in their procedural requirements. Whereas no-fault regulation is performed, in most cases, by the competition authorities and involves an expert administrative process, abuse-of-dominance cases are usually tried by the courts in a judicial process and suffer all its inherent limitations. Also, mere monopoly regulation shifts most of the complexities involved in regulation from the determination of liability to the framing of an appropriate relief. Once harm resulting from a dominant position is proven, relief can be granted. Although the question of relief is a difficult one, its resolution takes place in a more informal and flexible procedural setting than the judicial process.

The remedies also differ. Whereas no-fault regulation sets limitations on the monopolist's future conduct, abuse of dominance typically applies to conduct that took place in the past, although an injunction prohibiting future conduct can also be issued. In addition, in the former case relief is primarily of a regulatory character, while in the latter it is primarily quasi-criminal (mainly monetary fines). At bottom, no-fault regulation, if efficiently applied, is a better tool for regulating mere monopoly than regulation through abuse-of-power provisions. When small economies choose instead to follow the EC model, the law should strive to clarify, to the extent possible, its scope of application.

Summary:
Regulation of Mere Monopoly in Small Economies

Condemnation or regulation of mere monopoly has many drawbacks. Apart from distorting the incentives of firms to innovate and compete vigorously in the market, remedies are problematic. In the United States, the belief in the self-correcting forces of the market as well as in the disincentive effect have so far tipped the scale in favor of not regulating mere monopoly except in cases of essential facilities. In the EC, trading conditions are regulated only in rare cases that are deemed excessively unfair.

Small economies should not blindly adopt the approaches of large economies, given that some of the assumptions and considerations that hold in large economies do not hold in them. In small economies it cannot be assumed that market forces will deal effectively or efficiently with market power, and the effect of single-firm dominance on the economy is likely to be much more pronounced. Monopoly provisions posited on the assumption that once abuse of monopoly power is prevented the markets will operate efficiently have limited efficacy in small markets. These factors have rightly tipped the scale in many small economies in favor of regulating mere monopoly.

Table 3.2 indicates that all small economies surveyed have adopted some sort of mere monopoly conduct regulation, and some have adopted several methods cumulatively. Competition law in small economies is evolving in a new direction in which regulatory roles traditionally carried out by courts and direct regulators are undertaken by competition authorities. This implies that the borders between regulation, which in its widest sense is aimed at correcting market imperfections in a specific industry, and competition law, which is aimed at creating and maintaining the conditions for workable competition but leaves the decision-making process in the hands of market players, are not as clearly defined as they were in the past. Yet conduct regulation is still a highly problematic tool in that it creates a disincentive effect and thus should not be adopted lightly. I have suggested several limiting principles to ensure that conduct regulation is applied only when appropriate: it should be applied only to monopolies that can-

Table 3.2 Regulatory measures of mere monopoly adopted by different jurisdictions

Jurisdiction (listed by size)	Condemning mere monopoly	Structural regulation of mere monopoly	Conduct regulation of mere monopoly	Conduct as abuse of dominance	Regulation of essential facilities
United States	−	−	−	−	+
EC	−	−	−	+	+
Britain	−	−	+	−	+
Canada	−	−	−	−	+
Australia	−	−	+	+[a]	+
Sweden	−	−	−	+	+
New Zealand	−	−	+	−	+
Israel	−	+	+	+	+
Malta	−	−	+	+	+
Cyprus	−	−	+	+	+

a. Only when the monopoly is vertically integrated.

not be eroded by market forces in due time; it should distinguish between monopolies that are based on superior skill and those that are not; and it should be applied only if other regulatory methods are inefficient.

Abuse of Dominant Position

A dominant firm may use its market power to engage in practices that, instead of encouraging competition based on merit, further its dominance in the monopolized market or in an adjacent one. Such conduct creates artificial barriers to competition, which unnecessarily and unjustifiably exclude actual or potential competitors or raise their costs. By precluding the competitive check on its price and output decisions that these rivals provide, the dominant firm may further restrain output and raise price, leading to an additional efficiency loss. Such anti-competitive conduct can be horizontal or vertical, unilateral or imposed through an agreement.

Dominant firms may utilize different methods to exclude or prevent the expansion of their smaller rivals. Among other things, an established monopolist might use the power it has over existing retailers or wholesalers to deter them from carrying a new product by way of *exclusive dealing*. A dominant firm can also *refuse to deal* with a distributor who carries a competing brand. A rival firm would have to compensate the distributor for his losses in order to persuade him to deal with it. Such compensation can be very costly if the rival does not have sufficient capacity to meet all of the demand of the incumbent or if the products are differentiated. The incumbent monopolist might also use *fidelity or quantity rebates* to deter the entry or expansion of rivals. The monopolist may, under certain conditions, also have incentives to engage in *predatory pricing*. These examples are not inclusive.

To cite but one instance, in the Israeli case of *Yediot Aharonot*[73] the defendant, which held a monopoly in the market for daily newspapers, had conditioned the sale of its newspapers to some retailers and distributors on their consent not to sell competing newspapers or to display competing newspapers in disadvantaged display spots. The Competition Tribunal found that the newspaper's conduct strengthened its monopoly position based not on the legitimate and free choice of consumers but rather on the forced lack of competing newspapers at points of sale. The tribunal prohibited the firm from subjecting the sale of its newspapers to any obligation related to the manner in which other newspapers are sold at the distribution point.

When the monopolist is vertically integrated into another, potentially competitive market, it might also use its monopoly position to leverage its market power into the second market. The vertically integrated monopolist might leverage its power by giving its competitive arm(s) supply benefits over potential rivals *(discrimination)* or by *cross-subsidization.* The latter involves the use of profits earned from monopoly markets to fund competitive markets. By setting low prices in the competitive market, the firm can impose losses on its competitors and perhaps induce them to exit the industry. The integrated firm has the monopoly markets as a source of revenue to fund such activities. The same can be achieved by *tying*—refusing to provide supply to downstream consumers unless they also buy the competitive product from its affiliated competitive arm(s)—or by *exclusive dealing,* whereby the monopolist supplies only (or mainly) one or a number of firms, usually its affiliated competitive arm, and refuses to supply its competitors. Such conduct might have significant effects on economic efficiency as the differences in the terms on which competing customers are able to acquire supply—differences that are not explained by the relative costs of serving them—might distort competition. The incentives of a monopolist to leverage its monopoly power into a vertically related market by creating a comparative advantage for its competitive arm over its rivals, which is not based on real cost advantages, depend on the existing market conditions, which will be elaborated in Chapter 4.

Artificial restriction of competition by dominant firms may be especially damaging to small economies. Dominant position is much easier to achieve and, once achieved, much more difficult to erode in many markets in small economies, given that competition is already limited by the natural conditions of the market: high concentration levels protected by high natural barriers to entry. Unnatural barriers may strengthen a dominant position even further, to the point where it is almost impossible to challenge it. Moreover, downstream or upstream markets in small economies are often also concentrated, so that it might be easier for the monopolist operating at one level of the chain of supply to abuse its monopoly power in such markets. To illustrate, if there is room in the market for only one or two efficiently sized distribution or service outlets, and those enter into exclusive dealing contracts with a monopolist operating in a downstream or an upstream market, then a potential competitor would have to incur high costs to enter either market. Also, in a small economy a relatively small capital requirement or a rise in costs created by exclusionary conduct might constitute a barrier to entry, as there is a greater risk than in a larger economy that demand would not be sufficient to yield a normal return. Anti-competitive conduct may thus inhibit the (already limited) domestic competitive forces as well as the contestable effects of imports. Applying competition policy to eliminate, or at least to reduce significantly, business practices that artificially limit competition has the potential to increase efficiency.

My goal in this section is to analyze the abuse-of-dominance offenses that small size may render more significant from a regulatory point of view. General issues of abuse of dominance will be analyzed only as necessary to further this goal. The next section includes a broad overview of general issues of differentiating between use and abuse of market power. Small size emphasizes the need for setting clear requirements to be met when differentiating abuse from use. The subsequent discussion centers on specific types of conduct for which concentrated market structures protected by high entry barriers create a need for a more refined analysis of their effects. The final section focuses on remedies. It points to the pitfalls of using some traditional and conventional competition law remedies and suggests some ways to solve these problems. I argue that in markets with high barriers to entry and a small number of market players, competition authorities should be more cautious about preventing the elimination of an existing competitor when its elimination may significantly affect economic performance.

Abuse versus Use of Market Power

The main difficulty in preventing exclusionary business practices by dominant firms is distinguishing use from abuse—recognizing the nature and diverse forms of business efficiency and differentiating them from conduct that is designed primarily to exclude competitors. The difficulty arises from the fact that both involve deliberate injury to competitors and may even result in harm to competition. Yet a clear and correct definition is important to encourage firms to compete on merit and enhance productive efficiency. Otherwise firms might be prevented from exploiting their comparative advantages (e.g., economies of scale, government licenses, superior product) owing to the inevitable impact of such conduct on less efficient rivals.

The definition of abuse goes to the heart of competition policy: What should its fundamental objectives be? Should it prefer competition or its outcomes? Should it be narrowly defined in terms of consumer benefit, or should it be defined more broadly to include productive efficiency that may increase total welfare? As I argue throughout this book, small economies should favor efficiency over competition or specific competitors.

Jurisdictions differ in the terminology for, and the scope of, the prohibited conduct.[74] The tests for distinguishing competition from abuse range from considerations of public benefit to considerations of the negative effects of the conduct on competition not based on comparative merit. The ambiguity concerning the wrongfulness of harm to others has generally led to a rule-of-reason analysis of allegedly abusive practices. In most jurisdictions, to prevail in a claim, a plaintiff must satisfy a two-part test requiring that the defendant (1) have a dominant position in the relevant market, and (2) engage in conduct that protects, enhances, or perpetuates this power and is not based on comparative merit. Some jurisdictions also require exclusionary purpose or intent. Let us now analyze the suitability of these requirements for differentiating use from abuse.

A finding of dominant position in the relevant market is generally an essential prerequisite for abuse-of-dominance prohibitions. The reason is that it is assumed that unilateral anti-competitive conduct cannot be engaged in by firms lacking market power or that such conduct will have limited effect on market conditions if it is engaged in by such firms.

Most types of exclusionary conduct require preexisting market power to have any significant effect on the state of competition in the relevant market, but this is not always the case. Assume, for example, that a firm engages in a series of long-term exclusive contracts that lock up existing outlets or important inputs. A firm that possesses the resources necessary to suffer short-term losses in order to gain long-term monopoly profits may engage in such contracting even before it has market power.[75] This concern is especially applicable to network industries. Similarly, a firm that assumes that the current dominant firm is likely to lose its market position because, for example, its technology will soon become obsolete or an important input will become unavailable may engage in contracting that excludes its future rivals in the anticipation that it will have a comparative advantage over them in replacing the current monopolist.

Accordingly, small economies should prohibit certain acts that might potentially create a monopoly position from their incipiency.[76] Such prohibitions differ from regular abuse-of-dominance prohibitions in that the firm engaged in such conduct does not yet possess significant market power and thus cannot abuse this power. Rather, the conduct itself serves to create a competitive advantage to the firm not based on its comparative efficiencies. An injunctive order to restrain exclusionary conduct engaged in by a firm likely to achieve dominance can be more timely and effective and less costly than regulating dominance, once achieved. The importance of such regulation for small economies is strengthened by the fact that market power, once achieved, cannot usually be easily eroded. Another way to combat exclusive conduct in its incipiency is by adopting low thresholds for dominance.

The second requirement is that the dominant firm abuse its power. The task of differentiating use from abuse has proved to be one of competition law's most important dilemmas and is subject to much controversy. Abuse is often described as exclusionary in the sense that it impairs the opportunities of rivals by placing them at a significant economic disadvantage. The Australian Trade Practices Act and New Zealand Commerce Act both define abuse as occurring when a dominant firm takes advantage of its power for the purpose of eliminating or substantially damaging a competitor, preventing the entry of a person into the market or deterring or preventing competitive conduct.[77] But this definition is problematic as it is broad enough to include pro-competitive conduct such as innovation of a better product, which excludes competitors that have not achieved the same level of dynamic efficiency, or even the charging of a low price, based on productive efficiencies, which cannot be matched by a less efficient rival. If the goal of competition policy is to further efficiency and welfare, we must refine the definition to include exclusionary conduct that creates artificial barriers to competition not based on the competitive merits of the firm engaging in such conduct. This concept is elastic, encompassing almost any kind of behavior that would allow the dominant firm to put its rivals at a competitive disadvantage that cannot be justified by offsetting social benefits. It should be applied to prevent not only conduct that excludes a firm in the narrow sense but also conduct that prevents firms from expanding.

Similarly, the law should not center on the negative effects of the conduct on the state of competition in the market. For example, in U.S. law the basic test for abuse, found in *Griffith*,[78] postulates that the use of monopoly power "to foreclose competition, to gain a competitive advantage, or to destroy a competitor, is unlawful."[79] If construed literally, this formulation appears to condemn all conduct that creates entry barriers and thereby limits the process of rivalry, regardless of whether it is based on competitive merit. Such an approach may handicap the incumbent firm by requiring it to hold a price umbrella over the heads of its rivals or otherwise pull its competitive punches.[80] It also raises the possibility of condemning monopoly in the absence of identifiable exclusionary acts other than those ordinarily associated with a firm's operation.

Small economies should adopt a policy that furthers efficiency and welfare rather than a policy that promotes rivalry. Accordingly, the lack of rivalry in a market or the exclusionary effects of a conduct should not in themselves constitute an abuse if this were the consequence of new entrants' inability to match the efficiencies and investment performance of the incumbent monopolist. This does not mean that economic efficiency and inter-firm rivalry are to be regarded as being always mutually exclusive goals. Inter-firm rivalry is one means by which economic efficiency can be improved. But there may be substantial limitations on the extent to which economic rivalry can be attained and maintained in markets characterized by scale economies and entry barriers.

Small economies must therefore refine the test for abuse to prohibit only exclusionary conduct that creates artificial barriers to competition which are not based on the competitive merits of the dominant firm. Most jurisdictions have by now adopted such an interpretation, at least in theory. They also allow the dominant firm to justify its allegedly exclusionary conduct by legitimate commercial justifications, such as a refusal to deal with a customer with a bad credit record,[81] to avoid placing the dominant firm at a comparative disadvantage just because of its market position.

To prevent dominant firms from deterring pro-competitive conduct, the test must also be based on economic theory. This can be exemplified by the regulation of a firm that refuses to supply the spare parts for its products to its rivals in a downstream service market, a situation with which most jurisdictions have dealt. Economic analysis emphasizes competition in the product market as a restraining force in aftermarkets. When the consumer bases a decision on which product to buy not only on the initial price of the product but also on the price of replacement parts and service, a firm that faces competition in its product market will have limited ability, if any, to raise the prices of its parts and services. Its refusal to deal with independent service providers will thus most likely be motivated by business justifications (it provides more efficient service; the independent provider has a bad credit record) rather than as a way to abuse its power in the replacement parts market. Such analysis was the basis of the U.S. *Kodak* case.[82] The European Court of Justice, when confronted with a similar refusal to deal by a calculating machines provider that faced vigorous competition in the market for such machines, reached a different decision and found abuse of dominance.[83] This result does not adhere to economic principles and unnecessarily constrains business conduct.

Economic analysis dictates, however, that refusal to deal in a market for spare parts may amount to an abuse when inter-firm competition does not constrain the conduct of the firms involved. This can be illustrated by the Israeli case of the *Elevator Market*.[84] There, the relevant market was defined as the market for the supply of replacement parts for elevators. The defendants, the leading elevator producers, were found to jointly enjoy a monopoly position in replacement parts, and their refusal to supply the parts was found to be unreasonable. Although the court did not mention the effects of competition in the elevator market on the ability of the elevator firms to abuse their power in the service market, the decision can be justified on economic grounds. The elevator market might be unique in that the initial buyer (usually a building contractor) and the person requiring service (the resident) might base their decisions on different parameters. The contractor generally bases his decision on the cost of the elevator itself in order to reduce the overall cost of the building, as the price for the building is rarely affected by the quality of the elevator. The residents then have to bear the ongoing consequences of this decision with regard to the cost of maintenance and replacement parts for the elevator. Consequently, the costs of spare parts and service generally do not affect the decision as to which elevator is bought.

It is important for small economies that the negative effects test be applied broadly, to include probable future harm. Under such a standard, a firm's actions can be deemed anti-competitive even if its rivals have not already been harmed, and even if it is not clear which exactly will be the incumbent's rivals that may potentially be harmed in the future. The importance of such a standard stems from the fact that new entry could be blockaded if the incumbent were permitted to engage in anti-competitive conduct that creates artificial entry barriers before its potential rivals have entered the market. Enabling such barriers to be created might prevent, for example, the entry of foreign firms once trade barriers are lowered.

In particular, small economies should ensure that their laws are broad enough to capture conduct that creates obstacles to pro-competitive changes in market structure, as such dynamic forces may be the most important source of eroding market power. An interesting example that also illustrates the circularity of competition policy is found in the Irish case of *Independent Newspapers*.[85] The Irish Competition Authority found that Independent Newspapers had abused its dominant position in the newspaper market by providing a loan to and purchasing shares in a smaller rival. These actions had been deliberately designed to prevent the smaller rival from being acquired by an undertaking that could provide greater competition to it.

This discussion raises an interesting question for small economies: Can conduct that is otherwise abusive be justified by a market structure argument that, absent the practice, effective competition would still not exist because the market structure is oligopolistic or monopolistic? The answer should be negative. Abusive conduct must not be justified on the basis of relative performance arguments. Although concentrated markets can create allocative inefficiency, such inefficiency will result only if there are specific conditions in the market. Firms operating in concentrated markets may still compete vigorously for the benefit of consumers. But even if this were not the case, a dynamic long-term analysis dictates that it is highly important to prevent the foreclosure of markets for future potential competitors.

Another pitfall to be avoided is the inference of the competitive effects of a conduct from its adoption by firms in a competitive market. New Zealand and Australian case law exemplifies the dangers of applying such a test. In both abuse is defined as conduct that would not have been engaged in by a competitor operating in a competitive market structure but otherwise in the same circumstances.[86] It follows that a dominant firm, whatever its purpose, does not necessarily abuse its position merely by engaging in rivalrous conduct that harms other competitors, so long as such conduct could occur in a competitive environment.

Yet the question of whether a conduct could be maintained under a competitive structure and the question of whether it is conducive to economic efficiency or consumer welfare do not produce similar results. On the one hand, the competitive environment test is too broad and sweeping in nature and might prevent a monopolist from obtaining monopoly profits, even if no harm to competition results, since in a competitive market a would-be buyer might be able to obtain the use of a similar asset from another at a competitive price. This can be exemplified by the *ASX* case,[87] analyzed earlier. The test is especially difficult to apply when a dominant firm supplies more than one service in the chain of production, and is attempting to maximize its overall profits rather than the profits in the competitive market alone. On the other hand, this test might not be broad enough to prevent certain types of conduct that give a monopolist an advantage over its rivals that is not based on comparative merit. The danger in such analysis is that a conduct might be pro-competitive under one structure yet have dominating anti-competitive effects under another. Exclusive dealing contracts, for example, might be lawful in competitive markets. They might be motivated by the customer's need for a reliable source of supply and by the supplier's need for an assured outlet or loyalty in distribution. Both can be harmful and exclusionary, however, if they are engaged in by a dominant firm, they foreclose so much of the supply or the distribution channel that efficient firms must exit, and the harm is not outweighed by pro-competitive benefits.[88] The Australian *Melway* decision[89] can be read as injecting an economic efficiency test into the competitive environment standard in order to remedy this problem.

A small economy should thus adopt a test, based on economic analysis, which ensures that the monopolist's conduct actually reduces welfare before it is prohibited. Given the difficulties involved in proving in each case that a certain type of conduct has amounted to abuse of dominance, several small economies have included in their competition laws nonexclusive lists of practices that are presumed to constitute abuses of power if engaged in by a dominant firm.[90] Such presumptions shift the burden of proof from the plaintiff to the defendant and may be justifiable when economic theory suggests that there is a great likelihood of abuse or the information required to differentiate between abuse and use is known only to the defendant. In case the defendant has proven that its conduct does not necessarily harm competition, the court should analyze the effects of the conduct on actual and potential competition in both the short and the long run.

Most jurisdictions require anti-competitive purpose or intent to misuse market power as a fundamental underpinning of a violation.[91] In some jurisdictions the law can even be interpreted as focused on intent rather than on the economic effects of the conduct in question.[92] Intent, however, is an uncertain indicator, as the conduct is motivated in all instances by the same immediate objective: winning sales from competitors and gaining monopoly profits. Exclusionary purpose thus follows almost inevitably when there is use of market power. For example, a firm must anticipate that by exploiting economies of scale it would eliminate rivals. It would be surprising if the firm did not do so with that end in mind, as elimination of rivals is a natural consequence of expanding production to reduce costs. In acknowledging such difficulties, some jurisdictions have adopted a policy under which the intent requirement is all but redundant, and even those courts that do employ it consider questions of economic justification when examining the conduct.[93]

A small economy ought to focus on the economic effects of a conduct rather than on its intent. Even if a dominant firm had no specific anti-competitive intent (or it cannot be proven that it had such intent), the exclusionary practice should be prohibited. Otherwise, the goal of abuse-of-dominance provisions—to limit the creation of artificial barriers to competition—would be inhibited. The assumption that a firm intends the results of its conduct does not add much to the analysis. Nonetheless, proof of pro-competitive purpose may be useful in proving the legitimacy of the conduct by a monopolist. Also, the lack of an anti-competitive intent should be factored into the remedies granted. Otherwise the unclarity regarding the legal status of many types of conduct, given the case-specific analysis required, might reduce the incentives of firms to become monopolists or of monopolists to engage in pro-competitive conduct.

Specific Conduct That May Raise Special Concerns in Small Economies

Apart from the general importance of abuse-of-dominance provisions in preventing the creation of artificial entry barriers into markets protected by natural barriers, several specific practices may raise special issues in small economies. Such practices are the focus of this discussion. Chapter 4 elaborates on some other types of abuse-of-dominance conduct.

In regulating discriminatory policies adopted by a dominant firm, small economies may need to apply a different set of rules in order to achieve the goals of competition policy. Price and non-price discrimination, whereby a monopolistic supplier charges two or more customers different prices or applies different trade terms that have no direct relation to the costs of supplying these customers, is prohibited in most economies.[94] One of the main objections to price discrimination is that it may be used to punish an oligopolist that "acted out of line." To the extent that discrimination suppresses rivalry in particular segments of the discriminating firm's market, it may have negative dynamic effects on the state of competition in that market by retarding the normal downward slippage of oligopolistic prices.

In oligopolistic markets, discriminatory pricing or trade terms may, however, be part of pro-consumer market scenarios in which previously stable oligopolistic price structures are ultimately shaken loose and lowered, to the benefit of the public. Oligopolists often do not compete directly on price, but rather compete in other ways, principally through secret loyalty rebates and discounts that frequently discriminate among individual customers. Such discounts are generally to be encouraged. To forbid them would often reduce efficiency and slow reactions to changed market conduct.

This implies that if oligopolistic markets are caught under the abuse-of-dominance provisions—under a joint dominance or shared monopoly construction, or if the definition of dominance is broad enough to include duopolists or even triopolists—then scenarios in which discrimination is a means to the breakdown of oligopolistic price coordination should be distinguished from other scenarios wherein certain sellers succeed in using discrimination as a means of disciplining rivals and market prices are ultimately maintained or pushed up. An overly strict approach to discrimination in which all such practices are condemned as abusive might actually increase oligopolistic behavior as the sparse competition remaining is inhibited. Discrimination in small economies thus merits a deeper analysis of its real effect on the market. The downside of such a policy is that detailed prescriptions might demand accurate microeconomic predictions. Nonetheless, several factors can signal that a more cautious analysis should be performed before the effects of the discriminatory conduct are determined: the market is oligopolistic in nature, potential competitors adopt parallel pricing policies, and discrimination is secret in order to hide it from other oligopolists.

Small economies should also ensure that their rules against price discrimination do not prevent the achievement of the goals of competition policy. While analyzing the welfare effects of a prohibition against price predation are beyond the scope of this book, two comments are warranted. First, when the monopolist's potential customers operate in several different markets, price discrimination may enable the utilization of more efficient production techniques in some markets. If some of the monopolist's customers operate in one competitive market and some operate in another, and assuming that the monopolist is mandated to set only one price for all its customers, its profit-maximizing price might be so high as to serve only one market. This in turn might prevent customers in the second market from utilizing the most efficient production technique in which the monopolist's widgets are an essential element. In other words, discrimination increases total output when at the single-price equilibrium one group of consumers will not buy any inputs from the monopolist and demand of both groups is linear. This is Pareto-optimal: no one is harmed; one group of consumers is unchanged and the other group gains.[95] A simple method of achieving this result is by requiring that discrimination affect competition for it to be found anti-competitive, as many jurisdictions have done.[96]

The second comment is that a strict prohibition against price discrimination might prevent a domestic firm from meeting the competition of other producers, which may engage in "cream skimming"— serving only the most lucrative parts of the market. This can be illustrated by the Israeli case of *Nesher*. Nesher held a dominant position in the Israeli market for cement. Because of its market position, it was prevented from price-discriminating among its customers throughout Israel. While its position in the northern part of the country was relatively secure, the lowering of trade barriers with Jordan introduced competition from Jordanian cement manufacturers in the southern part of the country. After a campaign to influence the government to reestablish trade barriers had failed, Nesher requested that the Competition Authority enable it to meet Jordanian competition. The authority allowed Nesher to do so and lower its prices to specific customers.[97] The decision was based on interpretation of the legal prohibition, which defines discrimination among potential competitors as abuse when it might give some customers an unfair advantage over their rivals,[98] as not applying when such customers would have been served by lower-priced suppliers anyway. An exception to price discrimination to prevent "cream skimming" might be especially justified when otherwise a less efficient producer would be able to enter the market under the price umbrella created by the profit-maximizing price set by the monopolist.

Small size may also affect the occurrence and the analysis of predatory pricing. Although there is no universally accepted definition of predatory pricing, the definition provided by Posner is quite broad: "pricing at a level calculated to exclude from the market an equally or more efficient competitor."[99] Pricing at a level to exclude from the market less efficient competitors is, of course, what competition is supposed to achieve. Predatory pricing achieves the opposite. The theory of predatory pricing is based on the assumption that a predator will invest in losses for a period with the prospect of high returns upon becoming a monopolist or securing its current market position.

There is much debate in the economic literature regarding the profitability of predatory pricing, for two main reasons. First, the predator is almost always compelled to absorb larger losses in the short run than will the victim. This is because, after a price cut, the predator must increase output to satisfy new demand forthcoming at the lower price, and to take up the share of the existing market relinquished by its victim, it will sell many more units at a lower price than will its victim. Second, successful predation can occur only when entry barriers into the predated market are high. Otherwise the subsequent price increases would invite entry into the industry on a sufficient scale to ensure that price increases could not be sustained.

Small economies may, however, make a predatory strategy more attractive. First, high entry barriers, which are a prerequisite for predatory pricing, characterize many industries in small economies. Second, large conglomerates often operate in small economies. These conglomerates might use a predatory technique to signal to their actual or potential rivals in other markets that they are willing to abuse their market power to maintain or increase that power. Moreover, imperfect capital markets in a small economy may make early exclusion by way of predatory pricing more profitable. If an entrant is challenged shortly before or after entry and before it has the opportunity to achieve efficient scales of operation, then it might have insufficient resources to withstand a predatory price campaign. This is especially true if the cost structure of the incumbent firm is unknown to the entrant and to the capital market, as its costs may be perceived to be lower than they actually are. Finally, a relatively small capital requirement might constitute a barrier to entry, as there is greater risk in a small economy than in a large one that demand will not be sufficient to yield a normal return. It is also noteworthy that the focus on the costs of the predator might not capture exclusionary conduct when scale economies are significant and penalties for operating below such scales are high.[100] Under such conditions, the incumbent monopolist may not have to reduce its prices below its costs to engage in exclusionary conduct. Some commentators suggest that the definition of predation might need to be adjusted to capture such conduct.[101]

Exclusive dealing, whereby the monopolist conditions the sale of its product on an agreement with a distributor or a supplier to deal only with it, is one of the leading types of abuse found in small economies.

Although the foreclosure effects of exclusive dealing in large markets have been questioned, the nature of many markets in small economies—concentrated and protected by high entry barriers—makes exclusive dealing an important regulatory target. As all markets down the chain of supply tend to be more concentrated in small economies, it is much easier for a dominant firm to use its market power to coerce distributors or suppliers to enter into exclusive dealing contracts with it, especially if there are economies of scale in distribution or in the supply of an input. Such exclusive dealing contracts render a distributor or a supplier unavailable to other producers. By a series of exclusive dealing contracts with major customers, wholesalers, retailers, or suppliers, the monopolist can make entry of new firms into the industry more difficult than otherwise and can even drive existing firms out of the market. Whereas in large economies exclusive dealing by one or two leading firms will still leave to their competitors a sufficient number of uncommitted distributors, in small economies it might foreclose the market. Establishing a new distribution network may be uneconomical, given that it may involve distribution on sub-optimal scale.

For illustrative purposes, suppose that a dominant producer holds 70 percent of the relevant product market. Further assume that distribution scale economies amount to 40 percent of the market. This implies that the market can support only two efficient-sized distribution channels. It also implies that in order to realize low costs, both distributors need to do business with the monopolist (since the remaining producers fulfill only 30 percent of the demand). If the monopolist uses its market power to coerce the two distributors into exclusive dealing contracts (e.g., by threatening to establish its own distribution channel), then the remaining producers will have no outlet into the market. Existing distribution channels are blockaded, and establishing a new distribution network may not provide a solution when scale economies are significant and the producers have no significant cost advantage over the dominant firm. A similar outcome would have resulted if the monopolistic producer had entered into an exclusive dealing arrangement with duopolistic suppliers.

Exclusive dealing might, therefore, severely affect the ability of existing and potential competitors to compete with the monopolist on a merit basis. Existing competitors might lose their market share and even be driven out of the market, thereby strengthening the monopolist's market power. Alternatively, exclusive dealing might give rise to two or more parallel distribution systems when a single network would be more efficient.

The severity of the problems raised by exclusive dealing contracts in small economies can be exemplified by the Israeli case of *Eltam— Sheingoot*.[102] There it was found that Eltam, the dominant producer of throttles in the Israeli market (more than 80 percent), entered into exclusive dealing contracts with its largest customers, the dominant lighting equipment producers, under which the lighting producers committed themselves to buying their throttles exclusively from Eltam, and in exchange Eltam committed to charging them lower prices than those it charged their smaller rivals. Eltam's contracting system prevented import competition in the market for throttles, as import scale economies made imports profitable only for large quantities. The exclusive contracts were thus profitable to both Eltam and its large customers: Eltam faced no import competition, and its customers raised their smaller rivals' prices relative to their own. This gave them a comparative advantage over their rivals that made up for the higher prices they paid for throttles relative to their imported price.

The refusal-to-deal offense, which is analyzed in detail in Chapter 4, arises when a monopolist refuses to supply a product or a service without a valid business justification or on terms less favorable than those it gives its own competing arm or other firms. It raises similar issues to those raised by exclusive dealing. In both, a monopolist controls or has significant effect (directly or indirectly) over distribution or supply channels that are necessary for other competitors to compete with it. Under the refusal-to-deal scenario the monopolist owns the facilities or inputs or renders the services necessary for firms to compete, whereas under the exclusive-dealing scenario the facilities or services are supplied by another firm, which contracts with the monopolist. Both can be used to foreclose the market for potential competitors.

A Word on Remedies

Remedial powers may focus on one of three goals: deterrence, compensation, or restoration of competition. The goal of an enforcement system based on deterrence is to identify some level of violations that must be eliminated and to make it unprofitable by imposing costs on prospective violators. An optimal level of deterrence will make violation unprofitable precisely to the point that it is inefficient. The goal of an enforcement system based on compensation is to restore injured parties to the position they would have occupied had the violation not occurred. Although the focus is on the injured party, this remedy also has deterrent effects: the higher the cost to a violator, the higher the deterrent effect of such a remedy on future potential violators. A restorative remedy focuses on creating the market conditions necessary to restore competition in the specific market. All three goals have been adopted by different jurisdictions to remedy abuses of dominance. Most laws focus on restoring competition in the market, although deterrence and compensation may be cumulative goals. My remarks will be focused on the former, as it poses interesting and special issues for small economies.

In most cases courts attempt to achieve the goal of restoring competition simply by prohibiting the abusive conduct and depriving the dominant firm of the fruits of its anti-competitive behavior to ensure effective deterrence. Restoring the market to the situation that would have existed had the anti-competitive conduct not occurred may, however, require courts to undo various effects of the anti-competitive conduct that go well beyond depriving the dominant firm of the fruits of its abuse. The reason is that the abusive conduct has already changed the market equilibrium such that market conditions are different from what they would have been without the anti-competitive conduct. The court may need to use more extreme measures, such as monetary compensation of rivals, lowering of entry barriers created by the anti-competitive conduct, or even the divestiture of a dominant firm when other less intrusive remedies are not effective.[103]

If the goal of the remedy is to restore competition in the market, the concentrated nature of a market raises a structural consideration that is mostly absent in large economies. In using its remedial powers, a competition court in a small economy should take into account the effect of its remedy on the current market equilibrium.[104] If the court goes beyond what is necessary to restore competition and to eradicate the consequences of the anti-competitive conduct, it might create a situation that is counterproductive to competition, if the remedy necessarily leads to the exit of a firm from the market. For this to happen, four conditions have to be met. First, the market can support only a small number of firms that actually compete in the market. Second, entry barriers are high. Third, the judicial remedy should create such a comparative disadvantage to a competitor that it must exit the market. Fourth, the exiting firm's assets may not be utilized by a new firm such as a successor in bankruptcy, or it may take a new competitor a long time to establish itself in the market (for example, where reputation is an important factor in the consumer's decision). Put differently, although competition policy is designed to protect competition and not competitors, in some markets it might be important to exercise caution with regard to the viability of competitors if that viability is crucial for competition.

Take, for example, a market situation in which the relevant market can support only two firms. Assume that one firm is found to engage in anti-competitive behavior, and that the court does not exercise enough caution in its decision such that the firm has to exit the market owing to a significant comparative disadvantage created by the remedy. If a new entrant faces high barriers to entry, this change in market structure may affect the pricing behavior of the remaining firm in the market, given that it now enjoys a monopoly position. The exit of a competitor from the market may also have great economic impact when the market can or may support only one firm, and several firms engage in competition for the market. Efficiency dictates that the most efficient competitor ought to serve the market. If, however, a superior potential competitor engages in anti-competitive conduct while competing for the market, and the court hearing the case creates a significant disadvantage for this firm, the firm might exit the market. Consequently, efficiency will not be achieved.

This can be illustrated by the Canadian *Nielsen* case.[105] There, Nielsen was found to engage in anti-competitive exclusive dealing contracts with its suppliers and customers, which served to create artificial barriers to the entry of its potential competitors. The Canadian Competition Tribunal struck down the exclusivity clauses in its existing contracts, but without interfering with the rest of the contractual terms. The tribunal acknowledged that striking down the exclusivity clauses in Nielsen's contracts with its suppliers without addressing the current payment clauses of a blended nature (i.e., they contained a single payment for the data and exclusive access to them) might be problematic. The problem was that "Nielsen might have to continue its current level of payments, without receiving the benefits of exclusivity the payments were intended to secure, while its competitor makes payments at a lower level."[106] The tribunal chose to sidestep this issue, however, by making no comment on whether or not this was a valid concern for it to address. This remedy could have required Nielsen to suffer great losses and exit the market, were it not the case that Nielsen's incentives for de facto exclusivity were aligned with those of its suppliers, who shared some of the profits from Nielsen's position as a sole service provider.[107]

Conclusion

Monopoly markets pose some of the most important policy dilemmas for regulators in small economies. The prevalence of monopoly structures in small economies and the limited self-regulating powers of the market imply that regulation has a crucial role in limiting the welfare-reducing practices of monopolies. In this chapter I have analyzed the considerations that come into play in devising an efficient policy. On the basis of such considerations, I suggest that small economies adopt competition policy regimes that have the following features:

1. Monopoly should be defined with care to minimize false positives and false negatives. In particular, the scope of the relevant market in small economies should include current or potential imports which are real or significant substitutes for domestic products.
2. The *typical* or standard market share that signifies market dominance in small economies should be lower than that adopted in large ones because the elasticity of supply is typically lower, given the high prevalence of scale economies and oligopolistic interdependence in most of their markets.
3. Presumptions of market power should be based not only on market share indicators in absolute terms, but also on such market shares relative to the market shares of the largest competitors of the relevant firm. Dynamic factors are also important for a correct analysis.
4. Monopoly should be tolerated, as it is often necessary to achieve productive efficiency. Nonetheless, small economies should consider conduct regulation of monopolies more seriously than large ones. Conduct regulation is better performed by competition authorities rather than by the courts. Such regulation should follow the guidelines suggested.
5. Regulatory methods that enhance the transparency of the

monopolist's actions can assist the competition authorities as well as the general public to detect anti-competitive conduct.

6. Abuse-of-dominance provisions are highly important for small economies, as the peculiarities of small economies tend to make exclusionary conduct by dominant firms more profitable to the monopolist. Such provisions should be broad enough to encompass all types of abusive conduct engaged in by a dominant firm.

7. The analysis of abuse should be an economic one, in order to minimize false positives. Exclusionary practices should be interpreted in light of the need to enhance economic welfare.

8. Small economies should regulate exclusionary conduct that is likely to lead to the creation of market power rather than only exclusionary conduct that maintains or strengthens existing market power.

9. Intent should not play a significant role in determining the legal status of a certain type of conduct.

10. The special characteristics of small economies require that certain types of exclusionary conduct be analyzed differently than in large economies. For example, price discrimination should be allowed when it serves as a method for breaking oligopolistic coordination.

11. Courts in small economies should exercise caution when applying remedies to avoid creating a more concentrated market structure or increasing the height of entry barriers into the market.

Natural monopolies are a special kind of monopoly, which pose different dilemmas than mere monopolies for competition policy. They are the focus of the next chapter.

CHAPTER FOUR

The Regulation of Natural Monopolies and Essential Facilities

Natural monopolies are not a rare phenomenon in small economies. Especially in very small economies, natural monopolies may exist over a wide range of industries and may significantly affect the economic performance of their markets, of vertically interconnected markets, and of the economy as a whole. Accordingly, in this chapter I analyze the special characteristics of natural monopolies and their implications for the regulation that should be adopted.

I elaborate on the claim that competition laws should regulate the conduct of natural monopolies even when mere monopolies are not regulated. In fact, many jurisdictions regulate certain types of natural monopoly activity differently from the activities of other monopolies. Yet these regulatory tools are very limited and do not necessarily comport with the special characteristics of natural monopolies. Here I introduce and analyze a wide range of conventional and nonconventional tools that are available for competition authorities to regulate natural monopolies in order to achieve the goals of competition policy.

For illustrative purposes, suppose that a lawful monopolist owns and operates a port that is the only accessible one for many miles, owing to geographic constraints. Further assume that the port connects a cluster of manufacturers with their customers who live across the ocean and that no other method of transportation provides an economical alternative. The monopolist has the power to deny access to its port to any manufacturer, and it can also charge supracompetitive and discriminatory prices for such access.[1] This situation creates a host of regulatory dilemmas. Should the law regulate the terms governing access to the port? Should a different rule be applied if the port owner also operates a shipping service that competes with firms seeking access to its port? Should the regulatory policy change if the monopoly is created by a government-imposed barrier to the erection of a competing port? These are some of the questions addressed in this chapter.

Economic Characteristics of Natural Monopolies

Natural monopolies are, as their name indicates, first and foremost monopolies: a single *(mono)* firm has dominant market power. They are, however, a special kind of monopoly: a "natural" one.

The unifying characteristic of natural monopoly markets is the ability of a single firm to provide a good or a service at a lower cost than a set of firms in the market. Natural monopolies may result from unique natural conditions such as those in the port example. They may also result from large internal economies of scale relative to the size of the market: owing to an inherent and persistent tendency of decreasing long-run average unit costs over all or most of the extent of the market, no combination of several firms can produce the industry output as inexpensively as a single firm. The introduction of additional suppliers thus creates a wasteful duplication of facilities and an increase in costs.[2] Natural monopolies may also arise in network industries, in which the system becomes more valuable to a particular user as the number of other users is increased.[3] Under such circumstances, monopoly is accepted as the most appropriate industry structure. This is why such monopolies are termed "natural": they result from the natural conditions of the market. The natural monopoly market may encompass a region, the whole domestic market, or even the global market. Natural monopolies have arisen, for example, in connection with harbors,[4] airports,[5] local newspapers,[6] electricity transmission grids,[7] and bus terminals.[8]

A related phenomenon involves government-created facilities or services known as "essential facilities," which cannot be economically duplicated for policy reasons.[9] To illustrate, environmental objections or land-use restrictions may make it impossible to build a competing airport although market demand might be sufficient to support two airports. Other legal rules, such as intellectual property rights, may also restrict the ability of competing firms to operate in the market. Essential facilities may also exist when one competitor has assumed control over all the alternative sources of at least one critical element necessary to compete. They should be distinguished from natural monopolies. Essential facilities can often be eroded by removing the artificial barriers to entry that created them in the first place. Control of potentially competing facilities by one firm can be eliminated by separation of ownership. Natural monopolies, however, can lose their "natural" status only if one of the two market conditions that define natural monopolies change—either market demand grows significantly or technology erodes economies of scale. Yet because of the similar effects of both natural monopolies and essential facilities on the market and the fact that competition policy takes government-imposed barriers as a given, both are analyzed here together.

When market demand can support only one efficient-sized firm, a natural monopoly has an absolute advantage over other market structures: it is the only market structure that *takes full advantage of internal economies of scale.* Consequently, the costs of production can be lower under natural monopoly than under any other market structure.

Natural monopolies may create significant economic costs, however. They suffer from all the costs of monopoly. They may, for example, *charge monopoly rates* and *restrict output.* Although natural monopolists are able to charge the lowest price for a given widget, they have strong incentives to take advantage of their market power and charge supracompetitive prices. Because their position is generally secured by market conditions, they may even be able to price up to their profit-maximizing level. To return to the port example, the port owner may charge ship operators a monopoly price that is based on their own profit. Such conduct reduces allocative efficiency significantly; it creates a redistribution of profits from producers to the monopolist and might bring about additional economic and social malaise arising from market power.

When entry barriers into its market are prohibitive, the natural monopoly's ability to charge supracompetitive prices is constrained only by the demand elasticity and by technological innovation. For illustrative purposes, suppose that widgets and gadgets are perfect substitutes. Widgets are produced without utilizing the natural monopoly's output, whereas gadgets are produced by utilizing it. If the monopolist raises the price of its outputs, this will inflate the price of gadgets and create substitution effects to widgets. A rational monopolist, anticipating this effect, would price its input at a maximum price that, while sharing in its customers' profits, will still enable its customers to produce and sell gadgets at a competitive price.

The natural monopoly's ability to take advantage of its monopoly power may also be limited by competition *for* its market.[10] The most efficient firm will win the market and reduce productive inefficiency. The winner does not, however, necessarily have to reduce its prices to prevent entry. It can instead charge supracompetitive prices and engage in actual or threatened price changes whenever entry appears imminent. Still, lower production costs may lead to a lower equilibrium price to consumers.

For competition for the market to affect consumer welfare, it is also essential that no artificial barriers to entry exist and that no supplier or consumer has market power.[11] The Israeli case of *Passover Flour*[12] illustrates this point. Passover flour can be produced in any of the twenty-one flour mills operating in Israel. Such production is not profitable, however, for quantities smaller than five thousand tons, because diverting a flour mill from producing regular flour to producing Passover flour involves a large sunk cost. As yearly demand for Passover flour in Israel is approximately ten thousand tons, the market can support a maximum of two Passover flour mills. Nonetheless, given that any one of the existing twenty-one flour mills can potentially produce such flour, and that the flour market suffers from excess capacity, this creates competition for the market. Such competition would have regularly reduced prices to competitive levels. But the four largest buyers of Passover flour, whose combined demand exceeded 80 percent of total market demand, agreed to buy such flour from a specific mill. By so doing, the four created a de facto monopoly, since no other flour mill could sell enough flour to operate profitably. In exchange, the chosen mill agreed to sell the four conspirators Passover flour at low prices, and to sell to all other customers at a higher price. This arrangement prevented other market participants from enjoying the fruits of competition for the market.

Like all monopolies, natural monopolies also have incentives to *discriminate* in order to maximize their profits. In the port example, the port owner may maximize its profits by charging a higher price from an operator shipping a product that is produced by a monopolist than from one shipping a product that competes with substitutes. Natural monopolies also have incentives to engage in *predatory tactics* to prevent competition for their markets or the introduction of a new technology that might erode their position.

Another set of issues arises when the natural monopolist is vertically integrated with a competitor in a competitive segment of its industry, the danger being that under certain market conditions it might have incentives to use its power and profits from the natural monopoly segment to extend its monopoly power to, and exploit it in, the competitive segment(s).[13] The vertically integrated firm might leverage its monopoly power either by *cross-subsidizing* its competitive arms; by engaging in tying, exclusive dealing, or other *predatory or exclusionary conduct*; or by giving its competitive arms *supply benefits* over potential rivals. The effect of such practices on the economic viability and profitability of firms operating in the vertically related market may be significant as, by definition, they have no alternative but to use the natural monopoly's output and comply with its terms of trade.

Regulation of Mere Natural Monopolies

Natural monopolies were traditionally presumed to be outside the domain of competition law, since the main tool of competition policy—competition in the market—cannot regulate their activity. Instead, large, influential natural monopolies have traditionally been subject to sector-specific regulation. In practice, however, natural monopolies exist in markets that are not subject to direct regulation because they are too small or too insignificant to justify a special administrative solution. These natural monopolies usually come under the scope of competition policy by default. Moreover, the criticism of direct regulation for its substantial costs and limited effectiveness has caused some jurisdictions to transfer the regulation of large natural monopolies to the domain of competition laws.[14] Competition policy thus has an important role to play in regulating natural monopolies.

Natural monopoly regulation is much more important in small economies than in large ones. Limited market demand implies that natural monopolies will be found more commonly in small economies. High entry barriers further imply that competition for the market is often very limited and that monopoly position is relatively secure. Accordingly, their impact and effect is much stronger than in large economies. In addition, the relative prominence and strength of natural monopolies may affect other vertically interconnected markets. Thus, although the optimal policy toward natural monopolies should not be qualitatively different in different-sized economies, quantitative differences make the efficient regulation of natural monopolies in small economies more important.

In this chapter I explore a wide spectrum of conventional as well as nonconventional tools available to the competition authorities to regulate natural monopolies. These regulatory tools apply in addition to the competition rules that regulate the economic activity of all monopolistic firms operating in the market. Different regulatory tools sometimes affect one another. For example, price regulation or a prohibition of price discrimination may affect the monopolist's incentives to leverage its monopoly power into a vertically related market, and thus its activities should be much more closely regulated. Accordingly, in evaluating the effectiveness of regulatory tools, one should take into account not only their effectiveness in preventing a specific type of conduct but also their effect on the incentives and the ability of the regulated entity to circumvent such regulation.

In Chapter 3 we considered whether and how to regulate mere monopoly. Natural monopolies pose similar questions, but some of the considerations that were relevant in the case of unnatural monopolies have limited applicability where natural monopolies are concerned.

Drawbacks of Condemning Natural Monopoly Per Se

Any policy toward natural monopolies should not condemn the attainment or maintenance of a natural monopoly position per se. The specific intent to become a natural monopoly, when not accompanied by exclusionary practices, should also not be deemed anti-competitive. This policy prescription is based on the unique characteristics of a natural monopoly market. As the successful competitor for a natural monopoly market captures the entire market, all his conduct is exclusionary by nature. Condemning his intent to become a monopolist or his success at achieving his position will prevent the most efficient market structure—that of a natural monopoly—from being realized. It might also affect dynamic efficiency by removing incentives to grow through efficient performance.

Condemnation of natural monopolies per se is also problematic given the nature of available remedies. The basic remedy to restore the market to its position absent the violation is breakup. But breakup is not an efficient solution in the case of natural monopolies, since it would reduce productive efficiency and needlessly sacrifice economies of scale. Moreover, the tendency of resources to gravitate toward their most valuable uses when voluntary exchange is permitted would eventually recreate a natural monopoly by realizing economies. Thus, structural breakup of natural monopolies is costly and nonsustainable.

A rule that rejects condemnation of mere natural monopoly has been adopted, with limited variations, by all jurisdictions.[15] Under this rule, a natural monopolist violates the competition laws only if it acquires or maintains its power through the use of means that are exclusionary, unfair, or predatory. Competitive actions to win a natural monopoly market—even if they involve a clear attempt to become a monopolist—are not illegal.

Regulation of Anti-Competitive Practices in Achieving or Maintaining a Natural Monopoly

The special characteristics of natural monopoly markets raise an intriguing question: Can a natural monopolist claim that by engaging in predatory tactics it simply hastened the inevitable, that is, its becoming the sole supplier for a given market? Furthermore, given that coexistence creates wasteful duplication of resources, can the natural monopolist argue that it has in fact increased welfare by shortening the struggle to win the monopoly position? A similar set of questions can be posed with regard to the maintenance of a natural monopoly position: Can the natural monopolist's anti-competitive actions to remove a rival from the market in order to maintain its monopoly position be justified by the fact that the struggle to win the market would have resulted anyway in a sole supplier servicing the market, and that the incumbent's actions have reduced the costs of the elimination period?[16]

The answer to all of these questions should be negative. Anti-competitive methods used to achieve or maintain the position of monopoly should lead to a competition law violation, even if they serve to shorten the delays for realizing the low production costs. The main concern is that anti-competitive practices might prevent the most efficient competitor from winning the market. If a less efficient, higher-cost competitor achieves a position of monopoly power through anti-competitive practices, productive efficiency is reduced, and the monopolistic price might be higher.

Should this conclusion change if the firm that engaged in anti-competitive practices is the most efficient? Strong reasons still support condemning its conduct as anti-competitive. Once a court allows more efficient firms to shorten the struggle for the market by engaging in anti-competitive conduct, it must be able to ascertain which firm competing for the market is most efficient. Competition courts usually lack the tools to ascertain economic superiority. Especially in a world of rapid technological changes, it is impossible to require courts to play a determinative role in choosing the most efficient competitor. The very fact that private investors have chosen to compete for a natural monopoly market suggests that they believe they possess a comparative advantage over their rivals. It is thus better to put superiority to the market test by eliminating obstacles to efficient competition.

Moreover, there are benefits in setting clear and similar standards of conduct for all firms in the market, unless market conditions require otherwise. Consequently, small economies should condemn anti-competitive conduct that firms use to achieve or maintain a natural monopoly position, to ensure that the most efficient competitor wins the natural monopoly market and that the winner is constrained in the exercise of its legitimately obtained market power, to the extent possible, by market forces.

Regulation of Monopoly Pricing and Output

Natural monopolies may enjoy a market position that enables them to realize substantial profits by charging high prices and by limiting output. An important issue is whether competition law should prevent the monopolist from realizing supracompetitive rents by setting maximum prices for its goods or services and by setting output closer to competitive levels, provided that doing so is consistent with the economic viability of the firm. Price regulation by industry-specific regulators was the traditional solution to the problem of natural monopoly.

The arguments for and against pricing and output regulation have been extensively analyzed in the context of mere monopolies. The same arguments apply here, with some qualifications. The short-term effects on price and quantity in both natural and unnatural monopoly markets are qualitatively similar. At the same time, it is more likely that the natural monopolist would be able to set prices closer to their profit-maximizing level than most other monopolies, given that it is generally less restrained by market forces. If there is no competition or weak competition for the market, the natural monopolist is limited only by market demand and by technological innovation. Even when competition for the market is strong, the controlling monopolist will have incentives to charge supracompetitive prices and to price-discriminate among customers. The comparative inability of the market to regulate natural monopoly pricing thus points more strongly toward regulation in the case of natural monopolies than in the case of mere monopolies.

Pricing regulation is most strongly justified when the monopoly position was obtained and is maintained owing to a government license. The correlation between a legal franchise and the risk of monopoly pricing is likely to be high given the durability of the granted monopoly. Moreover, in such cases the legitimization of public controls is relatively straightforward. When monopolies are created by law, one can argue that the recipients are bound by consent to regulation through conditions contained within the original grant or the unique conditions artificially created by government intervention in the marketplace as a quid pro quo for government-protected market power. Pricing might also be justified when the natural monopoly position results from unique market conditions not based on dynamic efficiency. It is difficult to see the injustice of denying a "right" to indefinitely perpetuated monopoly profits and power, especially when this power is protected by unique market conditions.

If dynamic efficiency served to create the natural monopoly, the justification for price and output regulation is less straightforward. The incentives of a firm to invest resources in order to become a natural monopoly or to erode its position depend, to a considerable degree, on the price it can obtain. Clearly, such incentives are greatest when no price regulation is adopted. But even when the natural monopoly was created as a result of innovation, this does not necessarily entitle its owner to an indefinite stream of supracompetitive revenues. Given their relatively secure market position, natural monopolies can earn high returns and exist for very long periods of time. Limiting the revenues that can be obtained from the utilization of their assets will not necessarily reduce incentives to invest in natural monopolies, so long as the regulator ensures that the natural monopolist is appropriately compensated at least for the costs (including the risk factor) incurred in developing the asset. Such a policy will still reward the natural monopolist for investing in the product or service but at the same time decrease the ultimate price to consumers and ensure a more efficient allocation of investment resources in society. In cases in which the main cause for the creation of a natural monopoly cannot be easily determined, it should be assumed that the monopoly was created as a result of dynamic efficiency.

Yet regulation should be carefully structured so as to minimize the costs of intervening in the market. The same guidelines that applied in Chapter 3 should apply here as well. In particular, price regulation should be imposed only in cases in which the negative welfare effects of the natural monopolist's pricing is significant.

Australia and New Zealand have adopted a special set of rules that enables their competition authorities to regulate the price and output decisions of natural monopolies.[17] Other small jurisdictions empower their competition authorities to regulate natural monopolies by the same powers that regulate mere monopolies. As elaborated earlier, these include direct regulation of monopoly pricing and output or regulation of "unfair" or "inequitable" monopoly pricing and limitations of output or quality through the abuse-of-dominance provisions.

Cost Misallocations

Natural monopolies' conduct may encompass the whole range of predatory conduct engaged in by dominant firms. Nonetheless, in some situations natural monopoly raises unique issues. We shall focus on two. The first involves cost misallocations of a price-regulated natural monopoly into its competitive arm. The second involves refusal to supply, or discriminatory supply, by a vertically integrated natural monopolist.

If a vertically integrated natural monopolist cross-subsidizes its competitive arm in order to force its competitors out of the market, or if price cuts in the competitive segment are intended to discourage aggressive competition, such conduct may be condemned as anti-competitive predatory conduct.[18] A more complicated issue arises when the price-regulated monopolist misallocates some of the costs of its price-regulated competitive activities to its natural monopoly segments, thereby giving its competitive arm a price advantage.[19]

The most relevant economic offense involves predatory pricing. In applying predatory pricing provisions to combat cost misallocations, several difficulties may arise. Although the outcome of both the usual predatory pricing scenario and cost misallocations may be similar—driving competitors that have competitive advantages over the predatory firm out of the market—they are achieved in different ways. "Ordinary" predatory pricing involves temporary pricing below cost, whereas the natural monopolist might engage in cost misallocation for unlimited periods, as this does not entail a loss to the overall profitability of the firm; unlike "ordinary" predatory pricing, cost misallocation could be profitable to the monopolist even if it does not possess market power in the competitive market or if barriers to entry into the competitive segment are low. Assume, for example, that the "real" costs of its competitive arm are 100, while the monopolist succeeds in covering 50 percent of such costs by "smuggling" them into the cost structure of its regulated natural monopoly activities. It would be profitable for it to sell its product at any price above 50, whether or not there were barriers to entry into the predated market and whether or not it possessed market power in it.

It would thus be difficult, if not impossible, to establish some of the elements of the predatory offense, mainly, that the competing arm of the natural monopoly sets its prices at a predatory level. The fact that the monopolist "smuggles" some of the costs of its competitive arm or affiliate into its regulated rates enables it to sell its end product at a price that, although below the "real" cost of production, does not generate any loss for the firm as a whole. The crucial question then becomes whether a court will apply the economic criteria for predatory price levels to the costs of the competitive arm alone or will adopt a broader point of view that takes into account all the costs of the firm. The court may allow the firm to justify its actions on the grounds that it covers all of its costs and does not suffer any losses. Yet such justification will expose the firm to the scrutiny of the price regulator whose failure to prevent the monopolist from "smuggling" costs that were incurred by its competitive arm into its cost structure has enabled cost misallocation to occur in the first place.

In conclusion, the power to investigate and remedy predation is unlikely to be sufficient to regulate cost misallocations efficiently. Instead, price regulation should be corrected to limit these cost misallocations. One possible response would be for the regulator to impose "competitive safeguards" in related competitive segments, such as limitations on the pricing behavior of the natural monopolist's competitive affiliate, to ensure that the integrated firm does not leverage its market power. A regulator lacking expertise in the competitive process, however, might worsen the situation by interfering with that process. The efficient response is thus to tighten the regulatory measures to prevent cost misallocations in the first place.

Refusal to Supply and Discriminatory Supply Terms

Refusal to supply and discriminatory supply terms of vertically integrated natural monopolists raise an important concern for harm to competition. The concern is that through such conduct, the monopolist, competing in a vertically integrated market, might use its control over the natural monopoly facility to create artificial barriers for existing or new entrants to compete with its competitive arm in the potentially competitive market. It might do so by refusing to let its rivals use its asset, delaying their use of it, or charging them high and discriminatory prices.

Such conduct has been the basis for special rules and doctrines, adopted in many jurisdictions, which create a major exception to the liberal principle that monopolies can choose their customers and the terms on which they deal with them. Such legal regimes are analyzed in the discussion that follows. To set the basis for this discussion, I first introduce three different legal regimes governing such conduct. There are sufficient differences among them for a comparison to be a productive exercise. I then propose several methods for increasing the efficiency of these rules, some of which relate to the basic terms of the regulatory rules and others to the possible remedies.

The Legal Regimes
THE U.S. "ESSENTIAL FACILITIES" DOCTRINE
The best-known rule dealing with access to vertically integrated natural monopolies is the U.S. essential facilities doctrine, also known as the bottleneck monopoly doctrine. The doctrine imposes on a controller of an essential facility a duty to grant its competitors reason-

able and nondiscriminatory access to it. Its importance stems not only from its use in the United States but also from its adoption or use as a reference point in many small jurisdictions.[20]

The first U.S. Supreme Court case that dealt with access to an essential facility was *Terminal Railroad*.[21] There, the Supreme Court decided that a joint venture controlling all economical routes of access to and from a city must permit railroads wishing to use its facilities to do so on nondiscriminatory terms. A significant number of antitrust cases have been decided based on the same doctrine, which typically provides the principal legal justification for compulsory access when antitrust is the tool for facilitating competition in vertically interconnected markets.[22]

The doctrine's modern content can be largely understood from two cases—*MCI Communications*[23] and *Aspen Skiing*.[24] In *MCI* the plaintiff claimed that AT&T had improperly refused to allow it to connect its telephone lines with AT&T's nationwide telephone network and that such interconnection was essential for MCI to compete against AT&T in the long-distance market. The court identified four essential elements necessary to establish liability under the doctrine: (1) control of an essential facility by a monopolist; (2) a competitor's inability practically or reasonably to duplicate the essential facility; (3) the denial of the use of the facility to a competitor; and (4) the feasibility of providing the facility. *Aspen* is commonly interpreted as adding a fifth requirement, namely, the absence of a legitimate business justification for the refusal to deal at either the "micro level" or the "macro level."[25] Legitimate business justifications at the micro level focus on the circumstances of the particular case (such as past experience or technical problems of interconnection). The macro level focuses on legitimate justifications of a general policy of de facto exclusivity. The doctrine, applied to a single firm, must also meet the intent requirement necessary to constitute monopolization under section 2 of the Sherman Act. When the conditions of the doctrine have been met, the firm that controls an essential facility may not refuse to make the facility available to its competitors on nondiscriminatory and reasonable access terms.

A facility has been found to be "essential" if competitors cannot effectively compete in a market without access to it. It is not essential if it can, in fact, be technically and economically duplicated or is otherwise obtainable and if access is not vital and critical to competitive viability.[26] A municipal sports stadium,[27] an electricity distribution system,[28] and a uniquely situated commercial building[29] have all been found to be essential facilities. The strongest claims of essentiality are based on resources that constitute a natural monopoly or those whose duplication is forbidden by law.

Turning to the key issue of what constitutes a denial of access, we find that the case law implies that essential facilities must be made available on "fair and reasonable" or "nondiscriminatory" terms. "Access" was interpreted to mean actual use of the facility (i.e., allocating the scarce resource among users), subject to scarcity constraints. The doctrine in its current form focuses on nondiscriminatory terms. The intervention of the court in the facility controller's decisions is minimal and is usually limited to setting equal terms for all actual or potential competitors. This is because it is believed that the monopolist's profit-maximizing incentives will ensure that the market is served on reasonable—though profit-maximizing—terms, and because of the difficulties involved in price regulation. The reasonableness requirement should thus be read as prohibiting access terms that are discriminatory, de jure or de facto. For example, if a facility holder requires that competitors use one kind of equipment that is used only by some of the market participants, and such a requirement is not technically justified, then the court may require that all competitors be served without regard to their equipment.

Valid business justifications negate a presumption of intent to restrict competition. Access will not be granted if it will result in the diminution of service or the denial can be justified for technical or capacity reasons. In *Town of Massena,* for example, the district court concluded that the defendant had properly refused access to essential transmission lines when the plaintiff failed to resolve legitimate engineering concerns.[30] In *City of Groton* a refusal to consent to general requests to wheel which failed to specify the timing of a transaction or the quantity of power to be wheeled was sustained.[31] The *Massena* and *Groton* courts emphasized that the defendant utilities had not categorically refused to deal but had raised efficiency concerns in the course of good faith efforts to negotiate wheeling agreements. In general, the business justification for refusing access to an essential facility is limited to cases in which access would disrupt the monopolist's own business or the monopolist would incur substantial investments to accommodate its competitor. More recently courts have also upheld business justifications rooted in public policy issues such as equity concerns or the protection of captive consumers from the redistributional aims of a rent-seeking plaintiff.[32]

The essential facilities rule is essentially a take-it-or-leave-it rule in that the court does not balance the economic considerations present, but rather if one of the elements of the doctrine is not fulfilled, the case is dismissed. Most important, an absolute defense is created if there are valid business justifications for denials of access.

An important debate surrounds the issue of whether the controller of the essential facility must compete in a vertically related market for the doctrine to apply. The prevailing view is that vertical integration is an essential element of the doctrine.[33] The rationale behind this requirement is that access to the facility should be mandated only when the monopolist's conduct further entrenches or extends its monopoly into competitive markets.[34]

The essential facilities doctrine has nonetheless been applied, on rare occasions, to a non–vertically integrated natural monopolist.[35] These cases can be distinguished as involving the abuse of monopsony power (i.e., buyer monopoly power) to induce a natural monopolist to grant exclusive rights to its facility. It is questionable whether the essential facilities doctrine is the appropriate vehicle to use in such cases. Given that the monopolist is driven to its discriminatory conduct not by its own incentives to monopolize but rather by the incentives of a powerful buyer who uses its power over the monopolist to mandate discriminatory terms, the substantive anticompetitive offense as well as the remedy should relate to the monopsony buyer. This factual scenario raises an intriguing question. Given that the natural monopolist is the only firm operating in its market, how can a buyer abuse its power to induce a monopolist to engage in activities that are otherwise not to its advantage? The answer lies in specific constellations of facts, such as when the buyer can make a credible threat to compete for the market itself or to buy its inputs from another firm that will win over the natural monopoly market.[36] It also may threaten to use a different input. Such a threat may be credible when the alternative input or production techniques are still profitable if they allow the buyer to maintain a monopoly position in its market.

EC REFUSAL-TO-DEAL AND DISCRIMINATORY DEALINGS PROHIBITIONS

The general principle in European Community law is that there is no general duty of a monopolist to help its consumers or competitors. A firm is normally allowed to retain for its own exclusive use all the advantages it has legitimately acquired. Yet a monopoly is under special obligations not to engage in conduct that constitutes an abuse of dominance. Typical abuses are listed in Article 82 of the Treaty of Rome and include discriminatory trade terms. The discriminatory trade terms prohibition encompasses all the situations in which a monopolist discriminates among its customers (whether its competitors or not) requesting similar products or service, if the discrimination has significant effects on competition. This prohibition, along with the prohibition on setting monopolistic rates, creates strong incentives for monopolists to integrate vertically into another, potentially competitive market and exploit their market power there. Consequently, regulating access to essential facilities is of great significance in EC competition policy.

Under the EC refusal-to-deal prohibition, a firm in a dominant position is not permitted to refuse to supply a product or a service without justification or on terms less favorable than those that it gives its own competitive arm if this has significant effects on competition.[37] This duty includes both existing and potential competitors,[38] and it applies both to single-firm dominance and to joint ownership.[39]

Given the broad scope of this prohibition, there is no real need for a special doctrine that deals separately with situations in which access to a facility is essential for effective competition in a vertically connected market. Although the European Commission endorsed the creation of an explicit essential facilities doctrine,[40] the legal rules governing refusal to deal with regard to essential facilities have been present, in substance if not in name, for many years. Use of the doctrine may nonetheless be a useful label for some types of cases in which vertical integration is present, which create a subcategory of refusal-to-deal cases.[41]

The duty to deal arises only when supply is indispensable for the economic viability of the firm seeking supply and a refusal to supply would create an insuperable barrier to entry or a serious, permanent, and inescapable competitive advantage that would make its activities uneconomical. It arises only when the firm seeking supply is unable, physically or for some objective reason other than its own size or lack of funds, to provide corresponding facilities for itself. The indispensability applies to natural monopolies, to government-created monopolies, and to monopolies resulting from singular ownership, much as in the U.S. essentiality requirement.

The application of the indispensability requirement can be illustrated by the *Oscar Bronner* case.[42] The case involved a refusal by a press undertaking, which held a very large share of the daily newspaper market in Austria and operated the only nationwide newspaper home-delivery scheme, to allow the publisher of a rival newspaper to have access to its scheme for appropriate remuneration. The rival newspaper seeking inclusion in the home-delivery scheme was unable, by reason of its small number of subscribers (3.6 percent), to build up its own home-delivery scheme for a reasonable cost and to operate it profitably. The European Court of Justice was asked to determine whether such conduct constituted abuse of dominance on the ground that the refusal deprived the competitor of an essential means of distribution.

The court's analysis was based on the factual assumptions that a separate market exists in home-delivery schemes and that the press undertaking held a dominant position in that market. It stated that even if these factual findings were found to be true, for a refusal to constitute abuse, the plaintiff must establish "not only that the refusal of the service be likely to eliminate all competition in the market on the part of the person requesting the service and that such refusal be incapable of being objectively justified, but also that the service in itself be indispensable to carrying on that person's business, inasmuch as there is no actual or potential substitute in existence for that home-delivery scheme."[43] It then held that these conditions were not met in the case at hand. In the first place, other methods of distributing daily newspapers, such as by post and through sale in shops and at kiosks, even though they may be less advantageous for the distribution of certain newspapers, exist and are used by the publishers of other daily newspapers. Second, it did not appear that there were any technical, legal, or even economic obstacles making it impossible, or even unreasonably difficult, for any other publisher of daily newspapers to establish, alone or in cooperation with other publishers, its own nationwide home-delivery scheme and to use it to distribute its own daily newspapers. The court emphasized that for such access to be capable of being regarded as indispensable, it would be necessary at the very least to establish that it was not economically viable to create a second home-delivery scheme for the distribution of daily newspapers with a circulation comparable to that of the newspapers distributed by the existing scheme.

The court's decision limits compulsory supply in some important respects. First, the court analyzes all the options of the firm seeking access, including a joint venture operation with all other existing rivals. Thus, if a particular competitor were especially vulnerable or inefficient and could not compete without supply although other firms more normally situated could, it would not be granted supply. Access would not be granted if competitors, alone or jointly, could build a competing facility. Second, compulsory supply would not be granted if refusal to supply were to create a comparative advantage to the monopolist's competitive arm but would still allow a competitor to operate economically in the market, taking into account its overall commercial viability.

Another requirement of Article 82 is that the refusal to supply significantly affect competition. This condition was interpreted by the ECJ very narrowly to require that the conduct in question be likely to eliminate *all* competition in a vertically related market.[44] If there are a number of competitors in the downstream market and it is competitive, the refusal to supply one more competitor does not have a significant effect on competition. Thus, there is no duty to supply if the downstream market is competitive, even if it is technically feasible to supply another competitor, unless the firm seeking access can show that it is being discriminated against to discourage it from competing vigorously.

The duties imposed on the monopolist are farther-reaching than those imposed in the United States. The main duty is similar: to supply on nondiscriminatory terms. But an EC monopolist also has a positive duty to propose and seek solutions to meet a competitor's needs, to provide users with the timely information they need to exercise their rights, and to consult with users to make the necessary arrangements in order to maximize the overall benefits offered to consumers.[45] Moreover, the monopolist is mandated to share its facilities on equal terms with new and existing competitors on a nondiscriminatory basis.[46]

The court also looks at objective justifications for the firm's actions.

The basic test is whether a reasonable owner of the facility, were it not vertically integrated, would have refused supply. If so, the vertically connected facility may refuse supply, subject to the principle of proportionality.[47] In contrast to U.S. courts, the ECJ has recognized only very limited business justifications that could defeat a refusal-to-deal case. Objective reasons for refusal include shortages in supply as long as the asset controller has allocated the existing capacity in a nondiscriminatory way,[48] and having due regard to the controller's own requirements to provide supplies during periods of peak demand and his other long-term commitments; the relevant technical standards of the asset; and intellectual property rights. The last are applied very narrowly. An exclusive right of a proprietor to intellectual property rights did not constitute an acceptable business justification for refusal to deal when such refusal prevented the introduction of a new product for which there was potential consumer demand.[49] The greater the effect on competition, the harder it is to justify a refusal.

Another important difference between EC and U.S. case law is that the ECJ does not seem to recognize efficiency justifications for refusals to supply. The EC cases of *Hugin*[50] and *Commercial Solvents*[51] serve as good illustrations of this difference. Both cases involved decisions by an upstream supplier to undertake downstream activity and thereby undercut an existing competitor. In both cases the court analyzed the effects of the monopolist's decision on the existing supplier of such services, and it emphasized the fact that the monopolist's conduct would eliminate the only serious competitor that the monopolist's subsidiary could face, but it neglected to analyze and evaluate the scope economies that can result from such vertical integration and the net effect on welfare. A refusal by a supplier to supply a potential downstream competitor, even if it is efficient, is thus a serious abuse.[52] This concern with protecting competitors irrespective of the issue of welfare may well discourage businesses from efficient integration or efficient competition for fear of being characterized as anticompetitive.

AUSTRALIA'S DOUBLE REGIME OF SUPPLY TERMS

Australia's natural monopolies are regulated by a double regime. Section 46 of the Australian Trade Practices Act prohibits anti-competitive conduct, interpreted to include anti-competitive refusals to supply. In addition, more recent amendments to the act create a new regulatory regime, vested in the competition authorities, to ensure third-party access to essential facilities that a competitor cannot practically or reasonably duplicate, when such access would significantly increase competition.[53] This regime was based on the recommendations of a governmental committee that endorsed the establishment of a legislative regime to permit competitors to gain access to facilities that cannot be economically duplicated, given the problematic nature of granting access based on section 46 cases.[54]

Several Australian cases have involved refusals to deal by vertically integrated dominant firms. One of the best-known Australian cases, *Queensland Wire,*[55] involved a constructive refusal to supply. In this case, BHP was the sole domestic manufacturer of a steel fence post known as a star picket, which it produced from an intermediate steel product called a Y bar. Queensland Wire (QWI) competed with BHP in the rural fencing market comprising wire, fence posts, and hinges. QWI sought supplies of Y bar from BHP in order to manufacture its own star picket fence posts and thereby be in a position to deliver a full range of products to large consumers at competitive prices. BHP refused to supply QWI with Y bars other than at list price. The Australian court found an abuse of dominance, stating that the price set for the Y bars was unreasonably high, without an analysis of leveraging or the assessment of power gained over price. The court declined to accept the doctrine of essential facilities but left open the possibility of its application to "electric power, transport, communications or some other 'essential service.'"[56]

In *MacLean*[57] the relevant market was for the raw material cypermethrin, used in the production of an insect-killing chemical product for use on sheep, and the only effective source of supply was through the defendant. The defendant was prepared to supply raw material, but only if the plaintiffs entered into a joint venture with it. After the negotiations broke down, the defendant was prepared to supply only on new conditions that, the plaintiffs alleged, were not commercially viable and would effectively destroy their ability to compete in the downstream market. The Australian court was prepared to grant an interlocutory injunction restraining the defendant from failing to supply the raw material in accordance with the terms of the joint venture agreement. These cases incorporate a very broad compulsory supply rule, as they look not at the effect of the refusal on welfare but rather at the effect on specific competitors. Refusals used as part of a predatory tactic are also considered anti-competitive.[58]

Alternatively, natural monopolies that provide services can be regulated under Part IIIA of the Trade Practices Act. The act details a two-part process. The first step entails declaration of the service as essential by the responsible minister. The criteria for declaration require (1) that access promote competition in at least one market other than the market for the service; (2) that it would be uneconomical for anyone to develop another facility to provide the service (this was interpreted as determining the issue of essentiality from a social perspective rather than that of the person seeking access);[59] (3) that the facility be of national significance with regard to its size and its importance to trade, commerce, or the national economy; (4) that access to the service can be provided without undue risk to human health or safety; (5) that it not already be the subject of an effective access regime; and (6) that access would not be contrary to the public interest.

The second step involves setting access terms. If the parties cannot reach an agreement, the Australian Competition and Consumer Council (ACCC) engages in an arbitration process. Both the minister's decision on whether to accept a recommendation to declare a service essential and the ACCC's arbitration of the terms of access are subject to review by the Competition Tribunal. The ACCC is empowered to accept undertakings from service providers that bypass the declaratory process.

The Efficiency of Legal Requirements

Assuming that the laws governing supply by essential facilities are based on an economic rationale, an important question is whether they actually succeed, in their current form, in achieving economic efficiency. It is always tempting to respond favorably to a firm that complains of lack of access to a market. Yet to arrive at a balanced appraisal of regulation, it is necessary to apply limiting principles to ensure that competition laws achieve their goals. In this section I analyze the legal requirements in an attempt to evaluate their efficiency in light of traditional and new criticisms, in order to help formulate more efficient regulatory regimes.

THE HARM INFLICTED BY REFUSAL TO SUPPLY OR DISCRIMINATORY SUPPLY

An important element of compulsory supply provisions involves the harm inflicted by the monopolist's action. The U.S. and EC case law theoretically focuses on harm to competition, although some cases can be interpreted as focusing on harm to specific competitors. I will argue that neither should be the focus of compulsory supply. Rather, the focus should be on the results that competition is said to achieve, that is, economic welfare.

The EC cases of *Commercial Solvents*,[60] *CBEM*,[61] and *Bronner*[62] require that the conduct in question eliminate *all* competition in a vertically related market. A somewhat similar view can be attributed to several leading scholars who have suggested that a monopolist should not be forced to deal unless so doing is likely to improve competition in the marketplace substantially. Areeda and Hovenkamp, for example, suggest that the asset controller should not be forced to supply unless its discriminatory terms do, in fact, harm competition in a related market. No harm to competition exists if no monopoly is created or extended by the refusal. The purpose of the essential facilities doctrine, they argue, is not to permit particular rivals to survive but to make the market more competitive. Thus, a vertically integrated monopolist that discriminates among competitors should not be mandated to act otherwise unless its actions harm competition in the downstream market.[63] It follows that when the downstream market can support only one firm, merely substituting one competitor for another will not create or extend monopoly in the market, and access should not be mandated.

This suggestion suffers from an inherent flaw, given that it focuses on competition instead of on its results. A legal rule that looks solely to the *number* of existing competitors might create inefficient results by enabling the monopolist to eliminate its most efficient competitors. Assume, for example, that a natural monopolist deliberately refuses to serve its most efficient competitors in order to allow its own competitive arm to enjoy a comparative advantage. The monopolist's conduct may have a significant effect on welfare. Not only will productive efficiency not be achieved, but the incentives of future competitors to invest in and to utilize more efficient production techniques will be severely reduced as well. Requiring that *all* competition be eliminated might also create a duopoly structure, which is not always conducive to competition. Accordingly, an approach that depends solely on foreclosure of access to all competitors should be rejected.

Focusing on the harm to *specific competitors,* as the Australian abuse cases seem to do, also does not necessarily increase welfare, as it might protect inefficient competitors. Moreover, such an approach might block the vertical integration of a monopolist even if it would increase productive efficiency. In addition, when there is sufficient competition in the final product market, compulsory supply has no effect on the market price of the end product.

Instead, the focus should be on the welfare effects of compulsory access. An optimal rule would mandate that the monopolist supply only competitors that are more efficient than its competitive arm. Such a rule would, however, be extremely difficult to apply in practice, given that courts do not have the tools necessary to determine the relative efficiency of competing firms. The nondiscrimination rule, if applied correctly, serves in cases involving homogeneous products as a good approximation, since it implies that the monopolist will supply competitors that are more efficient than its competitive arm. A refusal to supply should thus not be deemed anti-competitive if nondiscriminatory, unless applied in an anti-competitive manner, for example, if the price is predatorily low. This will ensure that only the most efficient firms would be able to operate in the market.

The focus on welfare implies, too, that if granting supply will not reduce the price or increase the quality of products to the end consumer, then no compulsory supply should be granted. For example, a coal mine that can ship its coal into a coal market only by using an existing railway line should not be granted compulsory access to the railway if the coal market is already competitive and shipping its coal into the market would not reduce the price of coal to competitors. This rule should apply even if access is essential to the competitive viability of a competitor, and even if the asset controller has significant market power in the market for the asset.

Compulsory access also should not be mandated when adding users may reduce efficiency if the facility has reached an optimal size. In addition, a monopolist should be permitted to take over related operations if it is at least as efficient as the current operator. The monopolist will reap more profit, but the monopoly price to consumers may be lower.[64]

The differences among the divergent standards for compulsory access can be squarely presented in cases in which the monopolist refuses to deal with a firm that is in competition for a successive essential facility,[65] such that a monopoly is not created but merely transferred from one firm to the other. Under the elimination-of-competition standard, a refusal to deal would not be prohibited as it would not result in the elimination of competition, because the vertically related market can support only one firm anyway. Under the welfare standard, however, it would be prohibited. The reason is that a more efficient successive monopolist may well reduce productive inefficiency. Accordingly, the analysis focuses not only on the adverse effects on competitors or competition, as most courts typically do, but also on structural efficiency considerations. To minimize problems arising from information asymmetry, it is suggested that the burdens of proof be allocated as follows: the plaintiff should be required to establish a prima facie case for why the restraint reduces welfare. The burden then shifts to the defendant to prove that refusal to supply did not have such an effect.

Another condition for increasing welfare is that the business justification exception to the essential facilities doctrine, once recognized, not be applied as a complete excuse for not granting access, as is done in the United States. The EC approach, under which the monopolist has a positive duty to propose and seek solutions to meet a competitor's needs, to provide users with the timely information they need to exercise their rights, and to consult with them to make the necessary arrangements in order to maximize the overall benefits offered to consumers, is much preferable.

THE RATIONALE FOR COMPULSORY SUPPLY AND THE SINGLE MONOPOLY PROFIT THEORY

The presumption that a vertically integrated monopolist will seek to decrease competition in the vertically related market on which the essential facilities doctrine rests seems, at first glance, at odds with the single monopoly profit theory. The theory states that the monopolist of a single link in the chain of production can appropriate the entire chain's monopoly profits without having to refuse to deal with its competitors. Thus the monopolist is not necessarily motivated by predatory tactics in its decisions to discriminate between the competitors it serves and with which it also competes in a vertically related market. Rather, if the monopolist can duplicate monopoly conditions without refusing to deal, vertical restrictions serve efficient ends. It follows that mandating access to the facility might discourage efficient conduct without a corresponding benefit in terms of deterring anti-competitive conduct.

Several scholars thus suggest that refusals are generally efficient, not anti-competitive, as they are not necessary to extract monopoly profits. Accordingly, the law should presume that efficiency motivates monopolists absent any anti-competitive incentive for refusals to deal, instead of presuming that the monopolist has engaged in anti-competitive conduct. It follows that a plaintiff should establish an economic basis for why a refusal to deal is welfare-decreasing before a court imposes a duty to deal.[66]

The U.S. case of *Paschall*[67] illustrates the application of the single monopoly profit theory. In *Paschall,* Star held a monopoly position in the newspaper market in Kansas City, Missouri. For many years Star used independent carriers to deliver its newspapers, although it retained the right to distribute the papers itself. When it proposed a discontinuation of its independent delivery system, 250 independent newspaper carriers filed an antitrust suit, alleging refusal to deal and attempted monopolization of the carrier market. The district court granted an injunction preventing the termination of the independent carrier contracts.[68] On appeal, the Eighth Circuit affirmed.[69] Following Star's petition, the Eighth Circuit agreed to reconsider the case en banc. The court reversed its panel decision and found that Star's decision to integrate vertically did not violate the Sherman Act. Basing its decision on the single monopoly pricing theory, the majority concluded that Star's decision to integrate vertically would in fact result in lower prices and better service to consumers.[70]

Yet there are important limitations to the applicability of the single monopoly profit theory. Under most legal systems the monopolist is either prevented from charging discriminatory supply terms or is prevented from charging supracompetitive rates. This automatically limits the applicability of the single monopoly profit theory. When the monopolist is technically or legally prevented from extracting all its monopoly rents from vertically linked markets, it may impose restrictions on its competitors to create a competitive advantage to its own arm. The theory also does not apply in a host of other situations, such as when the asset is nearing the end of its life and the monopolist attempts to prolong its monopoly artificially by establishing a stronghold in an adjacent market or when the natural monopolist is under a threat of competition for the market.

The legal provisions, in their current form, do not differentiate between such situations. The essentiality requirement moves the focus away from the incentives of the monopolist to engage in predatory tactics or to evade regulation and toward the effect on competitors and competition.

ESSENTIALITY: THE IMPORTANCE OF A CORRECT MARKET DEFINITION

The criterion used to determine the scope of assets subject to compulsory access may also affect its efficient application. All jurisdictions surveyed adopt a narrow test, one that differentiates between assets that are merely advantageous to competitors and assets that are essential or indispensable to their competitive viability. This narrow criterion is based on the necessary balancing between competing dynamic and static considerations for compulsory access. Its application in specific cases raises some intriguing issues.

The identification of an essential facility often hinges on the relevant market definition. Even if the correct regulatory principles are set in place, the duty to supply may still produce inefficient results if markets are defined incorrectly. A narrow definition can easily result if the court tends to analyze the factual situation from the point of view of the firm refused supply. But even if a specific firm does not have any viable alternatives for its operation without access to the facility, this does not automatically imply that the refusal affects welfare.

Illustrative cases involve refusal to supply spare parts to third-party maintenance services or other after-sales service operators. In the EC *Hugin*[71] and the U.K. *Ford Body Panels* cases,[72] the competition authorities took a narrow view of the relevant market within which the plaintiff operated, defined as the market for spare parts of a specific product, although in both cases the plaintiff faced extensive competition from other original equipment manufacturers. Such a market definition almost automatically leads to a finding of essentiality. This definition is flawed in that although the manufacturer can increase short-term gains by taking advantage of locked-in consumers, it is constrained by competition from manufacturers of competing products. Consumers will take into account, when evaluating their alternatives, the costs of spare parts in making their initial decision. As elaborated in the previous chapter, a more economically based market definition would have looked at the competition facing the original manufacturer in its main market in defining the relevant market.

More recent EC case law seems to have taken a more economically based approach to market definitions. The case of *European Night*

Services[73] is a good illustration. The main railway companies in the United Kingdom, Germany, the Netherlands, and France formed a joint venture, European Night Services (ENS), to provide overnight passenger rail service between the United Kingdom and continental Europe by way of the Channel Tunnel. The commission, which defined the market as that of train services through the tunnel, found that the agreement infringed the Treaty of Rome and granted an exemption subject to the condition that train tracks and special locomotives be made available to third parties seeking access. The Court of First Instance reversed, basing its decision, inter alia, on the fact that ENS faced extensive competition in the market for the carriage of business and leisure passengers between the United Kingdom and the Continent, in which it held only a 5 percent market share. The court emphasized the need for a realistic analysis of the economic context and impact of a transaction.

FACTUAL SITUATIONS THAT CREATE ESSENTIAL FACILITIES

Some commentators argue that compulsory access should be limited to natural monopolies.[74] Indeed, monopoly power is a fundamental underpinning of the essential facilities doctrine. While natural monopolies pose some of the strongest cases for mandating access, the doctrine should also encompass other factual situations in which the facility cannot be economically duplicated. One such example involves situations in which government-created entry barriers make it impossible to duplicate supply, such as the grant of a legal monopoly.

Essential facilities may also result from the concentration of ownership of all potentially competing assets in one set of hands. *Terminal Railroad*[75] is a case in point. There, the defendants had acquired control of all viable competitive methods of transportation across the Mississippi into and out of St. Louis, including railways, bridges, and car ferries, which constituted potential competitive systems. In so doing, the defendants created a horizontal monopoly. A similar situation results when, for example, a taxicab operator controls all the existing taxi medallions. The same rules regulating compulsory supply in natural monopoly and government-created essential facilities should apply equally in such cases. The only difference is remedial: while natural monopolies and government-created legal monopolies cannot be eroded simply by dispersion of ownership, this is a viable solution in the case of a horizontal monopoly.

An intriguing set of cases involves those in which several firms produce outputs of the same kind that are essential complementary inputs for the operation of firms in an adjacent market. The output can be the firms' main product or a by-product of another market in which they may or may not have market power. These cases can be analyzed under the essential facility doctrine only if each output is analyzed as a separate product market. Whereas in most cases involving essential facilities the facility controller is the only firm operating in the downstream or upstream market, in this situation the facility controller is not the only firm producing output of the same type.

The EC *Magill*[76] decision is illustrative. *Magill* involved the refusal of two broadcasting firms operating in Ireland and Northern Ireland, together with the BBC, to sell their weekly scheduled television program listings to a third firm that was attempting to publish a comprehensive weekly TV guide. The court found that the two firms abused their dominant position by refusing to grant licenses for the publication of their weekly listings, necessary to meet consumer demand for a new product that would incorporate the listings of all firms broadcasting in Ireland, without an objective justification. The case is interesting in two respects. First, it involved placing limitations on the intellectual property rights of the broadcasting companies over their listings. Second, the input of each firm was unique in that the listings of all firms were necessary to create a comprehensive guide (what the commission termed a "factual monopoly"). The ECJ stated that the appellants were de facto monopolists because they were the only sources of basic information on program scheduling, which is indispensable for compiling a weekly television guide. Thus, although none of the firms had a dominant position in the broadcasting market, the fact that their inputs were necessary complements in the secondary market was sufficient for the court to deduce a dominant position.

The court's analysis is confusing. Instead of focusing on the dominant position that each firm held in its broadcast *listings* market, the ECJ chose to focus on the firms' positions in the broadcasting market. Such focus is misleading. Even if five or even ten firms with equal market shares operated in the broadcasting market, the weekly schedules of all or most of the broadcasting firms would still be essential inputs in the secondary market. Put simply, their position in their main market does not necessarily affect the essentiality of their input in a second market, when no marketable product could be created without their inputs. Moreover, the refusal to deal in the secondary market does not necessarily affect the consumer's decision to buy the main product (broadcasts). Consumers would most likely not stop viewing a TV channel just because it published its own program guide separately and did not participate in the publishing of some other firms' guide (unless such a guide were a main source of information for a significant number of consumers). A clearer analysis would focus on the control of each firm over an input that is a complementary essential input in a second market, as well as on the effect of the refusal to supply on the competitiveness of the firm in its main market.

ESSENTIALITY FOR THE ECONOMIC VIABILITY OF COMPETITORS

The test for essentiality in all jurisdictions focuses on the effect of refusal to supply on the economic viability of providing a similar service rather than on physical impossibility. Although jurisdictions use different terms, from "essentiality" to "indispensability," these tests generally focus on whether the handicap resulting from refusal to supply creates an insuperable barrier to entry, one that can reasonably be expected to make competitors' activities either impossible or seriously and unavoidably uneconomic. This is the correct test. Access to the facility should not be granted if the facility in question is better than the alternatives, but not so much better as to preclude totally the continued survival of excluded parties. Clearly, the effect of the refusal to supply on the competitor should be based on its overall viability in the *specific market*, rather than in all the markets in which it operates. A different rule would differentiate between well-established firms that operate in many fields of business and small ones that operate only in the vertically related market.

An interesting issue arises when supply is essential to the commercial viability of some competitors but not of others. Should the asset still be deemed essential, or does the fact that some competitors can compete without access negate the essentiality presumption? Strong considerations point toward the second view, at least in homogeneous product markets. The fact that a particular competitor needs access to a facility in order to enter the market is irrelevant if other, more normally situated competitors do not. A different rule would normally protect inefficient competitors and reduce the ownership rights of the asset controller. In addition, it would create uncertainty by requiring the dominant firm to assess the effect of its refusal on the specific characteristics of each firm requiring supply. The question should thus be whether the denial was one that would make it impossible for any competitor that is as efficient as the monopolist to enter the market and survive economically.

The Israeli *Dubek* case[77] is unique in that it finds a facility essential for some competitors but not for others. *Dubek* involved an attempt by a cigarette manufacturer to integrate vertically into distributional activities. The Israeli cigarette market was controlled by two main firms: Dubek, which held approximately 72 percent of the market and enjoyed a monopoly in the manufacture of Israeli cigarettes, and Elishar, the largest cigarette importer (25 percent market share). In addition, two small importers operated in the market (1 and 2 percent market share). For years all the firms distributed their cigarettes through a joint distribution network. The case involved Dubek's attempt to create a vertically integrated autonomous distribution network that would distribute only its cigarettes. Two justifications were set forth by Dubek for its actions. First, the joint distributorship operated under a conflict of interest, as the distributors enjoyed higher commissions on imported cigarettes. Second, a new distribution arrangement would enhance efficiency by realizing scope economies. These cost savings, it was argued, would more than offset the scale economies lost by serving a smaller portion of the market. The court emphasized that under the new arrangement, distribution costs for all the remaining firms would rise significantly. While Elishar would still be able to operate its own distribution network economically, the smaller importers would not be able to distribute their cigarettes economically and would be forced to exit the market. The public would be harmed both by the smaller range of products and by the higher distribution costs of all market participants. It then mandated Dubek, based on an essential facility doctrine, to grant access to its distribution facilities to the small importers.[78]

In fact, the Israeli court found that Dubek's distribution system constitutes an essential facility for only some competitors. Although the Israeli court did not recognize the implications of its ruling, its decision broadens considerably the scope of the essential facilities doctrine to situations that go far beyond those in which the doctrine is applied elsewhere. The EC *Oscar Bronner* case,[79] analyzed earlier, which is based on a very similar factual scenario, reached the opposite conclusion. There, the unique newspaper distribution system of one of Bronner's competitors was not found to be essential even though a small competitor could not, on its own, duplicate the facility, so long as a differently situated firm or a joint venture could create a competing distribution system. A similar principle was adopted in the U.S. case of *Paddock*.[80] There, Judge Easterbrook stated that when the plaintiff argued for compulsory supply of news services from one of three existing major competitors, the plaintiff's claim "was fundamentally an 'essential facilities' claim—but without any essential facility."[81] An essential facility claim must involve "a single monopoly that monopolizes one level of production and creates a potential to extend the monopoly to others."[82]

The *Dubek* outcome might nonetheless be justified, even if not under the essential facility doctrine, as the two remaining duopolists have a shared incentive to block their smaller rivals' access to their parallel distribution networks, as market conditions were such that the duopolists would have engaged in conscious parallelism at high price levels. This would not necessarily enable the most efficient competitors to operate in the downstream market. The test whether or not to grant access in such situations should focus on the welfare effects of the conduct. In markets with differentiated products, the fact that a monopolist has lower costs does not necessarily imply that it is more efficient than its higher-cost rivals. In such situations the nondiscrimination rule would not necessarily achieve welfare-increasing results.

A different rule should apply when the monopolist's product is essential for some customers but not for others and the two groups do not compete with each other. In such situations the essentiality requirement should focus on the conditions in each market separately. Otherwise a monopolist might refuse supply to eliminate its competitors from a most profitable vertically integrated market, in sharp contrast to the purpose of the refusal-to-supply prohibitions.

TEMPORARY ESSENTIALITY?

The EC *Aer Lingus* case[83] raises an interesting question: Can essentiality be temporary, or does the mere fact that it eventually ceases to exist negate the basic presumption of essentiality? The Irish airline Aer Lingus held a dominant position over the Dublin-London route. Once British Midland received a permit to fly this route, Aer Lingus terminated its interlining agreement with it. (Interlining enables a passenger to travel one leg of a trip with one airline and another leg with another airline.) The court recognized that interlining would not have a significant effect on Aer Lingus's costs, whereas a refusal to interline would impose a significant handicap on British Midland. It then mandated Aer Lingus to interline with British Midland, although it limited the time of the obligation to two years, until British Midland was established in the market.

In most cases the fact that time will reduce entry barriers for a new competitor should negate the essentiality requirement. Compulsory supply should not be based on the mere fact that a newcomer faces barriers to entry that result from the incumbent's first-mover advantage. A different rule would significantly reduce the long-term investment incentives of market participants.

Yet in some cases, recognition of temporary essentiality may be justified. This is the case when unique market conditions create insuperable entry barriers that are likely to be reduced over time. The clearest case is when the inability of competitors to duplicate a facility results from government-created barriers that will be reduced in the foreseeable future. The *Aer Lingus* case seems to fit this category. There, British Midland could not immediately provide a wide variety of flights owing to regulatory restraints imposed by airport facilities. Once its variety of flights was sufficient for an economical number of consumers to fly with it, compulsory interlining would no longer be required. The outcome should have been different if British Midland could have entered the market by providing a full line of flights but was not prepared to put in a comparable effort. Otherwise, compulsory dealing would amount to a form of artificial assistance to a new entrant.

EQUAL TREATMENT OF EXISTING AND POTENTIAL COMPETITORS
Although not specifically stated, all jurisdictions have been willing to take a more interventionist stance in complaints from existing trading partners than when asked to invoke refusal-to-deal principles to open up new market opportunities. Symmetric treatment of existing and potential trading parties is justified for the following reasons. One of the main potentials of the essential facility doctrine to affect market performance lies in its application as a tool to introduce new competition into the competitive market. There is no economic justification for granting competitors advantages that are based on their time of entry into a market alone, apart from the ones naturally resulting from first-mover advantages. The only apparent reason for such a distinction is some theory of vested rights: a firm that has committed capital to the production or distribution of a product utilizing a monopolized component is entitled to continue in business at least until

it has recovered its investment or received compensation. This theory is based on equity notions rather than competition arguments. The previous dealings of a monopolist have no bearing on competition policy, except when termination is part of a predatory strategy.

Similarly, there is no economic justification for asymmetric treatment of a situation in which the asset controller has not granted access to any of its competitors and one in which it has granted access to some. Adoption of such a rule might easily lead to decisions by an asset controller not to admit any rival to its facility for fear that this will open the door to a host of access demands from other potential competitors. Efficiency-enhancing trades may therefore be discouraged by fear of competition law intervention. Although devising a remedy is usually much easier in a case in which access is granted to at least one competitor, this does not justify such differentiation.

Alternative Remedies for Refusals to Supply

The desirability of applying competition laws to the regulation of trade terms of an essential facility is directly related to the adequacy of remedial tools at the competition court or the competition authority's disposal. This section provides a more detailed analysis of such legal remedies.

The difficulty in establishing an efficient remedy stems from two facts. One is that a facility, the use of which is essential for the economic viability of firms, cannot be duplicated. Accordingly, competition in the facility's market cannot be restored. Second, it is assumed, implicitly or explicitly, that the vertical integration of the monopolist is efficient, or that restructuring is not a viable solution. Accordingly, competition law cannot remedy the *core* of the problem but can only limit its negative effects. Endorsement of the essential facilities doctrine must therefore be based on acceptance, at the very least, of the need to regulate the terms and conditions of access to the facility. Some of the remedies explored here, such as joint ownership, can also solve other problems associated with natural monopolies.

SETTING EFFICIENT SUPPLY TERMS

When compulsory supply is mandated, the regulator should set trade terms and conditions. Such terms should not blockade efficient competitors from entering into the market, on the one hand, nor deprive the monopolist of its legal rights to enjoy profits obtained from its assets more than to the extent necessary, on the other.

The application of such remedies, however, raises great difficulties. Most important, courts are ill suited to perform regulatory functions, such as price setting, that require industry-specific expertise, exhibit a steep learning curve, and require ongoing supervision.[84] Also, the formula for calculating efficient access terms has proven to be one of the most controversial issues in regulatory economics. Should the trade terms compensate the monopolist for the net loss of revenue caused by third-party access so as to make the monopolist indifferent as to whether it shares its assets with competitors?[85] Or should the monopolist be allowed to charge its cost plus a specified profit that optimally provides a revenue stream that will remunerate the appropriate value of the asset? The first option may enshrine efficiency, while the second might reduce dynamic incentives. Because pricing is not the only factor that must be supervised, courts must also be prepared to arbitrate highly technical disputes. An analysis of case law reveals an attempt by courts to sidestep this thorny issue of access or supply terms.

A commonly favored solution is to require the facility to be made available to a third party and the monopolist's competitive arm on nondiscriminatory terms. The theory on which such a remedy rests is as follows: the monopolist may not take steps that merely make its competitors worse off in order to gain an advantage. Thus, discrimination in favor of its own competitive arm implies that its operations are less efficient than those of its competitors, and should be prohibited. The nondiscrimination principle may also reduce supracompetitive pricing by limiting the ability of the monopolist to extract the full monopoly price from each customer in accordance with his individual demand curve.

Determining what constitutes nondiscriminatory access terms is quite simple if the regulator can obtain accurate data on the real costs of providing supply or access to the vertically integrated arm or third parties, usually when there is genuine separation of decision making between the upstream and the downstream operations of the monopolist, or when standard terms apply in the specific industry (e.g., interlining). Trade terms are also easy to set when existing terms are altered so as to improve the monopolist's competing arm's arrangements, and such a change is not economically justified. In all other circumstances the nondiscrimination principle will not be easy to apply and will require an economic analysis of the monopolist's costs of "trading" with its competitive arm.

To combat leveraging, the nondiscrimination principle should not be applied literally. Rather, the regulator should ensure that the price set by the monopolist is not so high that the monopolist is cross-subsidizing its competitive arm. Otherwise the monopolist could abuse its market power by charging a price that, albeit on its face nondiscriminatory, would not enable a more efficient competitor to survive. Also, the nondiscrimination principle should be applied separately to different groups of customers competing among themselves. Otherwise the monopolist might prevent competition in the more lucrative market by setting the access or supply terms equal to those set in a market with less elastic demand.

When the regulatory task involves an in-depth economic inquiry into the costs of the monopolist, the task is best performed by the competition authorities. A court may suffer from several drawbacks.[86] Apart from those already noted, the newly established trade terms may necessitate careful ongoing scrutiny that it is ill equipped to perform. Litigation costs may make any relief inefficient when sought by large numbers of small competitors. Although in some jurisdictions class action suits can be initiated on behalf of all aggrieved parties, each party will still have to prove that it was afforded discriminatory terms. Moreover, since competition law litigation usually applies ex post, the monopolist's distortions might greatly affect the industry until the matter is finally resolved. Last, the benefits of case-by-case analysis might be overwhelmed by anti-competitive strategic behavior on the part of the monopolist. Delegation of the remedial power to the competition authorities to perform ex ante regulation, as was done in Australia and New Zealand, solves many of the problems inherent in regulation by the courts. An alternative solution is structural: to de-integrate industry segments to minimize incentives to discriminate. Although separation involves non-trivial transaction costs, it might sometimes provide for a more efficient overall outcome. Whatever the remedy, interim measures may often be suitable, because otherwise the new entrant might be excluded from the market as a result of strong first-mover advantages.[87]

SHARING PRINCIPLES: THE PROBLEM OF CAPACITY UTILIZATION
The principle governing the sharing of existing facilities to accommodate new entry also affects the efficiency of the access regime. If the facility controller is not required to share its facility in order to accom-

modate new entry, it may abuse its power to discriminate in favor of its competitive arm. But even if it is required to share its existing facilities, the sharing principle is important for achieving an efficient result.

Some facilities can support almost unlimited supply, such as access to information or patent licenses. If the capacity of the facility is not fully used, or if by its nature capacity is unlimited, compulsory supply poses no immediate dilemmas with regard to the asset sharing. Other assets have physical or other constraints that limit the number of their users. For example, narrow harbor docking slots and existing gas pipelines can support only a limited number of users. It may also be that some capacities are more valuable than others. For example, some landing and takeoff slots are more convenient to most airline passengers than others. Supply constraints may also result from the monopolist's decision to limit its production and supply to a given quantity or a given number of customers. When supply is limited, an important issue involves the sharing of the facility when access is essential for competing in the market.

One possible sharing principle, adopted by U.S. courts, is the first-come-first-served principle. Under this rule, the facility controller is not required to share its assets if such sharing would be impractical or would inhibit the controller's ability to serve its customers adequately, nor is it required to apportion the use of its facilities when operating at full capacity. Rather, courts have considered the non-feasibility of providing access to the competitor a sound business justification for the monopolist's refusal.[88] The asset controller is, however, required to share its facilities on a nondiscriminatory basis if no capacity constraints exist, so long as such sharing does not alter its ability to serve its customers adequately.

This sharing rule creates incentives and opportunities for its abuse by the monopolist. Assume, for example, a scenario in which the capacity constraints of an existing asset allow only the monopolist's competitive arm to operate in the market. A monopolist might use the power not to share and to prohibit entry of potential competitors. Also, if the monopolist can expand its assets at any time, it might avoid expanding its facilities at critical times when more efficient competitors seek to enter the market. The monopolist may also enter into long-term contracts that use the entire capacity of the asset. Thus, the first-come-first-served principle may prevent more efficient competitors from replacing existing ones if the monopolist has incentives to foreclose the market. Moreover, when some capacities are more valuable than others and the monopolist is prohibited from price-discriminating, it will have no incentive to share the most profitable slots with its more efficient competitors when the average price it sets is not high enough to capture all the monopoly profits to be had from utilizing these slots.

In jurisdictions in which the monopolist is prohibited from charging monopoly rates, the first-come-first-served principle may also impede the replacement of existing competitors with more efficient ones even if the monopolist has no incentives to do so. When the monopolist is not limited in its pricing decisions, it will set the price at such a level that only the most efficient competitors could pay it and still remain profitable. The market's natural selection mechanism will ensure productive efficiency. But when the price set by the monopolist does not reflect what the market can bear, incumbent competitors will have no reason to exit the market and free capacity on the essential asset, as they could still operate profitably. To be sure, if transaction costs are low, then more efficient operators will "buy their way" into the market, but their incentives to do so are reduced by the level of the transaction costs.

Richard Epstein has argued for the adoption of a proportioning rule that will distribute the monopolized asset between all potential users, much like the common law rule imposed on common carriers.[89] He argues that such a proportioning rule should work well from the point of view of overall consumer satisfaction, and he uses the common law *Consumers' Gas Trust* case[90] to exemplify his point. There, a natural gas company was placed under a strict obligation to supply service to a new customer along its route, notwithstanding unavoidable shortfalls in supply. The court's basic rationale was that there can be no such thing as priority or superiority of right among those who possess the right in common. Building on this case, Epstein argues that it is better to enable all residents to heat their houses to a low temperature than to enable only existing customers to heat their houses to the full extent and let all others freeze.

Some EC cases also adopt a proportionality sharing principle. In *Sealink*,[91] for example, the incumbent monopolist was required to change its ferry landing schedule to accommodate a new competitor. In another decision involving *Sealink*,[92] the natural monopolist port owner was not allowed to alter existing landing schedules if by so doing it harmed the consumers of a competing ferry service. Similarly, a European Community regulation controls the access of new airlines to congested airports by allocating some proportion of takeoff and landing slots at times of congestion to newly scheduled flights.[93] These sharing principles are much different from those adopted in the United States.

Although the proportionality rule has some appeal, the rule does not necessarily increase welfare and may even reduce it. If all the firms were required to reduce their operations sufficiently to let another competitor provide the same kind of product or service, then their total costs might increase if scale economies are present. In many situations it may well be that the monopoly's customers can operate economically only if some minimal capacity is granted to them, and thus if all customers were granted a lower capacity, all might be worse off. Take, for example, a situation in which the capacity is computer megabytes, and several users are hooked to the same computer. If all need a minimum number of bytes to operate a certain program, then all will be worse off if, to meet its proportionality obligation, the monopoly grants each customer a number of bytes that is below that minimum. This example can be easily carried over into other fields. A ferry operator needs a minimum number of landing slots to operate its business profitably. Incumbents should not be required to scale down or reorganize their existing activities unless an identifiable increase in welfare can be expected as a result.

This problem is partly solved when the monopolist is allowed to charge customers a supracompetitive price for utilizing its assets, as the price of supply set by the monopolist enables natural selection of the most efficient competitors. If the monopolist is price regulated, however, the proportionality test may reduce efficiency by enabling inefficient entrants to enter the market and increase total costs for all users. But even if the monopolist is not price regulated, the proportionality principle will create inefficiency when the monopolist is not allowed to price-discriminate among customers and some capacities are more valuable than others. The proportionality rule would enable inefficient competitors to share the most valuable capacity if the price set by the monopolist did not capture all of the monopoly rents from high valued capacity and transaction costs were high.

A proportionality rule would also not ensure existing customers of the constancy of their supply, because as more firms enter the market, each firm will be granted a smaller portion of overall output. This fact might have negative domino implications for industries and customers that rely on the continuing and constant flow of gadgets supplied by firms utilizing the monopolist's widgets. This in turn could lead to costly investments in the duplication of an essential facility or to costly use of alternative widgets. Furthermore, the monopolist's competitive arm will have a comparative advantage over its rivals based on its access to information regarding the possibility and probability of reduction in supply. Finally, the proportionality rule does not always allow a monopolist to enlarge the scale of its activities, even if so doing would reduce its own costs. Accordingly, a strict proportionality rule should be rejected.

A more efficient sharing principle, when a monopolist has incentives to foreclose a vertically related market, would focus on the welfare effects of altering an existing sharing pattern. The monopolist would be required to accommodate a new entrant or to share its most profitable slots only if this would increase welfare, either by reducing prices or by introducing better-quality products. Similarly, a monopolist should be entitled to expand its own operations at the expense of existing competitors if welfare would be increased. No sharing should be required if its only effect were distributive or if it reduced welfare.

MANDATORY EXPANSION OF EXISTING FACILITIES

A related issue involves the expansion of existing facilities to accommodate new entry. If the monopolist is not required to take positive steps to accommodate new entry, it might use this power as a strategic device to discriminate in favor of its competitive arm. It may also undersize the facility to reduce output and increase price. The monopolist's incentives to expand its asset's capacity parallel its incentives to foreclose a competitive market.

In the United States, for example, a legitimate business justification is recognized when existing capacity is incapable of serving all the existing and potential customers, and serving them would require the monopolist to incur additional costs in expanding its facilities. A monopolist is not required to expand its facilities even if such expansion is needed to allow its rivals to enter, survive, or expand in the market.[94] Once such justification is proven, there is no balancing of the social gains from refusing to deal with competitors against the losses resulting from the refusal. The effect of such a rule on potential competition may be compounded by some of the sharing principles I have surveyed. A similar approach has been adopted in many other jurisdictions.[95]

The reluctance of courts to require mandatory expansion might enable a monopolist to manipulate its capacity strategically to create an anti-competitive advantage for its competitive affiliate. Take, for example, a scenario in which the capacity constraints of an existing facility allow it to serve only the monopolist's arm. A monopolist might use the right not to expand its facilities to drive out efficient competitors. Alternatively, the monopolist might expand its capacity only after its more efficient competitors have exited the market.

One method of solving this problem is to mandate that the monopolist expand its assets to accommodate its competitors. A legitimate precondition for such expansion is that the competitors requiring expansion provide sufficient guarantees that they will cover the costs of the expansion minus any benefits it might confer on the monopolist by way of lowering average total costs. To be sure, the situation is still open to manipulation by the monopolist by way of charging its competitors a prohibitively high cost for the expansion, unless the costs of the monopolist are monitored.

Another problem associated with mandatory expansion involves its effects on the long-term dynamic incentives of firms to invest in or to create natural monopolies. If we recognize the natural monopolist's right to charge supracompetitive prices, this necessarily implies restricted output. If the monopolist is legally required to increase its output to accommodate its competitors, this might imply that the overall price the monopolist may charge for its product or service will decline. This is especially true if the monopolist can expand its capacity only by adding large increments of output. One solution to this problem is to require the new customers to compensate the monopolist for the difference in its revenues before and after the expansion, not taking into account revenues from anti-competitive foreclosure.

To reduce strategic manipulation by a monopolist, the monopolist should also be required to share the information regarding the addition of new capacity and any change in technology that might affect the business decisions of its competitors.

STRUCTURAL SOLUTIONS: BREAKUP OF OWNERSHIP

Structural solutions can often be most effective in increasing the incentives of market players to operate efficiently. Vertically de-integrating the natural monopoly from competitive segments or prohibiting the monopolist from integrating into downstream or upstream vertically related markets reduces the incentives or opportunities of the monopolist to leverage its monopoly power.[96] Nonetheless, separation is efficient only if the loss of scale economies resulting from de-integration of industry activities is lower than the costs imposed by vertical integration by impeding efficient competition. It also alters, to a large degree, the property rights of the natural monopolist and thus should be carefully applied.

JOINT OWNERSHIP

A relatively unexplored venue for regulating natural monopolies involves the joint ownership of their facilities by all competing downstream or upstream firms and the sharing of dividends in accordance with use.[97] Under this structural solution, production or service is unified and centralized to achieve scale economies, but ownership is decentralized among multiple owners who compete with one another in marketing the products or services produced from the common facilities or in producing products or services that utilize the service or the product of the common facilities. Joint ownership, if properly structured, solves the problem of foreclosure by granting all competitors jointly the power to determine the terms of supply. It also solves the resource misallocation problem, since the owners of the facility are also its users. Research and development to break the natural monopoly can be induced if common ownership rules require a share of the profits to be invested in such activity and if competing firms have a chance of making higher profits once new technologies are introduced. It can also be induced by granting the original facility owner a larger share in the profits.[98]

As Frederick Warren-Boulton and John Woodburt have argued, for joint ownership to be effective, certain requirements have to be met. First, ownership should be open to all the customers of the facility. Open membership ensures that the natural monopoly would be available to all actual or potential users. Second, each owner must independently market the products or services provided from its share of the joint venture. This may require specific constraints on certain kinds of information transfers between the owners. To reduce the risk of collusion, the facility should be managed by a separate operating company. Third, the operation of the joint facility should be subject to rules that are aimed at inducing competition among the owner-users in a manner that reduces the natural monopolist's exercise of market power by charging supracompetitive prices or by discriminating among competitors. Most important, each firm's ownership share should reflect its share in the output of the joint venture. This rule is necessary to minimize the strategic exercise of control by the owners. The higher the ownership share, the lower the private cost of using the facility. Yet the higher the share, the greater the incentive to maintain a resale price above the private marginal cost. If all owners engage in oligopolistic coordination, these two forces cancel each other out, so that all owners, regardless of their share, will set the joint-profit-maximizing price for their share of the joint venture's output.[99]

The joint venture proposal solves the dilemma between market power and efficiency issues. While leaving the number of independent competitors unchanged, it still retains the productive efficiencies of large scale. By so doing it offers competition authorities a new and innovative tool to bridge the horns of the market-power-efficiency dilemma. Yet joint ownership is a limited remedy. It can be applied only if the number of existing and potential owners is sufficiently low as to enable them to affect the supply policy of the natural monopoly. In addition, it may be difficult to detect and deal with coordination between competitors that extends beyond the specific venture. It is also an extreme remedy given that it interferes with the property right of the monopolist. Thus, it should be used only in appropriate cases.[100]

Conclusion

Natural monopolies pose major dilemmas for competition policy. Their special characteristics necessitate the adoption of distinctive rules framed especially to deal with these characteristics. The fact that a monopoly is the most efficient market structure and that market forces have restricted ability to regulate its conduct implies that outside control may be justified. In this chapter I have analyzed the tools available to competition authorities for regulating natural monopolies, in addition to the rules that regulate the activities of all monopolies alike. In fact, the essential facilities doctrine, adopted in many jurisdictions, applies stricter conduct rules to natural monopolies than to other monopolies. As the foregoing discussion demonstrates, however, the doctrine in its current form does not necessarily achieve efficiency. Several methods for increasing the doctrine's efficiency were suggested. The main policy suggestions put forward in this chapter can be summarized as follows:

1. Regulation of natural monopolies is much more significant in small economies than in large ones, given their prevalence in a large percentage of the markets and the higher barriers to their natural erosion.

2. Natural monopolies should not be condemned per se. Similarly, the specific intent to become a natural monopolist, when not accompanied by exclusionary practices, should also not be deemed anti-competitive.

3. Competition for the natural monopoly market should not be immune from monopolization allegations based on alleged anti-competitive conduct that served to achieve the monopoly position in the natural monopoly market.

4. The essential facilities doctrine is a major tool for regulating natural monopolies by competition law, especially when price discrimination by a monopolist is prohibited. The doctrine should be based on welfare considerations rather than the protection of competition or specific competitors.

5. For the essential facilities doctrine to be efficiently applied, the relevant market should be defined correctly, and the test should be based on the essentiality of the facility for the economic viability of a competitor who is inclined to put in a comparable effort.

6. Remedies for abuse of power should be crafted and applied to maximize welfare. Sharing principles should be based on welfare effects rather than on a technical proportionality rule. When appropriate, the natural monopolist may be mandated to expand its facilities to enable the expansion or the new entry of its rivals.

CHAPTER FIVE

The Regulation of Oligopoly Markets

Oligopoly markets create some of the principal competition policy dilemmas for small economies. Owing to limited market demand and high entry barriers, many markets in small economies are oligopolistic. Oligopoly market structures are characterized by rivalry among a small number of competitors in which no firm holds a dominant position. Rational behavior in such markets requires that each oligopolist take into account the effects of its actions on its rivals in its decision-making process. Interdependence among rival firms is thus inevitable. This inherent characteristic of oligopolies may reduce or eliminate competitive pressures by creating incentives for firms to coordinate their conduct. By avoiding competition among themselves, oligopolists can attain shared market power that may allow them to maintain prices above the competitive level. Depending on the existing market conditions, the level of interaction among oligopolists may vary from fierce rivalry through conscious parallelism (i.e., the unilateral decisions of oligopolists that simply take into account their mutual interdependence) to cooperative agreements, including cartels or joint ventures.

Market forces have limited ability to regulate many oligopolistic markets in small economies. Not only are concentrated market structures commonly justified by production efficiency considerations, but also the small size of the market may create additional high entry barriers that secure oligopolistic market positions even further. Entry of foreign firms may have only limited welfare effects unless the firms are willing to enter at a level that will change significantly the existing market equilibrium or they enjoy significant cost advantages. Regulation thus plays an influential role in bringing about more competitive outcomes in oligopolistic markets. Oligopolistic coordination in small economies may also be aided by their often close-knit business elite. Personal and business interactions on an ongoing basis between a small group of top managers and investors might create incentives for the preservation of traditional business spheres. (Of course, this is a matter not just of size but of the degree of centralism.)

Regulation of oligopoly markets raises difficult dilemmas for competition policy. Both equitable and practical obstacles limit the ability of competition authorities and courts to regulate conscious parallelism by traditional methods: prohibiting the parallel conduct or structural reorganization of the market. Most jurisdictions, therefore, do not regulate mere parallel conduct but require an agreement among firms to collude on which to base a prohibition. As it is extremely difficult, however, to distinguish between conscious parallelism and collusion, traditional competition law prohibitions may be difficult to rely on to regulate tacit agreements among oligopolists. Small economies should thus seek alternative ways to overcome these regulatory hurdles.

Coordination and cooperation among oligopolists is not, however, always welfare-reducing. Some forms of cooperation, such as specialization agreements or joint ventures for cooperative production, distribution, or research and development may have pro-competitive benefits that offset the potential anti-competitive effects resulting from cooperation. Allowing firms to participate in such arrangements is important for small economies, as they may be the most efficient or the only method for domestic firms to lower costs or to increase dynamic efficiency. Such agreements may also allow firms to achieve international competitiveness. Small economies should thus regulate these arrangements efficiently by allowing those that may enhance welfare.

This chapter is organized in two main parts. In the first I lay the foundation for the legal discussion by surveying the special economic characteristics of oligopolistic markets, focusing especially on the conditions that exist widely in small economies which enable firms to coordinate their conduct. In the second part I analyze the policy tools that are available to combat such conduct. Traditional approaches for regulating oligopolistic industries are analyzed as well as novel methods. In particular, I focus on two main remedies: the regulation of practices that facilitate coordination among oligopolists and do not have offsetting social virtues, and government support of a maverick firm to induce other firms to reduce allocative as well as productive inefficiency.

Special Economic Characteristics of Oligopoly Industries

Oligopoly means "few sellers." The main economic characteristic of oligopolistic markets is that each firm's decisions have a noticeable impact on the market and on its rivals. Although each firm may independently decide its strategic moves, any rational decision must take into account the anticipated reaction of its rival firms to its decisions. As Carl Shapiro states, "The hallmark of oligopoly is the presence of strategic interactions among rival firms."[1] An oligopolist's decisions may thus be interdependent though arrived at independently. Such mutual interdependence may forestall rivalrous conduct.

Economic theory on the relationship between oligopolistic market structure and economic performance is dominated by complex models that rely heavily on sensitive assumptions focusing on the conditions that are conducive to collusive or parallel conduct. These models do not yield a single economic theory of oligopoly but are highly context-specific and create a wide range of equilibria ranging from those that approximate competitive conditions to those that approximate monopolistic conditions, depending on the oligopolists' ability to coordinate their conduct.[2]

Oligopolists can coordinate their conduct in three major ways. First, they can form an agreement. The agreement can be overt or covert, verbal or tacit. We may further differentiate between collusive agreements with only anti-competitive effects (cartels) and collusive agreements with neutral or pro-competitive benefits. Second, conduct can be coordinated through recognition of oligopolistic interdependence by means of pure conscious parallelism. The third method consists of conscious parallelism aided by some facilitating practices. Such practices make it possible for oligopolists to coordinate their conduct sufficiently well to achieve noncompetitive outcomes.

Express or Tacit Collusive Agreements

Collusion is the joint determination of output, prices, or other terms of trade by ostensibly independent firms to elevate their profits. The colluding firms agree on trade terms in light of the costs and returns from tailoring such terms to the diversity of transactions, the elasticity of demand, and the conditions of entry.[3] Collusion may take numerous forms, including price fixing, bid rigging, geographic or product market allocation, and customer allocation.

Collusion can be express or tacit. Tacit collusion is collusion that is communicated by informal or nonverbal means, without any direct, explicit communication between the parties. "Tacit" therefore describes the process by which the agreement was achieved. Tacit agreements are less likely to produce detailed arrangements covering many variables and are thus less effectual than express collusion. Nonetheless, in highly concentrated markets with relatively homogeneous products, firms may not need more that a tacit agreement to achieve collusive outcomes.

Collusion is driven by the opportunity for firms in oligopolistic markets to elevate profits above the competitive level. The vitamin cartel of the 1990s serves as an example of a successful international cartel. The largest worldwide vitamin producers colluded to rig bids and divide up worldwide markets for vitamins. Overall, it is believed that the cartel boosted the price of products sold worldwide by more than $20 billion. Several jurisdictions, including the United States, Canada, Australia, and the EC, have successfully brought charges against the cartel members.[4]

Restrictive agreements might also result from the incentives of firms in vertical or adjacent markets to increase their profits. For example, assume that one bank finances all the oligopolists by giving them loans at fixed rates. To reduce its risks, the bank might impose conditions on the potentially competing firms which will reduce its risk if one of them should fail. For example, it might include in the loan contract a requirement that the price for their product will not fall below a certain amount, which would ensure that they can all cover their costs.

The colluding scheme is not a stable one. Rather, it creates a basic tension between competition and cooperation. Although the oligopolists' fates are interdependent, their individual self-interests are not perfectly consonant. Any collusive agreement that is based on a joint profit-maximizing scheme is thus inherently plagued by the natural temptation of each cartel member to "cheat" by deviating from the joint scheme. Cheating can take many forms including lowering price below the fixed one, granting secret rebates, entering into reciprocity agreements in which the cartel member buys something back from the customer at a supracompetitive price, or providing increased services. Such conduct by numerous cartel members would erode the joint profits and eventually undermine the agreement. The joint-profit-maximizing point is thus not an equilibrium but rather a modus vivendi.[5]

A successful collusive scheme must therefore overcome three main hurdles: reaching a joint-profit-maximizing agreement, detecting deviations from the agreed-upon trade terms, and enforcing the agreement by way of punishing such deviations.[6] Reaching an agreement requires the establishment of a mutual understanding or consensus regarding the controlled trade terms. This involves resolution of any disagreement between firms as to the "correct" trade terms and communication of the ultimate decision to all concerned parties.

The second task faced by colluding firms is to detect significant deviations from the agreed-upon terms. The more slowly and less completely deviations are detected, the weaker the collusion, as firms would have stronger incentives to cheat. Also, if market conditions are not conducive to exposing cheaters, colluders will have to incur substantial costs to detect cheating, which may reduce the overall attractiveness of the agreement in the first place. The ease of cheating varies considerably with the type of market. Cheating is most difficult in markets in which sales are large and results are publicly announced.

Punishment of deviations must simultaneously make cheating unprofitable without causing public discovery of the cartel. One interesting insight is that anything that makes more competitive conduct more feasible or credible actually promotes collusion, as the very competitive conduct is reserved as a threat to punish those who undermine the collusive scheme.[7] For example, when the colluding firms have excess capacity, it is more credible to threaten an overall increase in output that will significantly reduce prices for all colluders, including the defector.

The last two tasks promote mutual confidence that there will be adherence to the agreement reached. Detection and enforcement ensure a chain of events that the would-be price cutter anticipates and therefore resists the temptation to undercut prices. Once this is achieved, each firm has confidence that its adherence to the consensus price will not create strong incentives for its rivals to deviate from it.

Certain factors increase or decrease the likelihood of collusion and other types of coordinated conduct. These influence the initial formation of an agreement and its ability to survive temptations for chiseling. The relevant factors may vary within a market over time, and some of them, such as entrepreneurial attitudes toward the engagement in illegal activity, are intrinsically variable. None of the factors are deterministic in their ability to facilitate coordination. Rather, they all reflect general tendencies subject to random deviations. In reality, a combination of market conditions will determine the likelihood of collusion.

The importance of these factors from a legal perspective lies in their use as predictors of the conduct and performance of firms. Analysis of existing market conditions may, for example, serve to indicate situations that, absent a conspiratorial agreement, will most likely impede firms from attaining monopoly-like results through mere interdependence. In such cases, the presence of substantial noncompetitive trade conditions would be evidence of traditional conspiracy.[8]

Facilitating factors can be grouped into four broad categories: market structure variables (market concentration, entry barriers); the nature of the product (product and cost homogeneity, multiplicity of product variables); the nature of sales (lumpiness and secrecy); and the "personality" of the firms operating in the market. Although most of these factors are industry- or context-specific, two structural elements are more commonplace in small economies: a small number of competitors and high entry barriers.

The number of firms operating in the relevant market is one of the most important factors influencing the ability and incentives of firms to collude.[9] The reason is threefold. First, reaching an understanding to limit competition is easier and less costly if the number of firms accounting for a large proportion of total market output is small. Second, the incentives to cheat increase as the number of firms increases. In general, the smaller any firm's market share, the greater its incentive to deviate from the consensus price, as the profits from additional volume may dwarf any profits forgone on sales at the original price.[10]

Third, a small number of sellers makes the detection of chiseling easier. Enforcement of the agreement requires knowledge of transactions and of changes in market shares. Such knowledge is easier to come by the smaller the number of firms. Moreover, in highly concentrated markets, colluders are less likely to accept as a random demand fluctuation a loss in market share that occurs from a cheater's increased sales.[11] As a result, firms will have lower incentives to cheat in a concentrated market.

A small number of firms is conducive to collusive conduct only if there exist high entry barriers into the relevant market, as is often the case in a small economy. Without entry barriers, no reduction in competition among incumbents can successfully maintain supracompetitive prices in the long run. If entry barriers are low and potential rivals can easily enter or expand, they may increase output so long as the market price exceeds their costs and reasonable profits. Barriers to entry thus protect the monopoly profits of the cartel from external competition and subsequent erosion.

The Israeli gasoline market illustrates the importance of entry barriers for protecting an oligopolistic market. For several decades regulatory constraints limited the number of firms that were allowed to operate in the gasoline market. Then the market was opened to competition. Yet instantaneous new entry was blockaded owing to high entry barriers. Most of the existing gas stations were bound by long-term contracts to the three incumbent gasoline companies. Investment in new gas stations was also limited because of high costs and regulatory obstacles. New entrants were able to enter the market on a non-negligible scale only after the government relaxed some of the regulatory obstacles to building new gas stations and challenged the legality of the long-term contracts between station owners and the incumbent gasoline companies.[12]

By elevating prices above competitive levels, collusive agreements create the host of social costs associated with monopoly pricing. The principal evil created by a collusive strategy is persistent supracompetitive prices that are indicative of allocative inefficiency. At the extreme, the deadweight loss of horizontal price fixing may equal that of a single monopoly. Significantly for small economies, allocative inefficiency is increased when minimum efficient scales are high. Consider a situation in which there are three firms in a market and minimum efficient scale exceeds 30 percent of market share, scale advantages are significant, and sunk costs are high. The incumbents have less reason to fear new entry than firms in markets with lower minimum efficient scales. Any new entrant whose market share is less than 30 percent will have a cost disadvantage. The greater that disadvantage, the more room there will be for supracompetitive pricing by the firms already in the market.

Although both cartels and monopolies create allocative inefficiency, they differ in one important respect. Monopolies can realize internal economies of scale and scope that reduce productive inefficiency. In the case of a cartel there are no offsetting productive inefficiency gains, because the scale of the participating firms has not changed. Rather, the cartel might permit the perpetuation of high-cost inefficient producers. Consider a situation in which production on an efficient scale requires four production plants, each catering to 25 percent of the market, and the market currently consists of five equal-sized production plants. If the five plants are controlled by a single monopolist, it will have strong incentives to minimize its costs by closing down one of the plants. By contrast, if the five plants are controlled by five oligopolists, they may not be able to reach an agreement whereby only four plants will stay operational. No oligopolist would agree to close down its plant unless it can be satisfied that it will share the profits of the operational plants. Such an agreement would generally be illegal. Accordingly, bare cartels are unambiguously inefficient.[13]

Collusion may also reduce dynamic efficiency by reducing the incentives of firms to engage in research and development or to adopt new technologies that may change their cost structures and thus upset the market equilibrium. Two conditions must exist for dynamic incentives to be suppressed. Firms must have faith in the stability of the cartel; otherwise, the fact that potential rivalry may erupt creates strong incentives for firms to gain a comparative advantage. Also, the profits that firms seek to gain from adopting or developing new technologies must be lower than the profits gained through the collusive arrangement.

Collusive agreements may also distort incentive mechanisms in related markets by destroying or distorting the natural advantages of firms supplied by oligopolists. To illustrate, if oligopolistic firms collude to fix transportation costs, their customers lose the locational advantage they might have obtained otherwise.

The fact that collusive prices are set at a supracompetitive level does not necessarily imply, however, that oligopolists enjoy high profits.[14] Cartels often spend much of their anticipated profits on efforts to reach an agreement, to detect cheating, and to punish it. Such costs are wasteful as they do not enhance social welfare. Alternatively, oligopolists often spend much of their anticipated profits on non-price competition (e.g., packaging, advertising, and service). Aggressive non-price competition by colluding oligopolists produces an ambiguous effect on social welfare. To the extent that non-price enhancements increase the real or perceived value to consumers, they increase welfare. They may drive costs up, however, thereby reducing productive efficiency. In addition, such competition might create high barriers to entry by necessitating heavy promotional expenditures by an entrant wishing to differentiate its own brands from those of its competitors.

Agreements with Pro-competitive Effects

Agreements among competitors may achieve both private and socially valuable purposes. The welfare effects of strategic alliances to share certain facilities, joint ventures, and specialization agreements are ambiguous and pose more subtle and contentious analytical problems than bare cartels. Such agreements may enhance productive, dynamic, and even allocative efficiency. At the same time, they have the potential to restrict competition in the markets in which the cooperating firms actually or potentially compete.

Significantly for small economies, a cooperative agreement may enable its parties to achieve minimum efficient scales and to lower costs to levels that any single firm acting alone could not achieve under the existing market structure. Suppose, for example, that a certain widget can be produced at minimum efficient scale of 10,000 units. Further suppose that four firms each require 2,500 widgets in their production processes. If all four firms pool their resources to build a joint plant for producing the widgets, costs will be minimized. An example of a joint venture that allowed firms located in a small market to realize scale economies can be found in the Israeli case of *Poligar*.[15] There, two leading Israeli manufacturers of polyethylene covers for agriculture formed a joint sales venture for the distribution and marketing of their products. The venture allowed the two firms to achieve substantial cost savings through the realization of economies of scale in distribution that were necessary for them to compete effectively with imported products.

Cooperation may also allow firms to introduce new and superior products or services that would otherwise not be available or allow such products to be brought to market faster than would be possible absent the collaboration, thereby increasing dynamic efficiency. Such dynamic efficiency might be vital for competing in world markets.

Specialization agreements—under which each party agrees to discontinue producing an article or providing a service to allocate its scope of production or provision to another party—may also solve the production inefficiency problems that often characterize small economies. Markets in small economies frequently suffer from too fragmented a market structure, in which firms specialize in highly differentiated products that do not allow them to attain scale or scope economies. The result is inadequately short production runs, especially in industries in which the distribution system offers marketing advantages to firms producing full lines of products. In such cases maximum efficiency is unlikely to be achieved because each firm is producing a full line instead of specializing in a few items only, absent specialization agreements. Specialization agreements limit competition in the name of efficiency.

Cooperative agreements might also enable small firms to compete more effectively and therefore discipline their larger rivals. To give but one example, an agreement among several small producers to run a joint ad quoting similar retail prices would reduce advertising costs for each and allow them to compete more effectively with their large competitors. This can be illustrated by the Australian case of *Eastern Express*,[16] in which a group of suburban Sydney real estate agents had formed a firm to publish a newspaper to compete with an established real estate paper that had substantial market power. The court recognized the importance of creating such a firm for enabling small agents to compete effectively in a highly concentrated market. It nonetheless struck down the articles of association requiring the members to place a minimum amount of advertising in the new paper as it was unnecessary to achieve the pro-competitive benefits of the arrangement.

In oligopolistic markets, cooperative arrangements among existing or potential competitors may raise legitimate concerns regarding the restriction of competition. Agreements might limit the ability of the participants to compete effectively when key assets are engaged in joint collaboration. They might also limit the incentives of participants to compete, as the establishing parties are unlikely to compete aggressively, if at all, with a cooperative venture in which they have a substantial equity interest.[17] Competitor collaboration might also elevate prices, restrict output, or create market divisions. A major concern is that the parties to the cooperative agreement would have the power and the incentives to foreclose access to their competitors, thereby placing the latter at a significant disadvantage.[18]

Cooperative agreements among competitors might also have spillover effects into other competing or potentially competing activities in which the parties engage. The cooperative relationship creates, by its very nature, close relations between the parties. It puts the parent firms in dangerous proximity to discuss and act jointly on aspects of their business apart from the cooperative arrangement and creates an aura of team spirit. This concern is greater the stronger the market position the relevant parties enjoy and the more elaborate their ties with other firms or joint ventures.[19]

A situation of particular concern arises when a series of interlocking parallel joint ventures is established in which every two joint ventures have at least one common parent. Such a network could contribute to collective dominance and provide the opportunity for collusive exchanges of information, especially if all the members of an oligopoly were involved. This concern is especially critical to small economies in which a small number of large conglomerates account for very large proportions of industrial output. Conglomerates are often the main challengers of incumbent monopolies, given their substantial resources and varied experience, and this enables them to enter new lines of activity more readily than could a newly established or a highly specialized firm. Hence, cooperative agreements among conglomerates should be looked on with considerable skepticism. Joint ventures that may reduce future competition between these large players, even if they increase efficiency in a specific transaction, should be analyzed according to a broader perspective which takes into account the long-term dampening of competition.[20]

Conscious Parallelism

Conscious parallelism can best be described as actions of rivals that are based on the tendency, inherent in oligopolistic markets, to coordinate policies spontaneously and not as part of an agreement, and without the need for facilitating practices. Parallelism is reached when each oligopolist only assesses its rivals' behavior and reacts with a recognition of interdependence. Communication is merely aided through the actions and reactions of oligopolists toward one another and toward exogenous events. Conscious parallelism may manifest itself in many non-collusive ways, including an unwillingness to engage in aggressive price competition for fear of triggering a damaging price war or a willingness to tolerate a rival's price cutting that represents an attempt to restore lost market share. Of course, a market equilibrium might not ensue immediately, but might result from a trial-and-error period in which oligopolists test different strategies or determine the basic conditions of the equilibrium.

The Australian case of *Mobil Oil*[21] provides a useful example of conscious parallelism. There, several oil companies were charged with fixing gasoline prices. The allegations were based primarily on evidence of parallel pricing. The Australian court rejected the allegations, as gasoline retailing involves posting prices outside service stations, where they are as readily visible to competitors as they are to customers. Parallel conduct in such markets is thus as likely to follow from observation and independent action as from collusive agreement.

In small economies conscious parallelism is widespread. The number of firms in many industries is so small that even in the absence of formal agreements there is little room for effective domestic competition. Each firm makes its own independent decision based on the realization that if all oligopolists do not act competitively, they will all have some market power. Another Australian case can be used to illustrate this point. In *Email*,[22] two manufacturers of electricity meters potentially competed in the market. Both issued identical price lists and tendered accordingly. The explanations of the identical conduct by the two defendants that were accepted by the court involved the fact that Email had been a price leader since it was more efficient and better established. In addition, the largest customer had a policy of supporting two competitors in the market, irrespective of price. Under such market conditions, the less efficient market competitor can either try to undercut its more efficient rival's prices, which would lead to a price war in which the competitor has a comparative advantage, or follow its rival's pricing strategy. Both firms had a clear preference for the second type of conduct. As to several facilitating practices (the parties immediately sent each other their respective price lists whenever they changed prices or introduced any new meter or components), the court found that such actions simply helped facilitate a smoother non-collusive barometric price leadership by ensuring that the competitor had timely price information.

The social costs of conscious parallelism depend on the level of coordination reached by market participants. The price level yielded by oligopolistic interdependence may vary from a competitive price level to a monopoly-like outcome, depending on all the factors that make collusive or parallel conduct easy.

Under the Cournot model, which is the benchmark static model of conscious parallelism in output, each firm chooses its own output while taking into account the effect of its choice on the output decisions of its rivals.[23] An equilibrium is reached in which each firm equalizes its own marginal costs and marginal revenue. An important aspect of the theory is that each firm's markup is directly proportional to its market share, and market shares of firms are directly related to their efficiencies. Cournot equilibrium entails a higher aggregate output and lower price than does the collusive outcome. Yet Cournot equilibrium can be more stable than a cartel and thus create, in the long run, significant deviations from competitive price levels. Cournot stability is ensured, however, only if price cuts are visible. If firms are able to make secret price cuts, it becomes very difficult to predict what the resulting equilibrium will be, and prices may even be driven to competitive levels.[24] Cournot equilibrium can also lead to productive and dynamic inefficiency and wasteful non-price competition.

Cooperative Strategies with Facilitating Practices

Owing to the natural obstacles of reaching a profit-maximizing scheme and the illegal nature of collusion, firms seek strategies that reduce competitive friction and increase the likelihood of coordinated conduct. Such practices, often termed "facilitating practices," involve firms in specific, arguably avoidable acts rather than mere oligopolistic interdependence.

There are many types of facilitating practices, with varying degrees of success in promoting coordinated conduct. Steven Salop identifies two distinct effects of facilitating practices: information exchange and incentive management.[25]

Information exchange devices facilitate coordination by reducing the uncertainty about a rival's actions and intentions. They include inter-seller verification of price quotations and advance notice of price changes whereby detection lags are shortened or eliminated. When the market is oligopolistic, such exchanges may impair rather than invigorate rivalry, as they are necessary for reaching a profit-maximizing price or for increasing prices owing to changes in market conditions. At the same time, such information exchanges may have offsetting pro-competitive effects. They may provide firms with a more complete understanding of market conditions and may also improve market performance in more competitive settings. A complete prohibition of such information exchanges may thus not be warranted.[26]

Incentive management practices alter the structure of a firm's payoff matrix. In restructuring payoffs, the incentives of a firm to offer price discounts may be directly affected. Incentive management devices may take numerous forms. To illustrate, colluders may use contracts with customers or suppliers to make a binding commitment to their rivals to transform their incentives by formalizing a particular set of supply functions or reactions that yield collusive outcomes. Meeting competition clauses, for example, under which a firm announces that its price is the minimum of some stated price and the lowest price posted by another firm, may be used as facilitating devices. Such clauses automatically incorporate the aggressive responses to price cutting—the immediate matching of prices—which are needed to support collusion. Buyers police the arrangement, because the chance to receive price discounts creates incentives for them to ensure performance and bear the costs of monitoring the other oligopolists' conduct. These clauses may not be in the buyers' interest if their collective acceptance stabilizes the sellers' joint profit outcome and makes discounting less desirable or price increases less risky. Nonetheless, such clauses may be valued by each buyer individually, as they ensure that the buyer will enjoy the lowest price demanded by any firm operating in the market.[27]

Some facilitating practices may involve exclusionary acts that impede entry or expansion of rival firms. One interesting example of such practices is found in the U.S. *American Tobacco* case.[28] There, the major cigarette manufacturers purchased inexpensive tobacco that could not be used to produce their own cigarettes in order to drive up its price to their smaller competitors selling inexpensive brands. Other exclusionary conducts may include parallel vertical integration, exclusive dealings, or tying that may foreclose marketing opportunities for potential competitors. Some of these practices can be justifiable for their pro-competitive effects. The social costs of facilitating practices thus depend on the level of coordination they create among potential competitors and their offsetting pro-competitive effects.

Under market conditions that are omnipresent in small economies, market forces often have limited ability to regulate oligopolies. Accordingly, regulation plays a critical role in reducing their social costs. In the following sections I analyze the competition law tools available to regulate oligopolistic behavior. The sections are organized around the four main types of oligopolistic coordination, suggested earlier.

Regulation of Collusive Agreements

Despite the inherent instability of collusive agreements, many have proven to be reasonably durable and have imposed substantial costs on consumers. Since the natural conditions in small economies may facilitate collusion among oligopolists, prohibiting collusion is a central regulatory task for small economies. Prohibitions are generally based on two common elements: some form of meeting of minds among rival market participants, and a restraint of trade.

Most jurisdictions require some kind of meeting of minds to establish collusion, such as an agreement or arrangement among market participants.[29] The collusive agreement requirement shifts the focus from the outcome or effect of the collusive conduct to the method of achieving it in order to create a distinction (though sometimes vague) between collusion and mere conscious parallelism.

This distinction may result in the inability to prove a cartel, especially in small economies, for in highly concentrated markets both offer and acceptance can be crystallized by action alone. Mere parallel conduct is not conclusive evidence of a collusive agreement because firms will also be acting in parallel fashion when they are acting rationally in light of the conditions of the industry that make them interdependent. Alternatively, firms may have a common reason to act similarly, such as a rise in input prices.

Economic theory has a major role to play in such inferences by providing some insights into the market conditions that must exist for firms to coordinate their conduct by way of mere conscious parallelism. If these conditions are absent, it may be inferred that parallel conduct was facilitated by measures adopted by the parties to overcome natural obstacles.[30] One such example involves simultaneous identical bids to supply a made-to-order product not readily assembled from standard and conventionally priced items which are too close for coincidence and beyond explanation by mere recognized interdependence.[31] Similarly, a finding of collusive agreement may be supported by acts against self-interest, as when a firm declines an offer that is otherwise clearly welfare-enhancing for it.[32]

Alternatively, economic analysis may reveal that parallel conduct is not collusive when the market's natural conditions do not create insurmountable obstacles to conscious parallelism. While this analysis is in principle not affected by market size, small size affects the existence of several market conditions that are conducive to collusion, such as entry barriers and highly concentrated market structures. When such conditions exist, it may be much more difficult to prove the existence of a collusive agreement without direct evidence of collusion. As a result, small economies may face severe difficulties in proving tacit collusion.

The second element necessary to prove collusive agreement is restraint of trade. An agreement that involves no more than fixing prices or reducing output (a "naked" agreement) will usually restrain trade. An exception occurs when the parties possess no market power. An agreement to fix prices among several small retailers that engage in fierce competition with larger, more efficient competitors is unlikely to have any effect on price levels, unless such retailers have the capacity to serve their larger competitors' share of the market.

An important question is what legal standard should be adopted to prohibit collusive agreements. An agreement that can be judged a priori to have no pro-competitive benefits, such as one that pertains only to the price or quantity of a product, or an agreement that calls for bid rigging, should be considered under a per se rule. Under such a rule a collusive agreement is deemed illegal, without further inquiry into its effects on competition or the motivation of the agreeing parties. The logic of applying such a rule is that the types of agreements mentioned earlier appear on analysis to be inimical to the public interest and rarely if ever productive of any substantial public benefit. The costs of striking down those few instances of the practice that are capable of producing some net benefit to the public or that are neutral may be judged to be outweighed by the greater clarity and certainty of a per se ban, and thus such conduct should be categorically prohibited. Moreover, collusive agreements with no offsetting benefits undermine the most fundamental tenets of a market economy—that sellers will act independently in seeking competitive advantage.

Clear and strict prohibition of naked cartels is especially important for small economies, in which cartelistic behavior is widespread owing to underlying market conditions that are relatively more conducive to collusion. Australia,[33] New Zealand,[34] and Israel,[35] for example, have adopted a per se ban on price fixing under which it is legally assumed that the conduct is likely to have or already has the effect of restraining trade. Once such an agreement is found, it is not a defense that its members did not possess enough market power to reduce output profitably.

A rule of reason should apply to all other cases. Under the rule of reason, the effects of an agreement are analyzed in each specific case to ascertain whether it restrains trade. Such a rule is justified given that in many cases it is difficult to differentiate between naked cartels and agreements with pro-competitive benefits.

It is interesting to note that in many jurisdictions, agreements that relate exclusively to exports or to the supply of products outside their borders are exempted from the restrictions imposed on agreements.[36] While such rules may increase the international competitiveness of firms, they may raise serious concerns for small economies if adopted by their large trading partners, as elaborated in Chapter 6.

Regulation of Cooperative Agreements with Pro-competitive Benefits

Small economic size also exacerbates some of the issues involved in the regulation of agreements in restraint of trade that have certain redeeming virtues, such as specialization agreements or joint ventures and strategic alliances for shared research and development, production, or marketing functions. Such agreements may enable a group of firms to carry on an activity at a more efficient scale, to reduce information or transaction costs, to engage in expensive innovative projects, or to eliminate free rider problems. Absent such agreements, many firms in small economies would incur high costs given that they cannot reach scale economies on their own or would abandon these projects altogether, thereby reducing technical, productive, and the resulting allocative efficiency. Such agreements are also often a major tool for firms in small economies to meet the challenges of an increasingly competitive international environment. At the same time, these agreements may raise restraint of trade concerns, mainly as to the facilitation or enhancement of cooperation among competitors in an already concentrated market. Efficient regulation of such agreements is thus most important for small economies.

The dual nature of many cooperative arrangements requires that their existence serve only as an invitation to further analysis rather than a basis for automatic condemnation. Such agreements should be appraised in their economic context to determine their overall effects on competition. When such agreements operate on a lasting basis and preserve very limited competition between their parties, they might best be subject to the same rules that apply to mergers.[37]

The analysis should include three basic steps: determining the potential restriction of competition, determining the pro-competitive effects, and balancing the two. Small size gives rise to several important factors that should be granted sufficient weight in the analysis. First, the balancing of pro- and anti-competitive effects should include total welfare considerations to allow firms located in small economies to achieve the lowest production or distribution costs, which are important for productive efficiency, for competing effectively with imports, and for reducing inefficient product differentiation. Second, the balancing test should give much weight to dynamic efficiency considerations, which are vital for the ability of domestic firms to compete with foreign firms. Finally, the omnipresence of and the necessity for cooperative agreements in many markets create a need for a cost-effective and timely review of cooperative arrangements.

Determining the potential restriction of competition created by a cooperative arrangement is the first step in analyzing its effects. If the agreement has no restraining effects, then no competitive issue is raised. Factors to be taken into account include the structure of the market concerned and, in particular, the degree of concentration in the market, entry barriers into the market, the current and perceived future position of cooperators in the relevant market and other markets in which they operate, and historical data on collusive conduct in the relevant market.

The issue of whether competition will be harmed should be analyzed in light of the current and potential state of competition in the market absent the cooperative arrangement. This can be exemplified by the Australian case of *Melbourne Tug*,[38] in which authorization was sought for arrangements between two firms providing tug services in the Port of Melbourne to provide such services through a joint venture. The Australian Trade Practices Commission authorized the agreement, based on the public benefit resulting from it: fewer tugs would be required for servicing normal port operations, faster service of shipping would be possible during peak and emergency operations, and available tugs would be utilized more efficiently. Although the pooling arrangement eliminated the competition that would have existed between two independent operators, the commission recognized that given the duopoly structure of the market, competition would have been limited anyway. In other words, such an agreement increases productive efficiency while not necessarily changing allocative inefficiency. At the same time, if the agreement might foreclose the market to potential competition, this fact should not be overlooked.

The parties' ties with other firms should also be carefully evaluated. As noted earlier, this is especially important for small economies in which conglomerates are prevalent. When several conglomerates dominate the market, joint ventures must be scrutinized with care lest they be permitted to fortify the conglomerates' already substantial market power and increase entry barriers.

An agreement is unlikely to raise competition concerns, however, when there is still strong actual or potential competition with many suppliers or the market lacks significant entry barriers.[39] To minimize false positives and time-consuming, costly legal procedures, a de minimis rule can be applied in cases in which it is clear that the parties possess no market power (for example, when the combined market share of all parties to the agreement is less than 10 percent).[40] Such a rule is justified, given that not all oligopolistic market structures facilitate significant deviations from competitive conditions. In such cases the remaining part of the market itself will most likely regulate the conduct of the parties to the agreement and prevent them from imposing lasting unreasonable trading conditions. It also encourages pro-competitive collaborations by providing participants in future collaborations a degree of certainty in those situations in which anti-competitive effects are so unlikely that the arrangements can be presumed to be lawful without inquiring into particular circumstances. This is especially important in small economies, given the omnipresence of joint ventures and their importance to well-functioning markets. The de minimis rule should not apply, however, to cases in which the agreement's only purpose was to raise price or restrict output, even if the parties possessed no market power. The rule against such conduct should apply categorically.

Once it is determined that the agreement raises potential anti-competitive concerns, its pro-competitive effects should be ascertained. Small economies should place emphasis on increases in dynamic efficiency that result, for example, from each party's inability to finance or bear the risk involved in the joint operation independently, as well as the synergy between the parties' facilities, resources, or activities. The Israeli case of *Deta-Kar*[41] illustrates this point. Three large insurance companies created a joint venture for acquiring the rights to use a specialized data analysis software for insurance purposes that reduced the costs of evaluating damage to vehicles. The companies agreed to refrain from competing with the joint venture. The Competition Tribunal approved the venture, emphasizing the fact that none of the companies could have afforded to buy the software alone, and that the joint venture would reduce costs significantly.

Most important, small economies should base their evaluation of the agreement's pro-competitive effects on total welfare considerations. Increases in productive efficiency not only may allow firms located in small economies to reduce their costs and increase dynamic efficiency, but also may be vital to enabling domestic firms to compete effectively with larger foreign importers. This has been recognized by several small economies. The Canadian Competition Act,[42] for example, states that in considering specialization agreements, the Competition Tribunal must give weight to gains in efficiency that will result in a significant increase in the real value of exports or a significant substitution of domestic articles or services for imported products.

Australia has also recognized significant resource savings from rationalization as benefiting the public. In *Email*,[43] for example, the Trade Practices Commission authorized a specialization agreement to rationalize production. Two companies, Email and Simpson, had market control over the supply of certain household appliances in Australia. Under the agreement, Email would discontinue production of washing machines and Simpson would discontinue production of refrigerators and freezers. Each would purchase its supply of the discontinued line from the other, and repackage and sell it under its own label. The decision was based on the public benefits resulting from more efficient utilization of resources invested in manufacturing plants, higher productivity, and correspondingly lower unit costs of production, and the greater competitive effectiveness of Australian products against imports, which would lead to considerable savings of Australian foreign exchange.[44]

Given the potential pro-competitive effects of cooperative agreements, small economies should reject a per se rule under which all arrangements that restrict competition are prohibited. Instead, a rule should be adopted that balances the pro- and anti-competitive effects of the cooperative conduct and allows arrangements in which the pro-competitive benefits outweigh the restrictions on competition.

A rule of reason analysis of ancillary trade restrictions may, for example, enable small entities to compete effectively with larger groups in a way that would not be possible unless they joined in some cooperative scheme with other small businesses operating at the same level as themselves. Australia and New Zealand have recognized this. Both jurisdictions exempt joint buying and selling activities from per se illegality if the price fixing agreement relates to the price for goods or services to be acquired collectively by the parties or the joint advertising of the price for the sale of goods or services collectively acquired.[45]

The Australian attitude toward buying groups is reflected in the *Pharma-Buy* case,[46] in which the Trade Practices Commission granted clearance to a buying and promotion scheme involving forty pharmacies in Melbourne. The group accounted for a small portion of the relevant market, and outlets were geographically spread. The commission based its decision on the fact that the effect of the promotion was to enable this small group of outlets to compete more effectively against other, more substantial outlets in the market.

This can be contrasted with the U.S. case of *Topco*,[47] which involved an association of small and medium-sized retailers that desired to cooperate to obtain high-quality merchandise under private labels so as to compete more effectively with larger national and regional chains. The association required exclusivity through trademark licenses specifying the territory in which each member could sell such trademarked goods. The district court applied a rule of reason analysis and found that such restrictions were required in order to allow small retailers to compete effectively with larger ones and prevent members from free riding on other members' efforts to promote the trademark. The Supreme Court reversed, applying a per se rule to territorial restraints, and prohibited the conduct.[48] Application of a similar rule in small economies could be harmful, as small competitors would be prohibited from using certain competitive methods, in which the benefits strongly outweigh potential harmful conduct, to challenge dominant firms.

The rule of reason should be broad enough to encompass efficiencies and enable them to be balanced against the agreement's anticompetitive effects. Accordingly, a rule that categorially prohibits all agreements that restrict competition, such as that adopted by the EC, should be rejected outright. The EC has adopted a rule under which no joint venture will be allowed if it eliminates effective competition in respect of a substantial part of the market. The commission has defined this as occurring when the parties to the joint venture will or are likely to become dominant, so that a joint venture that creates a dominant position will never be permitted.[49]

To be operational, the rule of reason should also allow for a timely check. The Israeli law, for example, limits the discretion of the director of the Competition Authority to consider only the lessening of competition when authorizing a joint venture.[50] Only the Competition Tribunal is authorized to consider broader issues.[51] This is problematic since the legal procedure is often lengthy and costly.

Instead, the inquiry should focus on three questions: (1) whether the cooperative agreement is vital for the realization of the pro-competitive effects; (2) whether the potential costs of the cooperative arrangement are necessary to achieve the pro-competitive benefits; and (3) whether the pro-competitive rewards outweigh the anti-competitive effects.

The inquiry must first ascertain whether gains in efficiency would not be attained absent the agreement. This first step is important to ensure that pro-competitive goals neither are undervalued nor mask a reduction in competition. The cooperative arrangement is vital for the achievement of the pro-competitive effects, for example, when the technology and other resources provided by each of the parties are complementary and could not have been economically bought from another source, or when the cooperative agreement creates a new product that no firm acting alone would have created, given high costs or high risks. Several rules of thumb may be applied for ascertaining the true nature of the agreement. For example, it should be verified that each party will appropriate the benefits of its own investment. This ensures that the arrangement is not being used as a method to transfer profits among firms.

The necessity for the restraints should be evaluated in light of their contribution to achieving the pro-competitive goals. In some cases, for example, no party would make substantial investment unless each could ensure that it would appropriate the benefits of its investment by supplying an agreed-upon proportion of demand or by obtaining an agreed-upon capacity of supply. Limiting the ability of firms to impose such restraints would necessarily affect their incentives to engage in the cooperative conduct in the first place. In such cases, competition concerns are a byproduct of the agreement's benefits.

There are two main standards for evaluating restraints. One option is to allow the restraints as long as they are "reasonably necessary" to achieve the pro-competitive goal. Under U.S. law,[52] for example, ancillary restrictions need only be reasonably necessary, making the main transaction more effective in accomplishing its purpose, and it is irrelevant whether a slightly less restrictive provision could be devised with the advantage of hindsight. A second option allows restrictions only if there is no other less restrictive alternative that would allow the firms to achieve the pro-competitive benefits. Ancillary restrictions should be only as broad as necessary to make the basic transaction viable. The EC commission, for example, requires that the restriction on competition resulting from the challenged conduct be indispensable in the sense that it is the least restrictive solution consistent with obtaining the beneficial goals of the conduct.

The reasonable necessity test might be superior to the least restrictive alternative, as it reduces the danger of hindsight bias. Alternatively, the dangers of a false positive under the least restrictive alternative method can be mitigated if burdens of proof are allocated correctly. Once pro-competitive effects that possibly outweigh the conduct's anti-competitive effects are found, the plaintiff should be granted the option of identifying less restrictive methods to achieve the pro-competitive results. The burden then shifts to the defendant to prove that these methods were not open to it at the relevant time. The court should adopt an ex ante rather than an ex post perspective and ensure that the ultimate burden of proof remains on the plaintiff.

Whatever the test applied, it does not necessarily require a dichotomous determination of the agreement's legality, even for dealing with existing cooperative agreements. With regard to pro-competitive cooperative agreements, the regulator may allow the agreement to continue, subject to less restrictive conditions. Yet the new trade terms should not significantly reduce the incentives of the cooperating parties to engage in the cooperative conduct in the first place, if such cooperation has overall net positive welfare effects. In particular, the regulator should exercise caution that such conditions do not significantly affect the commercial balance of the agreement.[53] This is especially important when the legality of the cooperative agreement is determined long after the contract was negotiated. Otherwise parties may not be able to rely on the contract to appropriate the benefits of their investment. Changing the conditions of the agreement would also allow any party whose consent is needed to implement the change to renegotiate the agreement's terms under new bargaining conditions. Fear that such conditions might be imposed may deter some parties from forming cooperative agreements in the first place.

One of the chief concerns raised by cooperative agreements among oligopolists involves foreclosure of a market to existing or potential competitors. One way to solve this problem is to require that the parties to the agreement provide nondiscriminatory access to third parties if foreclosure might otherwise result. The analysis of such suggestions is similar, in many respects, to the regulation of an essential facility.[54] The duty to grant access should arise only if the lack of it would affect welfare significantly.

The third stage involves assessing whether the cognizable efficiencies would be sufficient to offset the potential of the agreement to create anti-competitive harms. This comparison is necessarily an approximate judgment, based on the perceived likelihood and magnitude of these effects. The standard of proof that the arrangement creates net pro-efficiency effects should be the preponderance of evidence.

The Israeli case of *Poligar*[55] may serve as an example of the dilemmas likely to be faced by small economies in balancing an agreement's pro- and anti-competitive effects. Recall that two leading Israeli manufacturers of polyethylene covers for agriculture created a distribution joint venture which allowed them to realize economies of scale in distribution that were necessary to permit domestic firms to compete efficiently with imported products. At the same time, it eliminated competition between the two manufacturers as it enhanced collusion with respect to prices and market division. In fact, the distribution function may have been even more important to competition than the manufacturing function, as it was the distribution venture that set the price for the manufactured products.

The Director of the Competition Authority cleared the joint venture. In reaching his decision, the director emphasized that the small size of the Israeli market does not enable firms the size of these two entities to attain scale economies in distribution and manufacturing. Importers, by contrast, produce on a much larger scale owing to their larger domestic demand. The venture thus enabled the domestic manufacturers to compete more effectively with foreign importers by reducing their distribution costs. Moreover, collusion was limited by foreign imports that placed a price cap on Israeli manufacturers. The director did, however, restrict the venture by prohibiting, inter alia, tying of products and exclusive dealing.

The decision is interesting because clearing the joint venture allowed the two manufacturers to overcome a comparative disadvantage vis-à-vis foreign importers in their *manufacturing* activities by allowing them to reduce their *distribution* costs. In fact, the decision sacrificed competition among Israeli firms in order to enable them to compete effectively with more efficient importers. While the joint venture would not necessarily reduce prices to consumers, it might prevent a price rise if domestic manufacturers would otherwise have to exit the market and importers could raise the price absent such competition. As long as there is potential effective import competition, the impact of such a joint venture on allocative efficiency is minimal, unless it creates high hurdles to the entry of foreign importers, for example, by controlling essential distribution outlets.

Regulation of Conscious Parallelism

The issue of conscious parallelism has generated a vigorous debate among economists and legal scholars. In this section I survey the theoretical arguments for and against the regulation of mere conscious parallelism and examine their validity and strength in the context of small economies. I propose an innovative remedy that can help overcome some of the obstacles to traditional regulation.

Most jurisdictions do not prohibit conscious parallelism.[56] Spain is the only jurisdiction known to the author that prohibits it outright.[57] As I will show, however, some EC and Israeli legal rules can be interpreted as prohibiting some forms of conscious parallelism.

Three main factors have tipped the scale against the regulation of conscious parallelism in most economies: equitable considerations, remedial issues, and the scope of the problem. Proponents of equitable considerations argue that it is unfair to condemn parallel conduct as such because the firms involved are acting rationally in light of the structure of the market whereby each firm's profit-maximizing price is directly affected by the prices of its rivals and their anticipated responses to its own price.[58] To ignore these issues would require firms to act irrationally by closing their eyes to the immediate and direct impact of their actions on the market equilibrium. Oligopolistic firms thus act as firms do in a completely competitive market. The rational oligopolist is simply taking another factor into account, which is the reaction of its competitors to any price or output change that it makes.

Several scholars have questioned the validity of these arguments. Richard Posner has argued that conscious parallelism is not an unconscious state.[59] Rather, in forbearing to seek short-term gains at one another's expense in order to reap monopoly benefits, the oligopolists are like parties to a unilateral contract, which is treated by the law as concerted rather than individual behavior. One seller communicates its "offer" by restricting output, and the offer is "accepted" by the actions of its rivals in restricting their outputs as well.[60] While such conduct is facilitated by market structure, it is not compelled by it. George Hay argued similarly that no less of a meeting of minds exists when oligopolists with identical costs and standard products select identical prices and recognize the folly of price cutting than when several manufacturers with widely different costs agree to charge an identical price.[61] Posner further argues that even if coordination is economically rational from the perspective of the individual actors, this is not a decisive objection. In terms of the substantive economic objectives of competition policy, it is merely a detail whether a cartel is buttressed by facilitating devices or achieves its end purely by conscious parallelism.

Yet even if we accept the view that conscious parallelism is not legally different from express collusion, the problem still remains of devising an effective and efficient remedy through the traditional remedial powers vested in the competition courts.[62] Most commentators concede that oligopoly pricing cannot be improved by a simple prohibition of mere conscious parallelism. This point was expressed by Justice (then Judge) Breyer, who found that oligopoly pricing does not constitute an offense "not because such pricing is desirable (it is not), but because it is close to impossible to devise a judicially enforceable remedy for 'interdependent' pricing. How does one order a firm to set its prices *without regard* to the likely reactions of its competitors?"[63]

The problematic nature of a simple prohibition of conscious parallelism can be illustrated by the Canadian *Atlantic Sugar* case,[64] in which three companies that produced almost all of the sugar refined in eastern Canada were indicted for a conspiracy to lessen competition unduly. The evidence pointed to parallel pricing as a result of independent decisions, based on historical market shares. The initiating firm decided to end the price wars by restricting price cutting so as to do no more than restore its historical market share. It felt confident that its competitors would recognize what was being done and would also be satisfied to keep their historical market shares. Not only were its competitors immediately aware of the firm's list price the moment it was posted in the lobby of its offices, but also they were able to discover its pricing formula by a process of deduction from available data. The Quebec Court of Appeal found tacit collusion, although this was presumably nothing more than conscious parallelism. The firms were acquitted on further appeal to the Supreme Court of Canada,[65] which recognized that when the product is homogeneous and the small number of firms operating in the market are protected by high entry barriers, conscious parallelism is almost inevitable. Once one firm raises its price, its competitors may learn of this price increase immediately through customers. They will then have a strong incentive to match the price. Requiring the sugar refineries to price their products without taking into account their rivals' prices is, under such market conditions, highly problematic.

Direct price regulation is also problematic, as it requires courts to fix prices for oligopolists at a "reasonable" or "competitive" level. Such a remedy raises important issues of competence and of monitoring.

The high costs of oligopolistic prices and the fact that they result from highly concentrated markets have led to several proposals for selective restructuring of persistently non-competitive oligopolistic markets, subject to an efficiency defense.[66] The essence of these proposals is that because oligopolistic interdependence is based on high concentration levels, reducing such levels by way of breaking up existing rivals into smaller competing units would hinder the natural conditions required to sustain oligopolistic interdependence. A variation on this proposal involves inhibiting the creation of market structures that predispose firms to oligopolistic interdependence.

Restructuring is, however, a limited remedy. Most important, a program of combating oligopoly by restructuring concentrated markets may result in a loss of productive efficiency when concentration is based on scale economies. This factor is especially significant for small economies. In view of the scale economies present in many of their markets, improvement of industrial structure usually means the creation of fewer and larger firms in each industry rather than divestiture. In addition, it is questionable whether a court of law would be able to differentiate between large firms that are based on scale economies and those that are not.

These considerations, and particularly the difficulty of devising an efficient remedy for combating conscious parallelism, have led most jurisdictions to leave conscious parallelism to the admittedly limited disciplining forces of the market. Large economies, such as the United States, have also based such decisions on the fact that the perceived occurrence of mere conscious parallelism is low. It is generally believed that the kind of oligopolistic interdependence that suffices to produce seriously noncompetitive performance in large economies is likely to be rare. In most industries complicating factors exist, and in their presence it is unlikely that an oligopoly will achieve joint-profit maximization absent some facilitating measures.[67]

This may not be true for small economies. Two of the most important market conditions that facilitate conscious parallelism—a small number of competitors and high entry barriers—are quite prominent in small economies. Accordingly, some degree of interdependence is omnipresent in various degrees in many markets.

The case for regulating conscious parallelism is strengthened by the fact that it is extremely difficult to prove and distinguish conspiratorial agreements from conscious parallelism. Jurisprudence indicates that the line differentiating the two is thin and elusive, as the mental process that characterizes much actual cartel bargaining closely resembles the process by which oligopolists come to settle on a particular supracompetitive price through recognized interdependence.

The problems involved in differentiating collusion from conscious parallelism can be illustrated by the legal treatment of price leadership, whereby one firm raises its price and this acts as a signal to the others to follow suit, based on an understanding that firms in the industry will follow the signal emitted by the price leader. In the United States, price leadership in the absence of evidence of collusion is lawful.[68] The Canadian *Atlantic Sugar* case[69] and the Australian *Email* case,[70] reviewed earlier, illustrate a similar position. In the EC[71] and in Israel,[72] such conduct is sometimes regarded as collusion.

Moreover, as a conspiratorial agreement constitutes, in most jurisdictions, a criminal offense, ambiguous cases are commonly decided in favor of defendants. These facts mandate a more serious debate over the regulation of conscious parallelism, especially in small economies. Alternatively, they underscore the need for clearer guidelines that will enable courts to distinguish between collusion and conscious parallelism.

The high costs involved in conscious parallelism and the difficulty in distinguishing it from tacit collusion have led to many proposals for alternative methods to regulate it. One involves the regulation of oligopolistic markets that act in a parallel fashion by using a "shared monopoly" or "joint dominance" construction. The Israeli Restrictive Trade Practices Act, for example, defines monopoly as including a collective dominance group that controls more than 50 percent of the market.[73] This provision applies to situations in which a small number of firms dominate the market by coordinating their activities and not competing among themselves. The provision was applied in the case of *Re Marketing and Selling of Vacation Units.*[74] There, six firms that marketed vacation units did not compete among themselves, and several even operated as agents for their potential competitors. The director of the Competition Authority found that all six firms could be treated as one group. As they controlled more than 50 percent of the market, they were declared a monopoly and were regulated as such.

The EC and the United States have also attempted to use a shared monopoly construction to regulate conscious parallelism.[75] In *Gencor/Lonhro,* for example, the EC Commission stated that joint dominance can occur when "a mere adaptation by members of the oligopoly to market conditions causes anti-competitive parallel behaviour whereby the oligopoly becomes dominant."[76] It is still unclear whether EC courts would apply a joint dominance construction to conscious parallelism.[77] Yet one of the challenges of using a joint dominance concept as a legal category in competition law is that it does not correspond to a clearly identifiable structural situation leading to a predictable market outcome. A concentrated market structure with high entry barriers is a necessary condition for anti-competitive parallel pricing, but it is not a sufficient condition.[78] Shared monopoly constructions are also limited by the extent of the power to regulate monopolies and share their difficulties. Regulating the prices of an oligopolistic market through abuse-of-dominance provisions raises the same equitable and practical considerations surveyed earlier.

The United Kingdom has attempted to overcome these equitable and remedial problems by creating an administrative process for the direct regulation of conscious parallelism, based on market failure rather than on specific conduct. The Fair Trading Act empowers the Competition Commission (and its predecessor, the Monopolies and Mergers Commission) to investigate a market when "two or more persons . . . whether voluntarily or not, and whether by agreement or not, so conduct their affairs, as to prevent, restrict or distort competition."[79] It thus allows for an investigation of an oligopoly whenever the market structure or the conduct of the oligopolists prevents or restricts competition, whether or not this amounts to an abuse of monopoly power. Its flexibility allows markets to be investigated without the requirement for blame, and as a result, a variety of factors that may have led to the competition breakdown can be assessed.

Once market failure is found, the commission may suggest remedies that include a wide range of behavioral restrictions together with the stronger structural remedy of divestiture.[80] It has been recommended, for example, that powerful buyers use their purchasing power more aggressively. Direct price control and the monitoring of industry prices for a specified period have also been recommended.

The MMC's policy toward oligopolistic markets can be demonstrated by its *White Salt Report.*[81] The U.K. salt production market essentially consisted of only two producers, British Salt and ICI, with broadly standardized products. Similarity of prices was found to reflect the lack of price competition, since British Salt was a lower-cost producer and thus could have priced its salt at significantly lower levels. The MMC concluded that the lack of price competition was against the public interest, as prices were higher than they would have been if effective price competition had existed. It considered a price control mechanism based on British Salt's costs to be the best method to break the link between ICI's high costs and prices. This implied that the industry price would be that of the more efficient producer. The less efficient producer would have to produce efficiently or else exit the market.

The pragmatic nature of this approach is its main virtue, as it enables the Competition Commission to devise an appropriate remedy for a market failure, allowing for the variety in structure of the oligopolistic markets and the associated anti-competitive practices. The legal assessment is not subjugated to the need for legal definitions for purposes of certainty and predictability. Rather, provisions are designed to provide for the investigation of and, when necessary, suitable prospective remedies for a situation of market failure in the public interest, irrespective of whether there has been collusion or other reproachable conduct. Yet this is also its main weakness. The approach attracted criticism, pertaining mainly to the uncertainty and unpredictability in the law and its highly interventionist implications.[82]

An important tool for changing the market conditions that are conducive to oligopolistic coordination involves the reduction or elimination of artificial entry barriers. The lowering of such barriers may enable new firms (both domestic and foreign) to enter the market and break down the oligopolistic conduct. Alternatively, it would reduce the ability of oligopolists to raise prices to supracompetitive levels. The British Monopolies and Mergers Commission, for example, recommended the reduction of government-created barriers to entry into the postal service market in order to reduce oligopolistic coordination.[83] Such a remedy is possible, of course, only in markets that are protected by artificial entry barriers.

Conscious parallelism can alternatively be regulated indirectly by a containment policy that prevents mergers that threaten to create oligopolistic market structures.[84] Such regulation is a limited remedy, as many concentrated market structures, especially in small economies, are created by the internal growth of the market that is not prohibited. In addition, productive efficiency considerations may justify mergers to more concentrated market structures.

Another way of reducing oligopolistic coordination is by constant regulation of many aspects of the firms' business activity. This may include requirements of notification of large deals, bids, prices, output, and product differentiation. Ongoing inquiries make cartels less attractive, thereby creating an incentive to merge or to compete. Such regulation may, however, be very costly in public and private resources and does not necessarily reduce conscious parallelism.[85]

Given the difficulties of regulating conscious parallelism by the methods surveyed here, small economies can potentially focus their policy on two additional tools: regulating facilitating practices and subsidizing a government-supported maverick.

Regulation of Oligopolistic Coordination with Facilitating Practices

The concern raised by facilitating practices is that they make it possible for firms to achieve supracompetitive pricing that would not otherwise occur so frequently or completely. Facilitating practices produce a consensus on trade terms or mutual confidence that oligopolists will adhere to such terms and make it individually rational for each oligopolist to behave in a parallel noncompetitive way. In light of the difficulty of preventing conscious parallelism, it may be useful to limit facilitating practices even when we cannot eliminate concentrated market structures or directly remedy supracompetitive pricing. Prohibiting facilitating practices might be particularly useful in small economies, in which highly concentrated markets are prevalent and firms are less likely to leave a well-marked trail of collusion.

Whether or not facilitating practices ought to be regulated depends on whether the anti-competitive effect resulting from the ability of a facilitating practice to overcome natural obstacles to coordination and thereby increase the likelihood of noncompetitive performance outweighs the redeeming values of the facilitating practice in serving business purposes other than the possible reduction of competition. If we can devise a set of rules that would create a high degree of certainty as to which facilitating practices should be prohibited and which should not without sacrificing legitimate business functions and without undue arbitrariness, excessive administrative costs, and unfair punishment, then such rules would be justified.

Facilitating practices can potentially be regulated by three legal methods. First, they may be condemned as part of a collusive agreement if they serve as a factual predicate for the inference of collusion.[86] This tool is practically limited, however, as the causal connection is magnified when the practice is deemed illegal, and criminal sanctions might be inappropriate.

Second, facilitating practices may be treated as possible restraints of trade. Under this approach, such practices are to be forbidden in themselves because of their anti-competitive tendencies, unless they have redeeming virtues. Accordingly, firms engaging in parallel conduct through facilitating practices should face antitrust liability if those practices have the effect of reducing competition.[87]

The third approach suggests the establishment of a new administrative reviewable matter that would enjoin avoidable facilitating practices that engender or are likely to engender substantially noncompetitive performance. Oligopolists would be liable when they engage in avoidable conduct, the tendency of which is to permit them to coordinate their conduct more closely than would otherwise be the case. Under this proposal, suggested by Areeda,[88] no finding of agreement is necessary. If the objective is to strike at practices or mechanisms that reduce uncertainty and help overcome natural hurdles to restricting competition, the law should focus on the effects of the practices as they operate in the context of specific markets.

The second and third approaches enjoy some advantages over the first one. Prohibiting facilitating practices triggered by one firm eliminates the problem of having to infer an agreement of other firms to follow that goes beyond mere conscious parallelism, by an artificial construction of facts. They also enable the competition authorities to prohibit and prevent anti-competitive conduct in advance, as a potentially facilitating practice may be enjoined from its incipiency. In addition, the remedy is relatively simple and effective: an injunction will often suffice to end the practice. The third approach enjoys some additional advantages over the second one. A civil route invokes no criminal sanctions or stigma and thus is especially well suited for the regulation of conduct that impairs competition without being morally blameworthy or reprehensible in any sense beyond having adverse economic consequences. Also, it does not require the heavy burdens of proof of a criminal approach.[89]

The benefits of the third approach are especially significant for small economies, as it enables the competition authorities and courts to deal more directly with practices that facilitate tacit collusion and have no offsetting pro-competitive effects without the additional hurdle of proving an agreement.

The following set of rules has been suggested by Areeda:

1. Facilitating practices that unambiguously or overwhelmingly serve to restrain trade should be prohibited.
2. The plaintiff must show that competition was substantially attenuated or that market structure is highly conducive to oligopolistic collusion.
3. The plaintiff must show (a) that the anti-competitive result could be traced to the challenged practices, or (b) that it would likely lead to such a result in a non-trivial way.
4. Facilitating practices that have offsetting benefits to total or consumer welfare should be judged on the balance of probabilities and prohibited where the benefits to welfare do not offset the effects of the practice on restraining competition or the benefits to welfare can be achieved in a less competition-restraining fashion.
5. The defendant must prove offsetting benefits or that the less restrictive alternative is significantly more costly or less effective (case [a]), or the greater cost or diminished effectiveness is not trivial (case [b]).
6. The sanctions should simply prohibit the facilitating practices and restore competition in the market.[90]

This set of rules overcomes some of the most difficult evidentiary problems that may arise. For example, as it is difficult to ascertain whether prices substantially exceed the competitive level, market structure should act as a surrogate for noncompetitive performance. Also, given the difficulties in proving a causal connection, especially where several facilitating practices have been adopted, proof of a tendency rather than of an effect of the facilitating practice should be sufficient. To offset some of the uncertainties involved in such a prohibition, however, the burden of proof on the defendant to show offsetting pro-competitive virtues should be lower.[91]

The most difficult analysis involves balancing the competitive harms and benefits that are both likely to be indistinct in magnitude. In most cases measuring pro- and anti-competitive effects in practice is impractical, except for grossly qualitative, intuitive judgments. The U.S. *Ethyl* case[92] clearly demonstrates the problems involved in characterizing certain business practices as facilitating restrictions of trade. There, the condemned practices—advance price

announcements, most-favored-buyer clauses, and delivered pricing—
were adopted by Ethyl when it was the only producer and when,
therefore, it was necessarily serving a business purpose other than
coordination with nonexistent rivals.[93] Because buyers favored these
practices, later entrants into the market adopted them. Under the new
oligopolistic market structure, however, these practices had the effect
of creating conditions favorable to collusion. The court rejected the
claim that the practices unfairly facilitated the reduction of price competition in the market. It stated that "before business conduct in an
oligopolistic industry may be labeled "unfair" . . . at least some indicia of oppressiveness must exist."[94] Facilitating practices should instead be analyzed in the context of their effects on current market
conditions rather than the initial incentives for their adoption.

It may be useful for small economies to adopt the "substantial effects" test with an offsetting virtues and a least restrictive alternative
defense, as suggested by Areeda in his proposed rules. Total welfare
considerations should be taken into account as well as consumer welfare considerations. The plaintiff would then have the ultimate burden of showing that the conduct had overall anti-competitive effects.
If the plaintiff can prove that the pro-competitive effects could be
achieved in an alternative way that is no more costly to the facilitator
or to society, then the defense should fail.

While small size should not affect the type of analysis, concentrated
market structures raise stronger concerns for collusive conduct than
would normally be raised in less concentrated markets. Accordingly,
a stricter policy toward facilitating practices should be adopted by
small economies.

Government Support of a Maverick Firm

This section sketches a novel solution to the oligopoly problem which
seeks to imitate the conduct of a maverick firm that reduces the incentives and the ability of oligopolists to coordinate their prices at supracompetitive levels, with one important difference: the maverick's pricing decision is based on total or consumer welfare considerations
instead of its own profit-maximizing considerations.[95] The proposal
requires government support of one of the firms operating in the oligopolistic market (the "maverick") for a limited period. During this
period, the maverick adopts a low-price strategy. Rival oligopolists

would have to follow its pricing strategy or else suffer great losses of market share. This proposal allows firms to compete vigorously on their merits without directly limiting their decision parameters. No firm is forced to act in a manner that is against its incentives, and there is no necessary ongoing control except for the prices charged by the maverick.

The central insight of the proposal is that the existence of a single competitive firm can dramatically affect the competitive conduct and performance of an entire industry. The compliance of the other firms is assured because competition forces them to match the offers of the maverick.

To illustrate how subsidizing a maverick can enhance competition and increase welfare, let us assume an industry with an almost perfectly homogeneous product in which three firms, A, B, and C, operate. Further assume that all firms' marginal cost of production is $10. In the pre-maverick situation the three firms engaged in conscious parallelism, and the equilibrium price charged for each widget was set at $13. Each firm enjoyed a market share of 33.3 percent. The government enters into an agreement with A in which A agrees to price its widgets at its marginal cost ($P = MC = \$10$), provided that the government pay it an additional $3 per unit sold. Assuming A can expand its output to meet increased demand for its products, B and C will have to reduce their prices to match A's price ($10) or lose their market shares. Price will be set near the level where it would have been set in a competitive market.[96]

One of the important features of the proposal is that it does not necessarily directly affect the cost structures of firms or the market structure. Rather, it affects the profitability of specific pricing strategies under given market conditions. Moreover, it interferes only with the pricing decisions of the maverick firm by creating an upper limit on the oligopolistic price. This in turn creates incentives for all other oligopolists to lower their coordinated price and compete vigorously on the merits.

An interesting issue involves A's incentives to cooperate with the government. Why would A agree to play the part of the maverick firm if it could continue to enjoy high profits by engaging in conscious parallelism? Each competitor has two conflicting incentives. On the one hand, if all the oligopolists decline to cooperate with the government, they could avoid the lowering of prices for all (at least until the government finds another way to enter the industry). On the other hand, if A does not agree to cooperate with the government but one of its competitors does, then A will incur great losses. The financial incentives offered by the government for the part of the maverick allow the chosen maverick to avoid at least most of the losses that would befall its rivals. Because A cannot ensure that all of its rivals will not agree to play the maverick role, as they might have other motives to do so (such as expanding their capacity by using government financial aid), it will have an incentive to agree. Therefore, so long as the competitors do not act collectively, each has an incentive to cooperate with the government. Furthermore, all firms might be better off in the long run if one of them agreed to cooperate with the government, as otherwise the government might seek alternative ways to enter the industry, such as establishing a new domestic competitor or subsidizing the entry of a new foreign competitor. Such a scenario might lead to a reduction in overall profits for all incumbents if capacity were increased.[97]

For the maverick strategy to be operational, two main conditions must exist. First, the maverick must create a credible threat to serve consumers who were previously served by its rivals if they do not follow its conduct and reduce their prices accordingly. It must therefore possess sufficient capacity, or should be able to add sufficient capacity, to serve all or most of the demand it will take away from its rivals. Yet the threat of added capacity may act, in itself, as a stimulus for firms to reduce their prices. The second condition is relative product homogeneity. Otherwise, the price of the maverick's product may have to be reduced considerably in order to affect the demand for competing products significantly. Nonetheless, conscious parallelism is most prominent in homogeneous goods industries.

Such conditions existed, for example, in the *Ethyl* case.[98] The relevant market was lead-based compounds used to prevent engine "knock," the premature detonation of gasoline in the engine's cylinders. The market had several characteristics that were conductive to oligopolistic coordination. During the relevant period, only four firms operated in the market, with two of them dominating the industry, and there were no significant imports into the United States. Thus, the industry was highly concentrated. The two larger firms had similar cost structures, and the product was relatively homogeneous. The product had no reasonably close substitutes, and demand was relatively inelastic. In addition, all firms had substantial excess capacity owing to a significant drop in demand caused by a change in government regulation.

As noted earlier, the FTC was not able to prove an illegal restraint of trade. The antiknock compound industry would have been a perfect candidate for the adoption of the maverick model, had it not produced lead-based products.[99] Each of the four firms had the ability to serve a much larger portion of market demand than it served, owing to significant excess capacity, thus creating a credible threat to take away market share from its rivals had they not matched its price. The product was relatively homogeneous, and the game was a continuous one. Government-induced price reductions would have served to lower price levels in the industry significantly.

The maverick model has several positive welfare effects. Allocative efficiency is positively affected by the maverick's price-reducing strategy, as price is reduced and output is increased. Cost reductions to consumers are much higher than the subsidy paid to the maverick because the government must compensate only the chosen maverick for its participation rather than all the firms operating in the market. The threat of repeated intervention in the post-maverick period may induce the oligopolists to continue to price their widgets at low levels. The model may also have indirect price-reducing effects on other oligopolistic industries because of the threat of government intervention. It can also reduce the problem of productive inefficiency created by sub-optimal plant size or inefficient firms. If the maverick's price is set at a level that could be profitable only if firms operated at efficient scales, then they will need to expand their operations to survive. In addition, the maverick model may destabilize the incentives of oligopolists to collude, as it creates obstacles to collusion by increasing uncertainty in the market.[100]

The model has some limitations, the most significant being that its application involves a high level of direct government intervention in the market. Although this objection is a serious one, several factors mitigate its significance greatly. First and most important, the model imitates conditions that might accrue in any oligopolistic market through the lowering of tariff barriers or the cost of inputs. Second, government intervention is limited to directly setting the prices of one firm in the industry. Third, no other less interventionist method has been proposed for dealing with conscious parallelism. This proposal intervenes in the firms' decision-making process to a much lesser extent than direct regulation of price and other strategic decisions by equating market conditions with those that would prevail in a more competitive setting.[101]

The risk that government intervention may increase costs instead of benefits can be reduced by judicial review to ensure that the choice of the maverick is based on clear and verifiable parameters. Nonetheless, given the positive steps necessary to intervene in the market, the proposal should not be applied unless there are clear benefits to its implementation and no other conventional regulatory tool can achieve efficient results. The proposal has the greatest potential to create efficient results in an industry in which three to six firms operate and produce a homogeneous product. Less interventionist variations on the maverick model, such as subsidizing the cost of any component in the production of the oligopolistic good, may also increase total or consumer welfare if applied in appropriate circumstances.

Conclusion

The omnipresence of oligopolistic market structures in many industries in small economies intensifies the need to regulate the conduct of oligopolists efficiently so as to minimize the welfare losses that can accrue from collusive or parallel conduct while maximizing the realization of benefits that collaborations among competitors might create. I have analyzed the legal tools available to a small economy for regulating oligopoly conduct. The major policy findings can be summarizes as follows:

1. Market conditions in small economies are more conducive than in large ones to collusive or cooperative conduct, given the limited number of firms operating in many industries that are protected by high entry barriers.
2. Collusive agreements with no offsetting pro-competitive effects should be strictly regulated. To avoid false positive and time-consuming, costly legal proceedings, a de minimis rule should be adopted in cases in which it is clear that the parties do not posses market power, unless the agreement pertains only to price or output, or involves bid rigging.
3. Trade restrictions might be a necessary byproduct of welfare-enhancing agreements that allow small firms to compete with

much larger ones. When the pro-competitive effects of such agreements outweigh their anti-competitive effects, they should not be prohibited. This dictates that a rule of reason analysis be applied to ancillary trade restraints.

4. Joint ventures should be evaluated on the balance of their pro- and anti-competitive effects. Especially in small economies, the finding of anti-competitive effects should be based on both the effects in the specific market and the spillover effects into other industries in which the parties to the venture operate. Total welfare considerations should be applied.

5. Practices that facilitate oligopolistic coordination should be regulated by way of a reviewable matter that would enjoin avoidable practices that engender substantially noncompetitive performance.

6. The maverick model may be applied, in appropriate cases, to increase significantly allocative and even productive efficiency in oligopolistic markets.

Oligopoly markets can also be regulated indirectly by merger policy. This may avoid the problems of differentiating between agreements and pure oligopolistic conduct by prohibiting structural changes that may facilitate either. Yet it may also prevent the realization of scale and scope economies. The next chapter focuses on optimal merger policy.

CHAPTER SIX

Merger Control Policy

Merger control is one of the most effective competition policy tools available to regulate market power. It acts as a safeguard against the strengthening or the creation of market structures that may lead to the exercise of such power and that are not justified by social gains. It does so by preventing certain changes in market structure rather than by conduct control methods.[1]

Merger policy is highly important for small economies, as mergers are one of the main driving forces behind changes in concentrated market structures. In particular, mergers are a major tool for the realization of potential efficiencies in oligopolistic markets that would otherwise remain unexploited owing to cooperative profit-maximizing strategies that limit the incentives of firms to grow to optimal sizes internally. In oligopolistic industries with homogeneous products that are protected by high entry barriers, a firm will invest in cost-reducing internal growth only when the increase in capacity would enable it to reduce its costs significantly so as to compensate for the loss of profits resulting from the increase in total market output, or when the other oligopolists will likely respond by lowering their own output levels. Merger, by contrast, enables firms to achieve optimal size without necessarily increasing output, thereby eliminating or at least reducing the tradeoff they face between reducing costs and maintaining supra-competitive prices. Mergers may also be the best—and sometimes the only—response of firms in small economies to the lowering of trade barriers and the entry of more efficient foreign competitors.

The unique market conditions in small economies influence the design of optimal merger policy. Concentrated market structures might need to become further concentrated to achieve minimum efficient scales. Accordingly, on the one hand, an overly aggressive or rigid stance toward mergers might prevent desirable efficiency-enhancing mergers from taking place while entrenching existing inefficient market structures. The need to rationalize is all the more significant as an economy becomes increasingly exposed to international competition.

On the other hand, an overly permissive merger policy might entrench monopoly elements in a small economy. Especially in industries characterized by high entry barriers, once market structures are in place, they are difficult to alter. Moreover, merger policy is the most powerful weapon available in the competition policy arsenal to combat tacit collusion or cooperative behavior. Because such conduct cannot generally be reached directly, preventing the creation of market structures that tend to facilitate such outcomes becomes more important. Merger policy in a small economy should thus comprise a set of flexible instruments to mitigate competition concerns while promoting economic efficiency.[2]

The practical effect of these policy prescriptions is that small economies should not rely on structural variables alone or on rigid and limiting structural assumptions as the main or only element to be considered in the design of merger control. Rather, they should base their policy on contestability considerations. They should also be more accommodating to efficiency considerations and rely more on a rule of reason analysis that takes into account the fact that concentration may be a necessary evil for achieving scale and scope economies.[3] Efficiency considerations should come into play at all stages of merger policy, from the formulation of legal thresholds to the balancing of competing considerations in specific cases. In this chapter I focus on the tools available to small economies to achieve these goals.

A flexible merger approach may also be justified by the role mergers play as catalysts for efficiency and new investments. The threat of takeover bids by another firm, which often come under the merger definition, creates significant incentives for management to run the firm more efficiently.[4] Limiting the ability of firms to take over inefficient ones reduces these incentives. Moreover, the incentive to set up a firm, invest risk capital, and develop new products may be diminished if the opportunities to sell the firm to the highest bidder are reduced. A strict merger policy that creates exit barriers for investors would thus have implications for the incentives to invest in firms in the first place. These considerations are especially important for small economies, in which mergers may often be the most realistic way to realize the firm's market value.

Despite its admitted regulatory importance, until recently merger control has been absent from the competition laws of most small economies. One possible explanation for this is the rejection of an absolute value of competition approach that was adopted in many large economies. This approach prohibited concentrated market structures that tended to create anti-competitive results without taking into account offsetting efficiencies. While this approach may have created overall efficient results in large economies, given that most of their industries include a large number of firms that have already realized scale and scope economies, the adoption of such a policy in small economies would have resulted in numerous false positive errors: many beneficial mergers would have been prevented. In recognizing this effect, most small economies instead opted for no merger control. This policy was based on the assumption that leaving merger control to the market would produce more efficient results than the absolute value of competition approach. Also, it was assumed that control of abuse of dominance, and specifically price and output regulation, would reduce the incentives of firms to merge and create dominant firms. The stress on ex post conduct regulation thus derived in part from the concern for false positives in merger control. Those small economies that did control mergers adopted very wide safe harbors.

This trend has changed profoundly since the mid-1980s as many small economies have added merger control to their competition policies. One of the major forces driving this trend was the development of economic theories and empirical tools that enable competition authorities and courts to perform a tradeoff analysis—though usually a crude one—between the harms to competition from increased concentration and the benefits from the realization of efficiencies. Still, merger control in many small economies diverges from merger policy in large ones in several ways that appear to reflect national size differences. As will be shown, large economies that recognize efficiencies adopt a policy that in practice leaves little room for their consideration. Small economies often seek policies that are more flexible and may take into account conflicting considerations in a way that will ensure that efficiency-enhancing increases in concentration are not blockaded.

The first section of this chapter includes an analysis of the theoretical and practical goals of merger policy in small economies. The next two deal with the appropriateness in small economies of adopting the absolute value of competition approach and the balancing approach, which weighs the benefits from increased concentration against the harms from increased market power on a case-by-case basis. I then analyze the suitability of different indicators of market power for small economies. In the last section I look at the effects of small size on mergers with international dimensions.

The Goals of Merger Control

Since policy goals determine which mergers are considered beneficial and which are considered harmful, it is necessary to analyze the goals of merger policy. I start by briefly examining the economic effects of mergers, which are key building blocks in determining the goals of merger control. I then analyze the effects of small size on the choice of illegality test for merger control.

The Economic Effects of Mergers

It is important in determining the goals of merger policy to recognize how changes in ownership and control patterns affect the performance of firms and industries in which they operate. Here I provide a brief overview of the major effects of mergers. A horizontal merger, that is, a merger among rivals operating in the same market, reduces, by definition, the number of competitors in the market,[5] and the merged entity ordinarily has a larger market share than either of the merging parties had before the merger. This reduction in the number of firms and increase in market shares may raise two basic competition policy concerns: unilateral market power and joint market power. Unilateral market power concerns focus on the creation or the strengthening of substantial market power of the merging entity, thus enabling it unilaterally to raise prices, restrict output, and behave otherwise strategically. Of course, if the increase in market share does not create efficiencies, market forces may eventually erode the merged entity's position. This process, however, may be lengthy or inhibited by artificial obstacles if competition law enforcement is not perfect and timely. Joint market power concerns, by contrast, focus on the strengthening of the ability of the market participants in the post-merger situation to coordinate their strategic choices (e.g., output, price, and quality) by engaging in explicit or implicit interdependent behavior.[6] What effects may result from changes in market conditions brought about by the merger depend on the factors that influence the firms' ability and incentives to act interdependently.

Vertical mergers, that is, mergers between firms with potential or actual buyer-seller relationships, raise concerns that focus mainly on the ability of the merged firm to increase its market power by controlling a vertical activity in the chain of production and distribution.[7] The main concern is that vertical integration may raise the price of entry of new competitors into the market, thereby increasing the market power of the vertically integrated entity. For example, if a dominant producer of a particular product were to merge vertically with the main wholesaler in that market, its rivals might face high barriers to selling their products in the market. Backwards integration with a dominant producer of an essential input may pose similar problems.

Several conditions have to be met for vertical integration to raise the cost of entry significantly: production at some stage of the industry is dominated by a vertically integrated firm; it is significantly costly for another firm to enter this stage of production; and the actual or perceived problems of purchasing from or selling to divisions of integrated firms compel firms to enter only as integrated operations. An increase in market power that results from a vertical merger also requires a significant probability that the integrated firm will not deal with independent firms or that any such dealings will be subject to strategic interruption or cost manipulations. The monopolist might not have incentives to foreclose competition unless it is prevented in some way from achieving monopoly profits. Vertical mergers should thus be evaluated carefully to reveal the real incentives and ability of the merged entity to raise prices.

Conglomerate mergers, defined to include all mergers that are neither horizontal nor vertical, might pose a threat to competition by the elimination of a potential rival. Some economists further argue that mergers between firms supplying a range of complementary or marginally substitutable products (e.g., detergents and food bought by supermarkets) might enable a firm that is dominant in one market to use its market power to leverage it into another, when competition in both markets is imperfect. This may include, for example, forms of exclusive dealing, such as full-line forcing.[8] Mergers between large, diversified firms may also reduce challenges to incumbent monopolies.

Mergers may raise additional concerns on the grounds that decisions taken by large corporations may have consequences that extend well beyond specific industries to produce political and social as well as "purely" economic results. Economic concerns about large absolute firm size derive from the potential for competitive disadvantages bestowed on the smaller firms by limited capital, distribution, advertising channels, and production factors. The concern is also not purely economic, in that large firms might translate financial strength into political power and influence legislation or regulation to their benefit at the expense of the rest of society. Other sociopolitical concerns focus on a strengthening of market power that may be antithetical to the balanced distribution of wealth, and effects on employment levels.

At the same time, a merger may enhance efficiency by integrating the firms' facilities and by allowing firms to achieve efficiencies that were not attainable under the pre-merger market structure because of firm interdependence, the absolute size of firms, or other obstacles. Most important for small economies, mergers may allow firms to overcome obstacles to efficient size that arise in oligopolistic structures. Permitting a sizable horizontal merger may increase long-run productive efficiency if the potential merging parties have strong respect for their mutual interdependence and would not build full-sized new plants independently for fear of either depressing prices or carrying too heavy an excess capacity burden. Some of the benefits of reduced costs may even be passed on to consumers in the form of reduced prices and higher product quality. Even a merger to monopoly can lead to price decreases. Achieving efficiencies is all the more important as domestic firms are becoming increasingly exposed to international trade.

Comparing the extent to which mergers will enable the parties to exercise market power and earn supracompetitive profits to the efficiencies created has been recognized as a highly complex and controversial subject in industrial organization economics. The original modeling of this tradeoff was undertaken by Oliver Williamson.[9] Williamson argued that only a fairly modest efficiency saving is required to outweigh the deadweight loss associated with empirically realistic price increases following a merger. Given the simplicity of the model, however, any application of the theory in practice requires a more complex analysis to account for various other factors, including pre-existing market power,[10] differing demand assumptions, and other firms' competitive responses to increased market power. Furthermore, the Williamsonian analysis has been concerned with static cost savings, without taking into account the temporal effects of an increase in market power. To the extent that good predictions can be made about the effects of a merger on technological progress, this information should also be incorporated. Despite these apparent weaknesses, the model still supports its basic message, which is that the potential benefits of mergers should be recognized in addition to their costs.

Can the internal growth of firms be relied on to regulate the incentives of firms to grow to optimal sizes effectively, so that merger policy can be more restrictive? Although internal growth may enable firms to attain minimum efficient scales, it cannot be relied on to regulate market growth effectively. Mergers take less time than internal growth. Also, internal growth may not enable the firm to achieve all of the efficiencies a merger may offer, such as better management or the use of complementary know-how and intellectual property. Finally, and most important for small economies, when demand is limited, the incentives of firms to attain efficient size are dampened by the incentives to limit total market output to monopolistic levels in order to maximize the profits of all oligopolists. Accordingly, merger policy is an important regulatory tool for small economies.

The Goals of Merger Review

The choice of goals for merger policy involves major value judgments. An important issue is whether merger control should focus mainly on achieving efficiency or on preventing concentrations of economic power. Other social or political goals may also impinge on merger policy. Although there is no "correct" set of goals, small size influences some of the tradeoffs that policy makers face when choosing among conflicting goals.

A small economy cannot afford to protect competition rather than its outcomes. The concern for ensuring that a sufficient number of competitors operate in each market should be subordinated in a small economy to the more compelling necessity of serving a small population efficiently. Given high concentration levels that are justified by scale and scope economies, protection of competition would blockade many mergers that have positive welfare effects. Producers would not, in many markets, be able to attain minimum efficient scales and thus reduce their costs, and consumers would not be able to enjoy lower prices that rest on lower costs. Similar arguments should prevent a small economy from giving paramount importance to considerations for the viability of small businesses as such.

Protecting competition might also prevent domestic firms from attaining the minimum efficient scales necessary for them to compete effectively with foreign firms in their domestic markets. Merger is often the best response of domestic firms to the reduction of trade barriers and the entry of foreign firms into their markets through imports or through local subsidiaries. This was acknowledged, for example, by the director of the Israeli Competition Authority in *Kelet/Taal*,[11] approving a merger that was essential to enabling two domestic firms to compete with imports. A proposed merger in the same market between two of the three domestic firms several years before, when trade barriers were higher, had not been approved.[12]

An argument often made in small economies concerns the need to enable firms to merge in order to increase their international competitiveness. The core of this argument is that merger policy should not prevent firms located in small economies from overcoming competitive disadvantages that result from limited domestic demand. It is also argued that an over-rigid merger policy might drive firms offshore, thereby preventing the development of large entities that can compete against the multinational firms operating in the domestic markets. These considerations should not be overlooked in a small economy. In a competitive international marketplace, mergers that significantly increase the international competitiveness of domestic firms should be treated favorably by small economies, even if they increase the level of concentration of acquiring enterprises. Australia and Canada, for example, include in their merger control regimes a specific instruction that a significant increase in the real value of exports should be considered an efficiency gain.[13] At the same time, considerations of international competitiveness should be balanced against harm to the domestic market.

The international competitiveness goal is often interpreted by businesspeople in small economies as requiring a merger policy that enables firms to reach large sizes. This "national champion" argument must be analyzed with caution. In many industries size is not a prerequisite for international competitiveness. This is demonstrated by the fact that exports are not the prerogative only of large businesses. Also, when it comes to international competitiveness, size is not the sole criterion. As Michael Porter has shown, domestic rivalry is more likely than national dominance to breed businesses that are internationally competitive, as it provides stimulus for the efficiency and innovation that are crucial for export success.[14] In addition, domestic consumers might not enjoy all the benefits of the domestic firms' success if international price discrimination were not prevented.

At the same time, in some industries in which penalties for operating below MES levels are high, achieving efficient size may be a necessary condition to enhance export opportunities. Size may affect not only production and dynamic efficiency but also the relative costs of the gathering and analysis of market information likely to be faced by smaller and medium-sized firms. In such cases small economies ought to balance the benefits from increased international competitiveness against the costs of the proposed merger in the domestic market. These should include not only competition in the specific market but also the effects of the merger on the ability of vertically connected firms to compete internationally. To reduce possible allocative inefficiency concerns, the competition authority may even require, as a condition for approving the merger, that the merging firm not charge a price in the domestic market that exceeds the price it charges in foreign markets, somewhat like an internally applied anti-dumping condition.

An important debate focuses on whether merger policy should maximize consumer welfare or total welfare. The consumer welfare approach strives to maximize consumer surplus, which is the difference between what consumers would willingly have paid for the product they consumed and the actual price they paid for it. This standard will be met only if in the post-merger situation the price will not increase beyond the pre-merger price, because the new efficiencies are sufficiently significant to cause the profit-maximizing price not to rise.

Under the total welfare approach, a merger is permitted if it increases total surplus, which includes both consumer and producer surplus. In economic terms, if the cost savings from the merger exceed the deadweight loss caused by the expected anti-competitive price increase (producer surplus minus consumer surplus), the merger should go through. Welfare transfers from consumers to firms do not count as a loss. The consumer welfare standard thus sets a much higher threshold for approving mergers than the total welfare standard. Yet it should be underscored that the total welfare standard is not easily met in markets with preexisting market power, as is commonly the case in small economies. Preexisting market power will increase the deadweight loss considerably and will make it more difficult to find efficiency gains that are larger in magnitude.[15]

Small size sharpens the dilemma posed by these two standards, since in a large percentage of cases the outcome will be determined by the choice of standard, given the already existing high concentration levels in many industries. Small size should tip the balance in favor of the total welfare standard for several reasons. First and foremost, given the concentrated nature of most markets in small economies, a policy that requires a high standard of proof of no negative effect on consumer welfare may well lead to market stagnation of oligopolistic structures that not only charge supracompetitive prices but do not achieve productive efficiency. The total welfare approach will thus reduce productive and even dynamic inefficiency.

Second, the consumer welfare approach may conflict with the goal of enhancing the international competitiveness of domestic firms. One interesting example involves rum producers from the Caribbean islands. The Caribbean domestic market for rum is very competitive. At the same time, high distribution and marketing costs in potential foreign markets create significant obstacles to the export of rum. A merger or a joint venture among rum producers that would enable them to realize scale economies in distribution and marketing abroad and to export rum would increase total welfare if the revenues from sales in other markets are significant. But unless domestic firms are prevented from charging different prices for their products abroad and in their home markets, consumers in the domestic markets will most likely be worse off, given probable cooperative conduct among rum producers, if the cost savings do not affect the production or distribution prices in the domestic market. In such situations the consumer welfare standard will clash with the goals of increasing total welfare as well as the international competitiveness of firms.

One should also note that the consumer welfare approach does not necessarily achieve distributional goals. A consumer welfare approach implies that the loss to each consumer and the benefit to each shareholder should be treated equally. Yet members of these groups may vary significantly in income and other socioeconomic traits. It might well be that customers of a specific firm (e.g., Mercedez-Benz) are, on average, more wealthy than the shareholders of the merging firms. Competition policy is therefore a blunt instrument for redistributional goals. The premise of the total welfare test, by contrast, is that wealth redistribution is best left for government instruments such as taxation and social insurance or welfare systems that are designed for that purpose, and through which redistribution is more directly observed or monitored by the voters to whom government is responsible.[16]

One problem with the total welfare standard is that in a world with high levels of international cross-holdings, it might reduce rather than increase domestic total welfare. If the merging entities are controlled mostly or solely by foreign shareholders or the production facilities are located outside the jurisdiction, then an approach that maximizes total welfare and ignores the nationality of shareholders may well increase total world welfare but not domestic welfare, because the cost savings and profits from the merger may accrue elsewhere.[17] Only when it can be assumed with a high degree of certainty that most of the profits earned by shareholders in the domestic market will be spent in it will this approach necessarily maximize total domestic welfare.

This problem can be at least partially overcome if the domestic economy creates incentives for the beneficiaries to reinvest their profits in the same jurisdiction. Alternatively, the total welfare standard can be applied selectively, to ensure that domestic producers benefit from it. Australia has applied a qualified total welfare approach under which all welfare benefits to be considered in the merger analysis must accrue to domestic firms or consumers. To the extent that wealth transfer is received by foreign owners, such welfare transfers are not taken into account in recognizing the merger's benefits, and the cost savings from the merger should be sufficient to offset both the deadweight loss and the wealth transfer enjoyed by the foreign owners. Similarly, if the production facilities are located abroad, the benefits from freeing assets for other productive uses will not be counted against the deadweight loss resulting from the merger.[18]

Adoption of a rule that applies a different standard to mergers between firms that are held primarily by domestic shareholders and to firms that are held primarily by foreign shareholders may, however, be problematic. Such a rule will most likely contradict the national treatment provision in international agreements. It also does not ensure that domestic producers would reinvest their profits in the domestic economy so that total welfare will, in fact, be maximized. While the adoption of a qualified total welfare approach raises some problems, the adoption of a consumer welfare standard may preclude many domestic welfare–enhancing mergers.

Total welfare predictions also involve a number of difficult analytical and qualitative issues that place a heavy burden on the regulator. Nevertheless, while it is true that total welfare is hard to predict, when such predictions can be made, there is a strong case in favor of adopting such a standard, especially in small economies, as it is the standard for reviewing mergers most consistent with promoting economic efficiency.[19]

It is noteworthy that while total and consumer welfare are commonly debated, one can also adopt a balancing approach that gives different weights to the consumer or producer surplus estimated to result from a merger. For example, a fall in consumer surplus might be weighted twice as heavily as the corresponding increase in producer surplus, consistent with society's preferences.[20] Such an approach serves as a middle ground between consumer and producer welfare, and as such it suffers from the advantages and the costs of both.

These arguments also have important implications for the selling of government assets as part of privatization programs. Privatization is often a positive step toward lessening government control in the market. At the same time, care should be taken that the wish to maximize immediate revenues from the sale of government assets does not overshadow long-term concerns about the effects of the sale on future competition in the market. Although such transactions often do not come under the merger review process of the competition authorities, the government should nonetheless consider the effects of a proposed acquisition in light of existing market conditions. It might sometimes be wise to forgo a high offer made by a firm or a consortium of firms in order to enjoy the benefits of competition in the long run.

Tests for Illegality

The small size of the market also influences which merger illegality test should be adopted. Two major tests can be identified. The first prohibits mergers that will or are likely to prevent or lessen competition in the market substantially.[21] This test is generally interpreted as preventing mergers that will significantly increase the market power of firms operating in the relevant market. The concerns center on the unilateral exercise of market power or implicit or explicit cooperative conduct. The second illegality test prohibits mergers that create or strengthen a dominant position in the market. Some jurisdictions rely on this test exclusively,[22] whereas others adopt both illegality thresholds as alternatives or complements.[23]

The behavioral lessening of competition test is more suitable for small economies than the structural creation or strengthening of dominance test. In a small economy, a larger percentage of mergers would tend to create a dominant firm. Yet these mergers do not necessarily lessen competition. For example, if a market is already characterized by a tight oligopoly that coordinates its conduct by reducing output and increasing price, a merger will not substantially lessen competition, as competition is nonexistent.[24] Rather, it may help remedy a situation in which firms do not realize scale economies, and it may also increase productive efficiency significantly. Such a merger should be allowed, unless a long-term analysis of the market points to some market conditions that might break down the existing oligopoly and introduce competition in the market. Similarly, when a merger enables the merging firms to compete effectively with an incumbent monopoly or with foreign importers, such a merger should be allowed, although it may create a dominant position for the newly merged entity (especially where dominance is defined to include firms with market shares equal to or lower than 50 percent). A different policy may well entrench a market structure in which one firm that attained minimum efficient scale has dominant market power and other firms are price followers and cannot compete with it effectively.

Moreover, mergers that do not create a dominant position may nonetheless lessen competition significantly. Most important, the dominance test might not prevent coordinated interaction of firms as a method of exercising market power, which is a major concern in small economies. Another situation that may not be caught under a strict application of the dominance approach occurs when after the merger there are at least two relatively evenly matched participants in the market. This can be exemplified by the Australian *Amcor* case, where Amcor and Visy Board had each bought 50 percent of the only remaining Australian corrugated fireboard manufacturer, Smorgon. This did not lead to dominance by either company, as each increased its market share proportionally, but it did substantially lessen competition.[25]

The practical implications of the differences between the two standards can be exemplified by the New Zealand case of *Progressive Enterprises*.[26] On May 26, 2001, New Zealand amended its 1986 Commerce Act. The new law changed the merger illegality threshold from the "creation or strengthening of a dominant position" to "substantial lessening of competition." The threshold was being strengthened to bring New Zealand's competition law into line with Australia's and to facilitate a more economic approach to defining anti-competitive conduct.[27] Australia had lowered its illegality threshold several years earlier, since the dominant position threshold did not apply to considerable rationalization and concentration within the Australian industry.[28]

On May 25, the day before the new test came into force, Progressive Enterprises, a company operating three supermarket chains, applied for clearance in respect of a proposed acquisition of the Woolworths New Zealand supermarkets. The Commerce Commission approved the merger under the old market dominance test. New Zealand case law interpreted dominance as involving "a high degree of market control."[29] The commission concluded that the proposed merger did not meet this high standard. It based its decision on the fact that the merger would result in a combined entity accounting for around 42 percent of all supermarket shopping in New Zealand, defined as the relevant market. Also, the merged entity would face competition from the Foodstuffs companies, which collectively accounted for a market share of about 58 percent.[30]

Foodstuffs, Progressive's main rival, appealed the decision. The High Court dismissed the challenge, but the New Zealand Court of Appeal allowed the appeal and declared that the commission was required to assess the Progressive application under the new substantial lessening of competition test.[31] The merger was then resubmitted to the commission to be decided under the new standard.[32] The commission stated that a lessening of competition and a strengthening of market power should be taken as being equivalent. It then acknowledged that the new test was broader than the dominance test, and that the commission is required to "have regard to such matters as the potential market power arising because of the differentiated nature of the market, the prospect of coordinated conduct and the elimination of a particularly vigorous or effective competitor."[33] It then found that as a result of the merger the supermarket retail market would be highly concentrated, with two firms of almost equal size, limited product differentiation, and price transparency. Thus the merger would facilitate "leader-follower" tacit collusion and discipline. Consequently, it prohibited the merger.[34]

The EC has attempted to broaden the limited scope of its dominance test by interpreting it broadly to include situations of joint dominance. Its experience exemplifies, however, the limitations of such an approach in applying the dominance test to prevent changes in market structure that increase parallel pricing. One difficulty centers on the kind of economic links that must exist between the oligopolists for them to be jointly dominant.[35] Another difficulty results from the linking of the concept of dominance, defined in the context of a single firm, to collective dominance. The definition of dominance requires that the dominant firm act independently of its rivals. In a non-cooperative equilibrium, however, the pricing of each oligopolist is constrained by the pricing of other oligopolists.[36] Under the lessening of competition test it would be enough to show that there is a high probability that the post-merger market equilibrium is likely to be further removed from the competitive equilibrium.

The Absolute Value of Competition Approach

Three major approaches toward merger control can be identified. The first is the absolute value approach. Under this approach, every merger that is likely to reduce competition is prohibited, regardless of the efficiencies it might create. The main rationale of merger policy under this approach is allocative efficiency, although it may also be based on decentralization of aggregate market power. This approach was predominant in most large jurisdictions around the world and is still predominant in some, including the EC and Japan.

The second, balancing approach weighs the anti-competitive effects of the merger against the efficiencies it creates or other sociopolitical goals. This approach views competition as an important but nonconclusive consideration and is basically neutral toward mergers that create firms of large size or with significant market shares. This is not to say that structural considerations play no role under this approach. Such considerations, however, make up only one of the relevant factors used in assessing the overall effects of the merger. The balancing approach has been adopted in most small economies, as well as by the U.S. competition agencies and most U.S. courts. The third approach leaves merger control to the market.

In this section and the next one I examine the absolute value and balancing approaches in detail to determine their effectiveness and efficiency in regulating mergers in small economies. The analysis will show that the absolute value approach is clearly unsuited to small economies. The balancing approach is most suitable for them, although much depends on the tools that implement it in practice, such as thresholds, burdens of proof, and the type of information deemed relevant to merger control.

The absolute value of competition approach places decisive weight on the reduction in actual or potential competition that may result from a merger by creating a per se violation whenever a merger is found to create anti-competitive effects. This approach is governed by paradigms that suggest that as industries become more concentrated, firms within them would find monopolistic or oligopolistic conduct more profitable, and the result would be poorer industrial performance. Accordingly, this approach implies that market power can be controlled by preserving a non-concentrated environment through the prohibition of mergers beyond a specific market share or size threshold.

Efficiencies play a role under this approach, if at all, in setting the thresholds for illegality and in predicting the competitive conduct of firms in the post-merger situation rather than as a counterbalance to anti-competitive effects. Any effect flowing from efficiencies is taken into account to the extent that it influences the abilities and incentives of firms to compete in the relevant market. If the merged firm has cost advantages in the form of lower production, marketing, or distribution costs, this might limit the ability of smaller rivals to achieve similar advantages. This is especially true when the smaller competitor cannot take advantage of comparable scale and scope economies.

Efficiencies may thus increase the market power of the merging firms.[37] Accordingly, if a merger achieves efficiencies that may further strengthen its position in the market, it will be prohibited even if it increases consumer or total welfare. An exception arises when efficiencies create incentives to new or existing competitors for increased competition. For example, where increased efficiencies act as an enhanced competitive constraint on the unilateral conduct of other firms in the market and thus undermine the conditions for collusive conduct, they will be relevant to the analysis.

To give a hypothetical example, suppose that four firms that produce a homogeneous product operate in a market, each with a production capacity of 10,000 units and a market share of 25 percent. Further assume that minimum production costs can be achieved at capacity levels of 18,000 units. A proposed merger between two of the firms operating in the market will most likely meet the standards for creating dominance or lessening competition. Although the merger achieves productive and possibly allocative and dynamic efficiency, it will be prohibited under the absolute value approach. The potential efficiencies may serve to indicate that the merger will strengthen market power, as it will create a dominant position of the merging parties based not only on their combined market shares but also on their strong comparative advantage vis-à-vis their rivals. It may also be feared that such a merger will create a trend toward further concentration in the market, as the two remaining firms will seek to merge in order to compete effectively with the newly merged entity. This will eventually lead to a duopolistic structure that is more likely to engage in collusive conduct, albeit with reduced costs and increased efficiency. The decision may be different if a dominant firm that can produce 18,000 units already operates in the market. In such a case, the merging of two potential competitors may well be a necessary condition allowing them to compete effectively in the market and increase competition. In this exceptional case, efficiency and competitiveness considerations may thus lead to the same outcome.

Most large economies tend, or have tended until recently, to apply this approach. The underlying assumption is that there is no need for high concentration levels in order to achieve efficiency, and therefore such concentration levels should be prohibited. Moreover, an erroneous assessment of the economic effects of a merger is likely to have a relatively smaller impact on a large than on a small economy. The following section provides a brief analysis of the merger control regimes in several large economies that have adopted the absolute value approach to exemplify its practical implications.

The U.S. Approach: Prima Facie Rules of Illegality

Section 7 of the Clayton Act is the controlling U.S. statute with respect to mergers. It prohibits any merger "where in any line of commerce, in any section of the country, the effect of such acquisition may be substantially to lessen competition, or to tend to create a monopoly." Until the 1980s this statute was interpreted as adopting the absolute value approach. Merger policy was based on rigid structural assumptions that implied that high degrees of concentration were harmful to the economy and thus should be prohibited, even if they entailed improved efficiency.[38] This approach not only was driven by administrative considerations that took into account the vast number of mergers that are subject to the jurisdiction of the courts, but also was rooted in a Jeffersonian structuralist and populist philosophy that gave decisive weight to concerns for preserving small businesses and to the dispersion of aggregate economic power, even if this meant occasional higher costs and prices.

This approach can best be illustrated by two landmark decisions of the U.S. Supreme Court in *Procter and Gamble*[39] and *Philadelphia National Bank*.[40] In the first, the Court stated that "possible economies cannot be used as a defense to illegality" in merger cases.[41] The rejection of efficiency arguments was based on an interpretation of the Clayton Act as favoring competition (rather than its outcome), which would be harmed if firms achieved economies by increasing levels of concentration in the market. Earlier, in *Philadelphia National Bank*, the Supreme Court had established that a merger "is not saved because, on some ultimate reckoning of social or economic debits and credits, it may be deemed beneficial."[42] In essence, the Court stated that there can be no defense once an anti-competitive finding has been established.

Following this choice of goals, competition agencies and courts developed unitary market share rules for prima facie illegality that applied to all industries equally, based on the presumption that high concentration creates negative effects on competition. *Philadelphia National Bank*[43] first established the market share–based presumption of illegality that had driven merger control until the 1970s. Under this rule, a plaintiff may make a prima facie showing that the merger will result in anti-competitive effects by establishing that the merged entity will have an undue share of the relevant market.[44] This burden of proof was especially easy to meet, as courts adopted extremely low levels of concentration as thresholds for illegality (as low as 5 percent) to prevent the agglomeration of market power in its incipiency.[45] Once such a showing is made, a presumption of illegality arises. To rebut this presumption, the defendant must produce evidence that the market share statistics provide an inaccurate account of the merger's probable effect on competition in the relevant market.[46] The defendant may rely on non-statistical evidence such as the "ease of entry into the market, the trend of the market either towards or away from concentration and the continuation of active price competition."[47] Additionally, the defendant may demonstrate unique economic circumstances that undermine the predictive value of the government's statistics.[48] If the defendant successfully rebuts the presumption of illegality, the burden of producing additional evidence of anti-competitive effects shifts to the plaintiff.[49]

The Supreme Court has not spoken on the issue of merger efficiencies since 1967. Courts, agencies, and academics have different interpretations of existing Supreme Court precedents, which oscillate between total rejection of efficiency claims to the recognition of their importance as a factor that should be weighed in determining the net effects of a proposed merger. The general trend has changed toward incorporating a limited efficiency defense. Yet the presumptions of illegality are still based on rigid market concentration assumptions.

The EC Approach: Focus on Dominance

The European Community serves as another example of a large economy that applies an absolute value approach. Since 1990, mergers with a "community dimension" have been regulated under the Merger Control Regulation.[50] A concentration has a community dimension if it meets the financial and scope of influence threshold set in the Merger Regulation. The test of legality is whether it "creates or strengthens a dominant position as a result of which effective competition would be significantly impeded in the common market or a substantial part of it."[51] The Merger Regulation sets forth criteria for considering whether mergers meet this test. The primary considerations involve the market position of the companies concerned and other static criteria, such as structural concentration and absolute size parameters.[52] Other issues, however, should be taken into account, such as the development of technical and economic progress and the effect on economic and social cohesion.[53]

Efficiency considerations have been interpreted as having little or no effect on the evaluation of mergers.[54] If a merger is found to create or strengthen a dominant position that results in a significant limitation of competition, efficiencies are not a defense. As EC officials clearly stated, "There is no real legal possibility of justifying an efficiency defense under the Merger Regulation. Efficiencies are assumed for all mergers up to a limit of dominance."[55] Some commentators go further, observing that the possibility that a merger might lead to static or dynamic efficiency gains which other non-merging firms are unlikely to achieve is interpreted as prima facie evidence that the merger would enable the merging firms to acquire a dominant position, incompatible with merger policy.[56]

The *Nordic Satellite Distribution* (NSD) case[57] is illustrative of the approach adopted by the commission with respect to efficiency arguments. Although the transactions could have generated significant efficiencies, the proposed merger was found to create or strengthen a dominant position and was thus prohibited. The case concerned a proposed joint venture for the distribution of satellite TV to the Scandinavian countries among TeleDanmark, the public Danish telecom operator, Telenor, the public Norwegian telecom operator, and Kinnevik, a Swedish industrial group with a large interest in media and in possession of some of the most popular TV programs in those countries. The commission prohibited the merger, as its operation would have created a highly vertically integrated structure ranging from program provision via satellite capacity to cable TV networks. Although NSD would undoubtedly have involved significant scale and scope efficiencies, it would also have resulted in the parties' achieving or strengthening dominant positions in several markets. Non-formally, however, efficiencies may sometimes be a consideration in approving a merger, conditional on appropriate structural or access remedies.[58]

The EC merger regime should be understood in light of the basic philosophy on which the Treaty of Rome is based, namely, that maintaining effective competition in the EC is a decisive goal. If dominance already exists in the market, that is, if competition is already fragile, the aim is to preserve at least some degree of remaining competition. Some comments made by high-ranking Commission officials and the issuance of the green paper on merger policy may signal, however, a more open approach towards efficiencies.[59]

The Inappropriateness of the Absolute Value
Approach to Small Economies

Adoption of an absolute value approach in small economies would necessarily produce harmful results, given that its inflexibility does not allow competition agencies and courts to screen only non-efficient mergers. Many mergers that are likely to create significant anti-competitive results, but at the same time would increase total or consumer welfare, will not be allowed.

Interestingly, several small economies have adopted the absolute value approach. The Australian and New Zealand merger control regimes that apply to mergers that were not reported to the relevant competition authorities do not include an efficiency defense.[60] The Israeli Restrictive Trade Practices Act can also be interpreted as applying the absolute value approach. Section 21 of the act mandates that the director of the Competition Authority prohibit any merger that raises a reasonable probability of significant harm to competition or the public in the specific market. Harm to the public is defined as higher prices, lower quality or output, or worse distribution terms. The wording of the act thus leaves no room for efficiency considerations. Accordingly, if the merger significantly increases the market power of the merging parties, it is generally not approved.[61]

The adoption of the absolute value approach in small economies is nonetheless often based on different assumptions and goals than in large ones. The Australian and New Zealand provisions should be read in light of the pre-merger authorization procedure, which balances public benefit considerations, interpreted to include efficiencies, against the risks of anti-competitive conduct arising from the merger. A merger is evaluated under the absolute value of competition approach only if the merging parties fail to notify the competition authorities of the proposed merger. It can thus be seen as a penalty that parties incur for failing to comply with the law.

The Israeli approach is based on the presumption that "monopolies are forever." That is, because market forces cannot easily erode

monopoly power once it is created, and regulatory tools have limited effect, such monopolies should be condemned from their in-
ception. Scale and scope economies can instead be realized through
internal growth. Also, given the administrative burden of verifying
efficiencies, such proof is not permitted. This approach ignores three
basic facts. First, especially in a small economy in which high concentration levels may be necessary to realize scale and scope economies,
the costs of market power can be balanced by efficiencies. Second,
internal growth is often prevented in oligopolistic markets by cooperative profit maximization. While large economies may assume
that scale and scope economies will normally be achieved over time
through normal market processes, this assumption often does not
hold true in small economies. The much higher level of market concentration there often implies that some potential efficiencies might
be achieved only through mergers that have anti-competitive effects.
Third, in markets in which cooperative conduct can be successfully
maintained, there is no major difference in consumer welfare between
one and three competitors because of strong mutual forbearance. In
such situations it might well be more efficient to let some or all market
participants reduce their costs.

Some of the limitations of the absolute value approach may nonetheless be reduced by coupling it with wide safety zones. By forgoing a
case-by-case analysis and increasing the level of legal thresholds for
challenging mergers, efficiency-enhancing mergers are allowed without the need to prove efficiencies explicitly. The Swiss Federal Act on
Cartels and Other Limitations to Competition is an illustrative example. The act does not contain an efficiency defense.[62] It does, however,
contain an extremely high threshold for dominance, which captures
only concentrations between major companies.[63]

The adoption of wide safety zones recognizes that in many concentrated markets mergers may well produce efficiencies that outweigh
the anti-competitive harm. It then takes account of other factors such
as the possibility of collusion and the degree of effectiveness of anti-
collusion measures. Such a policy eliminates the problems and the
costs inherent in a case-by-case analysis of anti-competitive effects
and efficiencies. Yet, to be efficient, safety zones must be correctly defined so as to capture most of the scale economy problems but nothing
more. This is problematic, because efficiencies and industry-specific
characteristics that affect market power differ significantly from one

case to another. Accordingly, the balancing approach is preferable for small economies.

The Balancing Approach

A balancing approach introduces another factor into the merger control equation: benefits from the merger. It recognizes that a merger should be permitted if the improvements in efficiency resulting from it are greater than and offset its anti-competitive effects. Accordingly, the regulator is empowered to balance in each specific case the benefits from efficiency and the harms that can come from the change in market conditions, once it is determined that the merger creates anti-competitive concerns. It should nonetheless be emphasized that efficiencies cannot be estimated in isolation from anti-competitive effects, as each affects the likely magnitude of the other.[64]

While balancing is a clear concept in theory, it raises some important practical issues, such as how to prove efficiencies. In this section I explore some practical aspects of the balancing approach, which may help explain why the defense is invoked relatively infrequently. To set the background for the analysis, the first section will contrast the approach adopted in the United States with that of Canada, Australia, and New Zealand. There are sufficient differences between these regimes for a comparison to be a productive exercise. The following section analyzes the suitability of the balancing approach to small economies. As will be seen, the small size of an economy is, in many cases, positively correlated to lower requirements for cognizable efficiencies.

Current U.S. Policy: Efficiencies as a Rebuttal

Since the early 1980s, U.S. merger policy has changed significantly, at least in theory, so as to acknowledge the benefits that can accrue from mergers, even if they bring about high levels of concentration. Despite early Supreme Court decisions and the fact that it has not ruled on a merger case for more than a quarter of a century, many federal courts examine efficiency considerations.[65] To date, however, no federal court has upheld an otherwise anti-competitive merger on the basis of efficiencies alone. At best, defendants succeeded in rebutting the government's prima facie case with evidence showing that the intended merger would create significant efficiencies.[66] In some cases efficiency defenses were found relevant but unnecessary, as the legality of the merger was determined without assessing the purported efficiencies.[67] In most cases the merger was found to be illegal because the efficiencies submitted were not sufficient to overcome the anticompetitive effects.[68]

The Eleventh Circuit Court of Appeals decision in *FTC v. University Health* is often cited as illustrative of a lenient approach toward efficiencies taken by a federal court.[69] There, the court stated that "whether an acquisition would yield significant efficiencies in the relevant market is an important consideration in predicting whether the acquisition would substantially lessen competition." The court went on to say, "We think, therefore that an efficiency defense to the government's prima facie case in section 7 challenges is appropriate in certain circumstances."[70] The Court, however, also stated that "of course, once it is determined that a merger would substantially lessen competition, expected economies, however great, will not insulate the merger from a section 7 challenge." Moreover, the difficulty involved in proving efficiencies has led the court to the conclusion that "a defendant who seeks to overcome a presumption that a proposed acquisition would substantially lessen competition must demonstrate that the intended acquisition would result in significant economies and that these economies ultimately would benefit competition and, hence, consumers."[71]

The competitive effects approach is also apparent in the Horizontal Merger Enforcement Guidelines published jointly by the Department of Justice and the Federal Trade Commission (FTC), which state their enforcement policy.[72] The guidelines allow for an efficiency defense so long as the merging parties can show that the proposed merger's efficiency benefits to consumers will outweigh the impact of increased concentration on consumer welfare. Publicly, however, the agencies have rarely acknowledged any decision not to challenge a merger that they believe anti-competitive on the basis of its efficiency-enhancing potential.[73]

The competition authorities[74] and most courts require that the following conditions be met in order to recognize efficiencies:

1. Efficiencies must be real rather than pecuniary. For example, cost savings due to avoiding taxes or negotiating lower output prices are regarded as transfers between the firm's owners and

other groups, as opposed to real cost savings. Production cost savings are cognizable, as are distribution cost savings and dynamic efficiencies.

2. Necessity: efficiencies must be realizable only through the proposed merger. The efficiency claims will be rejected if equivalent or comparable savings can reasonably be achieved by the parties through other means without the merger's potential adverse competitive effects.

3. Sufficiency: the expected net efficiencies must be sufficient to reverse the merger's potential to anti-competitive harm.

4. Efficiencies must be passed on to consumers rather than benefiting only the parties to the merger (consumer welfare standard).[75]

In addition, some courts have required that the claimed efficiencies be achieved in the relevant market rather than in other markets.[76]

U.S. courts have placed the burden of proof of efficiency claims on the merging parties, and many require clear and convincing proof of significant economies.[77] This strict evidentiary burden has, in practice, negated the availability of the efficiency exception. The Merger Guidelines seem to adopt a more lenient approach in requiring that the merging parties must substantiate efficiency claims so that the competition agencies can verify by reasonable means the likelihood and magnitude of each asserted efficiency, how and when each would be achieved (and any cost of doing so), how each would enhance the merged firm's ability to compete, and why each would be merger-specific.[78]

In 1997 the Merger Guidelines were modified to clarify the scope of efficiencies in merger analysis. Despite the modifications, efficiency claims are still restricted as the conditions for cognizable efficiencies are extremely hard to meet. The revised guidelines adopt a sliding-scale approach, stating that "when the potential adverse competitive effect of a merger is likely to be particularly large, extraordinarily great cognizable efficiencies would be necessary to prevent the merger from being anticompetitive . . . [E]fficiencies almost never justify a merger to monopoly or near—monopoly."[79]

Although courts and agencies alike have moved away from reliance on market share and concentration presumptions and toward an intense factual inquiry on the industry-specific characteristics of the market in which the merging entities operate, the basic rules, especially legal presumptions and burdens of proof, still convey an underlying presumption against concentration. Despite the increased sensitivity toward gains from production and distribution economies, the efficiency defense is very limited and hard to prove and could exonerate a merger only in the most extraordinary circumstances.

Canada: Efficiencies as an Explicit Legal Consideration

Canadian competition legislation is unique in providing for an explicit efficiency exception to otherwise anti-competitive mergers. When a merger is expected to be both anti-competitive and efficiency-enhancing, the Competition Act resolves the conflict in favor of the merger when the likely efficiency gains are greater than and offset the likely anti-competitive effects, and these efficiency gains would not be attained if the merger were prohibited.[80] The legislation makes it clear that if competition and efficiency conflict in merger review, the latter will prevail. The adoption of a balancing approach in Canadian legislation is based on the recognition of the importance of economic efficiency to the Canadian economy.

To be considered relevant, the act provides that the claimed efficiencies must not be realizable if the merger is prevented and must represent a savings of real resources rather than a redistribution of income.[81] Such efficiencies typically arise from economies of scale and scope in production or distribution, management-related efficiencies, and qualitative efficiencies, such as research and development or enhanced ability to respond dynamically to developments in the market.

The Canadian approach toward efficiencies was, at least until relatively recently, much more accommodating than its U.S. counterpart. The Canadian Competition Bureau recognizes efficiency gains from a merger that occur in markets other than the relevant market for competition analysis.[82] Also, the Competition Tribunal enables efficiencies to be established on the balance of probabilities in the usual way dictated by civil law.[83]

The *Superior* case, however, highlights the importance of the merger standard for recognizing efficiencies. In *Superior* the Canadian Competition Tribunal applied a total welfare standard and approved a merger despite its significant anti-competitive effects, based simply on likely offsetting efficiencies resulting from it.[84] In a much-criticized decision, the judgment was overturned by the Canadian Federal

Court of Appeal,[85] which limited the weight to be given to efficiency considerations.

Superior involved the merger of two firms in the propane retail and distribution industry which strengthened their market power significantly. Prior to the merger, Superior held approximately 40 percent and ICG approximately 30 percent of the market.[86] In numerous local markets the merger constituted a merger to monopoly.[87] In addition, there were high entry barriers into the market.[88] The Competition Tribunal concluded that the merger would remove an effective competitor from the market, such that the remaining competition would be incapable of effectively constraining the exercise of market power by the merged entity. In some markets the merged entity would have the ability to exercise market power by imposing unilateral price increases. Where there were at least three competitors including the merged parties prior to the merger, the merger would enhance interdependence and reduce competition.[89] Despite the significant impact on competition, the merger was approved in a majority opinion based on offsetting efficiency gains in management functions, customer support, and field operations. The estimated deadweight loss of $3 million Canadian per year was offset by gains in efficiency in the order of $29 million per year.

The decision of the tribunal endorses the total surplus criterion, which was also adopted by the Competition Bureau in its Merger Enforcement Guidelines. It based its decision on the interpretation of the act as endorsing efficiency and on the recognition that government instruments such as tax policy are more effective than merger policy as ways of meeting distributional objectives.[90]

The Court of Appeals reversed, replacing the total welfare standard with the more flexible and amorphous balancing weights approach. The Court of Appeals acknowledged the ultimate preference in the Competition Act for the purpose of efficiency, but it did not restrict the countervailing effects to deadweight loss. Instead, it interpreted the word "effects" to include all the anti-competitive effects to which a merger gives rise.[91] The court then instructed the tribunal to make broader public policy judgments beyond pure economic effects, but it did not prescribe the method by which the tribunal would perform its task. The new standard thus balances between economic efficiency and social goals such as distributive effects and loss of product choice, but none of these factors are assigned a fixed, a priori weight. This test significantly reduces the weight of efficiency considerations in evaluating a merger. It also creates uncertainty by enabling the Competition Bureau and the courts to exercise a high degree of discretion as to the weight given to different factors that will determine the merger's outcome.[92]

Interestingly, on remand the Competition Tribunal, in a majority opinion, applied the balancing standard to the facts of the case and approved the merger.[93] It found that the efficiencies created by the merger offset the deadweight loss as well as the redistributional effects created by it. The tribunal left open the question of how much weight should be given to efficiencies or to redistributional weights, as in this case "under any weighting scheme, the gains in efficiency . . . are greater than and offset all the effects of lessening and prevention of competition."[94] The decision was appealed.

Australia: Public Benefit Test in Authorization Proceedings

Australia serves as an example of a small economy in which efficiency arguments play a decisive role in various stages of merger analysis. Australia's merger regime has two tiers of control. Section 50 of the Trade Practices Act of 1974 is the principal section governing mergers and acquisitions. As noted earlier, efficiencies are relevant under this section only to the extent that they affect the level of competition in the market. As an alternative, parties to a proposed merger are provided with the option of seeking formal authorization of the merger by the Australian Competition and Consumer Commission. Authorization is the process of granting immunity, on public benefit grounds, for proposed mergers that would otherwise contravene section 50. Those dissatisfied with a commission decision may appeal to the Competition Tribunal for a rehearing of the application for authorization.[95]

The act does not define public benefits, except to the extent that it requires that significant increases in exports or import replacements be considered as public benefits and that the commission take into account international competitiveness.[96] The ACCC recognizes efficiency considerations as important aspects of the "public benefits" test in authorization proceedings. Public benefits include, inter alia, industrial rationalization resulting from more efficient allocation of resources and in lower production costs and improvement in the quality and safety of goods and services.[97] In *Davids,* for example, significant resource savings from rationalization, including warehousing and distribution facilities, advertising, and generic product ranges in grocery wholesaling, were recognized as public benefits.[98]

For authorization to be granted, an applicant must establish public benefits that outweigh the anti-competitive detriment of the proposed conduct. The applicant is not required to show that the acquisition is a necessary and sufficient condition of the public benefit claimed. Yet the benefit must be shown to have a causal relationship with the merger.[99] Cost savings from increased bargaining power that result merely in a transfer of wealth rather than any real resource savings for the community may not be considered substantial public benefits in themselves, unless such cost savings arise from the creation of countervailing power and may move the market outcome closer to a competitive one. The efficiencies should also be of a durable nature.[100]

The resulting benefit should be probable rather than possible or speculative, but need not be susceptible to formal proof. Nonetheless, while it is often difficult to measure public benefits in precise quantitative terms, general statements about possible or likely benefits will not be given much weight unless supported by factual material.[101]

As to the legality standard to be applied, the guidelines specifically recognize that "the concept of a benefit to the public is not limited to a benefit to consumers; a benefit to a private party which is of value to the community generally is a public benefit . . . A merger may result in economies of scale or other resource savings which may not be immediately available to customers in lower prices but may be of benefit to the public as a whole. The community at large has an interest in resource savings, releasing those resources for use elsewhere."[102] In *Du Pont* the commission accepted that improvements in the efficiency of sodium cyanide production resulting in resource savings, such as electricity and capital, constituted a public benefit, although consumers were unlikely to benefit from lower prices.[103] At the same time, the interests of the public as purchasers, consumers, or users are relevant. Lower prices for consumers and lower input costs for business, with potential ramifications for international competitiveness, are considered by the commission to constitute public benefits.[104] Nonetheless, if a merger benefits only a small number of shareholders of the applicant corporations through higher profits and dividends, this might be given less weight, because the benefits are not being spread widely among the members of the community.[105] The Competition Tribunal has also tended to define public benefits to include purely private benefits, such as reduction in production costs.[106]

New Zealand: Public Benefit Test in Authorization Proceedings

New Zealand has the most relaxed attitude toward the proof of efficiencies. Section 47 of the New Zealand Commerce Act of 1986 prohibits mergers that lessen competition significantly. As in Australia, however, the merging parties may apply to the Commerce Commission for authorization.[107] The commission is mandated to grant an authorization if the merger would lead to a public benefit that outweighs the lessening in competition.

Public benefit was interpreted, essentially, as an efficiency defense. Efficiency is the principal factor that the commission and, on appeal, the courts take into consideration under the act. The Commerce Commission stated that detriments from the loss of competition include losses of economic efficiency, incentives to innovate, and incentives to avoid waste. Benefits include tangible benefits, such as scale and scope economies, improved use of existing capacity, cost reductions due to reduced labor costs, greater specialization in production, decreased working capital, and reduced transaction costs. They also include intangible benefits, such as environmental and health improvements. Cognizable efficiencies must not be simple wealth transfers, and the gain must be shown to be dependent on the proposed acquisition.[108]

Until 1991 the New Zealand public benefit test was applied to require that the benefits accrued to a reasonable cross-section of the public. Since 1991 the courts have established that public benefits must be net gains in economic or social terms.[109] The distribution of gains and losses is thus irrelevant to their inclusion in the process of weighing benefits and detriments.

New Zealand has also adopted a low burden of proof standard that requires the merging parties to establish "a tendency or real probability" that claimed public benefits will materialize. The comparison between public benefits and detriments is, inevitably, largely a qualitative judgment, although quantification is encouraged.[110]

The Suitability of the Balancing Approach
for Small Economies

Optimal competition policy for a small economy requires the adoption of regulatory tools that acknowledge the benefits that can arise from the realization of efficiencies in certain market settings, even if they involve increases in market power. Given that efficiencies vary widely from one industry to another such that no general presumptions can be made based on market structure alone, this requires a case-by-case analysis of the potential efficiencies in each specific market setting. In theory, the balancing approach is best suited to regulate mergers in small economies. It should come as no surprise that the most advanced regulatory regimes for recognizing efficiencies were adopted in small economies.

Practice has shown, however, that the conditions for recognizing efficiencies play a decisive role in the practical implementation of efficiency considerations in merger decisions. The stricter the requirements, the less weight is given in practice to efficiencies and the more theoretical the ability to allow a merger based on efficiencies to go through. Several factors are positively correlated with the difficulty of proving an efficiency defense. The first is the stringency of the burden of proof placed on the merging parties to prove the alleged efficiencies that may result from the merger. The second involves the evidentiary weight attached to purely structural factors. In a small market characterized by scale economies, concentration levels are likely to be very high. If strong evidentiary weight is given to presumptions of illegality based on concentrated market structures, an efficiency defense may well become a theoretical possibility only. The third involves the balancing standard adopted, such as consumer or total welfare. The fourth factor involves other conditions for cognizable efficiencies, such as sufficiency and necessity. The higher the efficiencies must be to justify a merger, the harder it is to meet this standard. In recognizing the difficulty of proving efficiencies, small economies should take into account the impact of these factors on their competition policy and devise tools that would help overcome some of these obstacles.

The importance of the conditions for recognizing efficiencies can be exemplified by the unsuitability of the current U.S. policy to deal with concentrated market structures justified by scale economies. The U.S. health care industry suffers from many of the problems of markets in small economies: markets are regionalized such that scale economies are large relative to the market size and interdependent conduct is widespread. As David Gilo observes, in determining the legality of horizontal mergers in this industry, courts have exhibited little sensitivity to the unique characteristics of the market.[111] Even when courts acknowledge the small size of the market, the analysis resembles that of a large market: similar concentration ratios are used for presuming anti-competitive effects, and efficiency claims are treated with the same skepticism as claims in large markets.[112] Similarly, the Justice Department and FTC Health Care Industry Guidelines, while acknowledging the issues of small markets in the health care market, have adopted low concentration thresholds and count on an efficiencies defense to address the special characteristics of that market.[113] Since it is quite common in the health care industry for concentration ratios to be high, it is often the case that challengers of a merger are able to establish a prima facie presumption of anti-competitive effects. Hence, analysis of anti-competitive effects almost always produces strong inclinations toward the condemnation of a merger. This factor, combined with the often insurmountable obstacle of an efficiency defense based on the high burden of proof placed on the merging parties to show that the alleged efficiencies offset any loss in consumer welfare and could not be achieved in other ways involving lower allocative efficiency losses, cause the problems of scale economies in the health care industry to be systematically undertreated.[114]

Small economies generally take account of the special characteristics of a concentrated market characterized by scale and scope economies. While there has been a worldwide decline in views of concentration as the greater evil of competition law, small economies' competition policy may be bolder in accepting risks of greater concentration. In most small economies there is no a priori negative approach toward mergers. Rather, the approach is that mergers, in general, are positive phenomena that can serve the public interest. The relevant authorities are authorized to balance the benefits of efficiency and the harms from increased concentration that would likely result from the proposed merger. Moreover, as Table 6.1 clearly indicates, small economies, which have a stronger incentive to attempt to strike the optimal balance between the merger's benefits and detriments, are willing to exercise more leniency toward efficiency claims in order to overcome the practical problems in proving efficiencies. One example

Table 6.1 Requirements for cognizable efficiencies in different jurisdictions that have adopted the balancing approach

Requirement	United States	Canada	Australia	New Zealand
Onus of proof	Merging parties	Merging parties	Merging parties	Merging parties
Burden of proof	"Clear and convincing"[a]	Balance of probabilities	"Probable effect"	Tendency or real probability
Merger standard	Consumer welfare	Balancing weights	Total welfare	Total welfare
Real savings	Yes	Yes	Yes	Yes
Necessity	Yes	Yes	No	
Achievable in the relevant market	Yes	No	Unclear	Unclear

Note: Jurisdictions listed in order of size.

a. This standard was adopted by some U.S. courts. The competition agencies require a lower burden.

involves the balancing formula. A consumer surplus standard imposes a greater burden on an efficiency defense than a total welfare standard because it requires efficiency gains to be so substantial as to ensure that the merger will not result in a wealth transfer. Many small economies have thus opted for the lower total welfare standard. A similar tendency can be detected with regard to other requirements for cognizable efficiencies.

Still, an enforcement decision has explicitly turned on the efficiency-enhancing attributes of the transaction in question in a surprisingly small number of cases. Several reasons might explain this phenomenon.[115] Most important, the burden on the parties is still usually a difficult one. The merging parties must be prepared to articulate in detail the nature and size of the expected efficiencies, and they usually bear the burden of proving that achieving the efficiencies is probable and not reasonably attainable by less anti-competitive means. More often than not, parties to a merger do not reach such a detailed level of analysis in advance of their agreement, if only because it is risky to exchange during negotiations the extent of proprietary information necessary to make such calculations. They are left with having to generate their efficiencies study in the course of the review by the competition agency, a situation that the authorities view with skepticism, often rightly so. Moreover, the verification problems faced by competition authorities and the fact that the merging parties have incentives to overstate their claims often give efficiency claims limited credibility in the eyes of the authorities.

In addition, the defense is relevant only in cases in which a merger is found to be anti-competitive. Parties are understandably reluctant to admit that their merger is anti-competitive and to base their entire defense on efficiencies. Thus, when they make an efficiencies defense, it is in combination with a defense on competitive effects. An efficiencies defense, however, can be inconsistent with a competition argument, particularly one involving ease of entry. It is difficult to argue, on the one hand, that entry into the relevant market is easy and, on the other, that the claimed efficiencies cannot be achieved by internal expansion or by an alternative merger.

Moreover, from the perspective of the competition agency, the tradeoff analysis is difficult and imprecise. In practical terms, the efficiencies will have to exceed the agency's estimates of the merger's anti-competitive effects. Finally, the usually short period within which decisions on mergers must be made can preclude arguments of efficiencies, which are a time-consuming exercise.

The paucity of decisions approving mergers on efficiency grounds does not, however, necessarily mean that many beneficial mergers are being prevented. The safe harbors employed by most competition authorities encompass many efficiency-enhancing mergers. Mergers that fall within these limitations are ultimately adjudged to be competitive and are approved without the need to consider their efficiency benefits. Also, competition agencies are increasingly willing to employ innovative forms of relief, such as partial divestiture or technology licensing, that permit the underlying transaction to go forward, thereby achieving most or all of the efficiency gains. Finally, it is probably the case that efficiencies are an undisclosed factor, if not necessarily the deciding one, in some agency decisions approving mergers. Competition agencies may be reluctant to acknowledge that fact publicly, however, given the practical difficulties in applying the defense. In this regard the agencies face a challenge in providing sufficient information about their standards to the business community so that efficiency-enhancing mergers will not be unnecessarily discouraged.

The problem of verifying efficiencies can be partly overcome by ranking efficiency claims on the basis of their credibility. Proposed efficiencies would be weighed by the probability that they will occur (expected value). For example, efficiency claims resulting from increased capacity utilization are particularly credible in declining markets. Another solution may lie in the adoption of a sliding-scale approach in which, as the danger of an increase in the exercise of market power rises, the burden of proof of efficiencies rises accordingly.

Pre-merger consultation procedures, which enable market participants contemplating a merger to consult with the competition authorities before going forward with formal proceedings of notification, may also be useful. Such proceedings may be used as an informal device the aim of which is to verify, on a very preliminary level, whether the merger is likely to pose competition policy issues. Although the competition authority may reserve the right to change its mind and challenge a merger that did not seem likely to create anti-competitive concerns or to drop an investigation that seemed to be justified by the legal standards, it will most likely not reopen the issue for further evaluation, save in exceptional circumstances.

Pre-merger consultation procedures, while beneficial in an economy of any size, have greater significance in a small economy, given that the issues involved in balancing between efficiencies and anti-competitive conduct are often difficult for market participants to evaluate. Once the analysis goes beyond structural elements to an evaluation of the specific implications of each merger, preliminary proceedings can give the parties a general sense of which considerations are likely to be taken into account in evaluating their merger. Such a procedure enables parties to abandon a proposed merger without spending too many resources on its evaluation, or to go forward with merger proposals that, while raising anti-competitive concerns, may well enhance efficiency.

The balancing approach is superior to leaving the regulation of mergers to the market, as the latter does not differentiate between mergers that enable the realization of efficiencies and those that only increase market power.

Substantive Criteria for Analyzing Anti-competitive Effects

Both the absolute value and the balancing approaches have in common two steps in merger analysis: defining the market and evaluating the potential anti-competitive effects of the market. The balancing approach then adds a third step, in which the efficiencies involved in the proposed merger are analyzed and balanced against its anti-competitive effects.

Market definition serves to identify and establish the competitive constraints that the merging entities face from actual and potential competitors. Small size generally does not affect the methodology for or the definition of the relevant market. In fact, many small economies have followed in the footsteps of the United States[116] and adopted the SSNIP (Small but Significant and Non-transitory Increase in Price) test as a methodological tool to analyze demand and supply substitution.[117] Under this test, suppliers of other goods will be regarded as participating in the relevant market if consumers would switch to their products in response to a small but significant and non-transitory change in the relative price of the goods concerned. Similarly, where such a price increase will induce firms not currently operating in the market to switch or add production or marketing to compete in the relevant market, the value and volume of the products these suppliers would be able to produce and market if they switched or added production are taken into account in defining the relevant market. Although the methodology for defining the market is the same, in a small economy it is much more important to recognize that relevant markets may be defined to include foreign producers not currently operating in the market in appropriate cases.[118]

The next step, once the relevant market has been defined, is to analytically connect changes in market conditions that will likely result from the merger to market performance to determine the effects of these factors on competition. Modeling the effects of a merger on competition is not an easy task. While there is general agreement that high levels of market concentration are more conducive to anti-competitive conduct than low ones, there is an ongoing debate as to which specific market conditions are necessary to facilitate monopolistic or oligopolistic conduct. In this section I survey some of the methodologies that have been adopted to model changes in market structure in order to analyze their suitability for small economies.

Static market structure parameters that indicate the degree of concentration in the relevant market are often used as screening devices to identify those mergers that are likely to raise competitive concerns. Economists generally agree that there is a positive relationship between a decrease in the number of effective competitors in a market and the likelihood of the exercise of market power. High concentration levels may positively affect the incentives and ability of firms to engage in coordinated conduct, as they reduce the number of firms that may coordinate their conduct and increase the impact of each firm on the market equilibrium. Alternatively, a significant rise in market share may indicate the ability to exercise unilateral market power by the elimination of a substantial competitor. Moreover, when market shares are positively correlated to existing and potential production capacities, a large market share might indicate that the remaining producers may be too small to expand sufficiently to offset the output reduction within a reasonable time period. A firm with substantial market shares might therefore be potentially able to exercise market power unilaterally, regardless of the interdependent behavior of rivals in the market.

Another important structural consideration is the dispersion of firm size. If the feared threat is tacit or overt collusion, variations in firm size can make cartel bargains more difficult to reach and enforce. There might be more disagreement about the profit-maximizing price since firms with different cost structures compute different profit-maximizing processes and outputs. Changes in market structure that reduce size dispersions may thus allow firms to achieve comparable costs and increase the possibility for anti-competitive results.

Size dispersions may also indicate the comparable efficiencies of firms in the market. In oligopolistic homogeneous products markets, the Cournot model demonstrates that firms with the lowest marginal costs gain the highest market shares.[119] Accordingly, mergers among firms with high market shares leave firms with relatively small ones, and by implication high marginal costs, as competitors. Since such rivals are less able to discipline post-merger price increases, a merger among firms with high pre-merger shares may lead to a greater ability to exercise market power than a merger among low-share firms. Interpreting market shares when firms in a market produce differentiated products is less straightforward. In such markets, estimates of the substitutability of the products of the merging firms for one another relative to the substitutability of the products of competing firms with the products of the merging firms can be informative.

Therefore, many economies use structural measures as prima facie indicators of the competitive effects of a merger. Most indicators are based on the initial level of concentration and the predicted change in concentration due to the merger. The simplest and most common indicator is based on the post-merger market shares of the merging parties and the level of concentration in the market as measured by the aggregation of the market shares of the largest firms in the market. Because information about market share is often more readily available than other information, it is a relatively low-cost screening method.

In setting the threshold levels under which a merger will not be challenged, all economies should balance the possibility that the change will result in an increase of market power or the creation of market power against the need to enable firms to realize scale and scope efficiencies. If, on the one hand, the threshold is set too low, most mergers will be scrutinized, and positive market activity might be blocked. But if, on the other hand, threshold levels are set too high, many mergers with anti-competitive effects will be allowed. A small economy exacerbates the dilemmas of setting the threshold optimally, as many of its concentration-increasing mergers might be necessary to achieve productive efficiency.

Interestingly, the size of the economy is negatively correlated with the height of the legal thresholds it employs. For example, until the 1980s, U.S. courts and enforcement agencies employed a concentration ratio based on the combined market shares of the four largest firms operating in the relevant market (CR4). Under the original Merger Guidelines issued by the antitrust authorities in 1968,[120] a merger of two firms with 4 percent each or more operating in a market with a post-merger four-firm concentration of 75 percent was presumptively illegal. If the market was less concentrated, mergers involving firms of 5 percent each were presumptively illegal. These guidelines were substantially more tolerant than Supreme Court case law, which condemned mergers in unconcentrated markets of firms with combined post-merger market shares of less than 8 percent.[121] Hovenkamp suggests that more recently a vague consensus has emerged that a market in which the CR4 is less than 40 percent is a safe harbor. Also, if the CR4 is 75 percent or higher, a merger in which the combined market share of the post-merger firm exceeded 12 percent would be illegal.[122] These high thresholds were based on the assumption that mergers in such markets were generally unnecessary to achieve efficiencies and thus should all be blocked. Such an assumption does not hold true in small economies.

Compare this threshold to those adopted by small economies. The Australian guidelines employ a market share threshold for unilateral market power of 40 percent. A twofold test is employed for collusion-enhancing transactions: a merger will not be challenged if either the post-merger market share of the merged entity is below 15 percent or the four-firm concentration ratio is below 75 percent.[123]

New Zealand has adopted an even wider safe harbor. Under its revised guidelines, the Commerce Commission will not generally challenge a proposed merger when the merged entity will have less than a 20 percent share in the relevant market (or 40 percent including any interconnected or associated persons) and the three-firm concentration ratio is below 70 percent.[124]

The dangers of adopting too wide a safe harbor can be illustrated by the Israeli experience. The Israeli Restrictive Trade Practices Act provides that a merger will not be challenged unless the merged entity's post-merger market share will exceed 50 percent or the turnover rates of the parties exceed a legal threshold.[125] This safe harbor is quite problematic as it does not capture mergers that might strengthen oligopolistic coordination, although such mergers cause some of the most significant antitrust problems in small economies. To give but one example, suppose that four firms operate in the market, each with 25 percent market share. A merger between two competitors would not be scrutinized although it would create a much more concentrated market structure. Thus, small economies should adopt a two-part threshold that would capture increases in dominance or, alternatively, changes in oligopolistic market structures that have a high probability of creating or increasing coordinated policies.

Another commonly used methodological tool employed to measure concentration and screen mergers is the Herfindahl-Hirschman index (HHI). This static index indicates the level of concentration in the market based on both the number of firms operating in the market and their relative market shares. It is calculated by summing the squares of the individual market shares of all the participants. For example, a market with two firms of equal size, each with 50 percent market share, would have an HHI of 5,000.

The HHI levels adopted in the United States illustrate the importance of fine-tuning legal presumptions to economic size. Although the HHI is only a prima facie indicator of the anti-competitive effects of a merger, its thresholds are important for setting merger review standards since they create a presumption of illegality. The U.S. Merger Guidelines define moderately concentrated markets as those in which the post-merger HHI is between 1,000 and 1,800. An increase of more than 100 points potentially raises significant competitive concerns, depending on non–market share factors. For example, a market shared equally by eight firms has an HHI of 1,250. If two firms merged, the HHI would increase by 312.5 and the merger would probably be challenged. The guidelines define highly concentrated markets as those in which the post-merger HHI is 1,800 or more. When the HHI is increased by more than 100 points, it is presumed that the merger is likely to create or enhance market power or facilitate its exercise. For example, a market shared equally by five firms would have an HHI of 2,000. If two firms merged, the index would increase by 800 and the merger would be challenged. This choice of index is based on generalized predictions of gains from size as well as behavioral assumptions of the market, specifically oligopolistic coordination. As the chosen HHI threshold (1,800) is met in a market with five equal firms, it is presumed that, absent clear showings to the contrary, firms in such markets have already exhausted scale and scope economies. Thus, the cost savings from the merger will be very low.

The HHI has generated much criticism as it does not capture the effects of the size distribution of firms in facilitating anti-competitive conduct. Any amount in variation increases the HHI. That is, for any given number of firms, the HHI is minimized when all firms are exactly equal. This prediction is not consistent with the notion that collusion is most likely to succeed when all the firms are approximately the same size. Similarly, when firms cannot be assumed to be equally efficient, a greater dispersion of market shares may signal more rather than less competitive pressure and hence less concern for damage to consumers from the merger.[126]

Apart from these general criticisms that apply in jurisdictions of any size, the small size of a market and the resulting need to enable firms to grow relatively large in order to realize scale economies require the rejection of the U.S. concentration threshold in small economies. Adoption of the U.S. HHI levels will result, for example, in a presumption of illegality in a merger between the two smallest firms in a market with six businesses, four holding approximately 20 percent market shares and two holding approximately 10 percent each.

Objections to such a merger will not comply with the special economic conditions of a small economy. In small economies, especially when fixed costs and scale economies are substantial, it is not uncommon for firms to possess such market shares. Accordingly, many if not most proposed mergers would cross this threshold, although they would not always increase or create market power or facilitate its exercise, and most firms would be prevented from realizing scale economies.

Courts and agencies in small economies have thus rightly rejected the U.S. HHI levels as based on presumptions of market performance that lack sensitivity to the special characteristics of their markets. In the Israeli *Tnuva* case,[127] for example, a merger between the largest firm operating in the market (38 percent) and a relatively small competitor (5 percent) increased the HHI by 300 points, raising it from 1,700 to 2,000. The Israeli Competition Tribunal explicitly rejected the HHI test as well as the CR4 thresholds as an indicator of the lessening of competition, given the small size of the Israeli market. The tribunal stated that the choice of HHI levels and deltas is not universal but rather an attempt to create thresholds that would apply only to the U.S. market. In the United States, which is a large economy, the threshold of severe scrutiny is based on the presumption that firms have already exhausted scale and scope economies, and thus the cost savings from the merger will be very low. In a small market the number of firms should be lower, or firms will not be able to achieve scale economies.[128]

Whatever the structural indicators chosen by a small economy to indicate post-merger market power, it is crucial that the dynamic factors of the relevant market be analyzed to determine the real effects of the merger. Given that many markets in small economies cross illegality thresholds based on market structure considerations alone that are set by them, analysis of non-structural factors that affect the ability of firms to exercise market power in concentrated markets is crucial to a correct analysis of the effects of a proposed merger.

Reliance on structural indicators alone as an indicator of anti-competitive conduct is problematic, as high concentration levels are a significant but nonconclusive factor for the exercise of market power. Structural indicators merely increase the *probability* of such conduct. Even at very high levels of concentration it is not certain that competition will be impaired, even though its nature may change. In certain circumstances the reduction in the number of firms will lead them to achieve a non-cooperative equilibrium. In other situations the fact that the merger makes the cost conditions of the oligopolists more similar or leads to a more equal distribution of excess capacity may increase the probability of a cooperative outcome. When entry barriers are low, firms in a concentrated market might even act competitively. In still other situations increased levels of concentration may even facilitate competitive conduct. Consider, for example, a merger that creates a second large firm more able to compete with the existing dominant incumbent or a situation in which a maverick firm obtains sufficient capacity in the post-merger situation to restrain a dominant firm or to restrict collusive conduct. Alternatively, dynamic considerations come into play when a merger involves the removal of a relatively small market participant who has played a significant role in maintaining a competitive market by undermining attempts to coordinate market conduct. The conduct of firms in the market depends also on non-structural variables specific to each firm, such as whether or not they are risk averse (the more risk averse they are, the more sensitive to loss of profits as a result of retaliation) and whether they need an immediate large cash flow.

The implications for merger policy are that unless we intend to characterize all mergers in concentrated industries as anti-competitive, the effects of all existing forces that create contestability in the market should be carefully analyzed. Small economies should thus refine their preliminary analysis of the possible anti-competitive effects of a merger, based on structural factors, by considering non-structural factors that have a bearing on the competitive restraints placed on firms operating in the market. These factors may include, inter alia, entry barriers, excess capacity, sophistication of buyers, suppliers, or others in a position to discipline market players, the competitive nature of the merging firms, changing market demand or supply of inputs, and additional sources of potential competition. Dynamic considerations may justify mergers in concentrated markets in which rivalry will still significantly constrain the market power of the merging parties. Alternatively, they may also justify preventing a concentration trend in a market characterized by high entry barriers from its incipiency, absent efficiency justifications.

The importance of nonstructural factors in assessing the anti-competitive effects of a merger—both unilateral power and coordinated conduct—can be illustrated by two cases, the Canadian *Hillsdown* decision[129] and the EC *Kali & Salz* decision.[130] In *Hillsdown* the Canadian tribunal found that the merger of two rendering operations did not substantially lessen competition despite an increase in the HHI from 1,594 to 3,608 and the fact that the merging parties had in excess of 56 percent of the post-merger productive capacity to render red meat material.[131] Notwithstanding high concentration levels, the tribunal found that the merged entity could not exercise unilateral market power since market demand was declining and competitors of the merged entity could either shift production among facilities to free up capacity or easily expand capacity to serve the relevant market.

The shortcomings of an analysis of collective market shares of participants to indicate the likelihood of oligopolistic conduct was acknowledged by the European Court of Justice in its *Kali & Salz* decision.[132] The court rejected the EC Commission's conclusion that the proposed merger would likely create a joint dominant position, a conclusion that was based primarily on a static analysis of structural market characteristics, without seeking to evaluate their significance in light of firm-specific and industry-specific factors and their effect on the interdependence of oligopolists. The case involved the proposed merger of two suppliers of potash. The commission found that, as a result of the merger, the merged entity and a French producer would hold a joint dominant position in the relevant market.[133] In support of its conclusion it focused mainly on the increase in market share and the degree of concentration. The combined market share of the merged entity and the French producer would increase to more than 60 percent. It further found that the supply of rival firms was fragmented, as domestic and foreign producers had low market shares and limited capacity, which would prevent, at least in the short run, any increase in their market shares. The commission also pointed to other factors facilitating collusion, such as the transparency of the market, the homogeneous character of the relevant product, the absence of technical innovation, and prior anti-competitive conduct by the merging parties.

The European Court of Justice annulled the commission's decision, stating that it was based on static factors and failed to take account of the dynamic factors inherent in the market that would make it difficult to facilitate oligopolistic coordination. Specifically, it concluded that the commission had failed to demonstrate to a sufficient legal standard that the merger would create joint dominance because of the existence of significant asymmetries between the parties that might decrease the likelihood of collusion or conscious parallelism by giving rise to conflicting interests. In the case at hand, the oligopolistic parties differed significantly with regard to market shares (23 percent and 37 percent), production capacity (60 percent and 20 percent), and levels of capacity utilization and reserves. These factors, coupled with the market's being in decline, meant that the static elements relied on by the commission did not support a conclusive finding of joint dominance. The court concluded that the commission could not simply rely on a checklist of descriptive factors indicating the theoretical risk of a merger or on the fact that market shares exceeded a certain threshold. Rather, it must rigorously analyze these factors in the dynamic context of the relevant economic facts of each specific case. Since it had failed to do so, the commission's decision was annulled.

It is important for small economies to consider the regulating effects of potential domestic or foreign rivals on the conduct of incumbent firms. If entry barriers are low and importers enjoy a significant cost advantage over domestic producers, contestability might provide sufficient checks on the exercise of market power, even in highly concentrated markets. This can be exemplified by the Australian decision in the *Amcor/Associated Pulp and Paper Mills* merger.[134] This merger made Amcor the only domestic manufacturer of paper and gave it ownership of four of the five largest paper merchants in Australia. The merger was approved, although it created high concentration levels within Australia, owing to the competitive constraints imposed on the merging parties by importers, even though they did not have high market shares in the Australian market at the time of the merger.

Small economies may thus choose to adopt a legal rule similar to the one included in the Canadian Competition Act which explicitly provides that a merger may not be found to be anti-competitive "solely on the basis of evidence of concentration or market shares."[135] The act reflects an implicit legislative rejection of the structuralist approach to market performance, which was seen as inappropriate, given the size of the Canadian economy. The Canadian provisions place the initial burden of proof that a merger is likely to lessen competition substantially on the competition authorities, which must prove both structural and nonstructural elements of the relevant mar-

Table 6.2 Market structure variables in merger analysis

Jurisdiction (listed by size)	Market share threshold	HHI	Turnover threshold	Evidentiary weight of structural variables
United States	CR4 75%, merging parties 4%–12%	1,800 and an increase of 100 points		Prima facie illegality
EC	Merging parties 40%		Aggregate world-wide turnover at least 5,000 million ECUs and community-wide turnover 250 million of at least two understakings, or aggregate world-wide turnover more than 2,500 million ECUs and additional conditions are met	Judicial rejection of reliance on structural variables alone
Canada	Merging parties 35% or 10% if CR4 65%			Legislative rejection of market structure variables as sole indicators
Australia	Merging parties 40% or 15% if CR4 75%			Rule of reason
New Zealand	Merging parties 20% and CR3 below 70%			Rule of reason
Israel	Merging parties 50%		50 million shequels	Rule of reason

ket. This is a correct allocation of burdens. At the same time, it should not preclude placing significant weight on concentration data so long as dynamic factors are also considered.

Table 6.2 incorporates all the market structure variables that have been adopted by different jurisdictions.

Special Concerns Raised by Large Conglomerate Mergers

The high levels of aggregate concentration and interdependence between large market players that are characteristic of small economies may raise special concerns in mergers among large conglomerates or firms controlled by them. Beyond the issues generally raised by mergers,[136] mergers among firms controlled by large conglomerates may lead to interdependent cooperative conduct between the parties that extends beyond the specific agreement by placing the parent firms in dangerous proximity to discuss and act jointly on broad aspects of their business and by creating an aura of cooperative team spirit that is apt to dampen competitive intensity between the firms involved.[137] The danger is especially high when the merged entity constitutes a significant part of the business of one or more of the conglomerates, as it should not be expected that parties that share much of their economic interests in one market will compete as vigorously as before in another.[138]

Conglomerates are likely to be the main challengers in small economies of incumbent monopolies by engaging in competition for the market. The substantial resources and varied experience of conglomerates enable them to enter new lines of activity more readily than a smaller firm, especially when entry barriers are high. For example, their vast financial means and diversified holdings portfolios enable their business units to take more risk in product development programs or in entry into new markets. In general, where there are many diversified enterprises, the incentive to compete is substantial and the opportunity to collude is slight. Where there are a few diversified enterprises, collusion is easier. And in a small economy there is room for only a few large diversified enterprises. Hence, unless foreign trade is significantly influential, such mergers should be looked on with considerable skepticism. Business transactions that may reduce future competition between these large players, even if they increase efficiency in the specific transaction at hand, should be analyzed in a broader perspective, which takes into account the long-term dampening of potential competition between conglomerates that can reduce the degree of contestability in the relevant markets and may even amount to cooperative or collusive behavior.

The special issues raised by conglomerate mergers in a small economy can be illustrated by the Israeli case of *Columbus Capital/Cur Industries*.[139] Cur Industries was a large Israeli conglomerate that controlled many firms which held monopoly positions in their respective markets (its firms produced 7 percent of the Israeli GDP). Columbus Capital is part of the Claridge group, which is an international company with many holdings in the Israeli market, some of which were shared with other conglomerates. Columbus sought to acquire Cur in order to become a major player in the market. The director of the Israeli Competition Authority analyzed the effects of the proposed merger on horizontal competition in markets in which both firms operated, as well as on the potential and existing competition among the merging parties themselves and with other firms in the market.

The crux of the issue was the effect of the proposed merger on competition among the large conglomerates. Before the merger three main conglomerates operated in the Israeli market. Given that each controlled a large set of monopolies in markets characterized by high entry barriers which could not be easily overcome by small rivals, the fear of potential competition from other conglomerates was crucial for constraining the strategic decisions of incumbent firms. Any business ties between firms controlled by the conglomerates could potentially reduce their inclination to enter into new markets in which another conglomerate held a dominant position. Accordingly, the director conditioned his approval of the merger on the severing of all ties of the merged entity with the other large conglomerates and on the merging firms' agreement to obtain his approval for any future business ties with another conglomerate.

International Dimensions of Merger Analysis

Lowered national barriers to international trade create competition policy issues that go well beyond national frontiers. Whereas in the past competition law issues were largely contained within national borders, justifying doctrines that are based on the assumption that the law stops at a nation's borders, today's business is increasingly global.

One of the most fascinating and complicated issues created by increased levels of world trade involves the regulation of firm conduct (e.g., cartels, mergers, abuse of dominance) with extraterritorial effects. Firms in one country may engage in conduct that imposes costs or benefits on other jurisdictions. Beyond enforcement and jurisdictional power issues, substantial questions arise as to how the effects of the conduct on different jurisdictions should be evaluated and taken into account.

Small size exacerbates the importance of these issues. The large proportion of foreign-produced products traded in a small economy and the reduced ability of domestic market forces to regulate foreign importers effectively often imply that the anti-competitive conduct of dominant foreign importers will have strong negative effects on the small jurisdictions with which they trade, without significant offsetting efficiencies. In this section I use the example of mergers that have extraterritorial effects to identify the problems faced by small economies and to examine the legal tools available to them to combat anti-competitive conduct by foreign firms that affects them significantly.

Extraterritorial mergers can be divided into four main groups in accordance with their welfare effects. The first type reduces the welfare of both the home jurisdiction and other jurisdictions in which the firms trade. To illustrate, assume that two firms holding a dominant position in all or most of the markets in which they operate merge but without achieving significant efficiencies. The second type of merger enhances or has no negative effect on the welfare of all jurisdictions in which the merging parties trade. This can be the case when the merging firms face strong competition in all their markets. The third type creates mixed effects: the proposed merger has positive or neutral welfare effects on the home jurisdiction and negative effects on all or some foreign jurisdictions. This may occur, for example, when the merging firms face strong competition in their domestic market but face limited competition in certain countries in which they operate owing to limited demand and entry barriers. The fourth type creates the opposite mixed effects: negative welfare effects in the home jurisdiction and positive effects in foreign jurisdictions. This may be the case when high trade barriers at home prevent the entry of foreign producers that compete effectively with the merging parties in other markets.

The first two types of merger are easy cases. The decision of the home jurisdiction, assuming that merger control is interpreted and applied in all jurisdictions involved in a similar manner, coincides with the interests of the foreign jurisdiction. Major international mergers that fall under these categories are likely to be stopped by overseas authorities of large jurisdictions. The difficult cases arise in the third and fourth types of extraterritorial mergers, as different jurisdictions may have divergent interests and reach conflicting decisions. For example, if the firms of one jurisdiction have monopoly power in world markets, that jurisdiction may have strong incentives to promote anti-competitive activity, thereby increasing national wealth at the expense of foreigners.

Let us consider the Unilever–Best Foods merger, between a European and an American food producer. The merger was approved by the EC and the United States, as it did not raise anti-competitive concerns in their markets. Its effects on some small economies with which the merging entities traded were nonetheless significant. For example, the merger substantially lessened competition in the Israeli market, given that it was preceded by the merging of Best-Foods with the Israeli firm of Strauss Ice Creams, in which Elite is a shareholder, and the merger of the Israeli firm of Tami with Unilever. Elite and Tami are two dominant competitors in some Israeli food markets. The merger raised concerns regarding its effects on competition in the Israeli market—both the strengthening of a food conglomerate as well as the lessening of competition in several specific food markets, such as those for chocolate and snacks.[140]

Most jurisdictions adopt a concept of outbound extraterritoriality, which enables them to apply their own competition policy to regulate offshore conduct with significant domestic anti-competitive effects, even if the conduct occurred outside their borders.[141] Outbound extraterritoriality is, however, a limited tool in small economies. Small economies usually cannot prevent a merger with anti-competitive effects from occurring by unilateral action, as they face severe challenges to effective prosecution. The main problem is that small economies can rarely make a credible threat to prohibit a merger of foreign firms. Given that trade in the small economy is usually only a small part of the foreign firm's total world operation, were the small jurisdiction to place significant restrictions on the merger, the foreign firm would most likely choose to exit the small economy and trade only in other jurisdictions. That is, the foreign firm will exit the small economy if its loss of revenues from terminating its trade there is smaller than the increase of revenues it anticipates as a result of the proposed merger elsewhere. Also, the negative welfare effects of the foreign firm's exit from the small economy may well be greater than the welfare effects from the continued operation of the merged entity within its borders. Accordingly, a small economy usually does not have an incentive to prevent the firm from trading within its borders if it did merge. The foreign firm, acknowledging this, will not take into account in its merging decision the effect of that decision on the small economy. It will consider only the effects of the merger on its own profits in such a market.

In addition, political obstacles might also stand in the way of a small economy's attempt to prevent a merger among foreign firms. If the effects of such a merger are positive in the home jurisdiction or in other jurisdictions (e.g., higher taxes, lower unemployment, lower production costs), the small economy might encounter political resistance to its policy, especially because foreign firms have an advantage in shaping public opinion in their home jurisdiction. This consideration is based on a presumption that the small economy's size is positively correlated with its political power.

Unilateral enforcement of merger control by large jurisdictions does not provide a solution to the enforcement problems of small economies. While extraterritorial reach is generally wide with regard to the actions of foreign firms that harm domestic consumers and producers, it is generally extremely limited with regard to the regulation of the activities of domestic firms that have anti-competitive effects on foreign jurisdictions. Outbound extraterritoriality is rarely complemented by a national treatment principle for the nation's exporters and investors abroad, which mandates domestic authorities to regulate nationals that harm foreigners on foreign soil. Thus, most jurisdictions' evaluation of a merger is limited to the welfare effects of the merger on domestic consumers and/or producers and disregards the effects on foreign consumers and producers.[142]

Even if large jurisdictions were to adopt a national treatment rule, the standards or goals of merger review might still produce outcomes that do not coincide with the interests of small economies. For example, a merger policy that adopts an absolute value of competition approach may produce totally different results than a policy that adopts a balancing approach. Alternatively, nations may achieve adverse outcomes even if they apply similar principles owing to disagreements on underlying facts or different interpretations of common standards. Unilateral application of national law thus usually does not solve issues of extraterritorial mergers with mixed effects for small economies. Also, taking account of the effects of a merger on other jurisdictions in national courts is very problematic because the home jurisdiction does not have the tools or the information necessary to evaluate the effects of a merger on all the jurisdictions in which the merging entity trades or will potentially trade in the near future.

The problem of limited national vision affects small economies more significantly than large ones, as a large percentage of products in small economies is either imported from foreign jurisdictions or produced by subsidiaries of firms located in them. This fact, combined with the limited contestability exerted on foreign traders by domestic producers located in small economies, implies that mergers of dominant foreign firms that trade in a small economy may well reduce competition considerably without significant offsetting efficiencies. Even if the increase in market power is accompanied by increased efficiencies, these will rarely be realized by the small economy, as in many cases the production facilities are located outside its borders.

Small economies are very limited in their ability to prevent foreign extraterritorial mergers that negatively affect their domestic markets. Unilateral action is problematic, and most existing bilateral or multilateral agreements adopt positive comity principles, under which foreign nations and persons adversely affected by anti-competitive activities occurring in the territory of another party and contrary to the competition laws of that party may request it to investigate and, if warranted, to remedy these activities in accordance with its competition rules. Positive comity provides means to root out a common evil when there is a preexisting disposition to cooperate and to overcome the problem of nonenforcement or discriminatory enforcement by foreign jurisdictions. Yet it has limited effect when the merger policy principles adopted by the cooperating jurisdictions differ significantly from one another or such merger principles do not take into account the effects of the proposed merger on foreign jurisdictions. Positive comity thus does not reduce the concerns of small economies with regard to extraterritorial mergers with negative effects on their domestic markets.

Another alternative a small economy faces is political: to join forces with other jurisdictions to create a credible threat to a merger that reduces welfare in all of them. If a sufficient number of jurisdictions join forces to prevent such a merger, then this might create strong enough economic incentives for firms to abandon attempts to merge. For such an action to pose a credible threat, the prospect of limited access to such economies must have a sufficient effect on the merged entities' profitability to offset the gains from the proposed merger in other jurisdictions. Also, all jurisdictions must be prepared to block the entry of the merged entity into their markets in the event that the merger goes through. The fact that the welfare effects on one jurisdiction are not interrelated with the welfare effects on another eliminates some of the coordination problems that are present in other cooperative agreements. Political pressures from the merging entity's jurisdiction on some of the cooperating jurisdictions and informational problems may, however, reduce the possibility that they will act on their threat.

Alternatively, small economies should advocate the adoption of a multilateral dispute resolution system that would take into account the global effects of a merger. Such proposals are likely to be raised in the next round of WTO negotiations, which will focus, inter alia, on trade and competition policy.[143] Several obstacles may, however, stand in the way of the adoption of such a system. Even if it would be possible to reach a consensus on unified antitrust principles, nations would be reluctant to lose their sovereignty by relinquishing decision making to unknown and perhaps untrusted bureaucrats. It should also be noted that although this option can reduce the approval of extraterritorial mergers with negative domestic welfare effects, it would not prevent the approval of all mergers that have anti-competitive effects on a small economy. It may well be that a merger has positive effects in most of the jurisdictions in which it operates, in which case it will most likely be approved. Also, there are no clear guidelines as to how to quantify and measure the effects on different jurisdictions. Possible standards may include comparison of welfare effects on a per dollar basis, or of the proportional impact of the merger on total welfare in each jurisdiction.

The efficient regulation of merger policy was also the first item on the agenda of the International Competition Network, created in 2001, which strives to enhance cooperation among antitrust agencies around the world.[144] It was hoped that under this framework the issues of smaller economies would be dealt with effectively.

Until that happens, the most plausible way for small economies to treat extraterritorial mergers is to take changes in the market structures of their large importers as a given and to attempt to regulate the merged entities with the existing regulatory tools that relate to the actions of foreign firms within their domestic markets, although such tools are generally more costly and less effective than prohibiting the merger from occurring. This implies that conduct-regulatory measures play a more significant role in the competition policy of small economies than large ones.

One option is the imposition of structural and behavioral conditions on the merging parties that apply only to their operation within the small economy. In *Tozeret Mazon/Unilever*,[145] for example, the Israeli Competition Authority conditioned its approval of the merger between the U.S. and European food companies on limitations of joint business activity between Elite and Tami, the two Israeli food companies that became, as a result of the merger, parts of the same international food conglomerate. The conditions included limiting information transfer and maintaining a structural and personal division between the two Israeli firms. Similarly, when Unilever next acquired control over Ben & Jerry's and the merger raised concerns regarding competition in the Israeli ice cream market, the Competition Authority conditioned its approval on the distribution of Ben & Jerry's ice cream in Israel through an independent distributor that would be free to determine prices charged for the products. The authority also required that the quality and quantity of the products be at least as high as before the merger, and that any new product would be made available to the distributor.[146] These are limited remedies since they cannot totally erase the fact that both firms are controlled by the same entity that determines their strategic decisions. At the same time, the small economy often relies on the fact that an international firm will not change its strategic decisions (such as Ben & Jerry's introduction of a new product in world markets) only to reduce competition in the small economy.

In Australia, the ACCC has gone even further and imposed structural remedies to combat the anti-competitive effects of offshore mergers. The Australian case of *Rothmans/British American Tobacco*[147] provides an interesting and unique example in which a structural remedy was operational. The proposed acquisition of the Rothmans group by British American Tobacco did not create competition concerns in the major jurisdictions in which the firms operated and thus was not blocked. The merger nonetheless created significant competition concerns in Australia, as the market share of the merged companies would have been around 65 percent, with only one major competitor left in the cigarette market. The Australian competition authority agreed to approve the merger only after the merged parties agreed to divest cigarette brands and production and distribution facilities to an amount equal to 17 percent of the Australian market. The brands and facilities located in Australia were then acquired by a major international tobacco company that had not previously traded in the Australian market. The merger thus went ahead while competition in the domestic market was retained.

Conclusion

Merger policy is an important tool for regulating anti-competitive conduct by preventing the creation of market structures that are prone to increase the potential for such conduct. The limited efficiency of conduct-related measures in small economies increases the need for optimal merger control. At the same time, the special characteristics of small economies create difficult balances in the formulation of an efficient merger policy. As many industries are characterized by highly concentrated market structures justified by scale and scope economies in which further cost reductions can be achieved through merger, merger policy should be accommodating to efficiency considerations and at the same time wary of increased concentrations that are not justified by resource savings. Accordingly, a small economy does not enjoy the same elbow room in policy making that a larger economy does. The main policy prescriptions for small economies' merger policy that meet these goals can be summarized as follows:

1. Merger policy should be based on the recognition of the fact that mergers in small economies are a major tool for the realization of potential efficiencies in oligopolistic markets that would otherwise remain unexploited owing to cooperative profit-maximizing strategies that limit the incentives of firms to grow to optimal sizes.
2. Small economies should adopt an approach to merger policy that balances the anti-competitive effects of the merger against the efficiencies it creates or other sociopolitical goals.
3. Small size strengthens the case for the adoption of a total

welfare standard, which balances producer and consumer welfare.

4. Merger policy should avoid rigid structural presumptions that high concentration levels are necessarily welfare-reducing. Rather, nonstructural dynamic factors that have bearing on the competitive restraints placed on firms operating in the market should be given significant weight.

5. An important consideration that must be taken into account is the existing level of market power and the increase in such power that is likely to arise from the merger. Given that many industries are already concentrated, mergers should be evaluated not against a benchmark of theoretically competitive conditions, but rather against the rational market structure options in the specific market setting. A merger that merely preserves existing power over price should not be seen as lessening competition unless it limits potential foreseeable competition.

6. Strict assumptions and heavy burdens of proof may well reduce efficiency considerations to a theoretical possibility. Accordingly, the conditions for realizing efficiencies, including the stringency of the burden of proof, the evidentiary weight attached to structural factors, the balancing standard, and the conditions for cognizable efficiencies, should be set at a level that allows practical proof of offsetting efficiencies. The solution may lie in the adoption of a sliding-scale approach in which, as the danger of an increase in the exercise of market power rises, the burden of proof of efficiencies rises accordingly.

7. Pre-merger consultation proceedings can increase the number of welfare-increasing mergers and should be adopted by small economies.

8. Conglomerate mergers should be evaluated in light of the potential dampening of competition between the merging parties in other markets controlled by them.

9. Small economies have limited tools to combat extraterritorial mergers with anti-competitive effects. They should thus advocate the adoption of global effects rules or a multinational merger control regime, or join forces with other economies to prevent a welfare-reducing extraterritorial merger. Alternatively, they may use conduct or structural remedies that apply only within their economy.

As I have emphasized throughout this chapter, optimal regulation of merger activity is especially important in light of the lowering of trade barriers that create competitive pressures to adapt to new market conditions. Merger policy should thus recognize the valuable role mergers play in allowing industries to adapt to changing circumstances and the costs of inhibiting such transactions. At the same time, increased openness to trade creates new issues with regard to extraterritorial mergers with negative effects on small economies that are just beginning to be addressed in world forums.

Conclusion

Now, here, you see, it takes all the running you can do, to keep in the same place. If you want to get somewhere else, you must run at least twice as fast as that!

—LEWIS CARROLL, *Alice Through the Looking-Glass*

The goal of this book has been to determine whether the size of an economy matters for optimal competition policy. As has been shown, the answer is unequivocally affirmative: the high concentration levels and high entry barriers into many markets in small economies often require a different balancing of conflicting considerations than in large ones. Small economies have to "run at least twice as fast" as large economies: they have to keep up with ever-changing competition policy models, often formulated for large economies, and have to ensure that these models achieve the goals of competition policy in their own markets.

In this chapter I restate some of my policy prescriptions for small economies and analyze their practical and theoretical implications in a broader setting than was adopted throughout this book. The first section provides a brief reprise of the major policy prescriptions. It also points to several other elements that should complement substantive competition law, such as efficient institutions and educating the general public and the business community in the goals and tools of competition policy. The next two sections analyze the incentives for and the implications of the adoption of the laws of large jurisdictions by small ones, and the implications of this book for global or regional harmonization of competition laws. These two issues are related, given the ability of large jurisdictions to impress their will (and competition laws) on smaller economies. The chapter concludes with an analysis of the relevance of my findings for small markets within large jurisdictions.

Economic Size Matters for Optimal Competition Policy

The size of an economy affects optimal competition policy—from the choice of policy goals to rules of thumb. The main factor that creates the need to tailor competition law to economic size is that competition laws generally consist of "one-size-fits-all" formulations that are designed to best achieve the goals of the law in each category of cases to which they apply (mergers, cartels, dominant position, and so on), while recognizing that some false positives and false negatives will occur at the margin. The marginal cases of large economies, however, constitute the mainstream cases for small economies, as small size magnifies the occurrence of highly concentrated markets protected by entry barriers. This requires small economies to change the focus of their competition laws to regulate such markets efficiently. Accordingly, even if all economies reach a consensus that the basic objective of competition policy is to protect and preserve competition as the most appropriate means of ensuring the efficient allocation of resources, the natural conditions of the market—mainly the high degree of concentration and the height of entry barriers—affect the optimal rules that regulate the business conduct of market players.[1] Whether firms compete is very much a matter of the structure of the markets in which they operate, and structure is influenced primarily by the natural conditions of the market.

The thread that connects all the strands of this book is the need to recognize the inevitability of concentrated market structures that are protected by high entry barriers in many of their markets and that are often justified by productive and dynamic efficiency. Small economies should take the concentrated nature of their markets as a necessary evil while striving to reduce the occurrence of anti-competitive conduct by firms operating under such market conditions. This necessitates a more refined trade-off between production constraints on the number of sellers and the undesirability of certain types of conduct brought about by high degrees of concentration for allocative and dynamic efficiency. Most of the effects of small size require small but significant changes to existing doctrines, assumptions, or modes of enforcement that are adopted in large economies. Some changes nonetheless involve the adoption of regulatory methods that are absent from large economies. Here is a brief reprise of the main policy prescriptions for small economies.

Small size increases the importance of efficiency as a stand-alone goal, as small economies are less able than their larger counterparts to afford a competition policy that is prepared to sacrifice economic efficiency for broader policy objectives. Undeviating pursuit of wealth dispersion and small size of firms at the expense of efficiency will be costly in small economies because inefficient firms will be preserved in the market, and thus the market will operate inefficiently. When high concentration levels are justified by scale and scope economies, protection of competition would, for example, blockade many mergers that have positive welfare effects. In many markets producers would not be able to attain minimum efficient scales and thus reduce their costs, and consumers would not be able to enjoy lower prices that rest on such lower costs. Also, competition law efforts to preserve small business units over more efficient larger rivals would often be futile without costly ongoing regulation, because these inefficient firms would either exit the market or grow internally to efficient size. The importance of economic efficiency as a stand-alone objective is also highlighted in a small economy in which interdependencies in the interests of various stakeholders are likely to be more significantly affected by a particular market transaction. The risk of costly industrial policy in the guise of competition policy is increased when non-economic considerations play a role in competition law enforcement.

The highly concentrated nature of many markets, which is often justified by scale and scope economies, also has other implications for merger policy. A stringent merger policy might inhibit or preclude a broad spectrum of useful market structures that may increase efficiency by way of ownership of plants or firms of sub-optimal size which enables firms to achieve scale economies. In small economies mergers are a major tool for the realization of potential efficiencies in oligopolistic markets that would otherwise remain unexploited because of cooperative profit-maximizing strategies that limit the incentives of firms to grow to optimal size internally. Accordingly, presumptions of anti-competitive effects based on high levels of concentration, which almost always produce strong predispositions toward the condemnation of mergers in concentrated markets, should be rejected and much more emphasis should be placed on efficiency considerations. At the same time, an excessively lenient merger policy might make possible the creation of highly concentrated market structures that are not easily eroded by market forces and that reduce efficiency. Merger policy should thus be accommodating to efficiency considerations and at the same time wary of increased concentration that is not justified by resource savings or that might have long-term anti-competitive effects. I have also suggested that small economies should prefer a total welfare over a consumer welfare approach. Similar principles should apply to the regulation of joint ventures.

Small economies should be sensitive, too, to anti-competitive restraints that arise from their unique characteristics. To illustrate, a small economy should exhibit a strong concern toward the concentration of ownership of its conglomerates, beyond competition concerns in specific industries, as conglomerates are frequently the main challengers to incumbent monopolies, which are often controlled by other conglomerates.

The concentrated nature of the market also reduces the effectiveness of applying structural remedies to market imperfections. To try to restructure an inevitable monopoly is pointless and inefficient. After deconcentration, either some firm would expand to take advantage of the opportunity for lower costs with larger output until the market was again concentrated, or else the market would operate permanently at an unnecessarily high level of costs.

The limited effectiveness of structural remedies and the limited self-correcting powers of many markets in small economies increase the need for effective conduct regulation. Monopoly and oligopoly should be tolerated, as they are often necessary to achieve productive and dynamic efficiency. Nonetheless, their conduct should be closely scrutinized to minimize the creation of artificial barriers to competition.

An important task of competition policy in small economies is the regulation of monopolies, be they natural monopolies or not. Given the economic teachings that determine the incipiency of monopolies in a small market and the length of time it might take market forces to erode such monopoly power, a small economy might not be able to afford to leave the regulation of monopoly power to market forces alone. One regulatory method that might be employed by small economies involves conduct regulation that does not require anti-competitive intent, under which specified trading conditions constitute in themselves a cause for regulation. Such a law focuses solely on the harm to consumers or to competition. In so doing, the law creates safeguards from monopolistic activity while not condemning monopoly per se. Yet conduct regulation is a highly problematic tool in that it creates disincentive effects for firms to become monopolies. It should thus not be lightly adopted. Nonetheless, it may be justified in some situations, provided it meets some specified conditions.

Small size also dictates that certain types of exclusionary conduct be analyzed differently than in large economies. To give but one example, price discrimination should be allowed when it is necessary for a firm to break down oligopolistic coordination. Small economies should also regulate exclusionary conduct that is likely to lead to the creation of market power, as well as exclusionary conduct that maintains or strengthens existing market power. I argued, too, that given the limited effect of the market's invisible hand in many of their markets, small economies should exercise caution when applying remedies, to avoid creating a more concentrated market structure or increasing entry barriers into the market. I also suggested that small economies increase the early detection of abusive conduct by requiring large, dominant firms to report their major business activities to the competition authorities on a regular basis, or by creating alternative mechanisms that increase the personal incentives of managers in complying with the law.

Another important task involves the regulation of oligopolies. The limited number of firms that can operate in a small market necessarily increases their interdependence and their interdependent conduct. Even in the absence of explicit restrictive agreements, there is little room for effective domestic competition, as conscious parallelism may be all that is needed to facilitate interdependent conduct. Accordingly, the traditional prohibitions against collusion should be applied strictly. Such a policy may help break down oligopolistic coordination and induce oligopolists to operate at higher levels of output and lower prices than they would have but for the legal consequences. Yet the limited effectiveness of the prohibitions against collusive conduct in regulating conscious parallelism creates a strong need for the adoption of additional regulatory methods. One method that was suggested is the adoption of a prohibition against facilitating practices that have no or minimal offsetting pro-competitive effects. I also suggested that under certain market condition, small economies might introduce a government-supported maverick into an oligopolistic industry. This novel method may be used to combat oligopoly pricing by creating rivalry among the few that eliminates most of the problems of other proposed solutions. As I showed, the maverick model possesses great potential to increase allocative and even productive efficiency significantly in oligopolistic markets.

Small size also affects the accuracy of rules of thumb adopted by large economies, such as indicators of market dominance based on market share. In a small economy, the *typical* market share that signifies market dominance is smaller than in a large one, given the lower elasticity of supply owing to the prevalence of scale economies and oligopolistic interdependence. In other words, the smaller the market, the higher the barriers to entry usually are (lower elasticity of supply), and therefore the lesser the constraints that potential entry places on a firm that attempts to raise price above marginal cost, and the smaller the market shares necessary to infer dominant market power. Accordingly, given that the market's invisible hand has limited disciplinary power in concentrated structures, a specifically tailored competition law has an important role to play by setting clear rules of conduct and ensuring their effective application in practice.

Substantive law, on which this book focused, is the basic tool for competition policy. Nonetheless, several complementary elements have to be present to create a welfare-enhancing competition policy. These include competent and adequately empowered institutions as well as the creation of incentives and opportunities for all classes of market players to become familiar with the competition laws. Although such elements are beyond the scope of this book, several observations are noted here.

The creation of competent institutions that apply competition policy is highly important, as otherwise what has been gained by the creation of optimal competition policy will be lost by misguided enforcement. Many of the tasks that need to be performed by a competition authority or court in a small economy require careful balancing of competing considerations. In addition, large sectors of the economy are likely to come under the scrutiny of the competition authority, given high levels of concentration and high entry barriers in many industries. This implies that a competent competition authority and competition court are necessary elements to achieve the goals of competition policy and constitute a good investment for a small economy.

Reducing the extent of anti-competitive conduct engaged in by dominant firms by setting the "rules of the game" correctly in some exemplary cases and increasing levels of detection and enforcement may well prove much less costly than relying on market forces to correct market imperfections. Moreover, the fact that many competition rules apply similarly across different markets and that setting the rules correctly in one market creates positive enforcement externalities for other markets significantly reduces the costs of enforcing competition policy.

Enforcement is likely to be enhanced by appointing experts in industrial organization and competition policy to the competition authority; by creating a specialized judicial body that is empowered to hear competition law cases and is composed, inter alia, of economic experts; by ensuring that an appellate court has a limited mandate to overrule economic issues decided by the specialized judicial body; and by providing the competition authority with sufficient tools necessary to achieve its goals, such as investigatory powers and adequate resources.

Measures that are designed to educate the general public and the business community about the goals and the substantive content of competition policy are also very important for furthering the goals of competition policy. Such measures can increase detection and enforcement levels when resources are limited or when violations can easily be detected by consumers or competitors. They also lay the groundwork for understanding and appreciating the benefits associated with market regulation, and they familiarize market participants with the tools available to combat anti-competitive conduct. Educating the public in the benefits of competition might also be a fruitful investment as it may refocus the political interests of politicians on long-term and general goals and lead to the channeling of their private aspirations in more constructive and overall efficient ways. Even if politicians may not look beyond the next election, the interests of many who elect them may be long-term and non-sector-specific. Education thus has the effects of lengthening the politicians' time horizon.[2]

Antitrust authorities play an important role in this education process, as they may utilize their resources to make their decisions clear and open to all and to educate consumer groups, businessmen, and academia alike on the merits of antitrust enforcement. Such educational programs may include, for example, workshops and seminars for the executives of dominant firms to update them on significant changes in the legal regime; open communication lines for consumers and rivals to report alleged violations to the competition agency; and transparency and dissemination of information through the publication of important decisions.

Adoption of Competition Laws of Large Jurisdictions

The main thesis of this book is that the size of the economy should influence the content of its competition law. This conclusion raises the question whether small economies should, as they commonly do, adopt the laws or rely on the case law of larger jurisdictions.

Adopting the competition law of a large jurisdiction has many advantages, such as providing a ready basis for the law and a large body of comprehensive case law and commentary. In addition to these learning externalities, such adoption also generates network externalities that accrue to all jurisdictions utilizing the law. Network externalities are the increasing returns to users of a product as the number of users grows. As more decisions that apply the law to various factual settings begin to accumulate, legal certainty is increased. These network externalities are forward-looking. They are especially important in the area of competition law, which is characterized by elastic and open-ended notions that are often applied on a case-by-case basis. EC and U.S. competition laws, being the most widely used, thus have a value to other jurisdictions that exceeds their face value as judged by the clarity and comprehensibility of their provisions and current case law. Accordingly, adoption of the competition law of large jurisdictions will always confer an advantage on another economy.

Another possible reason for adopting the laws of large jurisdictions is herding behavior. If legislators are not certain what makes for optimal law, they may follow a popular trend. The complexity of the law and the fragile balance that must be struck between competing considerations make information about optimal laws costly. Jurisdictions may find following others to be a convenient alternative to incurring these costs. This has been exacerbated by the fact that there was no resource that systematically analyzed the policy implications of small size.

Adopting the competition laws of larger jurisdictions is also sometimes predicated on the existence of the hegemonic power of a large jurisdiction with the ability to impress its will, and its competition policy, on smaller and weaker jurisdictions. This phenomenon is especially pronounced in the EC. By requiring the adoption of an EC-compatible competition law as a condition for gaining access to its markets, either through trade agreements or outright membership,[3] the EC has been a driving force in the enactment of competition laws beyond its borders that are based on its model. As a result, many jurisdictions have adopted the EC model without changing it to be compatible with their special characteristics.

Accordingly, many small economies have adopted the statutes and regulations of large jurisdictions and refer to their case law for interpretation. Some small economies have gone further and adopted not just the current law of a large jurisdiction but future law as well, blindly committing themselves to future changes and court decisions.[4] This is not just politically problematic but creates a host of practical problems, such as the coherence of case law and the issue of retroactive relief when matters resolved by the importing economy's courts are subsequently resolved differently by the other economy's courts.

Adopting the laws of large jurisdictions thus involves major pitfalls. As I have demonstrated, the most important problem is that insufficient weight is given to the special characteristics of the small economy, which differ significantly from those of a large one. The costs of adopting the law of a large jurisdiction are influenced, inter alia, by the initial quality of the law and its variance from the optimal law for the small economy. When such laws are open-ended and flexible, they can be interpreted to fit the special characteristics of small economies. The price of such interpretation is, of course, the loss of some of the benefits of adopting the law of a large jurisdiction in the first place.

Harmonization of Competition Laws

The conclusions of this book also sharpen the question, which is the focus of recent debate, whether competition law can and should be unified and harmonized on a global or regional basis. To reduce obstacles to trade, many suggestions have been made—by both scholars and government officials—for bringing about a higher level of convergence of competition policies among jurisdictions. The proposed solutions range from national law enforcement that accounts for global impacts[5] to the harmonization of competition policies.[6]

Two developments have brought this debate to the forefront. The first is the recognition by the WTO Ministerial Conference of the need for a "multilateral framework to enhance the contribution of competition policy to international trade and development."[7] The second involves the establishment of an International Competition Network by the competition authorities of many jurisdictions for the enhancement of international cooperation and the reduction of trade barriers.[8] Will a unified competition law be welfare-maximizing for small economies? The answer is not straightforward.

An important consideration in favor of harmonization is a reduction in compliance costs. A patchwork of national antitrust rules has become a barrier to international business. Expanding trade by reducing multiple compliance costs may permit the realization of economies of scale in production and distribution, the attainment of network efficiencies, and the realization of regulatory economies. This consideration is especially important for small economies, as they stand to gain more from convergence than large ones. Harmonization may aid domestic firms located in small economies to export their products, as it reduces their costs of learning which competition law issues they might face in foreign economies. Export opportunities might be the only possible way for such firms to realize scale and scope economies. Moreover, if the competition laws of small economies diverge significantly from those of large ones, it might not be profitable for an importer to invest resources in learning the competition laws of small economies because the compliance costs may be high relative to the profits to be had from a small market. Imports are a pro-efficiency force because they can create contestability even in highly concentrated markets. Overall, small economies have a strong incentive to reduce compliance costs.

Several premises, however, motivate a relatively cautious view toward trade policy–driven harmonization. To achieve clear and unified rules, all jurisdictions might be required to adopt similar competition rules and ensure their harmonized interpretation and application. This implies the suppression of the particularistic policy choices of different jurisdictions as well as the loss of substantial national political autonomy. When negotiations occur between jurisdictions with asymmetric bargaining power, they also carry a serious risk of grossly discounting the considerations of smaller, weaker economies.

This book has revealed an additional cost of harmonization beyond general principles—the inadequacy of "one-size-fits-all" competition rules for different-sized economies, unless such principles are stated at a high level of generality. The differences in optimal competition policy between large and small economies may necessitate the setting of rules that are flexible enough to apply without jeopardizing the special needs of small economies.

Accordingly, there is an important trade-off between adopting clear competition rules that will apply similarly to all jurisdictions and adopting general principles that have the potential to increase domestic welfare in all jurisdictions but may be interpreted and applied in a dissimilar manner by different-sized economies. A wide array of options is available. At one end of the continuum lies complete deference to national sovereigns. At the other lies total harmonization. In between these extremes lie many alternatives that impose greater or lesser constraints on nations while still affording some opportunity for variations across nations. Under many of these options national authorities are largely free to pursue their own policy objectives but must do so subject to a set of broadly applicable legal constraints.

A relatively cautious approach to the harmonization or convergence of competition law might be justified. A bedrock of principles that could accommodate different shades of competition policy may be welfare-enhancing for small economies. The adopted policy should allow its administrators enough flexibility to deal with dissimilar situations in a different manner while creating a clear framework within which firms can operate efficiently. Otherwise the costs of policy convergence or equivalence may well outweigh its benefits and reduce domestic welfare.

Small size also affects the enforcement tools that should be adopted. As we have seen, small economies cannot always make a credible threat to prohibit a merger or an export cartel of foreign firms. Given that trade in the small economy is usually only a small part of the foreign firm's total world operation, were the small economy to place significant restrictions on the foreign firm's conduct, the firm would most likely choose to exit the economy. Also, the negative welfare effects of the firm's exit from the small economy may well be greater than the negative welfare effects from the continued operation of the firm within its borders. Thus, a small economy usually cannot credibly threaten that a firm will be prevented from trading within its borders if it does not comply with local competition laws. It will also not be welfare-enhancing to do so. The foreign firm, acknowledging this fact, will not take into account in its decision the effect of its conduct on the small economy. In addition, political obstacles might also stand in the way of a small economy's attempt to prevent a merger or an export cartel among foreign firms. If the effects of such conduct are positive in the home jurisdiction or in other jurisdictions (higher taxes, lower unemployment, lower production costs), it might encounter political resistance to its policy, especially since foreign firms have an advantage in shaping public opinion in their home jurisdiction. This consideration is based on a presumption that the small economy's size is positively correlated to its political power. Similarly, small economies often face problems in regulating the anticompetitive conduct of multinational firms that serve a large part of their domestic demand. Several large corporations, for example, have declined to sign an agreement that limits their conduct in Israel which contains the same terms that were included in the agreements they reached with the EC Commission.

One conclusion is that harmonized rules that rely for their enforcement on unilateral actions taken by the harmed jurisdiction would create a disadvantage to small economies. Such rules do not meet the concerns of small economies with regard to the negative effects of extraterritorial conduct on their domestic markets. To deal effectively with at least some of the enforcement problems of small economies, harmonized rules should include a regulation that forbids export cartels. Global or regional dispute settlement mechanisms that base their judgments on the welfare effects of the challenged practice on all economies affected may also solve some of the problems of small economies.

The practical importance of recognizing the differences between large and small economies arises from the fact that a large percentage of products produced in small economies is either imported from other jurisdictions or produced by subsidiaries of firms located in foreign jurisdictions, mostly large ones. This fact, combined with the limited regulatory pressure that is exerted on foreign traders by domestic producers located in a small economy, implies that the conduct of dominant foreign firms that trade in a small economy may well reduce competition significantly in the small economy without offsetting efficiencies. Even if the increase in market power is accompanied by increased efficiencies, these will rarely be realized by the small economy, as in many cases the production facilities are located outside its borders.

Recognizing the unique traits of small economies is thus crucial for the creation of a balanced multilateral antitrust regime. Laws that are based on a presumption that competition policies of all countries would have been similar absent political or social goals that impinge on efficiency-based policy prescriptions disregard some of the basic issues of harmonization. As the harmonization process has already begun to take shape, recognition of the differences between large and small economies is both important and timely.

The Relevance of Issues to Small Markets within Large Jurisdictions

Concentrated markets protected by high entry barriers can also be found within large economies. In some cases market conditions may create regional sub-markets within large economies, in which the supply price of products can vary, to a large degree, independently of price elsewhere. In other cases, though rare, demand conditions in an industry may support the operation of only a relatively small number of firms. The inherent characteristics of these two types of markets are similar, in many respects, to those of small-scale market economies.

Market segmentation can severely limit the competitive pressures on domestic firms in two ways. First, it limits producers' sales horizons, increases their dependence on one another's behavior, and inhibits the construction of optimal-sized plants. Second, it restrains the entry of outside producers and thus prevents distant suppliers from forcing local firms to hold down their prices and hence permit higher prices locally. These two effects can segregate sub-markets to the point where monopoly or oligopoly is inevitable. Thus, when a small regional market develops within a large economy, it is likely to have similar problems of market structure and performance as country-wide jurisdictions.

Several factors may subdivide national markets into small regional markets isolated from competition from firms operating in other regions. Regional sub-markets exist mainly because of geographic conditions (e.g., seas, high mountain ranges, isolated areas), which create high transportation costs. Transportation costs render trade with other regions irrelevant when such costs are high relative to the value of the good or service. The higher the transportation cost in relation to the price of the product, the freer firms are to charge supracompetitive prices. Crucial variables that affect transportation costs include the efficiency of available transportation modes, the geographic density and configuration of demand in relation to critical raw material sources, and the practices sellers formally or informally adopt to differentiate prices spatially and to make the best of the established price structure. Studies have shown that in several industries in large economies, transportation costs were sufficiently high that regional markets provided the main framework within which plant-scale decisions were made.[9] The cement market is one of the most striking examples. Because of relatively low costs of production and high costs of transportation, cement markets are usually local. Another fragmenting influence on national markets is caused by geographic conditions coupled with the perishability of products. When a product cannot be shipped over long distances, the market for it is inherently regional.

The small size of a market can also result from service markets that are local in the sense that consumers use the service at its location and usually do not travel great distances to obtain the service (e.g., gas stations, professional services). Yet the conduct of firms operating in local or regional markets might still be constrained by the contestability provided by competition *for* the market by firms operating at the national level. Isolation may also be created by the special needs of a regional market. The EC *Magill* decision[10] is illustrative. The case centered on whether the copyright in the television listings of the three Irish broadcasting companies should be regarded as an essential facility in the publication of weekly program guides. Although Ireland is part of the EC, the listings market is inherently a local one.

Issues of small-scale jurisdictions may also be relevant to large economies when scale economies exist over the whole range or a large part of the market. The market for large aircraft is one such example. Accordingly, natural monopolies or oligopolistic markets may exist in large economies. Such markets are likely to present similar problems of market structure and performance as those of small economies.

Of course, large economies can regulate such markets effectively by adopting sector-specific rules, as was done by the U.S. enforcement agencies in the health care industry. The U.S. health care industry is characterized by large minimum efficient scales of operation and high entry barriers. The American competition authorities recognized the special characteristics of this industry and the need to apply the competition rules in a manner that reflects those characteristics. The Statement of Enforcement Policy applied broad safety zones for mergers to enable hospitals to achieve scale economies.[11] The fact that special guidelines were issued for this industry reflects the belief of the competition authorities that general U.S. competition policy toward mergers is ill suited for dealing with mergers in this industry. At the same time, adopting sector-specific rules is costly and thus is rarely done. The U.S. experience with the health care industry, analyzed in Chapter 6, also indicates that exceptions are sometimes difficult to apply when the general framework is left unchanged.

There is, however, an important difference between concentrated markets within large economies and small economies, based on the occurrence of such market structures. In large economies highly concentrated market structures protected by entry barriers are exceptional, and the offsetting social costs are usually modest, whereas in small economies these market failures cannot go unattended without major efficiency losses. This difference requires, as I have shown, a difference in the focus of competition laws. The magnifying glass effect thus affects optimal competition policy.

Notes

Index

Notes

Introduction

1. Parts of this chapter are based on Michal S. Gal, "Size Does Matter: The Effects of Market Size on Optimal Competition Policy," 74 *S. Cal. L. Rev.* 1437 (2001).
2. Of course, this list is not exclusive. Consumption patterns, taste preferences, or income levels may also affect the level of concentration in some markets. Laws, regulations, and the availability of technology are also influential. Nonetheless, these three factors have the most significant influence on concentration levels in most or all industrially developed or relatively developed economies, with which this book is concerned.
3. Richard E. Caves, "Scale, Openness, and Productivity in Manufacturing Industries," in *The Australian Economy: A View from the North,* ed. Richard E. Caves and Lawrence B. Krause (Sydney: George Allen & Unwin, 1984), 313.
4. I. Svennilson, "The Concept of the Nation and Its Relevance to Economic Analysis," in *Economic Consequences of the Size of Nations,* ed. E. A. G. Robinson (London: Macmillan & Co., 1960), 1.
5. This famous expression was first used by Adam Smith in *An Inquiry into the Nature and Causes of the Wealth of Nations* (1776; reprinted New York: Modern Library, 1937) to indicate the process at work in a competitive market.
6. R. G. Lipsey and Kelvin Lancaster, "The General Theory of Second Best," 24 *Review of Economic Studies* 11 (1975). See also "Symposium: The Second-Best Theory and Law & Economics," 73 *Chicago-Kent L. Rev.* 1 (1998).
7. See John Fingleton, "Political Economy Insights from Competition Policy in

Ireland," in *International Antitrust Law and Policy*, ed. Barry Hawk (New York: Juris, 2002), 569.

8. Several regional competition regimes exist, including among the COMESA, CARICOM, and Mercusor countries. The EC competition regime can also be seen as creating a regional competition framework that deals with some issues and leaves others that have no significant effect on trade between member states to be resolved at the national level.

9. The seminal collection of studies on the economic and social characteristics of small economies is Robinson, *Economic Consequences*. See also United Nations, Department of Technical Co-operation for Development, *Development Problems and Policy Needs of Small Island Economies* (Kingstown, Saint Vincent and the Grenadines, no. 7–11, 1983); Bimal Jalan, ed., *Problems and Policies in Small Economies* (London: Croom Helm, 1982); J. Kaminarides, L. Briguglio, and H. Hoogendonk, eds., *The Economic Development of Small Countries: Problems, Policies, and Strategies* (Amsterdam: Eburon Publishers, 1989); *World Development*, Special Issue 21 (1993). For studies on specific economies, see, for example, John W. O'Hagan, ed., *The Economy of Ireland: Policy and Performance of a Small European Economy*, 7th ed. (London: Macmillan, 2000).

10. As of January 2002, the number of jurisdictions of less than 5 million population that had adopted a competition policy was thirty (30 percent of the total number of jurisdictions that have adopted a competition policy): Albania, Armenia, Costa Rica, Croatia, Cyprus, Estonia, Gabon, Georgia, Iceland, Ireland, Jamaica, Kyrgyzstan, Latvia, Liechtenstein, Lithuania, Luxemburg, Macedonia, Malta, Mauritania, Mauritius, Moldova, Mongolia, New Zealand, Nicaragua, Norway, Panama, Slovenia, Swaziland, Turkmenistan, and Uruguay. The number of jurisdictions of less than 10 million that have adopted a competition policy was forty-seven (47 percent): in addition to the above list, Austria, Azerbaijan, Benin, Bolivia, Bulgaria, Denmark, Dominican Republic, Finland, Hong Kong, Israel, Paraguay, Slovakia, Sweden, Switzerland, Tajikistan, Tunisia, and Zambia. This, of course, is a very crude figure for small economies, as it does not take into account the effects of population dispersion and openness to trade.

11. Ministerial Declaration of WTO Ministerial Conference, 4th sess., WT/MIN(01)/DEC/1.

12. International Competition Network, press release, October 25, 2001 (found on the Web at www.internationalcompetitionnetwork.org).

13. See, e.g., *Schumann Sasol (South Africa)(Pty) Ltd. and Prices's Daelite (Pty) Ltd.* (23/LM/May01) (South African Competition Tribunal, unpublished, July 18, 2001). Merger in candle industry prohibited because, inter alia, a price rise would affect the poorest members of society who use candles as a primary source of light.

14. Small size may also affect optimal policies in many other fields, such as

tax, intellectual property, and so on. These issues are, however, beyond the scope of this book and will be treated as exogenous factors. For the effects of small size on the intersection of competition policy and intellectual property, see Michal S. Gal, "The Intersection of Competition Policy and Intellectual Property: A Small Economy's Perspective," *Global Competition Review* 14 (2000).

1. The Economic Characteristics of Small Market Economies

1. Kenneth E. Train, *Optimal Regulation* (Cambridge, Mass.: MIT Press, 1991), 1.
2. Richard E. Caves et al., *Competition in the Open Economy: A Model Applied to Canada* (Cambridge, Mass.: Harvard University Press, 1980), 7–8.
3. E. A. G. Robinson, ed., *Economic Consequences of the Size of Nations* (London: Macmillan & Co., 1960).
4. *Report of Royal Commission on Corporate Concentration* (Ottawa: Printing and Publishing Supply and Services Canada, 1978).
5. These studies include, inter alia, Caves et al., *Open Economy* (Caves's co-authors were Michael E. Porter, A. Michael Spence and John T. Scott); Richard E. Caves et al., *Studies in Canadian Industrial Organization* (RCCC Study no. 24, 1978); and Christian Marfels, *Concentration Levels and Trends in the Canadian Economy, 1965–73* (RCCC Study no. 31, 1978).
6. MES should not be confused with the scale of operation that maximizes the revenues of the firm, taking into account demand and the interdependence of firms.
7. MES is generally assumed to be similar in all industries around the world. Such an assumption is, in some respects, simplistic. Plant MES can vary from one jurisdiction to another depending on the availability of natural and other resources necessary for the production of the good or service, as well as national policies that prohibit or make more expensive some methods of production, which may affect the choice of technology. Yet many studies have confirmed that the ranking of industries by concentration level tends to be quite similar from one country to another. The issue was first raised by Joe S. Bain, *International Differences in Industrial Structure* (New Haven: Yale University Press, 1966), and confirmed in additional studies, including P. L. Pryor, "An International Comparison of Concentration Ratios," 54 *Review of Economics and Statistics* 130 (1972), and John Connor et al., *The Food Manufacturing Industries: Structure, Strategies, Performance, and Policies* (Lexington, Mass.: Lexington Books, 1995).
8. For a good survey of scale economies, see Frederick M. Scherer and David Ross, *Industrial Market Structure and Economic Performance*, 3d ed. (Boston: Houghton Miffin, 1990), 97–141.
9. The idea originated in the work of Ronald H. Coase, "The Nature of the

Firm," 4 *Economica* 386 (1937). Oliver Williamson further refined and developed this approach in *Markets and Hierarchies: Analysis and Antitrust Implications* (New York: Free Press, 1975) and *Antitrust Economics: Mergers, Contracting, and Strategic Behavior* (Cambridge: Basil Blackwell, 1987).

10. This definition follows the "Bainian" definition of entry barriers as measuring "the extent to which, in the long run, established firms can elevate their selling prices above the minimal average costs of production and distribution [without] inducing potential entrants to enter the industry." Joe S. Bain, *Industrial Organization*, 2d ed. (New York: Wiley, 1968), 252. The main virtue of this definition to our analysis is that it includes all barriers that limit the ability of firms to expand or to enter the industry in order to reduce the high prices charged by existing market participants, which is a main concern of competition policy. It enables us, for example, to recognize the limitations that scale economies place on changes in market structure. This definition differs from the "Stiglerian" definition for entry barriers, which focuses on costs that must be borne by new entrants which those already in the market did not have to incur when they entered. George J. Stigler, *The Organization of Industry* (Homewood, Ill.: R. D. Irwin, 1968), 67.

11. Sunk costs should be distinguished from fixed costs. Fixed costs are those costs that are not reduced, even in the long run, by decreases in output so long as production is not discontinued altogether (e.g., rental costs of a plant). Sunk costs are those costs that cannot be eliminated, even by total cessation of production (e.g., investments in large-scale plant and equipment that cannot easily be converted for other uses). William J. Baumol and Robert D. Willig, "Fixed Costs, Sunk Costs, Entry Barriers, and Sustainability of Monopoly," 96 *Quarterly Journal of Economics* 365, 405 (1981).

12. Ibid., 418.

13. T. Scitovsky, "International Trade and Economic Integration as a Means of Overcoming the Disadvantages of a Small Nation," in Robinson, 282, 282–3.

14. F. M. Scherer et al., *The Economics of Multi-Plant Operation* (Cambridge, Mass.: Harvard University Press, 1975), 94.

15. Zeev Galmor, *The Quality of Competition in Israeli Manufacture Industries* (Commerce and Industrial Ministry, 1982), 15–16.

16. For studies on the Canadian economy that have reached similar results, see Marfels; Caves et al., *Open Economy,* chap. 3; R. S. Khemani, "The Extent and Evolution of Competition in the Canadian Economy," in *Canadian Industry in Transition,* ed. Donald McFetridge (Toronto: University of Toronto Press, 1986).

17. For Australia, see Richard E. Caves, "Scale, Openness, and Productivity in Manufacturing Industries," in *The Australian Economy: A View from the*

North, ed. Richard E. Caves and Lawrence B. Krause (Sydney: George Allen & Unwin, 1984), 312, 321. For an international comparison, see Pryor.

18. The data presented in Table 1.1 were derived from Scherer et al., *Multi-Plant Operation,* and Michael Shefer, *Calcalat Taasiya* (Industrial organization)(Tel Aviv: The Open University, 1992), chap. 4.3.3 (referencing Israeli data).

19. Given market size, as we make price competition tougher, equilibrium structure generally becomes more concentrated. See Partha Dasgupta and Joseph Stiglitz, "Learning-by-Doing, Market Structure and Industrial and Trade Policies," 40 *Oxford Economic Papers* 246 (1988).

20. The relationship between market size and the number of firms that can operate profitably in the market is not linear. This is because, inter alia, economies of scale might continue beyond the MES point. Also, the residual demand facing a new entrant must be at least equal to the incumbents' scales.

21. John Sutton, *Sunk Costs and Market Structure* (Cambridge, Mass.: MIT Press, 1991).

22. S. Kuznets, "Economic Growth of Small Nations" in Robinson, 18; Lino Briguglio, "The Economic Vulnerabilities of Small Island Developing States" (paper presented at the Regional Technical Meeting of the Global Conference on the Sustainable Development of Small Island Developing States, Port of Spain, Trinidad and Tobago, July 1993).

23. Harvey W. Armstrong et al., "The Role of Transport Costs as a Determinant of Price Level Differentials between the Isle of Man and the United Kingdom," 21 *World Development* 311 (1993).

24. C. D. Edwards, "Size of Markets, Scale of Firms and the Character of Competition" in Robinson, 117, 127.

25. J. S. Coleman, *Foundations of Social Theory* (Cambridge, Mass.: Belknap Press, 1990).

26. Scitovsky, 286; Briguglio, "Economic Vulnerabilities," 1617.

27. Edwards, 127–130.

28. For the seminal work on the subject, see H. C. Eastman and Stephan Stykolt, *The Tariff and Competition in Canada* (Toronto: Macmillan, 1967).

29. See, for example, Richard E. Caves, *Diversification, Foreign Investment, and Scale in North American Manufacturing Industries* (Ottawa: Economic Council of Canada, 1975), and studies cited by Douglas S. West, *Modern Canadian Industrial Organization* (New York: HarperCollins, 1994), to accompany Dennis W. Carlton and Jeffrey M. Perloff, *Modern Industrial Organization,* 2d ed. (New York: HarperCollins, 1994), 48–49.

30. Caves, *Diversification,* 34.

31. Eastman and Stykolt state that "[t]he main factor adversely affecting productivity in Canadian manufacturing is the prevalence of plant capacity of sub-optimal size." Eastman and Stykolt, vii.

32. Ibid.

33. Ibid. For additional studies on the Canadian economy reaching relatively similar results, see, e.g., Paul K. Gorecki, *Economies of Scale and Efficient Plant Size in Canadian Manufacturing Industries* (Ottawa: Minister of Supply and Services, Canada, 1976); Melvyn A. Fuss and Vinod K. Gupta, "A Cost Function Approach to the Estimation of Minimum Efficient Scale, Returns to Scale, and Suboptimal Capacity," 15 *European Economic Review* 123 (1981); and John R. Baldwin and Paul K. Gorecki, *The Role of Scale in Canada-U.S. Productivity Differences* (Toronto: University of Toronto Press, 1986).

34. See Bain; Scherer et al., *Multi-Plant Operation*, chap. 3; R. M. Colon, *International Transport Costs and Tariffs: Their Influence on Australian and Canadian Manufacturing* (Kensington, Australia: University of New South Wales, 1980), 115–145.

35. Caves, *Diversification*.

36. Scherer et al., *Multi-Plant Operation*, chap. 2.

37. Ibid., 256–257.

38. Ibid., 92.

39. Eastman and Stykolt, 26; Caves et al., *Open Economy*, 14–15.

40. Eastman and Stykolt, 104.

41. Caves, *Diversification*.

42. Scherer et al., *Multi-plant Operation*, 35.

43. Sutton, 29.

44. Scherer et al., *Multi-plant Operation*, 128.

45. See, e.g., R. S. Khemani, "The Dimensions of Corporate Concentration in Canada," in *Mergers, Corporate Concentration, and Power in Canada,* ed. R. S. Khemani, D. M. Shapiro, and W. T. Stadbury (Halifax: Institute for Research on Public Policy, 1988). Khemani found, for example, that the leading twenty-five enterprises in Canada held 42.5 percent of total corporate sector assets in 1977 and 45.3 percent in 1983. The leading one hundred enterprises held 64.8 percent of such assets in 1977 and 66.9 in 1983. A study conducted by Caves et al. found that in a sample of matched industries in the United States and in Canada, the largest four firms held market shares that were 47 percent higher in Canada than in the United States. Caves et al., *Open Economy*, 370.

46. See, e.g., Robert Pitofsky, "The Political Content of Antitrust," 127 *U. Penn. L. Rev.* 1051 (1979); Louis B. Schwartz, "Justice and Other Non-economic Goals of Antitrust," 127 *U. Penn. L. Rev.* 1076 (1979).

47. Galmor; Scherer et al., *Multi-Plant Operation*.

48. The seminal article is Harvey Liebestein, "Allocative Inefficiency v. 'X-Inefficiency'" 56 *American Economic Review* 392 (1966). The claim that monopoly firms do not always adopt the most efficient production methods can be traced back to Adam Smith, who remarked that "monopoly . . . is a great enemy to good management." Smith.

49. Richard A. Posner, *Antitrust Law: An Economic Perspective* (Chicago: University of Chicago Press, 1976), 8–18. This proposition is downplayed in the new edition of the book.

50. Ibid.

51. Jean Tirole, *The Theory of Industrial Organization* (Cambridge, Mass.: MIT Press, 1994), 77.

52. Unless, of course, its profits under a competitive market structure are higher than its profits in a monopoly market structure, owing to the significantly lower costs of production from utilizing the new technology.

53. Single-firm dominance is explained in Chapter 3. For the purposes of this chapter, it can be defined as arising when a firm has sufficient market power to raise price significantly above the competitive level without losing so many sales so rapidly that the price increase is unprofitable and must be rescinded.

54. Scherer et al., *Multi-Plant Operation*, 21.

55. This example is based on David Gilo, "Antitrust Policy in Small Economies" (LL.M. paper, Harvard Law School, 1994), 7.

56. Scherer et al., *Multi-Plant Operation*, 92–93.

57. Scherer and Ross, *Market Structure*, 394. Assuming, of course, that the firms operate only in the domestic market and are not part of a multinational corporation.

58. Gilo, 24.

59. G. Marcy, "How Far Can Foreign Trade and Customs Agreements Confer upon Small Nations the Advantages of Large Nations?" in Robinson, 265, 276.

60. Ricardo first clearly stated the importance of a comparative advantage for engaging in international trade. This has remained one of the basic principles of trade theory ever since. David Ricardo, *On the Principles of Political Economy and Taxation* (London: John Murray, 1817), chap. 7.

61. Armstrong et al. have found that growth success of micro-states is associated with a rich natural resource base or a strong service sector, notably in financial service and tourism. H. W. Armstrong et al., "A Comparison of the Economic Performance of Different Micro-States and between Micro-States and Larger Countries," 26 *World Development* 639 (1998).

62. Kuznets, 18.

63. Scherer et al., *Multi-Plant Operation*, 137.

64. Caves et al., *Open Economy*, 8–18.

65. Ibid., 16.

66. Ibid., 17–18; Eastman and Stykolt, chap. 7.

67. See, for example, Commonwealth Consultative Group, *Vulnerability: Small States in the Global Society* (London: Commonwealth Secretariat, 1985); Lino Briguglio, "Small Island Developing States and Their Economic Vulnerabilities," 23 *World Development* 1615 (1995), and "Towards the Construction of an Economic Vulnerability Index: Recent Literature with Spe-

cial Reference to Small Island Developing States" (paper presented at the Small States in the International Economy Conference, University of Birmingham, April 16, 1998).

68. Armstrong et al.

69. Empirical studies confirm the relative importance of trade for small economies. Foreign trade, and especially import, is of greater weight in the economic activity of a small economy than of a large one. As a broad generalization, the ratio of foreign trade to gross domestic product rises as the population size declines. The index of exports and imports as a percentage of GDP generally increases as the size of the population of an economy and the level of transport costs are reduced. To give but a few examples, in the period 1987–1989, the index was 83.43 for Malta, 51.37 for Jamaica, 38.2 for Israel, and 9.65 for the United States. Transportation costs also played a significant role: the index was 16.98 for New Zealand, which suffers from relatively high transport costs, and 58.60 for Ireland, with relatively lower transport costs. Briguglio, "Economic Vulnerabilities," 1628.

70. See, for example, the case of *Eltam-Seingoot,* analyzed in Chapter 3. *Eltam-Ein Hashofet Aguda Shitufit Haklait Baam VeHevrat H. M. Seingoot Baam* (Eltam-Ein Hashofet Association, Inc. and H. M Seingoot Company, Inc.) (M-4571) (Director of Israeli Competition Authority, unpublished, September 20, 2001).

71. Caves, "Scale, Openness, and Productivity," 370.

72. Bruce Dunlop, David McQueen, and Michael Trebilcock, *Canadian Competition Policy: A Legal and Economic Analysis* (Toronto: Canada Law Books, 1987), 60.

73. Until 2000, the Canadian Restrictive Trade Practices Commission recommended tariff reductions in only three cases. In only one of the cases the recommendation led to a reduction of 15 to 20 percent in customs duties.

74. Sections 99, 86(4), and 75(1) of the Canadian Competition Act of 1985. The British Monopolies and Mergers Commission also recommended the abolition of import duties in several of its investigations. See, e.g., *Report on Color Films HCP* (Monopolies and Mergers Commission, unpublished, 1966–67). The Australian case of *BHP/New Zealand Steel* also provides an interesting example. The case involved a bid by BHP, Australia's major steel company, to take over one its competitors, New Zealand Steel. The Australian Commission opposed the merger, as international trade was not strong enough to limit the market power of the merged entity. A practical solution emerged, however, when the Australian government agreed to reduce tariffs on an accelerated basis in relation to those parts of the market in which there could have been an anti-competitive effect, and the merger was eventually approved. Ross Jones, "Mergers and Competition in a Global Environment" (presentation given at the Victorian Commonwealth Executive Forum, August 31, 2000, Melbourne, Australia).

75. Innovation or investments to increase innovation are not, however, always

welfare-enhancing. Excess innovation owing to strategic manipulations might be harmful. This includes, inter alia, predatory innovation aimed at deterring entry by requiring rivals to invest in comparable products. See, e.g., Richard A. Posner, *Antitrust Law,* 2d ed. (Chicago: University of Chicago Press, 2001), 20–21.

76. Frederick M. Scherer, *International High-Technology Competition* (Cambridge, Mass.: Harvard University Press, 1992), 6.

77. Michael C. Porter, *The Competitive Advantage of Nations* (New York: Free Press, 1990), chap. 4; Scherer, *High-Technology,* 7.

78. The World Intellectual Property Organization (WIPO) statistical summary for 1999 indicates that a small percentage of the total patents granted were given to persons or firms in small economies. The following are some examples of patents granted to various countries as a percentage of the total patents granted in 1999: United States, 18.93 percent; Japan, 18.51 percent; Australia, 1.67 percent (most to nonresidents); New Zealand, 0.3 percent; Israel, 0.25 percent; Cyprus, 0.0 percent; Malta, 0.0 percent. www.wipo.org/ipstats/en/publications/a/xls/patents.xls. While these figures should be adjusted to reflect the size of the economy relative to the size of all markets surveyed (or at least those of relatively developed economies), they provide a crude illustration of the innovative activities of small economies. See also Briguglio, "Economic Vulnerabilities." This, of course, is a broad generalization. Israel, for example, exhibits high levels of innovative activity, especially in computer software developments, which require copyrights rather than patents. Human capital thus provides it with a comparative advantage that overcomes some of the obstacles of small size. It is interesting to note that while innovative activity does take place in Israel, most of the products and processes developed there that require large-scale production or distribution are implemented elsewhere.

79. For an overview, see Wesley M. Cohen and Richard C. Levin, "Empirical Studies of Innovation and Market Structure," in *Handbook of Industrial Organization,* ed. Richard Schmalensee and Robert D. Willig, vol. 2 (Amsterdam: Elselvier Science Publishers, 1989), 1060. Sang-Seung Yi, "Market Structure and Incentives to Innovate: The Case of Cournot Oligopoly," 65 *Economic Letters* 379 (1999).

80. See, e.g., Frederick M. Scherer, *Innovation and Growth: Schumpeterian Perspectives* (Cambridge, Mass.: MIT Press, 1984).

81. This argument is often labeled "the Schumpeterian Argument," after Joseph A. Schumpeter, *Capitalism, Socialism, and Democracy,* 3d ed. (New York: Harper and Row, 1950). Schumpeter also argued that monopoly position affords the security needed to ensure the appropriation of sufficient rewards to justify innovative activity.

82. Scherer and Ross, *Market Structure.*

83. Arrow was one of the first to show that given enforceable property rights, the incentive to innovate will be smaller under conditions of monopoly than

under competitive conditions. Kenneth E. Arrow, "Economic Welfare and the Allocation of Resources for Invention," in *The Rate of Direction of Inventive Activity,* ed. R. R. Nelson (Princeton: Princeton University Press, 1962), 609. For a more recent study on the effects of competition on innovation, see Philippe Aghion et al., "Competition, Imitation, and Growth with Step-by-Sep Innovation" (working paper, October 2000).

84. *Report of Royal Commission, 57–60*; D. G. McFetridge and R. J. Covari, "Technology Diffusion: A Survey of Canadian Evidence and Public Policy Issues," in *Technological Change in Canadian Industry,* ed. D. G. McFetridge (Toronto: University of Toronto Press, 1985).

85. Cornelis W. A. M. van Paridon, "Technology Policy in a Small and Open Economy: The Case of the Netherlands," in *Entrepreneurship, Technological Innovation, and Economic Growth,* ed. Frederic M. Scherer and Mark Perlman (Ann Arbor: University of Michigan Press, 1992), 105.

2. The General Implications of Small Size for Competition Policy

1. This chapter builds, in part, on Michal S. Gal, "Size Does Matter," 74 *S. Cal. L. Rev.* 1437 (2001).

2. John E. Calfee and Richard Craswell, "Some Effects of Uncertainty on Compliance with Legal Standards," *Va. L. Rev.* 965 (1984).

3. Phillip E. Areeda and Herbert Hovenkamp, *Antitrust Law: An Analysis of Antitrust Principles and Their Application,* 2d ed. vol. 1 (New York: Aspen Law & Business, 2000), 96, 103–111.

4. R. Shyam Khemani, "Merger Policy and Small Open Economies: The Case of Canada," in *Perspectives in Industrial Organization,* ed. B. Dankbaar et al. (London: Kluwer Academic Publishers, 1990), 216, 223.

5. Similarly, Australia's competition policy underwent significant microeconomic reform in the 1980s. As part of the reform, several significant changes were made to Australia's competition law regime, intended to bring increased economic focus to competition policy. These are elaborated throughout the book.

6. Canadian Competition Act of 1985, sec. 1.1.

7. This can be exemplified by the *Superior* case, which is analyzed in Chapter 6. See *Canada (Commissioner of Competition) v. Superior Propane, Inc. and ICG Propane, Inc.* [2001] 3 F. C. 185.

8. See the Israeli Restrictive Trade Practices Act of 1988.

9. See, e.g., the decision of the director of the Israeli Competition Authority in *Hescemei Habiladiut Bein Hevrot Hadelek Levein Mafilei Tahanot* (Exclusivity arrangements among the petrol companies and petrol station operators), in *Hegbelim Iskiim* (Antitrust), ed. Tova Olshtein, vol. A (Tel Aviv: Vaad Mechoz Tel-Aviv-Yafo, 1994), 19, 38–39; *Tivol (1993) Baam neged Shef Hayam (1994) Baam veach* (Tivol [1993] Ltd. v. Shef Hayam [1994] Ltd. et al.) (DNA 4465/98), *Piskei Din* (Court decisions) 50(1), 56 (Israeli Supreme Court, 2000).

10. Michael Shefer, "Guidelines for Legislation on Monopolies and Restrictive Practices in Small Economies," 15 *Antitrust Bull.* 781, 793 (1970).

3. The Regulation of Single-Firm Dominance

1. George A. Hay, "Market Power in Antitrust," 60 *Antitrust L. J.* 807 (1992); idem, "Market Power in Australian Antitrust: An American Perspective," 1 *Comp. and Cons. L. J.* 215 (1994).

2. For the seminal article on this subject, see William M. Landes and Richard A. Posner, "Market Power in Antitrust Cases," 94 *Harv. L. Rev.* 937, 937 (1981). Some courts have adopted an additional test for market power that focuses on the ability to exclude competitors. See, for example, the U.S. case of *United States v. E. I. du Pont de Nemours & Co.*, 351 U.S. 377 (1956); the EC case of *Europemballage Corp. and Continental Can Co. Inc. v. Commission* (6/72) [1973] ECR 215, [1973] CMLR 199; the Israeli case of *Hamemune Al Hahegbelim Haiskiim neged Yediot Aharonot Baam Veacherim (Psak Din Mashlim)* (Director of Competition Authority v. Yediot Aharonot, Inc. et al.) (complementary decision) (M 2/92) (Israeli Competition Tribunal, unpublished, June 7, 2000). The exclusion benchmark is problematic in that it can capture pro-competitive actions that exclude less efficient competitors. See discussion in text accompanying notes 77–81.

3. Landes and Posner make the argument that when a foreign producer imports into a local market, all its (actual or potential) production capacity should be included in the relevant market, once it meets some specified conditions (e.g., the foreign producer has had nonnegligible sales in the market for a continuous period of several years). They reason that if firms can sell significant quantities of the product in a given national market, they will be able to sell additional units at no appreciably higher cost simply by diverting sales from one market to the other. This approach will tend, however, to overstate market power in cases in which foreign producers do not sell in the market at present but could do so if prices were even slightly higher. In addition, the Landes-Posner conclusion depends on the product's being homogeneous. If products are at all differentiated, only certain classes of consumers will find the foreign products attractive at any given price level. See Louis Kaplow, "The Accuracy of Traditional Market Analysis and a Direct Adjustment Alternative," 95 *Harv. L. Rev.* 1817 (1982), and Timothy J. Brennan, "Mistaken Elasticities and Misleading Rules," 95 *Harv. L. Rev.* 1849 (1982). Instead, potential and actual imports should be evaluated in light of the existing conditions in the market.

4. Small economies often recognize the importance of imports in defining the relevant market. See, e.g., the Israeli case of *Bakashat Ptor Meishur Beit Hadin Lehesder Covel Shutafut Poligar* (Request for the director's waiver for the agreement for the creation of Poligar), in *Hegbelim Iskiim* (Antitrust), ed. Tova Olshtein, vol. A (Tel Aviv: Vaad Mehoz Tel-Aviv-Yafo,

1994), 108, 108; and the Australian case of *D&R Byrnes (Nominees) Pty Ltd. v. Central Queensland Meat Export Co. Pty Ltd.* (1990) ATPR 41–028.

5. Landes and Posner, 944–945. The Lerner Index was first developed in Lerner, "The Concept of Monopoly and the Measurement of Monopoly Power," 1 *Review of Economic Studies* 157 (1934). It assumes Cournot competition between firms. The index is appropriate when the market is characterized by a single large firm and a competitive fringe. When the market is characterized by firms that act interdependently, the index will understate market power, as it neglects the relationship between market power and the interdependence of large firms in an industry. Janusz A. Ordover, Alan O. Sykes, and Robert D. Willig, "Herfindahl Concentration, Rivalry, and Mergers," 95 *Harv. L. Rev.* 1857 (1982).

6. Landes and Posner.

7. Ibid., 958.

8. For such criticism, see, e.g., Kaplow; Jonathan B. Baker and Timothy F. Breshnahan, "Estimating the Residual Demand Curve Facing a Single Firm," 6 *International Journal of Industrial Organization* 283 (1988).

9. *Yediot Aharonot.* For another example of the effect of market shares on the profitability of anti-competitive fidelity rebates, see the European Commission's decision in *Soda Ash–Solvary* (Commission decision, unpublished, December 13, 2000).

10. Assume, for example, that before the strategy was implemented, the distributor regularly bought twelve copies of Yediot, sold ten and returned two; bought six copies of Yediot's largest rival and sold five. The regular commission per newspaper was 30 cents, increased by Yediot to 1 shequel. Further assume that the price of a newspaper to readers is 2 shequels. Under the target discount strategy, the distributor would have to buy twelve copies of Yediot for 1 shequel each. If he sold his regular quantity, he would earn 8 shequels from selling Yediot (since he could not return the two unsold newspapers) and $0.30 \times 5 = 1.5$ from selling the rival's newspaper (total 9.5). If he sells all twelve copies of Yediot, his profit is 12 from Yediot and $0.3 \times 3 = 0.9$ from the rival (total 12.9). To offset this strategy, the rival would have to provide its newspaper to distributors for a lower price, since if it just matched the strategy, the distributor's profits would be 12 $(5 \times 2 - 6 + 10 \times 2 - 12 = 12$ or any other combination of a total of fifteen newspapers sold).

11. *U.S. v. Microsoft Corporation*, 84 F. Supp. 2d 9 (D.D.C. 1999)(findings of fact); 87 F. Supp. 2d 30 (D.D.C. 2000)(conclusions of law); 97 F. Supp. 2d 59 (D.D.C. 2000)(final judgment); on appeal 253 F. 3d 34 (D.C. Cir. 2001), cert. denied 2001 U.S. Lexis 9509.

12. This argument can be quite simply proven by using algebraic formulas. Using the Lerner index formula, we see that when we hold Li (the degree of market power) and Edm constant and we vary Esj, the higher Esj is, the higher the Si needed to offset its effect.

13. *Mark Lyons Pty Ltd. v. Bursill Sportsgear Pty Ltd.* (1987) ATPR 40–808.
14. The EC has adopted a similar approach. In *Michelin,* for example, the dominant firm was found to have a market share of 57 to 65 percent, compared with shares of 4 and 8 percent for its main competitors. The dispersion of market shares constituted "a valid indication of Michelin's preponderant strength in relation to its competitors." *Michelin v. Commission* (322/81) [1983] ECR 3461, [1985] 1 CMLR 282. A fragmented fringe market may signify that the dominant firm is more efficient than its rivals.
15. EC Treaty of Rome, 1957, sec. 82; New Zealand's Commerce Act of 1986, sec. 3(8).
16. U.S. Sherman Act, sec. 2.
17. Sec. 79 of the Canadian Competition Act of 1985, dealing with "abuse of dominant position."
18. Sec. 77(2) of the Canadian Competition Act, dealing with exclusive dealing and tied selling.
19. Australian Trade Practices Act of 1974, sec. 46.
20. Israeli Trade Restrictive Practices Act of 1988, sec. 26.
21. For Australia, see, e.g., *Queensland Wire Industries Pty Ltd. v. BHP Co Ltd.* (1989) 167 CLR 177, 178, ATPR 40–925 ("A large market share may well be evidence of market power"). For the EC, see *Hoffman La Roche v. Commission* [1979] 1 ECR 461, para. 41 ("Very large shares are in themselves, and save in exceptional circumstances, evidence of the existence of a dominant position"). For Canada, see *Canada (Director of Investigation and Research) v. D&B Companies of Canada Ltd.* (1995) 64 C.P.R. (3d) 216 (hereafter *Nielsen*)("A prima facie determination of whether a firm likely has market power can be made by considering its market share. If the share is very large, the firm will likely have market power although, of course, other considerations must be taken into account").
22. For an elaboration of the use of market shares as an indicator of market power in different-sized economies, see Michal S. Gal, "Defining Market Power in Small Markets" (paper presented at the Competition and Competition Law in Small Jurisdictions, International Conference, Valetta, Malta, May 1998).
23. "'Dominant' refers to a position in a market where a 'prevailing,' 'commanding,' 'governing' or like influence can be exercised over production." *Port Nelson Ltd. v. Commerce Commission* [1996] 3 NZLR 554, 573; *Telecom Corp. of New Zealand Ltd. v. Clear Ltd.* [1992] 3 NZLR 429 (CA).
24. Divrei Hesber Lehatzaat Hok Hahegbelim Haiskiim, 1984 (Explanatory memorandum of the Trade Restrictive Practices Act, 1984), *Hatzaot-Hok* (Legislative proposals), 41.
25. See Tzav Hahegbelim Haiskim (Hachraza Al Monopol Beshuk Hagaz) (Competition Law Decree [declaration of a monopoly in the gas market]), 1982, *Kovetz Takanot,* (Regulations), 1339.
26. *Yediot Aharonot,* para. 68.

27. This discussion builds, mainly, on Phillip E. Areeda and Herbert Hovenkamp, *Antitrust Law,* 2d ed., vol. 3 (New York: Aspen Law & Business, 2002), 44–66, and on Phillip E. Areeda and Louis Kaplow, *Antitrust Analysis: Problems, Text, Cases,* 4th ed. (Boston: Little, Brown, 1988), 549–557.

28. Robert H. Bork, *The Antitrust Paradox: A Policy at War with Itself,* 2d ed. (New York: Free Press, 1993), 175–178.

29. See Oliver E. Williamson, "Dominant Firms and the Monopoly Problem: Market Failure Considerations," 85 *Harv. L. Rev.* 1512, 1520 (1972); William G. Shepherd, "Dim Prospects: Effective Competition in Telecommunications, Railroads, and Electricity," 42 *Antitrust Bull.* 151 (1997).

30. Areeda and Hovenkamp, 58–62.

31. Donald Turner, "The Scope of Antitrust and Other Economic Regulatory Policies," 82 *Harv. L. Rev.* 1207, 1216, 1220 (1969); Williamson.

32. Areeda and Kaplow, 556.

33. Turner, 1213–15. This is also the position taken by the current director of the Israeli Competition Authority.

34. Ibid.

35. For the first cases establishing this approach, see *Standard Oil Co. v. U.S.,* 221 U.S. 1 (1911)(Sherman Act omitted "any direct prohibition against monopoly in the concrete"); *U.S. v. United States Steel Corp.,* 251 U.S. 417, 440–441 (1920).

36. *United States v. Grinnel Corp.,* 384 U.S. 563, 571 (1966). See, e.g., *Berkey Photo v. Eastman Kodak Co.,* 603 F. 2d 263 (2d Cir. 1979) cert. denied, 444 U.S. 1093 (1980).

37. *Standard Oil.*

38. Areeda and Hovenkamp, 52 –53 (emphasis added). For the seminal cases establishing this view, see *Standard Oil* and *United States v. American Can Co.,* 230 F. 859, 901–902 (D. Md. 1916). This view is not, however, universally shared. Over the years there have been several suggestions to regulate mere monopoly. The proposals were seen as an attempt to fill a perceived gap in the law dealing with monopolies and other concentrated market structures that the market does not succeed in eroding in due time and that have adverse consequences. These proposals reject the argument that structure will take care of itself as it is based on average tendencies. Although the market can correct dominance in most cases, aberrations can and do appear, and the implied time horizon for self-policing to be efficient may be unacceptably long. For such suggestions, see, for example, Walter Adams, "Corporate Power and Economic Apologetics: A Public Policy Perspective," in *Industrial Concentration: The New Learning,* ed. Harvey J. Goldschmid, H. Michael Mann, and J. Fred Weston (Boston: Little, Brown, 1974), 360; Carl Kaysen and Donald Turner, *Antitrust Policy: An Economic and Legal Analysis* (Cambridge, Mass.: Harvard University Press, 1959), 266–272; Phil C. Neal et al., "Report of the White House Task Force on Antitrust Policy," 2 *Antitrust L. & Econ. Rev.* 11 (1968–69), adopted in

S. 2614, 92d Cong. (1971); S. 1167, 93d Cong. (1973). Reintroduced as S. 1959, 94th Cong. (1975). These proposals were never accepted.

39. Israeli Restrictive Trade Practices Act of 1988, sec. 30.

40. See, e.g., *Tzav Hahegbelim Haiskiim (Sidrei Tashlum Veaspaka Lemelet) 1981* (Restrictive trade practices decree—concrete market [payment and supply terms], 1981), *Kovetz Takanot 1355*; *Tzav Hahegbelim Haiskiim (Darchei Yiitzur Veaspaka Shel Nyar) 1981* (Restrictive trade practices decree—paper market [terms for the supply and production of paper], 1981), *Kovetz Takanot* 1276. Most conduct of dominant firms nowadays is regulated by the director as part of the firms' compliance programs, elaborated in the text.

41. Israeli Product and Service Surveillance Act of 1957. Similar laws can be found in other economies, including Australia and Cyprus. Such laws are remnants of more interventionist eras. In recent years the scope of direct price regulation in most economies has been substantially reduced.

42. Israeli Restrictive Trade Practices Act of 1988, sec. 30(F).

43. U.K. Fair Trading Act of 1973. The power to refer a scale monopoly to the Competition Commission was retained in the introduction to the Competition Act of 1998.

44. See, e.g., *Reports on Contraceptive Sheaths* (Monopolies and Mergers Commission, unpublished, 1974 and 1982); *Report on Opium Derivatives* (Monopolies and Mergers Commission, unpublished, 1989)(MMC recommended a prohibition against any price increase for three years). *Classified Directory Advertising Service* (Monopolies and Mergers Commission, unpublished, 1996) (recommendation for price cap and prohibition to publish more than one directory in any particular area to be placed on a large producer in order to enable smaller ones to develop and eventually compete effectively).

45. In parliamentary discussions before the adoption of the 1998 Competition Act, the government explained that in the future its powers under the Fair Trading Act of 1973 would be used only in exceptional cases, when a firm had abused its monopoly power and the Office of Fair Trade believed that future abuses were likely, since the Competition Commission could then propose a structural remedy. House of Lords Committee, November 13, 1997, col. 300, and House of Lords 3R, March 5, 1998, col. 1333.

46. Maltese Competition Act of 1995, section 11.

47. See *Transpower New Zealand Ltd. v. Meridian Energy Ltd.* [2001] NZLR Lexis 22, 44.

48. For discussion of the rationale behind this light-handed regulation, see *Vector Ltd. v. Tanspower New Zealand Ltd.* [1999] 3 NZLR 646.

49. See Michal S. Gal, "Reality Bits (or Bites): The Political Economy of Antitrust Enforcement," in *International Antitrust Law and Policy,* ed. Barry Hawk (New York: Juris, 2002), 605.

50. Israeli Restrictive Trade Practices Act of 1988, sec. 27(A).

51. Austrian Cartel Act of 1988, sec. 36(d).

52. Israeli Restrictive Trade Practices Act of 1988, sec. 26.

53. Ibid., secs. 43(E) and 26(A).

54. Such obligations are sometimes imposed on merging parties as part of the conditions for the approval of a merger. See, e.g., the Israeli case of *Ishur Mizug Betnaim Columbus Capital Corporation Mikvutzat Klaridge Cur Taasiot Baam* (Conditioned approval of a merger between Columbus Capital Corporation from the Klaridge Group, Cur Industries Ltd.) (Director of Israeli Competition Authority, unpublished, January 5, 1998).

55. Israeli Restrictive Trade Practices Act of 1988, sec. 48.

56. Restrictive Trade Practices Act of 1988, sec. 31. Similarly, the Irish Competition Act of 1991, sec. 14, empowers the Minister for Industry and Commerce "to prohibit the continuance of a dominant position" or "require the adjustment of a dominant position" once an investigation indicates abuse of such power. Any such order requires confirmation by both houses of Parliament. As of mid-2002, this power had not been used. The 1975 version of the New Zealand Commerce Act included provisions that enabled a court to divest firms with market power. These provisions were repealed in 1986.

57. *United Brands Co. v. Commission* (27/76) [1978] ECR 207, [1978] 1 CMLR 429.

58. Some of the member states that adopted provisions based on Article 82 of the Treaty of Rome of 1957 in their domestic competition laws have also interpreted this provision. For an interesting case, see *Napp Pharmaceutical Holdings Ltd. v. Director-General of Fair Trading* (U.K. Competition Commission Appeals Tribunal, unpublished, January 15, 2002). The court found abuse of unfairly high prices based on several comparisons, taken together: Napp's prices with its costs, Napp's prices with those of its competitors, and Napp's prices with prices charged by it in other markets. These comparisons supported a conclusion that Napp's prices in the relevant market were well above what would have been expected in competitive markets.

59. *General Motors v. Commission* (26/75) [1975] ECR 1367, [1976] 1 CMLR 95.

60. The EC erred in its market definition in *General Motors*. The definition disregarded the effects of inter-firm competition on intra-firm competition. The discussion in the text takes these market definitions as given, as the correct market definition is irrelevant to the substantive tests established for excessive pricing once market power is established.

61. *General Motors*.

62. *British Leyland v. Commission* (226/84)[1986] ECR 3263, [1987] 1 CMLR 185. The market definition suffered from the same flaw of the analysis noted in *General Motors*.

63. *United Brands Co. v. Commission.*
64. Ibid., 302.
65. *Ministere Public v. Tournier* (C-395/87)[1989] ECR 2521, [1991] 4 CMLR 248, sec. 38.
66. E. Susan Singleton, ed., *Comparative Laws of Monopolies* (London: Kluwer Law International, 1988, updated 1998), 325.
67. European Commission, Fifth Report on Competition Policy (1975), point 3: "Measures to halt the abuse of dominant positions cannot be converted into systematic monitoring of prices." See also European Commission, Twenty-fourth Report on Competition Policy (1994), point 207: "The Commission in its decision-making practice does not normally control or condemn the high level of prices as such."
68. Maltese Competition Act of 1995, sec. 9(5).
69. This section draws heavily on Kathryn McMahon, "Refusals to Supply by Corporations with Substantial Market Power," 22 *Australian Bus. L. Rev.* 7 (1994).
70. For an application of the test by the High Court of Australia, see *Melway Publishing Pty Ltd. v. Robert Hicks Pty Ltd.* [2001] ATPR 41–805.
71. This is, however, a very simplistic application of this test. The same standard could have been applied more narrowly in that in essence both the monopolist and the firm operating in a competitive market are taking the maximum price that the market will bear. This interpretation was adopted by New Zealand courts. See, e.g., *Clear Communications.*
72. *ASX Operations Pty Ltd. v. Pont Data Australia Pty Ltd.* [1991] ATPR 41–069. See also *Queensland Wire.*
73. *Hamemune Al Hahegbelim Haiskim Neged Yediot Aharonot Baam veacherim (Psak Din Helki)* (Director of the Competition Authority v. Yediot Aharonot, Inc. et al.) (partial decision) (M2/96) (Israeli Competition Tribunal, unpublished, 1999).
74. The terminology includes "abuse of power" (e.g., Israeli Restrictive Trade Practices Act of 1988, sec. 29A; Maltese Competition Act of 1994, sec. 9); "taking advantage of market power" (e.g., Australian Trade Practices Act of 1974, sec. 46); "use of power" (e.g., New Zealand Commerce Act of 1986, sec. 36); "activities contrary to the public interest" (e.g., Belgian Act on Protection against the Abuser of Economic Power of 1960, sec. 2); and "monopolization" (U.S. Sherman Act, sec. 2).
75. See, e.g., the Canadian *Nielsen* case. For its analysis, see Michal S. Gal "The *Nielsen* Case: Was Competition Restored?" 29 *Canadian Bus. L. J.* 17 (1997).
76. Section 2 of the U.S. Sherman Act prohibits acts of attempted monopolization, interpreted to include acts that create a dangerous probability of success of monopolization. See, e.g., *Microsoft,* Court of Appeal decision, 62–67. The U.S. threshold might not be low enough for small economies, however, as the defendant firm should have at least a 35–40 percent market

share. As noted earlier, in small economies such high shares almost always signify a dominant position in the market.

77. New Zealand Commerce Act of 1986, sec. 36; Australian Trade Practices Act of 1974, sec. 46.

78. *U.S. v. Griffith,* 334 U.S. 100 (1948).

79. Ibid.

80. See *Olympia Equipment Leasing Co. v. Western Union Telegraph Co.,* 797 F. 2d 370 (7th Cir. 1986) 375. The decision in the U.S. case of *Alcoa* can be interpreted as defining the progressive embracing of each new business opportunity as exclusionary. *United States v. Aluminum Co. of America,* 148 F. 2d 416 (2d Cir. 1945).

81. This does not imply, however, that the dominant firm can require securities that its rivals cannot receive, thereby harming them. The Israeli case of *Shogul* is illustrative. There, Bezeq, the monopolistic telecommunications company, conditioned the continuation of the supply of its telephone services to a firm in bankruptcy on the provision of securities for the payment of its past debts. The district court held that the conduct amounted to an abuse of dominance: a monopolist may not gain an advantage over other suppliers of a firm in bankruptcy by using its dominant position to receive securities for past debts. Civil Case (Tel Aviv) 112/92, *Baruch Shogul v. Bezeq,* Takdin District Court Decisions, vol. 92 (2), 1350 (1992–93).

82. *Eastman Kodak Company v. Image Services, Inc.,* 504 U.S. 451, 112 S. Ct. 2071 (1992).

83. *Hugin Kassareigister AB et al. v. Commission* (22/78) [1979] ECR 1869. Case dismissed on other grounds.

84. *Hamemune Al Hahegbelim Haiskiim Neged Electra (Israel) Baam Veacherim* (Director of Competition Authority v. Electra [Israel] Ltd. et al.)(M/343) (Israeli Competition Council, unpublished, July 9, 1982).

85. "Interim Report of the Study on the Newspaper Industry" (Irish Competition Authority, unpublished, 1994).

86. See, e.g., the New Zealand cases of *Telecom Corporation of New Zealand Ltd. v. Clear Communications Ltd.* [1995] 1 NZLR 385, 403 (PC) and *Port Nelson* [1996], 577 and also the Australian cases of *Queensland* and *Melway Publishing,* 42,758.

87. *ASX Operations.*

88. See generally Dennis W. Carlton, "A General Analysis of Exclusionary Conduct and Refusal to Deal: Why *Aspen* and *Kodak* Are Misguided," 68 *Antitrust L. J.* 659 (2001); *Microsoft.*

89. *Melway Publishing.*

90. See, e.g., Israeli Restrictive Trade Practices Act of 1988, sec. 29A(a); Canadian Competition Act of 1985, sec. 79; Maltese Competition Act of 1994, sec. 9.

91. See, e.g., Canadian Competition Act of 1985, secs. 78–9; the New Zealand case of *Vector,* 646; the U.S. case of *Spectrum Sports v. McQuillan,* 506 U.S. 447, 113 S. Ct. 884 (1993).

92. See earlier discussion of the Australian *ASX Operations* case. See also Michael O'Bryan, "Section 46: Law or Economics?" 1 *Competition and Consumer L. J.* 64 (1993); Stephen Corones, "Section 46 of the Trade Practices Act: What Are the Rules of Battle?" 29 *Australian Bus. L. Rev.* 175 (2001). In *Melway* this approach was rejected in obiter dictum. *Melway Publishing,* 42,754–55.

93. See, e.g., the EC case of *Hoffman La Roche;* the Israeli case M—1/93 *Hamemune neged Hevrat Dubek Baa'm veach* (Director of Competition Authority v. Dubek, Inc. et al.), in *Hegbelim Iskiim,* vol. B, 194; the U.S. case of *Microsoft,* Court of Appeals decision.

94. See, e.g., Canadian Competition Act of 1985, sec. 34; Israeli Restrictive Trade Practices Act of 1988, sec. 29A(b)(3); EC Treaty of Rome, 1957, sec. 82; Maltese Competition Act of 1994, sec. 9.

95. Kip Viscusi, John Vernon, and Joseph Harrington, *Economics of Regulation and Antitrust* (Toronto: D. C. Heath and Co., 1992), chap. 9.

96. See, e.g., Israeli Restrictive Trade Practices Act of 1988, sec. 29A(b)(3); Maltese Competition Act of 1994, sec. 9; Swedish Competition Act of 1993, sec. 19; EC, Treaty of Rome, 1957, sec. 82(c).

97. Press release, "The Antitrust Authority Allowed Nesher to Grant Price Reduction to Customers" (Israeli Competition Authority, March 12, 2002).

98. Israeli Restrictive Trade Practices Act of 1988, sec. 29A(b)(3).

99. Richard A. Posner, *The Robinson-Patman Act: Federal Regulation of Price Differences* (Washington, D.C.: American Enterprise Institute for Public Policy Research, 1976).

100. Areeda and Turner see the problem as one of comparative statics and condemn prices when they fall below short-run marginal cost. Phillip Areeda and Donald F. Turner, "Predatory Pricing and Related Practices under Section 2 of the Sherman Act," 88 *Harv. L. Rev.* 697 (1974–75). The Areeda-Turner suggestion did not lack critics. For some criticism and other suggestions, see, e.g., Frederick M. Scherer, "Predatory Pricing and the Sherman Act: A Comment," 89 *Harv. L. Rev.* 869 (1976); William Baumol, "Quasi-Permanence of Price Reductions: A Policy for Prevention of Predatory Pricing," 89 *Yale L. J.* 1 (1979); Patrick Bolton, Joseph B. Brodley, and Michael H. Riordan, "Predatory Pricing: Strategic Theory and Legal Policy," 88 *Georgetown L. J.* 2239 (2000); Richard A. Posner, *Antitrust Law,* 2d ed. (Chicago: University of Chicago Press, 2001), 217–223.

101. Aaron S. Edlin, "Stopping Above-Cost Predatory Pricing," 111 *Yale L. J.* 941 (2001). See also the case of *U.S. v. AMR Corp.,* 140 F. Supp. 2d 1141 (D. Kan. 2001), rejecting this view. The U.S. Department of Justice subsequently announced its intention to challenge the decision.

102. *Eltam—Ein Hashofet Aguda Shitufit Haklait Baam VeHevrat H. M Sein-goot Baam* (Eltam—Ein Hashofet Association, Inc. and H. M. Seingoot Company, Inc.)(M-4571)(Director of the Israeli Competition Authority, un-published, September 20, 2001).

103. See, e.g., the U.S. case of *Microsoft* for the difficulty in creating effective and efficient remedies.

104. For an extended analysis of this consideration, see Michal S. Gal, "Harmful Remedies: Optimal Reformation of Anti-Competitive Contracts," 22 *Cardozo L. Rev.* 91 (2000).

105. *Canada (Director of Investigation and Research) v. D & B Companies of Canada Ltd.*

106. Ibid., 282.

107. See Gal, "The *Nielsen* Case."

4. The Regulation of Natural Monopolies and Essential Facilities

1. This example is partially based on an actual EC case, *B and I Line/Sealink Harbours* [1992] 5 CMLR 255. There, Holyhead port was the only available British port in the central ferry corridor between Great Britain and Ireland and could not be duplicated owing to geographic constraints. Holyhead port was owned by Sealink and was the base for a ferry service operated by it which competed with other ferry operators.

2. See Kenneth E. Train, *Optimal Regulation: The Economic Theory of Natural Monopoly* (Cambridge, Mass.: MIT Press, 1991).

3. See Oz Shy, *The Economics of Network Industries* (Oxford: Cambridge University Press, 2001). See also *U.S. v. Microsoft Corporation*, 84 F. Supp. 2d 9 (D.D.C. 1999)(findings of fact), recognizing that computer operating systems have significant positive network effects.

4. See, e.g., the EC cases of *Sealink* and *Sea Containers/Stena Sealink (Holyhead)*, OJ 1994 L 15/8, [1995] 4 CMLR 273.

5. See, e.g., the Israeli case of *TWA et al. v. Sherutei Teufa et al.* (Haifa District Court, undecided) and the EC case of *Disma*, Twenty-third Report on Competition Policy (1993), points 223–224. Both cases involve the only network of pipelines for distributing airline gasoline. See also the New Zealand case involving access of rental car companies to Auckland airport, *Auckland Regional Authority v. Mutual Rental Cars (Auckland Airport) Ltd.* (1988) 2 NZBLC 99–110.

6. See, e.g., the U.S. case of *Lorain Journal Co. v. U.S.* 342 U.S. 143 (1951). A single newspaper was a natural monopolist in the daily newspaper market in Lorain, Ohio.

7. See, e.g., the New Zealand case of *Transpower New Zealand Ltd. v. Meridian Energy Ltd.* [2001] NZLR Lexis 22, [2001] 3 NZLR 700.

8. See, e.g., the Israeli case of *Hachrazot al Monopolin Beinyan Natzba Hachzakot 1995 Baam Veach (Declaration of monopoly of Natzba*

Hachzakot 1995 Ltd. et al.), in *Hegbelim Iskiim* (Antitrust), ed. Tova Olshtein, vol. D (Tel Aviv: Vaad Mehoz Tel-Aviv-Yafo, 2001), 11.

9. See, e.g., the EC case of *Centre Belge d'Etudes de Marche-Telemarketing S.A. v Compagnie Luxembourgeoise de Telediffusion et al.* (311/84) [1985] ECR 3261, [1986] 2 CMLR 558. There, the defendant had a legal monopoly to operate the only television station.

10. Competition for the market was first thoroughly analyzed in Harold Demsetz, "Why Regulate Utilities?" 11 *J. Law and Econ.* 55 (1968).

11. For an example of the latter, see the Canadian *Nielsen* case, *Director of Investigation and Research v. D&B Companies of Canada Ltd.* (1995) 64 C.P.R. (3d) 216 (Competition Tribunal). (hereafter *Nielsen*).

12. *Hesder Covel Behitkashruyot LeAspaka Velerechisha Shel Kemach Kasher Lepesach Hatashnad* (Cartel for the supply and acquisition of Passover flour, 1994), in *Hegbelim Iskiim (Antitrust),* ed. Tova Olshtein, vol. A (Tel Aviv: Vaad Mehoz Tel-Aviv-Yaffo, 1994), 57.

13. See, for example, the U.S. case of *Griffith.* The defendant owned several movie theaters in small towns that were capable of supporting only one theater. He attempted to use the purchasing power he possessed in the natural monopoly markets to obtain exclusive-run and first-run movies for his theaters in competitive towns. *U.S. v. Griffith,* 334 U.S. 100 (1948).

14. New Zealand is an illustrative example. There, deregulation of the electricity supply industry was accompanied by the transfer of the regulatory functions to the Commerce Commission, under the supervision of the Minister of Commerce. New Zealand Commerce Act of 1986, Part IV.

15. See, e.g., the U.S. case of *Lamb Enterprises, Inc. v. Toledo Blade Co.,* 461 F.2d 506, 514 (6th Cir. 1972) cert. denied, 409 U.S. 1001 (1972); the Canadian *Nielsen* case; the Israeli *Passover Flour* case; the EC *Sealink* case; the New Zealand case of *Union Shipping New Zealand Port v. Port Nelson* (1990) 2 NZLR 662; *Port Nelson Ltd. v. Commerce Commission* (1996) 3 NZLR 554.

16. Neil W. Hamilton and Anne M. Caufield, "The Defense of Natural Monopoly in Sherman Act Monopolization Cases," 33 *Depaul L. Rev.* 465 (1984).

17. New Zealand Commerce Act of 1986, Part IV; Australia Trade Practices Act of 1974, sec. 44G.

18. For example, see the EC case of *Deutsche Post AG* (C/35.141) OJ 2001 L 125/27.

19. This discussion builds on Michael J. Trebilcock and Michal S. Gal, "Market Power in Electricity Restructurings," 22 *World Comp. L. and Econ. Rev.* 119 (1999).

20. For Australia, see, e.g., *Queensland Wire v. BHP* (1989) ATPR 40-925. For Israel, see, e.g., Monopoly File 1/93, *Hamemune al Hahegbelim Haiskiim Neged Hevrat Dubek Baam Vehach* (Director of Competition Authority v. Dubek, Inc. et al.), in *Hegbelim Iskiim* (Antitrust), ed. Tova Olshtein, vol. B (Tel Aviv: Vaad Mehoz Tel-Aviv-Yafo, 1996), 194.

21. *U.S. v. Terminal Railroad Ass'n,* 224 U.S. 383 (1912).

22. For a long list of cases in which the doctrine has been applied, see Abbott B. Lipsky, Jr., and J. Gregory Sidak, "Essential Facilities," 51 *Stanford L. J.* 1187 (1999).

23. *MCI Communications v. AT&T,* 708 F. 2d 1081 (7th Cir. 1983).

24. *Aspen Highlands Skiing Corp. v. Aspen Skiing Co.,* 738 F. 2d 1501 (10th Cir. 1984), aff'd on other grounds, 472 U.S. 585 (1985). It is questionable whether Aspen was, in fact, an essential facility, given that the mountain ski market comprised many other competing ski facilities.

25. Ibid.

26. *Illinois ex rel. Hartigan v. Panhandle E. Pipe Lineco.,* 730 F. Supp. 826 (C.D. Ill. 1990) aff'd 935 F. 2d 1469 (7th Cir. 1991) cert. denied 502 U.S. 1094 (1992).

27. *Fishman v. Wirtz,* 807 F. 2d 520, 539 (7th Cir. 1986).

28. *City of Groton v. Conneticut Light & Power Co.,* 662 F. 2d 921, 932 (2d Cir. 1981).

29. *Gamco, Inc. v. Providence Fruit and Produce Bldg., Inc.,* 194 F. 2d 484 (1st Cir. 1952).

30. *Town of Massena v. Niagara Mohawk Power Corp.* (CCH) P63,526 (N.D.N.Y. 1980).

31. *City of Groton v. Connecticut Light & Power.*

32. See, e.g., *City of Anaheim v. Southern California Edison Co.,* 955 F. 2d 1373 (9th Cir. 1992), and *City of Vernon v. California Edison Co.,* 955 F. 2d 1361 (9th Cir. 1992).

33. See, e.g., *Olympia Equipment Leasing Co. v. Western Union Telegraph Co.,* 797 F. 2d 370, 375 (7th Cir. 1986).

34. *MCI Communications.*

35. *United States Football League,* 842 F. 2d 1335 (2d Cir. 1988); *Hecht v. Pro Football, Inc.,* 570 F. 2d 982 (D.C. Cir. 1977) cert. denied 436 U.S. 956 (1978).

36. The Israeli *Passover Flour* case is an interesting example.

37. For a thorough analysis of existing EC case law up to 1995, see John Temple Lang, "Defining Legitimate Competition: Companies' Duties to Supply Competitors and Access to Essential Facilities," in *International Antitrust Law and Policy* (Irvington-on-Hudson, N.Y.: Transnational Juris Publications, 1995), 245. For a more recent analysis, see John Temple Lang, "The Principle of Essential Facilities in European Community Competition Law: The Position since *Oscar Bronner,*" 1 *Journal of Network Industries* 375 (2000).

38. *Sealink; Irish Continental Group/CCI Morlaix* (IV /35) [1995] 5 CMLR 77.

39. *IGR Stereo Television—Salora,* Eleventh Report on Competition Policy (1981), point 94. See also *Amadeus/Sabre,* Twenty-first Report on Competition Policy (1991), points 73–74.

40. *B and I Line* and *Sealink.*

41. Lang, "Position since *Oscar Bronner.*"

42. *Oscar Bronner v. Mediaprint* (C-7/97) [1998] ECR I-7791, [1999] 4 CMLR 112.

43. Ibid.

44. See *CBEM v. CLT and IPB* (311/84) [1985] ECR 3261, [1986] 2 CMLR 558; *Bronner,* para. 38.

45. *Bronner.*

46. *Sealink.*

47. Lang, "Position since *Oscar Bronner.*"

48. *BP v. Commission* (77/77) [1978] ECR II-1513, [1978] 3 CMLR 174.

49. *RTE and ITP v Commission* (C-241/91 and C-242/91 P) [1995] ECR I-743, [1995] 4 CMLR 718.

50. *Hugin Kassareigister AB et al. v. Commission* (22/78) [1979] ECR 1869. Case dismissed on the grounds of no effect on trade between member states.

51. *Commercial Solvents v. Commission* (6 and 7/73) [1974] ECR 223, [1974] 1 CMLR 309.

52. *Napier Brown/British Sugar* OJ [1988] L 284/41, [1990] 4 CMLR 196.

53. Australian Trade Practices Act of 1974, sec. 44G.

54. *National Competition Policy, Report of Independent Committee of Inquiry* (August 1993).

55. *Queensland Wire v. BHP.*

56. Ibid., 49,076–77.

57. *MacLean and Anor v. Shell Chemicals (Australia) Pty Ltd.* (1984) ATPR 40-462.

58. See, e.g., *TPC v. CSR* (1991) ATPR 41-076.

59. "Discussion Paper: Application by Robe River Iron Associates for Declaration of a Rail Service Provided by Hamersley Iron Pty Ltd." (Australian National Competition Council, unpublished, 1998).

60. Phillip E. Areeda and Herbert Hovenkamp, *Antitrust Law,* vol. 3A (New York: Aspen Law & Business, 2002), 204–207.

60. *Commercial Solvents v. Commission.*

60. *CBEM v. CLT and IPB.*

62. *Oscar Bronner v. Mediaprint.*

64. *Buyars v. Bluff City News Co.,* 609 F. 2d 843, 861 (6th Cir. 1979).

65. In the U.S. case of *Fishman,* both the defendant and the plaintiff sought to purchase the Chicago Bulls—the city's only National Basketball Association franchise. The defendant, who controlled the city's only appropriate basketball stadium, refused to lease the facility to the plaintiff. The court imposed a duty to deal notwithstanding the fact that only one NBA team would be in Chicago regardless of who owned the franchise. For a different position, see *Almeda Mall, Inc. v. Houston Lighting & Power Co.,* 615 F. 2d 343 (5th Cir. 1980) cert. denied, 449 U.S. 870 (1980).

66. Robert Bork, *The Antitrust Paradox: A Policy at War with Itself* (New York: Basic Books, 1978), 141; David J. Gerber, "Rethinking the Monopo-

list's Duty to Deal: A Legal and Economic Critique of the Doctrine of 'Essential Facilities,'" 74 *Va. L. Rev.* 1069, 1085 (1988).

67. *Paschall v. Kansas City Star Co.*, 605 F. 2d. 403 (8th Cir. 1979).

68. *Paschall v. Kansas City Star Co.*, 441 F. Supp. 349 (W.D. Mo. 1977).

69. *Kansas City Star Co. v. Paschall*, 695 F. 2d 322 (8th Cir. 1982)(panel opinion).

70. *Paschall v. Kansas City Star Co.*, 727 F. 2d 692 (8th Cir. 1984)(en banc). The dissent pointed out that many customers would suffer price increases and reduced service. It also noted the desirability of preserving the 250 independent businesses. Ibid., 705–706.

71. Relevant market defined as that of Hugin's cash register spare parts in Britain, in which Hugin held 100 percent. Yet Hugin accounted for only approximately 13 percent of cash registers sold in Britain. Case dismissed by ECJ on other grounds. *Hugin*.

72. *Ford Motor Co.* (Monopolies and Mergers Commission, unpublished, 1985).

73. *European Night Services and Others v. Commission* (T-375, 384 and 388/94) [1998] ECR II 3141, [1998] 5 CMLR 718. See also *Silvano Raso* (C-163/96) [1998] ECR 1-533, [1998] CMLR 737.

74. See Gregory Werden, "The Law and Economics of the Essential Facility Doctrine," 32 *St. Louis U. L. J.* 433 (1987).

75. *U.S. v. Terminal Railroad.*

76. *RTE and ITP v. Commission.* See also the Canadian case of *Nielsen.*

77. *Competition Authority v. Dubek.*

78. Ibid.

79. *Oscar Bronner v. Mediaprint.*

80. *Paddock Publications, Inc. v. Chicago Tribune Co. et al.*, 103 F. 2d 42 (7th Cir. 1996).

81. Ibid., 44.

82. Ibid. See also *Flip Side Productions, Inc. v. JAM Productions, Ltd.*, 843 F. 2d 1024, 1032–34 (7th Cir. 1988).

83. *British Midland v. Aer Lingus* OJ [1992] L 96/34, [1993] 4 CMLR 596.

84. This was acknowledged by many courts. See, e.g., the U.S. case of *Town of Concord v. Boston Edison Co.*, 915 F. 2d 17, 25–29 (1st Cir. 1990) cert. denied, 111 S. Ct. 1337 (1991); and the New Zealand case of *Telecom Corporation of New Zealand Ltd. v. Clear Communications Ltd.* (1995) 1 NZLR 385.

85. This option, also known as the Baumol-Willig Rule, was adopted in the New Zealand *Clear* case. For criticism of this approach, see, for example, Alfred E. Kahn and William E. Taylor, "The Pricing of Inputs Sold to Competitors: A Comment," 11 *Yale J. Regulation* 225 (1994).

86. Lipsky and Sidak also recognize the problems involved in granting mandatory access. They suggest, however, that the competition authorities should not try to create through injunction or consent decree what Congress and

the state legislatures have declined to create through a regulatory agency. This suggestion is problematic since many natural monopolies that do not have great national significance are not regulated by specialized regulators and come under the scope of competition law. Accepting Lipsky and Sidak's suggestion would mean that access to many essential facilities would be denied.

87. Lang, "Position since *Oscar Bronner.*" This was acknowledged in the EC cases of *IGR-Salora* and *Stena Sealink.* The *Telecommunications Access Notice* OJ 1998 C262/2, para. 87–95, is also based on a similar principle.

88. See, e.g., *City of Anaheim.*

89. Richard Epstein, *Principles for a Free Society: Reconciling Individual Liberty with the Common Good* (Reading, Mass.: Perseus, 1998).

90. *State ex Rel. Wood v. Consumers' Gas Trust Co.,* 61 N.E. 674, 677 (1901).

91. *Sea Containers/Stena Sealink.*

92. *B and I Line/Sealink Harbours.*

93. Community Regulation no. 2299/89, OJ 1989 L220/1, as amended by Council Regulation no. 3089/93, OJ 1993 L14/1.

94. See, e.g., *Oahu Gas Serv., Inc. v. Pacific Resources, Inc.,* 838 F.2d 360 (9th Cir. 1988), cert. denied, 488 U.S. 870 (1988).

95. For a Canadian ruling, see *R. v. Allied Chemicals* (1975) 69 D.L.R. (3d) 506 (B.C.S.C.).

96. Structural separation was imposed by the EC Commission on the German postal operator, which abused its legal monopoly in the letter market to engage in anti-competitive fidelity rebates and predatory pricing in the market for business parcel service. *Deutsche Post.*

97. The idea was developed at the Antitrust Division of the U.S. Department of Justice, and first proposed in 1976 as a solution to the competitive problems posed by the large economies of scale present in large deepwater ports. "Report to the Attorney General Pursuant to Section 7 of the Deepwater Port Act 1974 on the Application of LOOP, Inc. and Seadock, Inc., for Deepwater Port for Licenses" (U.S. Department of Justice, unpublished, November 5, 1976). For an analysis, see Lucinda M. Lewis and Robert J. Reynolds, "Appraising Alternatives to Regulation for Natural Monopolies," in *Oil Pipelines and Public Policy,* ed. Edward J. Mitchell (Washington, D.C.: American Enterprise Institute for Public Policy Research, 1979), 135.

98. Frederick R. Warren-Boulton and John R. Woodburt, "The Design and Evaluation of Competitive Rules Joint Ventures for Mergers and Natural Monopolies" (paper prepared for the Conference on Policy Approaches to the Deregulation of Network Industries, American Enterprise Institute, October 10–11, 1990).

99. Ibid.

100. New Zealand has adopted such a solution for its electricity distribution network. The proposed remedy also does not go much further than remedies that have been granted by U.S. courts. The U.S. *Terminal Railroad* case can

be read as mandating a quasi-structural remedy of joint control. There, the U.S. Supreme Court mandated the association controlling the facility to permit all railroads to share the ownership of the assets on equal terms as existing owners. *Associated Press* can also be read as granting a competitor an equitable share in an association. *U.S. v. Associated Press,* 326 U.S. 10 (1945). Although these two cases already involved associations of owners, requiring a single monopoly to give or sell an equity interest in itself to actual or would-be competitors does not go much further, on a theoretical level. The fact that a facility is owned by one, two, or a hundred owners does not reduce the strength and the validity of the property rights to a facility.

5. The Regulation of Oligopoly Markets

1. Carl Shapiro, "Theories of Oligopoly Behavior," in *Handbook of Industrial Organization,* ed. Richard Schmalensee and Robert D. Willig, vol. 1 (Amsterdam: Elselvier Science Publishers, 1989), 329.
2. Ibid.
3. For the seminal work on this subject, see George Stigler, "A Theory of Oligopoly," 72 *Journal of Political Economy* 44 (1964).
4. See, e.g., U.S. Department of Justice press release, "F. Hoffmann–La Roche and BASF Agree to Pay Record Criminal Fines for Participating in International Vitamin Cartel" (Release 196–199, May 20, 1999); EC press release, "EC Imposes Fines on Vitamin Cartel" (Release IP/01/1625, November 21, 2001); *Australian Competition and Consumer Commission v. Roche Vitamins Australia Pty Ltd. et al.* (Federal Court of Australia New South Wales District, unpublished, February 28, 2001).
5. Steven Salop, "Practices That Credibly Facilitate Oligopoly Co-ordination," in *New Developments in the Analysis of Market Structure,* ed. Joseph Stiglitz and Frank Mathewson (Cambridge, Mass.: MIT Press, 1986), 265.
6. Alexis Jacquemin and Margaret Slade, "Cartels, Collusion, and Horizontal Merger," in Schmalensee and Willig, *Handbook,* 415. For additional economic studies on collusion, see, for example, George A. Hay, "Facilitating Practices: The Ethyl Case," in *The Antitrust Revolution: Economics, Competition, and Policy,* ed. John E. Kwoka, Jr., and Lawrence J. White, 3d ed. (New York: Oxford University Press, 1999), 182; Andrew R. Dick, "When Are Cartels Stable Contracts?" 39 *J. of Law and Econ.* 241 (1996).
7. Shapiro, "Oligopoly Behavior," 357.
8. Phillip E. Areeda, *Antitrust Law: An Analysis of Antitrust Principles and Their Application,* vol. 6 (New York: Aspen Law & Business, 1986), p. 220.
9. For the seminal work on this issue, see John S. McGee, "Cartels: Organization and Functions," 27 *U. Chi. L. Rev.* 191 (1960). For cases acknowledging this relevant factor, see, for example, the Canadian case of *Di-*

rector of Investigation and Research v. Air Canada et al. (1989) 27 C.P.R. (3d) 476; the U.S. case of *E. I. du Pont and Ethyl Corp. v. FTC*, 729 F. 2d 128 (2d Cir. 1984); the Israeli case of *Bakashat Ptor Meishur Beit Hadin Lehesder Covel Shutafut Poligar* (Request for the director's waiver for the agreement for the creation of Poligar), in *Hegbelim Iskiim (Antitrust)*, ed. Tova Olshtein, vol. A (Tel Aviv: Vaad Mehoz Tel-Aviv-Yafo, 1994), 108.

10. Stigler.

11. Ibid.

12. Appeal 1-3/93, *Delek Baam Veach neged Hamemune al Hahegbelim Haiskim* (Delek Ltd. et al. v. Director of Israeli Competition Authority), in Olshtein, *Hegbelim Iskiim*, Vol. A, 283.

13. Several economists have raised thought-provoking challenges to the welfare effects of collusion. Donald Dewey has argued that when collusion is present, information costs and variance as to future rates of return are lowered. This may lead to fewer price changes, lower inventories, and lower uncertainty. The result is expanded production leading to higher total welfare. Dewey's model is limited, however, when entry barriers exist, and it does not apply to mere price fixing. Donald Dewey, "Welfare and Collusion: Reply," 72 *American Economic Review* 276 (1982). For a somewhat similar proposition, see S. Y. Wu, "An Essay on Monopoly Power and Stable Price Policy," 69 *American Economic Review* 60 (1979).

14. Empirical studies of cartels have indicated that their members do not necessarily earn more than the competitive rate of return. See, e.g., Peter Asch and Joseph J. Seneca, "Is Collusion Profitable?" 58 *Review of Economics & Statistics* 1 (1976), finding collusion and profitability negatively correlated though rejecting an outright causal explanation.

15. *Poligar Agreement.*

16. *Eastern Express Pty Ltd. v General Newspapers Pty Ltd.* (1991) 30 FCR 385.

17. In some jurisdictions competing with a joint venture amounts to a breach of contract, even if the contract did not specifically prohibit competition. See, e.g., the Israeli decision *Deta-Kar Baam neged Hamemune Al Hahegbelim Haiskiim* (Deta-Kar Ltd. v. Director of Competition Authority) (456/96) (Israeli Competition Tribunal, unpublished, July 7, 1996), 21.

18. See, for example, the EC case of *Tetra-Pak I*, OJ [1988] L272/27, [1990] 4 CMLR 47; the Israeli case of *Director of Competition Authority v. Vitamed* (Israeli Competition Tribunal, unpublished). Vitamed, a monopolistic manufacturer of veterinary drugs, entered into an exclusivity contract with Hahaklait, a cooperative that provides veterinary services to agricultural markets and that incorporates almost all of the veterinarians. The arrangement created a monopoly for the cooperative in the market for veterinary services.

19. See the U.S. case of *Northern Natural Gas Co. v. Fed. Power Comm'n*, 399 F. 2d 953, 972 (D.C. Cir. 1968); Israeli decision of *Hachlata al Ei Matan*

Ptor Meishur Beit Hadin Lehesder Covel: Energiyat Hamizrach Hatichon (Non-approval of clearance to Middle East Energy) (Director of Israeli Competition Authority, unpublished, May 13, 1997).

20. *Ishur Mizug Betnaim Columbus Capital Corporation mikvutzat Klaridge, Cur Taasiot Baam* (Conditioned approval of a merger between Columbus Capital Corporation from the Klaridge Group, Cur Industries Ltd.) (Director of Israeli Competition Authority, unpublished, January 5, 1998).

21. *ACCC v. Mobil Oil Australia Ltd.* (1997) ATPR 41-568.

22. *Trade Practices Commission v. Email Ltd.* (1980) 43 FLR 383.

23. A. A. Cournot, *Researches into the Mathematical Principles of the Theory of Wealth* (New York: Kelley, 1838).

24. For the seminal work on this subject, see George Stigler, *The Organization of Industry* (Homewood, Ill.: R. D. Irwin, 1968), 39–63.

25. Salop, "Practices."

26. Ibid.

27. Ibid.

28. *American Tobacco Co. v. U.S.*, 328 U.S. 781 (1946).

29. For example, the Australian Trade Practices Act of 1974 and the New Zealand Commerce Act of 1986 require an "agreement, arrangement or understanding"; the Canadian Competition Act of 1985 requires a "conspiracy, combination, agreement or arrangement"; the Israeli Restrictive Trade Practices Act of 1988 requires "an arrangement"; the Maltese Competition Act of 1994 and the 1957 EC Treaty of Rome require "an agreement" or "a concerted practice." The U.S. Sherman Act requires "an agreement."

30. See, e.g., the Australian case of *Trade Practices Commission v. Nicholas Enterprises Pty Ltd.* (1979) ATPR 40-126. The failure to provide another explanation for parallel pricing conduct was an important consideration in finding that an understanding had been reached.

31. See, e.g., the Canadian case of *R. v. Canadian General Electric Co.* (1976) 15 O.R. (2d) 360, 75 D.L.R. (3d) 664, 34 C.C.C. (2d) 489 (H.C.J.).

32. See, e.g., the U.S. case of *Alvord Polk v. F. Schumacher & Co.*, 37 F. 3d 996 (3d Cir. 1993).

33. Trade Practices Act of 1974, sec. 45C.

34. Commerce Act of 1986, sec. 30.

35. Israeli Restrictive Trade Practices Act of 1988, sec. 2(b).

36. For a legislative exemption, see, e.g., Australian Trade Practices Act of 1974, sec. 51. Other jurisdictions generally base their exemption on interpretation of the requirement that the agreement restrain trade as applying within their domestic borders only.

37. The EC, for example, differentiates between full-function joint ventures, which are analyzed under the EC Merger Regulation, as amended, and others that are treated as restrictive agreements under Article 81. Full-function joint ventures are defined as autonomous economic entities that operate on a lasting basis and perform all the functions of such entities and that have a

"community dimension." See EC Commission, *Notice on the Concept of Full-Function Joint Ventures under Regulation 4064/89*, OJ 1998 C66/1. The U.S. antitrust agencies also apply merger control when certain conditions are met. See *Antitrust Guidelines for Collaborations among Competitors* (Federal Trade Commission and the U.S. Department of Justice, unpublished, April 2000), sec. 1.3.

38. *Application of McIlwrath McEacharn Ltd.* (A4460) (Trade Practices Commission, unpublished, July 31, 1980).

39. See, e.g., the Australian case of *Ampol Petroleum Ltd. and Newbold General Refractories Ltd.* C933-4 14 (1975). Joint venture cleared on the basis that entry into the market was relatively easy and producers could easily expand their production, even though the effect of the joint venture was to bring about increased market concentration.

40. See, e.g., the Israeli regulation *Clalei Hahegbelim Haiskiim (Ptor Sug Lehescemim Shepgiatam Batacharut Kalat Erech)* (Competition law regulation [block exemption for agreements with minor effects on competition]), 2001, sec. 2. An agreement is presumed to be legal if the aggregate share held by the parties to the agreement does not exceed 10 percent of any relevant market. The exemption does not apply to agreements the intent of which is to harm competition or agreements that contain restrictions that are not necessary to achieve their goals. Broader safe harbors exist for joint ventures or research and development agreements under specific block exemptions. See, e.g., *Clalei Hahegbelim Haiskiim (Ptor Sug Lemeizamim Meshutafim)* (Competition law regulation [block exemption for joint ventures]), 2001.

41. *Deta-Kar v. Director of Competition Authority.*

42. Canadian Competition Act of 1985, sec. 96.

43. *Trade Practices Commission v. Email.*

44. For additional Australian cases based on such considerations, see, e.g., *Federal Springs Ltd.* (1987) ATPR 50-054; *Davids* (1995) ATPR 50-185; and *Davids* (1996) ATPR 50-224.

45. New Zealand Commerce Act of 1986, sec. 33; Australian Trade Practices Act of 1974, sec. 45.

46. *E. F. Found Pty Ltd. & William Hodge Pty Ltd.*, (C4272) (Australian Trade Practices Commission, unpublished, July 11, 1975). See also *Eastern Express Pty Ltd. v. General Newspapers Pty Ltd.* [1991] 30 FCR 385. The joint venture enabled small real estate agents to compete effectively with an established real estate paper.

47. *U.S. v. Topco Associates, Inc.*, 405 U.S. 596, 607–608, 92 S. Ct. 1126 (1972). Several lower courts have nonetheless applied a rule of reason when horizontal market division was found to be ancillary to a joint venture. See, e.g., *General Leaseways, Inc. v. National Truck Leasing Ass'n*, 744 F. 2d 588 (7th Cir. 1984).

48. *U.S. v. Topco*, 607–611.

49. European Commission, *Guidelines on Horizontal Cooperation Agreements* OJ 2001 C3/2, sec. 36. Lang considers the test to be even stricter than that of dominance. John Temple Lang, "International Joint Ventures under Community Law," in *International Antitrust Law and Policy*, ed. Barry Hawk (New York: Juris, 2000), 381.

50. Israeli Restrictive Trade Practices Act of 1988, sec. 2. See also Appeal 1/97 *Iscur Sherutei Pladot Baam Veach v. Hamemune al Hahegbelim Haiskiim Veach* (Iscur Sherutei Pladot Inc. et al. v. Director of Competition Authority et al.) (Israeli Competition Tribunal, unpublished, December 11, 1997).

51. Israeli Restrictive Trade Practices Act of 1988, sec. 10.

52. *Antitrust Guidelines for Collaborations*, 8–9.

53. See, for example, the conditions imposed by the European Commission on the parties in *De Laval/Stork* OJ 1977 L215/11, [1977] 2 CMLR D69. The commission provided that when the agreement was terminated, each party would be entitled to a license for the technology that had been available to the joint venture. The condition affected the commercial balance of the agreement since most of the technology came from one of the partners.

54. See, for example, *Eurotunnel III* OJ 1994 L354/66, [1995] 4 CMLR 801. The EC applies a lower threshold than when the essential facility principle applies to a single dominant firm. In determining access issues in the context of agreements, the test is whether not granting access would eliminate competition in a substantial part of the market. A dominant firm normally has no duty to supply if there is even one alternative source available. Lang, "International Joint Ventures."

55. *Poligar Agreement*, 108.

56. For the United States, see, e.g., *Theatre Enterprises, Inc. v. Paramount Film Distrib. Corp.*, 346 U.S. 537 (1954); *E. I. Du Pont de Nemours & Co. v. FTC*, 729 F. 2d 128, 139 (2d Cir. 1984); for Malta, see Maltese Competition Act of 1994, sec. 5; for Australia, see *ACCC v. Mobil Oil Australia Ltd.* (1997) ATPR 41-568; *Trade Practices Commission v. J J & Y K Russell Pty Ltd.* (1991) ATPR 41-132; for New Zealand, see *ARA v. Mutual Rental Cars (Auckland Airport) Ltd.* (1987) 2 NZLR 647; *NZ Magic Millions Ltd. v. Wrightson Bloodstock Ltd.* (1990) 1 NZLR 731, 765. For a survey of the ways different jurisdictions treat conscious parallelism, see *Oligopoly*, OECD Committee on Competition Law and Policy, DAFFE/CLP(99)25 (1999).

57. The Spanish act prohibits "knowingly parallel activities, whose object or whose effect is to prevent, to limit, or to distort competition." Spanish Act against Restraints of Competition of 1989, Art. 1(1).

58. Donald F. Turner, "The Definition of Agreement under the Sherman Act: Conscious Parallelism and Refusals to Deal," 75 *Harv. L. Rev.* 655 (1962).

59. Richard A. Posner, "Oligopoly and the Antitrust Laws: A Suggested Approach," 21 *Stan. L. Rev.* 1562 (1968); idem, *Antitrust Law: An Economic Perspective*, 2d ed. (Chicago: University of Chicago Press, 2001), 55–60.

60. Posner, "Oligopoly"; Posner, *Antitrust Law.*
61. George A. Hay, "Oligopoly, Shared Monopoly, and Antitrust Law" 67 *Cornell L. Rev.* 439 (1982). For criticism of this approach, see Donald Baker, "Two Sherman Act Section 1 Dilemmas: Parallel Pricing, the Oligopoly Problem, and Contemporary Economic Theory," 39 *Antitrust Bull.* 143, 150–169 (1993).
62. See, e.g., *Report on Parallel Pricing* (Cmnd. 5330) (British Monopolies Commission, unpublished, 1973), 38; *Oligopoly.* The European competition commissioner and the EC national antitrust authorities discussed the difficulty in applying traditional competition principles to parallel pricing in the gas retailing sector. The conclusion reached by the EC authorities was that "where national markets are dominated by a narrow oligopoly . . . competition law alone does not provide a satisfactory remedy." "Commission, National Authorities Discuss Competition Policy in EC Motor Fuel Sector," 79 *Antitrust and Trade Reg. Rep. (BNA)* 345 (2000).
63. *Clamp-All Corp. v. Cast Iron Soil Pipe Institute,* 851 F. 2d 478, 484 (1st Cir. 1988).
64. *Atlantic Sugar Refineries Co. Ltd. et al. v. A. G. Canada* (1980) 54 C.C.C. (2d) 373 (S.C.C.).
65. Ibid.
66. See, for example, *White House Task Force on Antitrust Policy* (1968), reprinted in "Report, Comments, and Separate Statements," 2 *Antitrust L. Econ. Rev.* 11 (1968–69), which recommended the reduction of concentration in any industry in which four firms or fewer have an aggregate market share of 70 percent or more, subject to an efficiency defense. Article 13 of the Munich Code provides for restructuring firms in anti-competitive, highly concentrated markets. Draft International Antitrust Code, 64 *Antitrust and Trade Reg. Rep. (BNA)* S-17 (1993).
67. See, e.g., David Scheffman, "Commentary on 'Oligopoly Power, Coordination, and Conscious Parallelism,'" in Stiglitz and Mathewson, *New Developments,* 295.
68. See, e.g., *U.S. v. International Harvester Co.,* 274 U.S. 693 (1927); *U.S. v. National Malleable and Steel Castings Corp.,* 385 U.S. 38 (1958).
69. *Atlantic Sugar Refineries.*
70. *Trade Practices Commission v. Email.*
71. *Belgian Roofing Felt* OJ 1986 L32/15, [1991] 4 CMLR 130, upheld on appeal; *Belasco and Others v. Commission* (246/86) [1991] 4 CMLR 96.
72. Israeli Restrictive Trade Practices Act of 1988, sec. 6.
73. Ibid., Art. 26(D). See also the Canadian Competition Act of 1986, sec. 79 ("one or more persons"); Maltese Competition Act of 1994, sec. 9.
74. *Kvia Lefi Saif 43(a)(4) Lefia Kvutzat Rikuz hina Baal Monopolin Shivuk Umechirat Yechidot Nofesh* (Decision in accordance with section 43[A][4] that a group of firms is a monopoly—marketing and selling of vacation units) (Director of Israeli Competition Authority, unpublished, 1996).

75. For the United States, see *Electric Generators Investigation* (Department of Justice, unpublished, 1977). For the EC, see, e.g., *Compagnie Maritime Belge Transport NV v. Commission* (T-24/93, etc.) [1996] ECR II-1201, [1997] 4 CMLR 273, appeal dismissed, (C-395 & 396/96P) [2000] 4 CMLR 1076; *Gencor v. Commission* (T-102/96) [1999] ECR II-879, [1999] 4 CMLR 971.

76. *Gencor.* The commission has stated that it recognizes the need to provide further clarification of its approach to oligopolistic dominance. *Twenty-ninth Report on Competition Policy* (European Commission, 1999), point 155.

77. Lang argues that EC court decisions can be interpreted as moving in the direction of applying the joint dominance concept to parallel conduct. John Temple Lang, "Oligopolies and Joint Dominance in Community Antitrust Law," in *International Antitrust Law and Policy,* ed. Barry Hawk (New York: Juris, 2002), 269. Whether there need be any greater connecting factors between the oligopolists than may arise from the characteristics of a tight oligopolistic market remains unclear. *Bellamy and Child European Community Law of Competition,* Peter M. Roth, ed., 5th ed. (London: Sweet and Maxwell, 2001), 716.

78. Frederic Jenny, "Collective Dominance and the EC Merger Regulation," in Hawk, *International Antitrust Law and Policy.*

79. Sec. 6(2) of the U.K. Fair Trading Act of 1973, as amended by the Competition Act of 1998.

80. U.K. Fair Trading Act of 1973, pts. 1 and 2 of Schedule 8.

81. *A Report on the Supply of White Salt in the U.K. by Producers of Such Salt* (Cmnd. 9778) (Monopolies and Mergers Commission, unpublished, 1986). For some more recent investigations, see *New Cars* (Cmnd 4660) (Competition Commission, unpublished, 1999); and *Supermarkets* (Cm 4842) (Competition Commission, unpublished, 2000).

82. See, e.g., Jeremy Lever, "U.K. Economic Regulation: Use and Abuse of the Law," 2 *European Competition Law Review* 55 (1992).

83. *A Report on the Supply, Maintenance, and Repair of Postal Franking Machinery in the U.K.* (Cmnd 9747) (Monopolies and Mergers Commission, unpublished, 1986).

84. See *Oligopoly.*

85. For an interesting suggestion to regulate oligopoly pricing by way of freezing the price of each oligopolist after it has submitted its future price in a secret bid to the government, see William Bishop, "Oligopoly Pricing: A Proposal," 28 *Antitrust Bull.* 311 (1983).

86. Several U.S. cases have gone along these lines. See, e.g., *United States v. Container Corp. of America et al.,* 393 U.S. 333 (1969), 89 S. Ct. 510; *Airline Tariff Publishing* (unpublished, 1994).

87. Most jurisdictions have been very cautious in applying this approach. See, e.g., the Australian case of *Email;* the U.S. cases of *E. I. Du Pont and Ethyl* and *FTC v. Abbott Laboratories,* 853 F. Supp. 526 (1994).

88. Areeda, 237–262.
89. Ibid.
90. Ibid., 239–240.
91. Ibid., 254–256.
92. *E. I. Du Pont and Ethyl.*
93. It is conceivable, but not always probable, that a monopolist would adopt business practices in anticipation of a change in market structure when co-ordination would be desirable.
94. *E. I. Du Pont and Ethyl.*
95. For an extended analysis of this proposal, see Michal S. Gal, "Reducing Rival's Prices," 7 *Stan. J. of L., Bus., and Fin.* 73 (2001).
96. Ibid., 80–81.
97. Ibid., 82.
98. *E. I. Du Pont and Ethyl.*
99. Yet the FTC still pursued the case. A court victory would have meant that prices for antiknock products would have been reduced.
100. Gal, "Reducing Prices," 88–93.
101. Ibid., 98–102.

6. Merger Control Policy

1. Merger is generally defined to include changes in ownership or control between different business entities that enable one entity to control, directly or indirectly, de jure or de facto, a significant part of the assets or the decision process of another firm. Some jurisdictions (e.g., Australia, Canada, EC, Belgium) extend the definition to encompass some types of joint ventures among firms in which all parties share control over another entity.
2. Shyam Khemani, "Merger Policy and Small Open Economies: The Case of Canada," in *Perspectives in Industrial Organization,* ed. Ben Dankbaar et al., (Dordrecht: Kluwer Academic Publishers, 1990), 215; idem, "Merger Policy in Small vs. Large Economies," in *Canadian Competition Policy at the Centenary,* ed. Shyam Khemani and W. T. Standbury (Halifax: Institute for Research on Public Policy, 1991), 205.
3. Khemani, "The Case of Canada," 223.
4. For the seminal works on this subject, see Henrey G. Manne, "Mergers and the Market for Corporate Control," 73 *Journal of Political Economy* 110 (1965); Frank Easterbrook and Daniel Fischel, "The Proper Role of a Target's Management in Responding to a Tender Offer," 94 *Harv. L. Rev.* 1161 (1981). New Zealand courts have recognized this consideration. See *Power New Zealand Commerce Commission* [1997] 2 NZLR 669.
5. An exception occurs when one of the merging entities is a failing firm that would otherwise exit the market.
6. R. D. Jacquemin and M. E. Slade, "Cartels, Collusion, and Horizontal Mergers," and Carl Shapiro, "Theories of Oligopoly Behavior," in *Handbook of Industrial Organization,* ed. Richard Schmalensee and Robert

Willig, vol. 1 (Amsterdam: Elselvier Science Publishers, 1989), chaps. 7 and 6, respectively.

7. See, for example, Martin K. Perry, "Vertical Integration: Determinants and Effects," in Schmalensee and Willig, *Handbook,* 183; Jean Tirole, *The Theory of Industrial Organization* (Cambridge, Mass: MIT Press, 1988), chap. 4.

8. The issue of whether or not conglomerate mergers among firms that hold a dominant position in at least one market raise special issues that go beyond traditional concerns raised by horizontal or vertical mergers is the center of a debate between U.S. and EC competition authorities created by their divergent views on the *GE/Honeywell* case. The EC Commission blocked the merger based on a potential leveraging argument (also known as "portfolio effects"). *GE/Honeywell* (Comp/M. 2220)(EC Commission, unpublished, July 3, 2001). For additional EC cases based on the portfolio effects argument, see, e.g., *Coca-Cola Company/Amalgamated Beverages GB* (M.794) OJ 1997 L218/15 and *Guinness/Grand Metropolitan* (M.938) OJ 1998 L288/24. The U.S. Department of Justice allowed the GE-Honeywell merger, rejecting the portfolio effects argument and arguing that the policy implication of the EC theory condemns competition based on efficiencies. *GE/Honeywell* (U.S. Department of Justice, unpublished, November 29, 2001). Australia also seems to accept the portfolio effects argument in some cases. See "Contribution by Australia," OECD Mini-Roundtable on Portfolio Effects in Conglomerate Mergers (October 18–19, 2001); *Coca Cola and Cadbury Schweppes* (ACCC, unpublished, March 31, 1999).

9. Oliver E. Williamson, "Economies as an Antitrust Defense: The Welfare Tradeoffs," 58 *American Economic Review* 18 (1968); and idem, "Economies as an Antitrust Defense Revisited," 125 *U. Penn. L. Rev.* 699 (1977), his legal exposition of the theory. Some commentators reject this view, based on the role it would grant courts of law in deciding on complex economic arguments and the difficulty of balancing future and uncertain efficiency gains versus immediate and certain anti-competitive effects. See, for example, Richard Schmalensee, "Horizontal Merger Policy: Problems and Changes," 1 *Journal of Economic Perspectives* 41 (1987).

10. Oliver E. Williamson, "Economies as an Antitrust Defense: Correction and Reply," 58 *American Economic Review* 1372 (1968).

11. *Ishur Mizug Kelet (1991) Baam ve Taal Taasiot Etz Lavud Kvutzat Mishmarot Baam* (Approval of a Merger between Kelet [1991] Ltd. and Taal Taasiot Etz Lavud Kvutzat Mishmarot Ltd.) (Director of Israeli Competition Authority, unpublished, February 2, 2002).

12. *Hitnagdut Lemizug Shebein Taal Levein Levidei Ashkelon Baam* (Non-approval of a merger between Taal and Levidei Ashkelon, Inc.) (Director of Israeli Competition Authority, unpublished, October 14, 1998).

13. Australian Trade Practices Act of 1974, sec. 90(9A); Australian Competition and Consumer Commission, *Exports and the Trade Practices Act*

(ACCC, 1997); Canadian Competition Act of 1985, sec. 96(2). Israel, by contrast, focuses solely on the effects of the merger on the domestic market. Israeli Restrictive Trade Practices Act of 1988, sec. 21; Civil Appeal 2247/ 95 *Hamemune al Hahegbelim Haiskiim neged Tnuva Baam* (Director of the Competition Authority v. Tnuva, Inc.), *Piskey Din* (Court decisions) 52 (5), 213.

14. "Few roles of government are more important to the upgrading of an economy than ensuring vigorous domestic rivalry." Michael Porter, *The Competitive Advantage of Nations* (New York: Free Press, 1990), 662. This view is not universally shared. Some scholars argue that large, strong enterprises are better suited to meet international competition because they will be able to compete in those markets if they have a strong home market that gives them the critical mass to become world players. C. D. Foster, *Privatization, Public Ownership, and the Regulation of Natural Monopoly* (Oxford: Blackwell, 1992); Kenneth E. Train, *Optimal Regulation* (Cambridge, Mass.: MIT Press, 1991), 156.

15. Williamson, "Correction and Reply"; Jeffrey R. Church and Roger Ware, *Industrial Organization: A Strategic Approach* (San Francisco: McGraw-Hill/Irwin, 2000), 719.

16. Roger Ware, "Efficiencies and the Propane Case," 3 *International Antitrust Bulletin* 14 (2000); Frank Mathewson and Ralph A. Winter, "*Superior Propane*: Correct Criterion Incorrectly Applied," 20(2) *Canadian Competition Policy Record* 88 (2001).

17. Stephen F. Ross, "Did the Canadian Parliament Really Permit Mergers That Exploit Canadian Consumers So That the World Can Be More Efficient?" 65 *Antitrust L. J.* 641 (1997).

18. Australian Competition and Consumer Commission, *Australian Merger Guidelines* (Canberra: ACCC Publications Unit, 1999).

19. In the U.S. *Staples* case econometric estimates of the degree of post-merger market power served as a basis for determining the effects of the proposed merger. *FTC v. Staples, Inc.,* 970 F. Supp. 1066 (D.D.C. 1997).

20. Proposal of Professor Townley cited in the Canadian *Superior* case. *Canada (Commissioner of Competition) v. Superior Propane, Inc.,* 7 C.P.R. (4th) 385 (Competition Tribunal, 2000) (hereafter Tribunal decision I).

21. See, for example, sec. 96 of the Canadian Competition Act of 1985; sec. 50 of the Australian Trade Practices Act of 1974; sec. 47 of the New Zealand Commerce Act of 1986; sec. 21 of the Israeli Restrictive Trade Practices Act of 1988.

22. For example, European *Council Regulation (EEC) 4046/89 on the Control of Concentrations between Undertakings* OJ 1989 L395/1 and OJ 1990 L257/14 (hereafter EC *Merger Regulation*), Art. 2.

23. For the two standards as alternatives, see, e.g., sec. 7 of the U.S. Clayton Act. For the two standards as complements, see, e.g., the Swiss Federal Act on Cartels and Other Limitations to Competition of 1995.

24. Such a merger might also not create or strengthen a dominant position, unless a structural approach to dominance is applied.

25. For this and other cases that substantially lessen competition but do not fall under the dominance test, see Allan Fels, "The ACCC Attitude to Mergers" (presentation given at the Institute of Public Affairs Seminar, Melbourne, July 24, 1998). *Amcor Ltd. v. Visy Board Pty Ltd.* 18 IPR 621.

26. *Progressive Enterprises Ltd. and Woolworths (New Zealand) Ltd.* (New Zealand Commerce Commission, Decision 438, unpublished, July 13, 2001).

27. New Zealand Commerce Amendment Bill (no. 2), 2001.

28. See "Mergers, Takeovers, and Monopolies: Profiting from Competition" (Griffiths Report, 1989).

29. *Commerce Commission v. Port Nelson Ltd.* (1995) 5 NZBLC 103, 762 (HC) at 103,787. Approved by the New Zealand Court of Appeal in *Commerce Commission v. Port Nelson Ltd.* (1996) 5 NZBLC 104,142, 104,161.

30. *Progressive,* Decision 438, 13.

31. *Foodstuffs (Auckland) Ltd. v. Commerce Commission and Progressive Enterprises Ltd.* (CA163/01) [2001] NZCA 294 (Court of Appeal of New Zealand).

32. *Progresive Enterprises Ltd. and Woolworths (New Zealand) Ltd.* (New Zealand Commerce Commission, unpublished, December 14, 2001).

33. Ibid., paras. 79–84.

34. Ibid., paras. 222–226.

35. For an extensive survey and analysis of all the EC cases applying or interpreting the concept of joint dominance and the problems they raise, see John Temple Lang, "Oligopolies and Joint Dominance in Community Antitrust Law," in *International Antitrust Law and Policy,* ed. Barry Hawk (New York: Juris, 2002), 269.

36. See Frederic Jenny, "Collective Dominance and the EC Merger Regulation," in Hawk, *International Antitrust Law and Policy,* 361. In June 2000 the European Commission decided to launch a major review of the *Merger Regulation.* In December 2001 a Green Paper outlining possible avenues for reform of the regulation was adopted by the commission. The EC Green Paper launched a wide discussion and solicited views on the merits of the EC dominance test and the proper role and scope of efficiency considerations in the area of merger control. "Green Paper on the Review of Council Regulation (EEC) No. 4064/89" (European Competition Commission, unpublished, December 11, 2001).

37. See, e.g., *Coca Cola.*

38. Hovenkamp goes further to suggest that mergers were prohibited *because* they might have improved efficiency and thus created higher entry barriers into their markets. Herbert Hovenkamp, *Federal Antitrust Policy: The Law and Its Practice,* 2d ed. (St. Paul: West Publishing, 1999), 499–500.

39. *FTC. v. Procter and Gamble Co.,* 386 U.S. 568 (1967).

40. *U.S. v. Philadelphia Nat'l Bank,* 374 U.S. 321 (1963). See also *Ford Motor Co. v. U.S.,* 405 U.S. 562 (1972).
41. *Procter and Gamble,* 580.
42. *U.S. v. Philadelphia National Bank,* 371.
43. Ibid.
44. Ibid., 363. See also *United States v. Citizens and Southern National Bank,* 422 U.S. 86, 120 (1975). For more recent cases still using this prima facie rule, see *FTC v. Cardinal Health, Inc.,* 12 F. Supp. 2d 34 (D.D.C. 1998); *FTC v. Swedish Match et al.,* 131 F. Supp. 2d 151, 166 (D.D.C. 2000).
45. See, e.g., *Brown Shoe Co. v. U.S.* 370 U.S. 294 (1962); *U.S. v. Von's Grocery Co. et al.,* 384 U.S. 270 (1966); *U.S. v. Continental Can Co. et al.,* 378 U.S. 441 (1964); *United States v. Aluminum Co. of America et al.,* 377 U.S. 271 (1964).
46. *Philadelphia National Bank,* 363; *Cardinal Health,* 54; *Swedish Match,* 167.
47. *Kaiser Aluminum and Chemical Corp. v. FTC,* 652 F. 2d 1324, 1341 (7th Cir. 1981).
48. See, e.g., *U.S. v. General Dynamics Corp.,* 415 U.S. 486 (1974). Proof of an industry-wide decline in demand deemed relevant.
49. *Unites States v. Baker Hughes, Inc.,* 731 F. Supp. 3 (D.D.C. 1990) aff'd 908 U.S.F. 2d 981, 982 (D.C. Cir. 1990).
50. EC *Merger Regulation.* Prior to the enactment of the regulation, mergers were mostly regulated under Article 81 of the Treaty of Rome of 1957, which prohibits agreements that restrict or distort competition. *British American Tobacco Co. Ltd. v. Commission* (142 & 156/84)[1987] ECR 4487.
51. EC *Merger Regulation,* Art. 2. See also EC, *Notice on the Concept of Concentration under Council Regulation (EEC) No. 4056/89 on the Control of Concentrations between Undertakings* OJ 1998 C66/5.
52. The decisive criterion is one of dominance, interpreted as a firm's "ability to act to an appreciable extent independently of its competitors, customers and ultimately its consumers," as linked to the ability to raise prices. *Renault/Volvo* (M.004) [1991] 4 CMLR 297. The Merger Regulation requires that the concentration also "significantly impede effective competition."
53. EC Merger Regulation, Art. 2(1)b and Recital 13.
54. See, for example, J. P. Griffin and L. T. Sharp, "Efficiency Issues in Competition Analysis in Australia, the European Union, and the United States," 64 *Antitrust L. J.* 649 (1996); Simon Bishop and Mike Walker, *Economics of E.C. Competition Law* (London: Sweet & Maxwell, 1999), 160–161. Some early cases, however, mention the conditions for recognizing efficiencies: efficiencies must be substantial and merger-specific with the burden of proof resting on the parties and should reasonably be passed on to the consumer on a permanent basis, in terms of lower prices or increased quality. *Aerospatiale-Alenia/de Havilland,* (M.053) OJ 1991 L334/42, [1992] 4

CMLR M2; *Accor/Wagons-Lits* (M.126), OJ 1992 L204/1, [1993] 15 CMLR M13.

55. Contribution from the Commission of the European Union, in "Efficiency Claims in Mergers and Other Horizontal Agreements" (OECD/GD [96]65 Competition Policy Roundtable, 1996), 53. More recently, the EC Green Paper launched a wide discussion and solicited views on the proper role and scope of efficiency considerations in the area of merger control.

56. Frederic Jenny, "EEC Merger Control: Economies as an Antitrust Defense or an Antitrust Attack?" in *International Antitrust Law and Policy,* ed. Barry Hawk (Irvington-on-Hudson, N.Y.: Juris, 1993), 591, 597.

57. *Nordic Satellite Distribution* (M.490) OJ 1996 L53/21.

58. Some EC Commission decisions can be interpreted as allowing efficiencies when the merging parties provide undertakings to ensure that competition in their market will not be harmed. See, e.g., *Vodafone Airtouch/ Mannesman* (M.1795)(EC Commission, unpublished, April 12, 2000). The merger raised competition concerns, as Vodafone's acquiring of Mannesmann would give it mobile networks throughout Europe, creating the possibility of a seamless, pan-European mobile telecommunications service, which would grant it advantages over its competitors. The commission found Vodafone dominant in this prospective market. It nonetheless allowed the merger after Vodafone agreed to give its competitors nondiscriminatory access to its integrated network for three years, a period that would allow competitors to replicate the Vodafone network.

59. Remarks made by Phillip Lowe at the Fordham International Antitrust Conference, October 30, 2002; EC green paper.

60. See sec. 50(3) of the Australian Trade Practices Act of 1974. Efficiencies are relevant only inasmuch as they affect the competitiveness of markets. Australian *Merger Guidelines,* sec. 5.171.

61. Based on discussions with the former and current directors of the Israeli Competition Authority. Some decisions, however, can be interpreted as opening the door to efficiencies considerations. See *Nimukim Lehitnagdut Lemizug Haribua Hacahol Israel Baam—Yarkon (Plus 2000) Sitonaut Mazon Baam* (Non-approval of a merger between Haribua Hacahol Israel Ltd.—Yarkon [Plus 2000] Sitonaut Mazon Ltd.) (Director of Israeli Competition Authority, unpublished, October 10, 2001).

62. The merging undertakings can, nonetheless, apply to the Federal Executive Council for exceptional admission owing to predominant public interest.

63. The threshold for merger notification and review consists of two criteria. The first is an extremely high turnover of the merging parties. The second criterion requires notifications of all concentrations with a participating undertaking already found to possess a dominant position under the act. In addition, the legality test requires that the merger eliminate competition.

64. This can be demonstrated by the Canadian *Imperial Oil* case. There, the magnitude of the efficiency gains depended on the reaction of existing rivals and potential entrants to the removal of a competitor from the market. If

they were to expand capacity and effectively duplicate the exiting firm's assets, there would be no efficiency gain. *Canada (Director of Investigation and Research) v. Imperial Oil et al.* (CT-89/3) (Canadian Competition Tribunal, unpublished, January 26, 1990).

65. These court decisions rely on an interpretation of the Supreme Court decisions as rejecting only efficiencies that are based on insufficient or speculative evidence and on more recent Supreme Court cases that were based on an economic analysis, such as *Continental T.V., Inc. v. GTE Sylvania, Inc.*, 443 U.S. 36, 97 S. Ct. 2549 (1977). For a discussion of some of the differing views, see, e.g., *FTC v. University Health, Inc.*, 938 F. 2d 1206 (11th Cir. 1991).

66. The only decision that came close to recognizing offsetting efficiencies was the decision of the D.C. District Court that declined to issue a temporary injunction against a proposed merger, based on efficiency considerations. *FTC v. H. J. Heinz, Co.*, 116 F. Supp. 190 (D.D.C. 2000). The decision was overturned by the Court of Appeals. *FTC v. H. J. Heinz Co.*, 246 F. 3d 708, 711 (D.C. Cir. 2001).

67. See, e.g., *U.S. v. Country Lake Foods, Inc.*, 754 F. Supp. 669, 680 (D. Minn. 1990); *U.S. v. Carilion Health Systems*, 707 F. Supp. 840, 849 (W.D. Va. 1989) aff'd 892 F. 2d 1042 (4th Cir. 1989).

68. See, e.g., *University Health; U.S. v. United Tote, Inc.*, 768 F. Supp. 1064 (D. Del. 1991).

69. *University Health.*

70. Ibid., 1222.

71. Ibid.

72. U.S. Department of Justice and Federal Trade Commission, *Horizontal Merger Guidelines*, 4 Trade Reg. Rep. (CCH) 13,104 (1992, rev'd 1997) (hereafter U.S. Merger Guidelines).

73. Discussion "Efficiency Claims in Mergers," in OECD Roundtable, 8.

74. U.S. *Merger Guidelines*, sec. 4.

75. For a reiteration of this standard, see *Swedish Match.*

76. See, for example, *RSR Corp. v. FTC*, 602 F. 2d 1317, 1325 (9th Cir. 1979) cert. denied, 445 U.S. 927 (1980); *U.S. v. Ivaco, Inc.*, 704 F. Supp 1409, 1427 (W.D. Mich. 1989).

77. See, e.g., *University Health*, 1223; *U.S. v. Long Island Jewish Medical Center and North Shore Health System, Inc.*, 938 F. Supp. 121, 147 (E.D.N.Y. 1997).

78. U.S. *Merger Guidelines*, sec. 4. The FTC staff report advised not to return to the "clear and convincing" burden of proof. "Anticipating the Twenty-first Century: Competition Policy in the New High-Tech, Global Marketplace: A Report by the FTC Staff," *Antitrust & Trade Reg. Rep. (BNA)*, vol. 70, no. 1765, Special Supplement (June 6, 1996).

79. U.S. *Merger Guidelines*, sec. 4. In the 2000 *Swedish Match* case the court stated, "Even assuming that [the efficiencies defense] is a viable defense in some cases [to rebut the government's prima facie case], however, the Court

finds that the defense is inappropriate . . . [when] the acquisition would generate undue market power and increased concentration." *Swedish Match,* 171.

80. Canadian Competition Act of 1985, sec. 96.
81. Ibid.
82. Director of Investigation and Research, *Merger Enforcement Guidelines* (Ottawa: Canadian Bureau of Competition, 1991), sec. 5.2.
83. *Canada (Director of Investigation and Research) v. Canadian Pacific Ltd.* (1997) 74 C.P.R. (3d) 55, 63; *Superior,* Tribunal decision I.
84. *Superior,* Tribunal decision I.
85. *Canada (Commissioner of Competition) v. Superior Propane, Inc. and ICG Propane, Inc.* [2001] 3 F.C. 185 (hereafter Appeals Court decision).
86. *Superior,* Tribunal decision I, para. 206.
87. Ibid., paras. 110 and 117.
88. Ibid., para. 150.
89. Ibid., para. 308.
90. Ibid., paras. 437–438.
91. *Superior,* Appeals Court decision, para. 92.
92. Michael J. Trebilcock and Ralph A. Winter, "The State of Efficiencies in Canadian Merger Policy," 19(4) *Canadian Competition Policy Record* 106 (2000).
93. *Canada (Commissioner of Competition) v. Superior Propane, Inc.* (Competition Tribunal, unpublished, April 4, 2002) (hereafter Tribunal decision II). The decision was appealed by the Competition Bureau.
94. Ibid., para. 371.
95. Australian Trade Practices Act of 1974, secs. 88, 90, 101.
96. Ibid., sec. 90(9A).
97. Australian *Merger Guidelines,* sec. 6.38.
98. *Davids Ltd.* (1995), ATPR 50–185; *Davids Ltd.* (1996), ATPR 50–224.
99. Australian *Merger Guidelines,* secs. 6.30, 6.37. For the basic case establishing these propositions, see *Queensland Co-operative Milling Association Ltd. and Defiance Holdings Ltd.* (1976), ATPR 40–012, 17, 242–243, 25 FLR 169 (hereafter *QCMA*).
100. Australian *Merger Guidelines,* sec. 6.40; *Wattyl (Australia) Pty Ltd., Courtaulds (Australia) Pty Ltd. and Others* (1996) ATPR (Com.) 50–232.
101. Australian *Merger Guidelines,* secs. 6.48–49.
102. Ibid., secs. 6.42–44, based on *Re Rural Traders Co-operative (WA) Ltd. and Others* (1979) ATPR 40–110, FLR 244.
103. *Du Pont (Australia) Ltd. and Others* (1996) ATPR (Com.) 50–231, 56,493.
104. *QCMA,* 17,242.
105. *Re Howard Smith Industries Pty Ltd.* (1977) ATPR 40–023, 17,334, 28 FLR 385.
106. *Re Queensland Independent Wholesalers Pty Ltd.* (1995) ATPR 41–438, 132 ALR 225.

107. Commerce Act of 1986, sec. 67.
108. *Guidelines to the Analysis of Public Benefits and Detriments* (New Zealand Commerce Commission, 1997). The Guidelines are being revised in line with the changes in legislation from a dominance standard to a substantial lessening of competition one. It is unlikely, however, that the commission's views on efficiencies will change as a result of the new legislation. For case law, see, e.g., *Health Waikato Ltd./Midland Health* (Decision 275)(New Zealand Commerce Commission, unpublished, August 1, 1995).
109. *Telecom Corporation of NZ Ltd. V. Commerce Commission* [1992] NZLR 193.
110. New Zealand *Business Acquisition Guidelines.*
111. This discussion builds, mainly, on David Gilo, "Competition Policy in Small Markets" (LL.M. thesis, Harvard Law School, 1994), 165.
112. See, e.g., *University Health.*
113. Department of Justice and Federal Trade Commission, *Statements of Enforcement Policy and Analytical Principles Relating to Health Care and Antitrust,* 4 Trade Reg. Rep. (CCH) 13,152 (September 30, 1994).
114. Gilo, 179–181.
115. See "Background Note of Secretariat," in "Efficiency Claims in Mergers," OECD Roundtable, 7–8.
116. U.S. *Merger Guidelines,* sec. 1.
117. See Australian Merger Guidelines, secs. 5.44–46; New Zealand's *Practice Note 4: The Commission's Approach to Adjudicating on Business Acquisitions under the Changed Threshold in Section 47—A Test of Substantially Lessening Competition* (Commerce Commission, 2001), sec. 3; Israel's Competition Authority, *Proposed Guidelines for Market Definition* (2002), 3.
118. Many small economies have recognized this need. See, e.g., the Canadian case of *Director v. Hillsdown Holdings (Canada) Ltd* [1992] 41 C.P.R. 3d 289. For a list of Australian mergers not opposed when import competition was substantial, see ACCC, *The ACCC's Approach to Mergers: A Statistical Summary* (ACCC Publications Unit, 1998).
119. A. A. Cournot, *Researches into the Mathematical Principles of the Theory of Wealth* (New York: Kelley, 1838).
120. U.S. Department of Justice, *Merger Guidelines,* reprinted in 2 *Trade Reg. Rep.* (CCH) 4510 (1968).
121. *Von's Grocery Co.; U.S. v. Pabst Brewing Co.* 384 U.S. 546, 86 S. Ct 1665 (1966) on remand 296 F. Supp. 994 (E.D. Wis. 1969).
122. Hovenkamp, 499–500. For a table of cases indicating the market shares of the firm, the market structure, and the decision, see Phillip E. Areeda, Herbert Hovenkamp, and John L. Solow, *Antitrust Law: An Analysis of Antitrust Principles and Their Application,* vol. 4, rev. ed. (New York: Aspen Law & Business, 1998), 102.
123. Australian *Merger Guidelines,* sec. 5.95.

124. New Zealand *Business Acquisition Guidelines,* sec. 4.4.
125. Israeli Restrictive Trade Practices Act of 1988, sec. 17.
126. See, e.g., John Kwoka, "Large-Firm Dominance and Price/Cost Margins in Manufacturing Industries," 44 *S. Econ. J.* 183 (1977); Frederick Warren-Boulton, *Vertical Control of Markets: Business and Labor Practices* (Cambridge, Mass.: Ballinger, 1978), 350.
127. Appeal 2/94 *Tnuva neged Hamemuna al Hahegbelim Haiskim (Tnuva v. Director of Competition Authority)* in *Hegbelim Iskiim (Antitrust),* ed. Tova Olshtein, vol. B (Tel Aviv: Vaad Mehoz Tel-Aviv-Yafo, 1994), 159. Ireland, by contrast, has adopted HHI levels that are similar to those of the United States.
128. Zdaka and others show that for similar economic surplus, a merger in the U.S. market that increases the HHI from 1,700 to 2,000 (i.e., reduction from six equivalently sized firms to five such firms) is similar to a merger that increases the HHI from 3,300 to 5,000 (from three equivalently sized firms to two) in the Israeli market if the cost reduction is 0.5 percent (if we assume that the profit was previously set at 5 percent). They recommend the adoption of an HHI threshold of 5,000 in Israel. Efraim Zdaka et al., "Monopolim ve Mizugim Betnaei Hasifa" (Monopolies and mergers in exposure conditions), 152 *Israeli Economic Quarterly* 53 (1992).
129. *Director v. Hillsdown Holdings (Canada) Ltd.* [1992] 41 CPR 3d 289.
130. *France v. Commission* (C-68/94 & C-30/95) [1998] ECR I-1375, [1998] 4 CMLR 829.
131. See also *Imperial Oil.*
132. *France v. Commission.*
133. *Kali and Salz/MdK/Treuhand* (M.308) OJ 1994 L186/30, [1994] 4 CMLR 526.
134. *Amcor/Paper Mills* (ACCC, unpublished, November 1993). See also *Email/Southcorp* (ACCC, unpublished, March 11, 1999).
135. Canadian Competition Act of 1986, sec. 92(2).
136. As noted, some jurisdictions argue that conglomerate mergers may also create portfolio effects.
137. See the U.S. decision in *Northern Natural Gas Co. v. FTC,* 399 F. 2d 953, 972 (D.D.C. 1968).
138. *Hachlatat Hamemune al Ei Matan Ptor Meishur Hesder Kovel: Energiat Hamizrach Hatichon* (Decision of the director of Competition Authority not to grant an exemption to Middle East Energy) (Director of Israeli Competition Authority, unpublished, May 13, 1997).
139. *Ishur Mizug Betnaim Columbus Capital Corporation Mikvuzat Klaridge, Cur Taasiot Baam* (Conditioned approval of a merger between Columbus Capital Corporation from the Klaridge Group, Cur Industries, Ltd.) (Director of Israeli Competition Authority, unpublished, January 5, 1998).
140. *Hachlatat Hamemune Bedvar Ishur Mizug Betnaim Tozeret Mazon Israelit*

Baam/Unilever N.V. (Conditioned approval of the merger between Tozeret Mazon Israelit Baam and Unilever N.V.) (M/4006) (Director of Israeli Competition Authority, unpublished, September 27, 2000).

141. See the U.S. case of *Hartford Fire Insurance Co. v. California*, 509 U.S. 764, 113 S. Ct. 2891 (1993); the EC *Wood Pulp* case, *Ahlstrom Osakeyhtio v. Commission*, (89/85, etc.) [1988] ECR 5193, [1988] 4 CMLR 901; the Israeli case of *James Richardson—Shuk Habsamim Haseliktiviim* (James Richardson—the selective fragrance market), in *Hegbelim Iskiim* (Antitrust), ed. Tova Olshtein, vol. D. (Tel Aviv: Vaad Mehoz Tel-Aviv-Yafo, 2002), 97.

142. The U.S. Foreign Trade Antitrust Improvements Act of 1982, for example, states clearly that the Sherman Act does not apply to exports not affecting U.S. citizens.

143. World Trade Organization, Ministerial Declaration of WTO Ministerial Conference, 4th sess., WT/MIN(01)/DEC/1.

144. International Competition Network, press release, October 25, 2001 (on the web at www.internationalcompetitionnetwork.org).

145. *Tozeret Mazon/Unilever.*

146. *Tnaim LeMizug Ben & Jerry's Homemade, Inc. uvein Unilever N.V.* (Conditions for the approval of a merger between Ben & Jerry's Homemade Inc. and Unilever N.V.)(Director of Israeli Competition Authority, unpublished, December 16, 2001).

147. *Rothmans/British American Tobacco* (ACCC, unpublished, June 3, 1999).

Conclusion

1. This has been acknowledged by many small economies. See, for example, the Israeli decision of *Iscur.* The tribunal stated that the significant difference in size between the Israeli and U.S. market necessitates a difference of perspective and emphasis. Appeal 1/97 *Iscur Sherutei Pladot Baam Veach v. Hamemune al Hahegbelim Haiskiim Veach* (Iscur Sherutei Pladot Inc. et al. v. Director of Competition Authority et al.) (Israeli Competition Tribunal, unpublished, December 11, 1997). See also the New Zealand case of *Fisher & Paykel:* "Despite the common ancestry which both the New Zealand and Australian statutes derive from the United States antitrust statutes, caution has to be exhibited before adopting uncritically developments in law and economics from that country." *Fisher & Paykel Limited v. Commerce Commission* [1990] 2 NZLR 731, 756.

2. Michal S. Gal, "Reality Bites (or Bits): The Political Economy of Antitrust Enforcement," in *International Antitrust Law and Policy,* ed. Barry Hawk (New York: Juris, 2002), 605.

3. EC Commission, *The European Union's Pre-accession Strategy for Associated Countries of Central Europe* (1996).

4. See, e.g., the Maltese Competition Act of 1994.

5. Eleanor M. Fox, "International Antitrust: Against Minimum Rules; for Cosmopolitan Principles," 43 *Antitrust Bull.* 5 (1998).

6. Report of The Group of Experts, *Competition Policy in the New Trade Order: Strengthening International Cooperation and Rules* (1995).

7. Ministerial Declaration of WTO Ministerial Conference, 4th sess., WT/MIN(01)/DEC/1.

8. International Competition Network, press release, October 25, 2001.

9. For example, Weiss estimated that the U.S. continental market comprised six regional markets in beer brewing, nine in glass bottles, twenty-four in cement, six in steel, and six in storage batteries. Leonard W. Weiss, "The Geographic Size of Markets in Manufacturing," 54 *Review of Economics and Statistics* 245 (1972).

10. *RTE and ITP v. Commission* (C-241 & 242/91P) [1995] ECR I-743, [1995] 4 CMLR 718.

11. Department of Justice and Federal Trade Commission, *Statement of Enforcement Policy and Analytical Principles Relating to Health Care and Antitrust,* 4 Trade Reg. Rep. (CCH) (September 30, 1994) 13,152.

Index of Legislation

Australia

Trade Practices Act (1974), 294n29; Part IIIA, 131; sec. 45, 174; sec. 46, 65, 96, 129–130, 283n74; sec. 50, 221, 301n21; sec. 50(3), 214, 304n60; sec. 51, 294n36; sec. 88, 221; sec. 90, 221; sec. 101, 221; sec. 90(9A), 201; sec. 45C, 170; sec. 44G, 287n17

Austria

Cartel Act, 81

Belgium

Act on Protection against the Abuse of Economic Power (1960): sec. 2, 283n74

Canada

Competition Act (1985), 294n29; sec. 1.1, 50–51; sec. 31, 42; sec. 34, 285n94; sec. 50, 301n21; sec. 75(1), 274n74; sec. 77(2), 65, 279n18; sec. 78–79, 285n91; sec. 79, 65, 279n17, 284n90; sec. 86(4), 274n74; sec. 96, 173, 219; sec. 96(2), 201; sec. 99, 274n74

England

Competition Act (1998): sec. 6(2), 183
Fair Trading Act (1973), 78, 183, 281n43

European Community

Community Regulation no. 2299/89, 291n93
Community Regulation no. 3089/93, 291n93
Treaty of Rome (1957), 137, 213, 294n29; Article 81, 303n50; Article 82, 126, 128; sec. 82, 65, 285n94; sec. 82(a), 83–84; sec. 82(b), 85; sec. 82(c), 285n96

Ireland

Competition Act (1991), sec. 14, 282n56

Israel

Competition law regulation [block exemption for agreements], 295n40
Product and Service Surveillance Act (1957), 281n41
Restrictive Trade Practices Act (1988), 51, 67, 294n29; sec. 2, 296n50; sec. 2B,

Index of Cases

Australia

General Index

Absolute value of competition approach, 196, 208–216

Abuse of dominance, 91–106, 117–118, 122–152; defined, 86, 91, 94–101; and economic analysis, 97–98; incentives to engage in, 115, 117–118; and intent, 100–101; and market power, 30–31, 95; and regulation of, 55, 83–88, 91–109, 122–152. *See also* Cross-subsidization; Discrimination; Essential facility; Exclusive dealing; Monopoly pricing; Predatory pricing; Rebate; Refusal to deal; Tying

Adoption of laws, 8, 257–258

Areeda, Phillip, 70–71, 75, 132, 186, 187

Australia: and abuse defined, 87–88, 96, 99–100; characteristics of, 2–3, 15, 19, 26; and collusion, 170; and conglomerates, 300n8; and conscious parallelism, 165–166, 182; and cooperative agreements, 163, 172, 173–174; and dominance, 64, 65; and essential facility, 129–131, 145; and mere monopoly, 87, 88; and merger, 201, 204, 207, 214, 221–223, 232, 237, 238, 246–247, 274n74, 300n8; and monopoly pricing, 86–88; and natural monopoly, 120, 129, 130, 131, 132–133; and refusal to deal, 129–131, 132–133; and vertical integration, 133

Austria, 81, 127–128

Bain, Joe S., 270n10

Balancing approach, 208–209, 216–228

Barrier to entry. See Entry barrier

Belgium, 84

Bork, Robert, 70

Breakup. *See* Remedy, structural

Canada: characteristics of, 15, 19, 24, 272n45; and conscious parallelism, 180, 182; and cooperation agreements, 173; and dominance, 65; and exclusive dealing, 108–109; and goals, 50–51; and merger, 201, 219–221, 236, 237–239

Caribbean, 203

Cartel. See Collusion

Caves, Richard, 14

Collusion: and conditions for success, 32, 157–159; defined, 157; express, 157; and facilitating factors, 159–160; and meeting of minds, 168–169; and merger, 198, 206, 232, 233, 236–237; and per se rule, 169–170; and restraint of trade, 169; regulation of, 41, 54, 56, 168–170, 192, 254; and rule of reason, 170; social costs of, 33, 157, 160–162, 293n13; tacit, 157. *See also* Oligopoly

Competition: contestable, 14, 21; perfect, 13–14

Compliance program, 82

Concentration: and abuse of market power, 99; and aggregate, 27–28; and Australia,